Student Workbook for the

Insurance Handbook for the Medical Office

5th edition

Marilyn Takahashi Fordney, CMA-AC, CMT

Formerly
Instructor of Medical Insurance, Medical Terminology,
Medical Machine Transcription, and
Medical Office Procedures
Ventura College
Ventura, California

Student Workbook for the Insurance Handbook for the Medical Office

5th edition

W.B. SAUNDERS COMPANY
A Division of Harcourt Brace & Company
Philadelphia London Toronto Montreal Sydney Tokyo

W.B. Saunders Company
A Division of Harcourt Brace & Company

The Curtis Center
Independence Square West
Philadelphia, Pennsylvania 19106

Student Workbook for the Insurance Handbook for the Medical Office, Fifth Edition — ISBN 0-7216-6991-3

Printed in the United States of America

Last digit is the print number: 9 8 7 6 5 4 3 2 1

Preface

This *Workbook* has been prepared to assist the learner in a practical approach of doing insurance billing and understanding insurance programs. It uses a method of progressing from easy to more complex issues within each chapter. Read the Instruction Guide to the Workbook. After the introductory section, each chapter begins with performance objectives so the reader will know what will be accomplished. Next is a repeat of the key terms for quick reference when studying. Each chapter outline will serve as a lecture guide to use for note taking. Review questions in the form of short answer, true/false, multiple choice, and matching are presented to reinforce learning key points for each topic. Assignments are given with some critical thinking problems for certain sections that the instructor may use for class discussion. Patients' medical records, ledgers, and encounter forms are presented as they might appear in the doctor's files, so the learner may discover how to extract information to complete claim forms properly and accurately. Many medical record entries contain physicians' handwritten notes. All the material included in the assignments have been altered to prevent identification of the cases or parties involved. The patient records are presented in an abbreviated manner. No evaluation of medical practice, nor medical advice, nor recommendations for treatment or prescribed medications are to be inferred from the assignments. Easily removable insurance claim forms and other sample documents are included in the *Workbook* for typing practice. Some assignments give students hands-on experience in typing forms for optical character recognition (OCR) computer equipment, which is used in many states for insurance claims processing and payment. Current procedural and diagnostic code exercises are used throughout to facilitate and enhance coding skills for submitting a claim or making up an itemized billing statement. Tests are provided at the end of the *Workbook* to provide a complete, competency-based educational program. Special appendices appear at the end that include a mock fee schedule with index and an alpha/numeric Medicare Level II HCFA Common Procedure Code System (HCPCS). The appendices may be used as reference tools to complete the procedural code problems.

Since many medical practices use computer technology to perform financial operations, user-friendly computer software has been developed to accompany the textbook and workbook. Key terms are integrated into five cases, and definitions may be accessed from a glossary. The goal is to complete the HCFA–1500 claim form for each case and insert accurate data, including diagnostic and procedural code numbers. A simulated electronic transmission of a Medicare insurance claim is included. An ongoing summary of scores achieved on completed cases may be brought up on screen to keep the student and instructor informed of progress made. Detailed scoring reports may be printed out so that the instructor has access to the information from time to time. The instructor may wish the student to do the first four cases strictly for learning and use case five for testing and grading.

An enhancement to the software for the 5th edition allows the user to complete the HCFA–1500 claim form for any assignment in the *Workbook* and print it out for evaluation.

The author hopes that by using this *Workbook* the student will learn by doing and, with the stepping stones of practical experience and knowledge, be able to obtain a job and embark on a successful career as an insurance billing specialist.

MARILYN TAKAHASHI FORDNEY, CMA-AC, CMT
Oxnard, California

Acknowledgments

This edition of the *Student Workbook for the Insurance Handbook for the Medical Office* has had considerable input from many medical professionals. Expert consultation has been necessary due to the complexities of the managed care environment, intricacies of procedural and diagnostic coding, impact of technology on insurance claims processing, and the more sophisticated role the insurance billing specialist has in today's work force. I wish to express an immense debt of gratitude to the following:

To my husband, Alan, who offered support, encouragement, and ran Federal Expresses almost on a daily basis for many months and was so understanding of the priority this edition had on my time.

To Alison Zaintz, editor and owner of The Production House, Inc. in Winter Springs, Florida who expedited the project to meet target dates in preparing the *Student Workbook*.

To Linda French, CMA-C, who acted as a technical consultant and helped me enhance many sections of the *Student Workbook* to assist the learner as well as the instructor using the material.

To my assistant, Nina Janis, who enthusiastically and competently did the typing, filing, and many other tasks necessary to meet the deadlines. Lastly, and most importantly, I express overwhelming gratitude to the professional consultants who provided vital information to make this Workbook better than the last edition, and they are:

Deborah Emmons, CMA
President
S.T.A.T. Transcription Service
Port Hueneme, California

Ronna Jurow, M.D.
Active Staff and Attending Physician in Obstetrics
Gynecology and Infertility
Community Memorial Hospital
Ventura, California

Margaret Kirby, CMA
Office Manager
Ventura Ear, Nose, and Throat Medical Group, Inc.
Drs. Arthur S. Peters and John M. Edison
Ventura, California

Lucille M. Loignon, M.D., F.A.C.S.
Diplomate American Board of Ophthalmology
Oxnard, California

Maria Reyes
Ventura Anesthesia Medical Group
Ventura, California

Walter A. Shaff
President
CPR
Lake Oswego, Oregon

Lita Starr
Office Manager and wife
of William E. Starr, M.D.
Oxnard, California

Paul Wertlake, M.D.
Medical Director and Chief Pathologist
Unilab Corporation
Tarzana, California

Shirley Wertlake, CLS
Technical Specialist
Clinical Laboratories
UCLA Medical Center
Los Angeles, California

Contents

Instruction Guide to the *Workbook*

Learning Objectives

The student will be able to

- Define and spell key terms for each chapter.
- Answer review questions for each chapter of the textbook.
- Complete assignments to enhance and develop better critical thinking skills.
- Define abbreviations as they appear on a patient record.
- Prepare legally correct medicolegal forms and letters.
- Code professional services properly, using the *Current Procedural Terminology* (CPT) code book or Appendices A and B.
- Select diagnostic code numbers, using the *International Classification of Diseases (9th Revision) Clinical Modification* (ICD–9–CM).
- Locate errors on insurance claims before submission to insurance companies.
- Locate errors on returned insurance claims.
- Complete an insurance claim tracer form.
- Execute financial management procedures for tracing managed care plans.
- Abstract information necessary to complete insurance claim forms from patient records and billing statement/ledger cards.
- Complete insurance claim forms commonly used in medical offices.
- Post payments, adjustments, and balances to patients' statement/ledger cards when submitting insurance claims.
- Compute mathematic calculations for Medicare and CHAMPUS cases.
- Analyze insurance claims in both hospital inpatient and outpatient settings.
- Prepare a cover letter, résumé, job application, and follow-up letter when searching for employment.

INSTRUCTIONS TO THE STUDENT

This *Workbook* has been prepared for those who use *Insurance Handbook for the Medical Office* (hereafter referred to as the *Handbook*) as a textbook. Performance objectives are presented for each assignment. Key terms are presented for each chapter, and definitions may be located in the Glossary at the end of the textbook. Your instructor may wish to select certain words for study.

Patient records are presented as they might appear in the physician's files so that you may learn how to abstract data from them to complete a claim properly and accurately. Many contain the physician's own handwritten notes. Easily removal sample insurance forms are included for typing practice.

Optical character recognition (OCR) computer equipment has been introduced for insurance claims processing and payment. The forms presented in each chapter will assist you in typing forms for this purpose.

As an introduction to the use of procedure code numbers, obtain the *Current Procedural Terminology* (CPT) *Code Book*, published annually by the American Medical Association, or use Appendix A of this *Workbook*. Beginning with Chapter 6, assume that you have been hired as an insurance billing specialist and that you will be working for an incorporated group of medical doctors, other allied health specialists, and podiatrists. You will be asked to complete various assignments. These doctors will be on the staff of a nearby hospital.

Patient records, statement/ledger cards, encounter forms, and blank insurance forms have been provided. In some instances it was necessary to omit a lengthy physical examination from the patient record to give you pertinent and concise information. Refer to Appendix A for doctors' fees for the statement/ledger cards and to provide you with experience in totaling up the charges and properly recording the appropriate information on the ledger when the insurance claim is submitted. The names and addresses are fictitious, and no reference to any person living or dead is intended. No medical advice is to be inferred from the patient records, or is any recommendation made toward alternative treatment methods or prescribed medications.

To learn how to abstract and read doctors' notes, refer to the abbreviation list at the end of this Introduction to decode any abbreviations that you do not understand or that are unfamiliar to you. To reinforce learning these abbreviations, write out their meanings on the Assignment pages. If possible, type all insurance forms, since this is the format in which the insurance carriers wish to receive them for processing. However, if you do not have access to a typewriter, neatly write in the information on the insurance form as you abstract it from the patient record. If you have a computer, use the diskette and complete each assignment and print it out for evaluation. Some of the records are handwritten and some are typed to give you a chance to abstract from both types. As each patient record is used for a particular insurance form, the doctor's signature will appear after the last entry that has been made on the record.

If you do not have a background in medical terminology, it might be wise to use a good medical dictionary as a reference.

Remember: Always read the assignment entirely before beginning to answer the questions. To complete each type of insurance form properly, refer to Chapter 6 in the *Handbook* that describes in detail the correct information to be put in each blank or box. Table 1 is a guide to match assignments with the corresponding chapters in this *Workbook* and the *Handbook*.

Note Taking

Taking notes is an important key to success in studying and learning and helps an individual pay attention during class. Each chapter has a study outline for organizational purposes, and this may be used as a guide for writing down key points during lectures or when studying or reviewing from the textbook for tests. Use file cards, note

Table 1 Table of *Workbook* Assignments

Handbook Chapter	Corresponding *Workbook* Chapter	Assignments
1	A Career as an Insurance Billing Specialist	1
2	Legal Issues Affecting Insurance Claims and Medical Records	2
3	Basics of Health Insurance	3
4	Procedural Coding	4 through 11
5	Diagnostic Coding	12 through 16
6	The Health Insurance Claim Form	17 through 21
7	Electronic Data Interchange (EDI)	22 and 23
8	Tracing Delinquent Claims and Insurance Problem Solving	24 through 26
9	Managed Care Systems and Special Plans	27 through 29
10	Blue Cross and Blue Shield Plans	30 through 34
11	Medicaid and Other State Programs	35 through 37
12	Medicare	38 through 45
13	CHAMPUS, CHAMPVA, and TRICARE	46 through 49
14	Workers' Compensation	50 through 52
15	Disability Income Insurance and Disability Benefit Programs	53 through 57
16	Hospital Billing	58 through 62
17	Seeking a Position as an Insurance Billing Specialist	63 through 67

pads, or a notebook for taking notes. Underline or highlight important words or phrases. To improve the usefulness of notes, try this format.

1. On a notepad sheet or file card, draw a margin 3 inches from the left.
2. Use the right side for notes and the left side for topic headings.
3. Skip a few lines when there is a change in topic.
4. Write numbers or letters to indicate subideas under a heading.
5. Be brief; do not write down every word except when emphasizing a quote, rule, or law. Write notes in your own words, since that is what you will understand.
6. Use abbreviations that you know how to translate.
7. Listen carefully to the lecture.
8. After the lecture, reread your notes. Highlight the word(s) on the left side of the page to identify the topic of the notes on the right.
9. For study purposes, cover the right side and see if you can explain to yourself or someone else the topic or word.
10. Remember—learning is by doing, and doing is up to you. So take notes for better understanding.

REFERENCE MATERIAL

To do the assignments in this *Workbook* and gain expertise in coding and insurance claims completion, an individual must have access to the books listed here. Addresses for obtaining these materials are given in parentheses. Additional books and booklets on these topics as well as CHAMPUS, Medicaid, Medicare, and more are listed in Appendix B of the *Handbook*.

Dictionary

Dorland's Illustrated Medical Dictionary, 28th edition, W.B. Saunders Company, 1994. (6277 Sea Harbor Drive, Orlando, FL 32821-9989; 1-800-545-2522.

Code Books

Current Procedural Terminology, American Medical Association, published annually. (515 North State Street, Chicago, IL 60610; 1–800–621–8335).
International Classification of Diseases (9th Revision) Clinical Modification (an inexpensive soft cover generic physician version of Volumes 1–3 is available from Channel Publishing Limited, 4750 Longley Lane, Suite 100, Reno, NV 89502; 1–800–248–2882).

Word Book

Medical Abbreviations and Eponyms by Sheila Sloane, W.B. Saunders Company, 1997 (6277 Sea Harbor Drive, Orlando, FL 32821–9989; 1–800–545–2522).

Pharmaceutical Book

An optional book might be the *Physician's Desk Reference* (PDR) for pharmaceutical drug names, descriptions, and so forth. Medical Economics Company, published annually. (5 Paragon Drive, Montvale, NJ 07645; 1–800–432–4570.

Physicians' Identification Numbers

Insurance companies and federal and state programs require certain identification numbers on claim forms of individuals who provide and bill for services to patients. Because there are so many different numbers, this can be confusing to the beginner as well as someone experienced in insurance billing procedures. Therefore, an explanation will be given here.

To practice within a state, each physician must obtain a *state license number*. Sometimes this number is requested on forms.

Example: A 12345

In a medical group or solo practice, each physician must have his or her own *federal tax identification number* issued by the Internal Revenue Service for income tax purposes.

Example: 77–1234567

In addition, each physician must have a *Social Security number* (SSN) for other personal and financial reasons as well. A physician in solo private practice is issued a *taxpayer's identification number* (TIN) which is identical to a taxpayer's Social Security number.

Example: 123–00–1234

Physician groups practicing together at one location are issued an *employer identification number* (EIN) by the Internal Revenue Service. This number may be used by physicians when submitting insurance claims forms.

Example: 95–3664021

Medicare

In 1997 the Health Care Financing Administration (HCFA) began issuing each provider a Medicare lifetime ten-digit National Provider Identifier (NPI) that replaces the unique physician identification number (UPIN) and provider identification number (PIN) numbers. It is recognized by Medicare, CHAMPUS/TRICARE, CHAMPVA, and Medicaid programs.

Example: **0123456** **7** **89**

NPI Root Base | Check Digit | Locator Code

Providers who charge patients a fee for urinary catheters, ostomy supplies, surgical dressings, and so forth must bill Medicare using a durable medical equipment, *DME supplier number.*

Health Insurance Claim Form HCFA–1500 (Figure 1)

Block 17a: NPI • When services are ordered or referred by another physician for a consultation, the referring physician's national provider identifier is placed in Block 17a.
Block 24j: Enter the first two digits of the NPI.
Block 24k: Performing Physician • In a group practice, if several physicians are involved in submitting services on one claim form, then place the individual national provider identifier (NPI) remaining 8 characters of the performing physician on the line indicating the procedure or service rendered. Solo practitioners leave this block blank.
Block 25: Federal Tax ID# • The federal tax identification number of the group or physician who is billing is placed in this book.
Block 33: NPI# or GRP# • Solo practitioners enter the national provider Identifier (NPI). Group or clinic practices enter the group practice number, which is composed of seven digits and two alpha characters (0000000 AB). Do not enter both a NPI and GRP identification number in this block.

Most claims require three NPI numbers: the referring physician, the rendering physician, and the billing entity. It is possible the NPI is the same for all three, but sometimes three separate numbers are required, depending on the circumstances of the case.

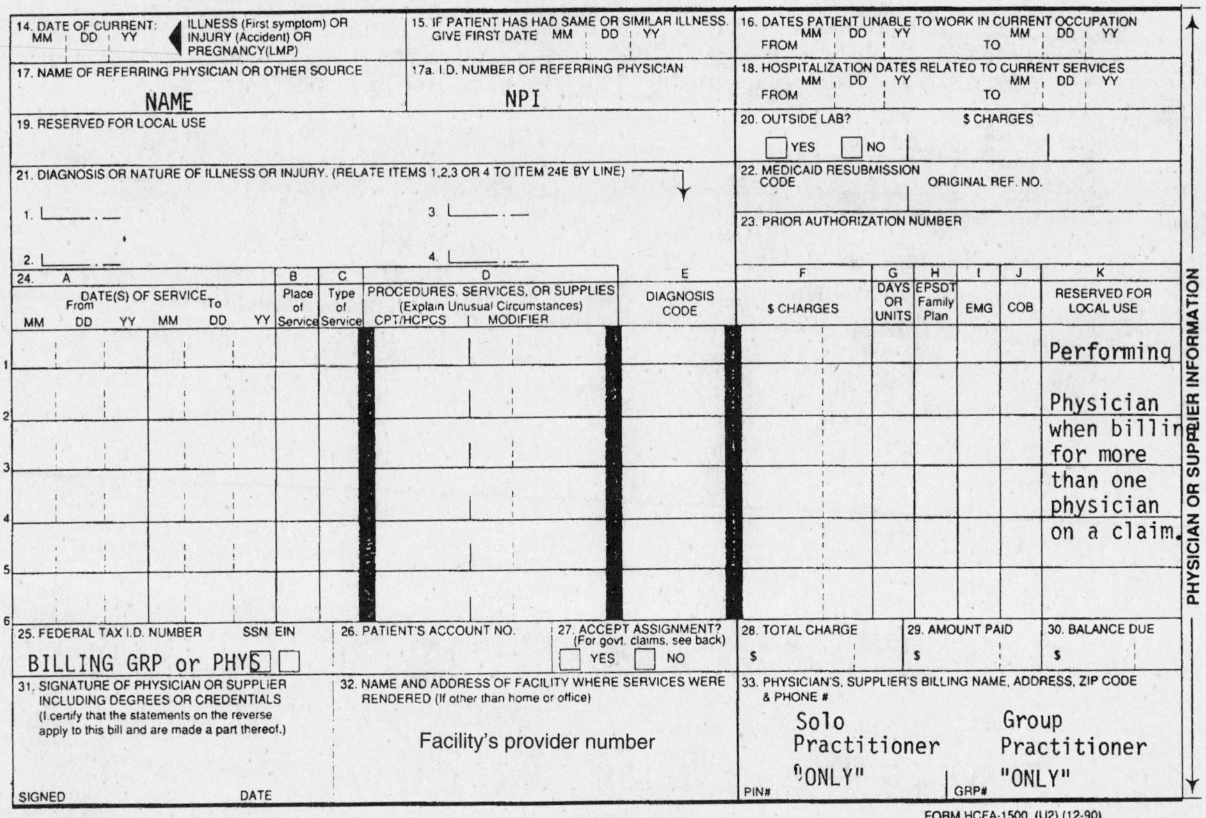
14. DATE OF CURRENT: MM DD YY ◀ ILLNESS (First symptom) OR INJURY (Accident) OR PREGNANCY(LMP)
15. IF PATIENT HAS HAD SAME OR SIMILAR ILLNESS. GIVE FIRST DATE MM DD YY
16. DATES PATIENT UNABLE TO WORK IN CURRENT OCCUPATION FROM MM DD YY TO MM DD YY
17. NAME OF REFERRING PHYSICIAN OR OTHER SOURCE — NAME
17a. I.D. NUMBER OF REFERRING PHYSICIAN — NPI
18. HOSPITALIZATION DATES RELATED TO CURRENT SERVICES FROM MM DD YY TO MM DD YY
19. RESERVED FOR LOCAL USE
20. OUTSIDE LAB? YES NO $ CHARGES
21. DIAGNOSIS OR NATURE OF ILLNESS OR INJURY. (RELATE ITEMS 1,2,3 OR 4 TO ITEM 24E BY LINE) 1. 2. 3. 4.
22. MEDICAID RESUBMISSION CODE ORIGINAL REF. NO.
23. PRIOR AUTHORIZATION NUMBER
24. A DATE(S) OF SERVICE From MM DD YY To MM DD YY | B Place of Service | C Type of Service | D PROCEDURES, SERVICES, OR SUPPLIES (Explain Unusual Circumstances) CPT/HCPCS MODIFIER | E DIAGNOSIS CODE | F $ CHARGES | G DAYS OR UNITS | H EPSDT Family Plan | I EMG | J COB | K RESERVED FOR LOCAL USE
Lines 1–6 — K: Performing Physician when billing for more than one physician on a claim.
25. FEDERAL TAX I.D. NUMBER SSN EIN — BILLING GRP or PHYS
26. PATIENT'S ACCOUNT NO.
27. ACCEPT ASSIGNMENT? (For govt. claims, see back) YES NO
28. TOTAL CHARGE $
29. AMOUNT PAID $
30. BALANCE DUE $
31. SIGNATURE OF PHYSICIAN OR SUPPLIER INCLUDING DEGREES OR CREDENTIALS (I certify that the statements on the reverse apply to this bill and are made a part thereof.) SIGNED DATE
32. NAME AND ADDRESS OF FACILITY WHERE SERVICES WERE RENDERED (If other than home or office) — Facility's provider number
33. PHYSICIAN'S, SUPPLIER'S BILLING NAME, ADDRESS, ZIP CODE & PHONE # — Solo Practitioner "ONLY" PIN# | Group Practitioner "ONLY" GRP#
PHYSICIAN OR SUPPLIER INFORMATION
(APPROVED BY AMA COUNCIL ON MEDICAL SERVICE 8/88) PLEASE PRINT OR TYPE FORM HCFA-1500 (U2) (12-90) FORM OWCP-1500 FORM RRB-1500

FIGURE 1

COLLEGE CLINIC

You are employed as an insurance billing specialist for an incorporated group of medical doctors, other allied health specialists, and podiatrists. These doctors are on the staff of a nearby hospital, College Hospital. Reference information to complete insurance claim forms for each assignment follows.

Office address:
College Clinic
4567 Broad Avenue
Woodland Hills, XY 12345–0001
telephone: 013–486–9002
FAX: 013–487–8976
Group practice (employer) tax identification number: 3664021CC
Clinic's Medicaid provider number: HSC12345F
Medicare Durable Medical Equipment (DME) supplier number: 34007

Hospital address:
College Hospital
4500 Broad Avenue
Woodland Hills, XY 12345–0001
telephone: 013–487–6789
FAX: 013–486–8900
Hospital provider number: 95–0731067
Hospital's Medicaid provider number: HSC43700F

College Clinic Staff (Table 2)

Patient record in this *Workbook* include the doctors' names, specialties, subspecialties, and physicians' identification numbers of the College Clinic staff (see Table 2).

LEDGER CARD

An example of how a ledger card should be completed is shown in Figure 2. A good bookkeeping practice is to take a red pen and draw a line across the ledger card from left to right to indicate the last entry billed to the insurance company. You will notice that there are abbreviations at the bottom of the ledger card that pertain to Evaluation and Management CPT codes and types of professional services. However, physicians have this section personalized to their particular practice so that some of these abbreviations may change from time to time.

The following applies to Medicare and may apply to some other insurance plans. Following major operative procedures, preoperative visits (hospital or office), intraoperative procedures, complications not requiring surgery, and postoperative visits during a 90-day follow-up period are included in the "package" or global fee. Following minor surgery, same-day visits, the procedure, and some postoperative visits during a 10-day follow-up period are included in the "package" or global fee. These services may be listed on the ledger card for documentation purposes, and an entry of NC (no charge) may be posted. Many medical practices do not list these on the insurance claim form as it is an optional policy depending on the insurance carrier and/or medical practice.

STUDENT REFERENCE NOTEBOOK

You may want to make up a personal reference three-ring binder with indexes so you can access information quickly to help you complete the *Workbook* assignments.

TABLE 2 College Clinic Staff

Name	Specialty (abbr)	Soc. Sec. #	State License #	Federal Tax ID #	Medicare HCFA-Assigned National Provider Identifier (NPI)
Concha Antrum, MD	Otolaryngologist (OTO) or Ear, Nose, and Throat Specialist (ENT)	082–19–1707	C 16021	74–1064090	1245897700
Pedro Atrics, MD	Pediatrician (PD)	134–80–7600	D 60123	71–3206151	3764001700
Bertha Caesar, MD	Obstetrician and Gynecologist (OBG)	230–80–6700	A 18174	72–5713051	4305675700
Perry Cardi, MD	Internist (I) *Subspecialty:* Cardiovascular Disease (CD)	557–46–9980	C 21400	70–6421710	6780502700
Brady Coccidioides, MD	Internist (I) *Subspecialty:* Pulmonary Disease (PUD)	670–54–0874	C 48211	75–6732101	6421106700
Vera Cutis, MD	Dermatologist (D)	409–19–8620	C 60021	71–8056112	7056871700
Clarence Cutler, MD	General Surgeon (GS)	410–23–5630	B 76005	71–5737291	4305004700
Dennis Drill, DDS	Dentist	240–47–8960	7061	72–4650312	7430108700
Max Glutens, RPT	Physical Therapist (PT)	507–40–4300	8761	79–3650028	6513227700

TABLE 2 College Clinic Staff ***Continued***

Name	Specialty (abbr)	Soc. Sec. #	State License #	Federal Tax ID #	Medicare HCFA-Assigned National Provider Identifier (NPI)
Cosmo Graff, MD	Plastic Surgeon (PS)	452–57–9899	C 81046	74–6078992	5030711700
Malvern Grumose, MD	Pathologist (Path)	470–67–2301	A 16025	72–7365114	
Gaston Input, MD	Internist (I) *Subspecialty:* Gastroenterologist (GE)	211–09–6734	C 80016	75–6721022	3278312700
Adam Langerhans, MD	Endocrinologist	447–90–6720	C 60511	60–5783128	4768065700
Cornell Lenser, MD	Ophthalmologist (OPH)	322–75–8963	C 60466	61–7894119	5403721700
Michael Menter, MD	Psychiatrist (P)	210–60–5302	C 71402	73–6657712	6730123700
Arthur O. Dont, DDS	Orthodontist	102–30–4566	8053	90–5117821	4537824700
Astro Parkinson, MD	Neurosurgeon (NS)	210–42–8533	C 26002	75–4453014	4678937700
Nick Pedro, DPM	Podiatrist	233–08–4300	E 83400	62–7410931	5402228700
Gerald Practon, MD	General Practitioner (GP) or Family Practitioner (FP)	123–45–6789	C 14021	70–3459766	4627889700
Walter Radon, MD	Radiologist (R)	344–09–6540	C 50013	95–4613782	4003722700
Rex Rumsey, MD	Proctologist (Proct)	337–88–9743	C 30421	95–3260111	0199904700
Sensitiv E. Scott, MD	Anesthetist (Anes)	220–45–5655	C 20411	72–5420305	9999926700
Raymond Skeleton, MD	Orthopedist (ORS, Orthop)	432–11–4589	C 45612	74–6541270	1267854700
Gene Ulibarri, MD	Urologist (U)	990–70–3245	C 64303	77–8653124	256788310

STATEMENT

College Clinic
4567 Broad Avenue
Woodland Hills, XY 12345-0001
Telephone: 013-486-9002
Fax: 013-487-8976

Mrs. I. M. Hurt
1300 Injury Street
Wound, XY 123345-0201

DATE	PROFESSIONAL SERVICE DESCRIPTION	CHARGE		CREDITS PAYMENTS		CREDITS ADJUSTMENTS		CURRENT BALANCE	
-6-9X	CPX, EKG	145	--					145	--
-9-9X	Rec'd ck #230			145	--			-0-	
-10-9X	OC	35	--	35	--			-0-	
-14-9X	HV	50	--					50	--
-15-9X	Closure of vesicovaginal	450	--					500	--
-16 to	21-9X HV	NC							
-30-9X	Billed Prudential Insurance Company 4-6 through 5-21							500	--
-33-9X	ROA Ins ck #7421			305	--			195	--

e and payable within 10 days. Pay last amount in balance column ⇧

y: **PF:** Problem-focused **SF:** Straightforward **CON:** Consultation **HCD:** House Call (Day)
EPF: Expanded problem-focused **LC:** Low complexity **CPX:** Complete Phys Exam **HCN:** House Call (Night)
D: Detailed **MC:** Moderate complexity **E:** Emergency **HV:** Hospital visit
C: Comprehensive **HC:** High complexity **ER:** Emergency Dept. **OV:** Office Visit

FIGURE 2

Besides these suggestions for content, you may wish to tear out or make photocopies of other sections of the textbook or workbook for your personal use. In addition, your instructor may give you handouts pertaining to regional guidelines to place in your notebook.

Content suggestions

Textbook:

E & M Codes	Tables 4–1 and 4–2
Laboratory Abbreviations	Table 4–5
Glossary	end of textbook

Workbook:

College Clinic information	page 6
Abbreviations and Symbols	pp. 11–14
College Clinic Staff	Table 2
Mock Fee Schedule	Appendix A
Medicare Level II HCPCS Codes	Appendix B
HCFA–1500 claim form	for photocopy use

INSURANCE PROCEDURAL MANUAL

If you are presently working in a medical office and taking this course, you may custom design an insurance manual for your physician's practice as you complete insurance claims in this *Workbook*. Obtain a three-ring binder with indexes and label them Blue Cross/Blue Shield, Medicaid, Medicare, CHAMPUS, managed care plans, State Disability, Workers' Compensation, Group Plans, and Private Carriers. If many of your patients have group plans, complete an insurance data or fact sheet (Figure 3) on each one and organize them alphabetically by employer under Group Plans. For managed care plans, type a form as shown in Chapter 9, Figure 9–4 of the *Handbook*.

As you complete the assignments in this *Workbook*, place them in the insurance manual as examples of completed claims for each particular program. An insurance manual with fact sheets listing benefits can keep you up-to-date on policy changes and ensure maximum reimbursement. Fact sheets can be prepared from information obtained when patients bring in their benefit booklets. Obtain and insert a list of the procedures that must be performed on an outpatient basis and those that must have second opinions for each of the insurance plans.

ABBREVIATIONS AND SYMBOLS

Abbreviations and symbols may appear on patient records, prescriptions, hospital charts, and patient ledger cards. Abbreviation styles differ, but the current trend is to omit periods in capital letter abbreviations except for doctors' academic degrees. For information on official American Hospital Association policy, refer to page 136 in the *Handbook*. Following is a list of abbreviations and symbols used in this *Workbook* and their meanings.

Abbreviations

A	allergy
Abdom	abdomen
abt	about
a.c.	before meals
Adj*	adjustment
adm	admit, admission, admitted
adv	advise
aet	at the age of
agit	shake or stir
$AgNO_3$	silver nitrate
ALL	allergy
a.m.	ante meridian (time)
ant	anterior
ante	before

*Bookkeeping abbreviation

INSURANCE DATA

1. Employer's name__________
2. Address__________ Telephone Number__________
3. Insurance Company Representative__________
4. Insurance Carrier__________
5. Address__________ Telephone Number__________
6. Group Policy Number__________
7. Group Account Manager__________ Telephone Number__________
8. **Insurance Coverage:**

   Annual Deductible__________ Patient Copayment Percentage__________

   Noncovered Procedures__________

   Maximum Benefits__________
9. **Diagnostic Coverage:**

   Limited Benefits__________

   Maximum Benefits__________

   Noncovered Procedures__________
10. **Major Medical:**

    Annual Deductible__________ Patient Copayment Percentage__________

    Limited Benefits__________

    Maximum Benefits__________

    Noncovered Procedures__________

Mandatory Outpatient Surgeries__________

Second Surgical Opinions__________

Preadmission Certification Yes_____ No_____

Payment Plan:

UCR__________ Schedule of Benefits__________ CPT__________ RVS__________

Send claims to:__________

____

Date Entered__________ Date Updated__________

FIGURE 3

AP anterior-posterior, anteroposterior
approx approximate
apt apartment
ASA acetylsalicylic acid (aspirin)
ASCVD arteriosclerotic cardiovascular disease
ASHD arteriosclerotic heart disease
asst assistant
auto automobile
AV atrioventricular
Ba barium (enema)
Bal fwd* balance forward
B/F* balance forward; brought forward
BI biopsy
b.i.d. 2 times daily
BMR basal metabolic rate

*Bookkeeping abbreviation

BP	blood pressure
Brev	sodium brevital
C	cervical (vertebrae); comprehensive (history/exam)
Ca, CA	cancer, carcinoma
c/a*	cash on account
CAT	computed axial tomography
cau	Caucasian
CBC	complete blood count
CBS	chronic brain syndrome
cc	cubic centimeter
CC	chief complaint
chr	chronic
ck*	check
cm	centimeter
CO	complains of
comp, compl	comprehensive, complete
Con, CON, Cons	consultation
Cont	continue
CPX	complete physical examination
Cr*	credit
cs, CS*	cash on account
C-section	Cesarean section
CVA	cardiovascular accident; cerebrovascular accident
Cysto	cystoscopy
D	diagnosis; detailed (history/exam)
D & C	dilatation and curettage
dc	discontinue
DC	discharge
DDS	Doctor of Dental Surgery
def*	charge deferred
Del	delivery, OB
Dg	diagnosis
dia	diameter
diag	diagnosis, diagnostic
dil	dilate (stretch, expand)
Disch	discharge
DNA	does not apply
DNS	did not show
DPM	Doctor of Podiatric Medicine
DPT	diphtheria, pertussis and tetanus
Dr	Doctor
Dr*	debit
DRG	diagnosis-related group
Drs	dressing
Dx	diagnosis
E	emergency
EC*	error corrected
ECG	electrocardiogram, electrocardiograph
ED	emergency department
EDC	estimated date of confinement
EEG	electroencephalograph
EENT	eye, ear, nose, and throat
EGD	esophagogastroduodenoscopy
EKG	electrocardiogram, electrocardiograph
E/M	Evaluation and Management (CPT code)
EMG	electromyogram
EPF	expanded problem-focused (history/exam)
epith	epithelial
ER	emergency room
Er, ER*	error corrected
ESR	erythrocyte sedimentation rate
est	established (patient)
Ex, exam	examination
exc	excision
Ex MO*	express money order
ext	external
24F, 28F	French (size of catheter)
FH	family history
ft	foot, feet
FU	follow-up (examination)
fwd*	forward
Fx	fracture
gb, GB	gallbladder
GGE	generalized glandular enlargement
GI	gastrointestinal
Grav	gravida
GU	genitourinary
H	hospital call
HBP	high blood pressure
HC	hospital call or consultation; high complexity (decision making)
HCD	house call (day)
HCN	house call (night)
Hct	hematocrit
HCVD	hypertensive cardiovascular disease
Hgb	hemoglobin
hist	history
hosp	hospital
H & P	history and physical
hr, hrs	hour, hours
h.s.	before bedtime
HS	hospital surgery

*Bookkeeping abbreviation

Ht	height
HV	hospital visit
HX, hx	history
HX PX	history and physical examination
I	injection
IC	initial consultation
I & D	incision and drainage
I/f*	in full
IM	intramuscular (injection)
imp	impression (diagnosis)
inflam	inflammation
init	initial (office visit)
inj, INJ	injection
ins, INS*	insurance
int	internal
intermed	intermediate (office visit)
interpret	interpretation
IUD	intrauterine device
IV	intravenous (injection)
IVP	intravenous pyelogram
K 35	Kolman (instrument used in urology)
KUB	kidneys, ureters, bladder
L	left; laboratory
Lab, LAB	laboratory
lat	lateral
LC	low complexity (decision making)
LMP	last menstrual period
LS	lumbosacral
lt	left
ltd	limited (office visit)
L & W	living and well
M	medication; married
MC	moderate complexity (decision making)
med	medicine
mg	milligram(s)
ml	milliliter
mo	month(s)
MO*	money order
N	negative
NA	not applicable
NAD	no appreciable disease
NC, N/C*	no charge
NEC	not elsewhere classifiable
neg	negative
NOS	not otherwise specified
NYD	not yet diagnosed
OB, Ob-Gyn	obstetric
OC	office call
occ	occasional
OD	right eye
ofc	office
OP	outpatient
Op, op	operation
OR	operating room
orig	original
OS	office surgery; left eye
OV	office visit
PA	posterior-anterior, postero-anterior
Pap	Papanicolaou (smear, stain, test)
Para I	woman having borne one child
PC	present complaint
p.c.	after meals
PD	permanent disability
Pd, PD*	professional discount
PE	physical examination
perf	performed
PF	problem-focused (history/exam)
PH	past history
Ph ex	physical examination
phys	physical
PID	pelvic inflammatory disease
p.m.	post meridian (time)
PND	postnasal drip
PO, P Op	postoperative
post	posterior
postop	postoperative
preop	preoperative
prep	prepared
PRN	as necessary *(pro re nata)*
Proc	procedure
Prog	prognosis
P & S	permanent and stationary
Pt, pt	patient
PT	physical therapy
PTR	patient to return
PVT ck*	private check received
PX	physical examination
q	every
qd	one time daily, every day
qh	every hour
q.i.d.	four times daily
QNS	insufficient quantity
qod	every other day
R	right; residence call; report
RBC, rbc	red blood cell (count)
rec	recommend
rec'd	received
re ch	recheck
re-exam	re-examination
Reg	regular

*Bookkeeping abbreviation

ret, retn	return
rev	review
RHD	rheumatic heart disease
RN	registered nurse
R/O	rule out
ROA*	received on account
RPT	registered physical therapist
rt	right
RTC	return to clinic
RTO	return to office
RX, Rx, R_x	prescription, any medication or treatment ordered
S	surgery
SC	subcutaneous
SD	state disability
SE	special examination
SF	straightforward (decision making)
Sig	directions on prescription
SLR	straight leg raising
slt	slight
Smr	smear
SOB	shortness of breath
Sp gr	specific gravity
SQ	subcutaneous (injection)
STAT	immediately
surg	surgery
T	temperature
T & A	tonsillectomy and adenoidectomy
Tb, tb	tuberculosis
TD	temporary disability
temp	temperature
tet. tox.	tetanus toxoid
t.i.d.	three times daily
TPR	temperature, pulse, and respiration
Tr, trt	treatment
TURB	transurethral resection of bladder
TURP	transurethral resection of prostate
TX	treatment
u	units
UA, ua	urinalysis
UCHD	usual childhood diseases
UCR	usual, customary, and reasonable (fees)
UGI	upper gastrointestinal
UPJ	ureteropelvic junction or joint
UR	urinalysis
URI	upper respiratory infection
Urn	urinalysis
UTI	urinary tract infection
W	work; white
WBC, wbc	white blood cell (count); well baby care
wk	week; work
wks	weeks
WNL	within normal limits
Wr	Wassermann reaction (test for syphilis)
Wt, wt	weight
X	xray, x-ray(s); times (e.g., 3X = 3 times)
XR	xray, x-ray(s)
yr	year

Symbols

c̄,/c	with
s̄,/s	without
c̄c, c̄/c	with correction (eye glasses)
s̄c, s̄/c	without correction (eye glasses)
–	negative
ō	negative
+	positive
Ⓛ	left
Ⓡ	right
♂	male
♀	female
– *	charge already made
Θ*	no balance due
✓*	posted
($0.00)*	credit

*Bookkeeping abbreviation.

CHAPTER 1

A Career as an Insurance Billing Specialist

Key Terms

Your instructor may wish to select some specific words pertinent to this chapter for a test. For definitions of the terms, further study, and/or reference, the words, phrases, and abbreviations may be found in the Glossary at the end of the Handbook. *Key terms for this chapter are:*

American Academy of Procedural Coders (AAPC)
American Association of Medical Assistants, Inc. (AAMA)
American Association for Medical Transcription (AAMT)
American Health Information Management Association (AHIMA)
American Medical Association (AMA)
certification
Certified Claims Assistance Professional (CCAP)
Certified Coding Specialist (CCS)
Certified Electronic Claims Professional (CECP)
Certified Medical Assistant (CMA)
Certified Procedural Coder (CPC)
Claims Assistance Professional (CAP)
continuing education (CE)
ethics
etiquette
group practice
insurance billing specialist
National Association of Claims Assistance Professionals, Inc. (NACAP)
nonprivileged information
privileged communication
privileged information
Professional Association of Health Care Office Managers (PAHCOM)
recertification
Registered Medical Assistant (RMA)
reimbursement specialist

Performance Objectives

The student will be able to

- Define and spell the key terms for this chapter, given the information from the textbook Glossary, within a reasonable period of time and with enough accuracy to obtain a satisfactory evaluation.
- Answer the review questions after reading the chapter with enough accuracy to obtain a satisfactory evaluation.
- Use critical thinking to write one or two grammatically correct paragraphs with sufficient information to obtain a satisfactory evaluation.

Study Outline

INTRODUCTION
EDUCATION AND TRAINING REQUIREMENTS
CAREER ADVANTAGES
PERSONAL QUALIFICATIONS
MEDICAL ETIQUETTE
MEDICAL ETHICS
  Confidentiality
  Professionalism
    Personal Image
    Certification
KEEPING CURRENT

Review Questions

Review the objectives, key terms, and chapter information before completing the following review questions.

1. Identify three career opportunities (job titles) available after training in diagnostic and procedural coding and insurance claims completion.

   a. ____________________

   b. ____________________

   c. ____________________

2. List the duties an insurance billing specialist might perform.

   a. ____________________

   b. ____________________

   c. ____________________

   d. ____________________

   e. ____________________

   f. ____________________

3. List duties of a claims assistance professional.

   a. ____________________

   b. ____________________

   c. ____________________

4. Skills required for an insurance billing specialist are

a. ______________________________

b. ______________________________

c. ______________________________

d. ______________________________

e. ______________________________

f. ______________________________

g. ______________________________

h. ______________________________

i. ______________________________

j. ______________________________

5. Standards of conduct by which an insurance billing specialist determines the propriety of his or her behavior in a relationship are known as ______________ .

6. Complete these statements with either the words *illegal* or *unethical.*

a. To report incorrect information to the Aetna Casualty Company is __________ .

b. To report incorrect information to a Medicare fiscal intermediary is __________ .

c. It is __________ for two physicians to treat the same patient for the same condition.

7. A confidential communication that may be disclosed only with the patient's permission is known as ______________.

8. Exceptions to the right of privacy are those records involving

a. ______________________________

b. ______________________________

c. ______________________________

d. ______________________________

e. ______________________________

f. ______________________________

g. ______________________________

9. Define the following abbreviations that stand for validations of professionalism:

CCAP ______________________________

CPC ______________________________

CCS ______________________________

CECP ______________________________

10. Name three ways an insurance billing specialist may seek to keep knowledge current.

a. ______________________________

b. ______________________________

c. ______________________________

11. Give the names of two national organizations that certify coders.

a. ______________________________

b. ______________________________

CRITICAL THINKING

To enhance your critical thinking skills, problems will be interspersed throughout the *Workbook*. Thinking is the goal of instruction and a student's responsibility. When trying to solve a problem by critical thinking, it is desirable to have more than one solution and take time to think out answers. Remember that an answer may be changed when additional information is provided in a classroom setting.

ASSIGNMENT 1

This assignment is presented to help you develop your critical thinking skills. Write one or two paragraphs describing why you are training to become an insurance billing specialist. Or, if enrolled in a class that is part of a medical assisting course, explain why you are motivated to seek a career as a medical assistant. Make sure grammar, punctuation, and spelling are correct.

CHAPTER 2

Legal Issues Affecting Insurance Claims and Medical Records

Key Terms

Your instructor may wish to select some specific words pertinent to this chapter for a test. For definitions of the terms, further study, and/or reference, the words, phrases, and abbreviations may be found in the Glossary at the end of the Handbook. *Key terms for this chapter are:*

abuse
arbitration
assumption of risk
bonding
breach of confidential communication
breach of contract
breach of duty
civil law
embezzlement
felony
fraud
grievance committee
invasion of privacy
libel
litigation
medical record
negligence
phantom billing
qui tam action
respondeat superior
statute of limitations
subpoena
subpoena duces tecum

Performance Objectives

The student will be able to

- Define and spell the key terms for this chapter, given the information from the textbook Glossary, within a reasonable period of time and with enough accuracy to obtain a satisfactory evaluation.
- Answer the review questions after reading the chapter with enough accuracy to obtain a satisfactory evaluation.
- Select the correct medicolegal form letters and properly prepare them for the physician's signature, given the patients' chart notes and ledger cards, within a reasonable period of time and with enough accuracy to obtain a satisfactory evaluation.

Study Outline

INTRODUCTION
EMPLOYER LIABILITY
INSURANCE POLICIES (CONTRACTS)
PATIENT/PHYSICIAN CONTRACTS AND FINANCIAL RESPONSIBILITY
PHYSICIAN AND MANAGED CARE CONTRACTS
CONFIDENTIALITY
- Medical records
- Medical record guidelines
- Facsimile (FAX) Communication
- Principles for release of information

RETENTION OF RECORDS
- Medical records
- Accounting records

SUBPOENA
INSURANCE CLAIMS
- Guarantor
- Assignment
- Time limits
- Signature authorization

INSURANCE CLAIM FRAUD AND ABUSE
FORGERY
CLAIM AUDITS AND REVIEW
EMBEZZLEMENT
CREDIT AND COLLECTION LAWS
APPEALS
STATUTE OF LIMITATIONS
MEDICAL PROFESSIONAL LIABILITY PREVENTION
- Prevention Commandments of American Medical Association Committee on Medicolegal Problems

PHYSICIAN/PATIENT AGREEMENT
TERMINATION OF A CASE
MEDICOLEGAL REFERENCES
INSURANCE COMMISSIONERS
STATE BOARDS OF MEDICAL EXAMINERS

Review Questions

Review the objectives, key terms, glossary definitions to key terms, chapter information, and figures before completing the following review questions.

1. When a physician is legally responsible for an employee's conduct performed during

   employment, this is known as ______________________________

   ____

2. A claims assistance professional neglects to submit an insurance claim to a Medicare supplemental insurance carrier within the proper time limit. What type of insurance is

   needed for protection against this loss for the client? ______________________________

   ____

3. What is meant by a challenged policy? ______________________________

   ____

4. The time period that must elapse before an insurance policy may not be challenged is

____

5. When a patient seeks and accepts professional medical care, this is referred to as a/an

______________________________ contract.

6. The type of case when the contract exists between the physician and insurance company

is a/an ______________________________ case.

7. Written or graphic information about patient care is termed a/an ______________

____

8. When faxing a patient's medical records, a signed document for ______________

______________________________ must be obtained from the patient.

9. Action to take when a faxed medical document is misdirected is ______________

____

10. What must the former physician have from the patient before a record can be given to

a new physician? ______________________________

11. What must an insurance billing specialist do if he or she receives a request from another

physician for certain records? ______________________________

12. What must a physician have from the patient before he or she can give information to

an attorney? ______________________________

13. What is (are) the exception(s) to the Right of Privacy and Privileged Communication?

a. ______________________________

b. ______________________________

c. ______________________________

14. Indicate either *indefinite retention* or *number of years* for keeping records in the following situations.

a. Computer data ______________

b. Insurance claim for Medicare patient ______________

c. Medical record of a deceased patient ______________

d. Active patient medical records ______________

e. Letter to a patient about balance due after insurance paid ______________

15. An individual promising to pay for medical services rendered is known as a/an ____

____

16. A document signed by the insured directing the insurance company to pay benefits directly to the physician is known as a/an _______________

17. Guidelines for avoiding unauthorized use and preventing problems when a medical practice uses a facsimile signature stamp are:

a. _______________

b. _______________

c. _______________

d. _______________

e. _______________

f. _______________

19. Indicate whether the situation is one of *fraud* or *abuse* in the following situations.

a. Billing a claim for services not medically necessary. _______________

b. Changing a figure on an insurance claim form to get increased payment. _______________

c. Dismissing the copayment owed by a Medicare patient. _______________

d. Neglecting to refund an overpayment to the patient. _______________

e. Billing for a complex fracture when the patient suffered a simple break. _______________

20. State three bonding methods.

a. _______________

b. _______________

c. _______________

21. How should an insurance billing specialist correct an error on a patient's record?

____

22. Can a physician terminate a contract with a patient? _______________ If so, how?

____

23. Can an insurance billing specialist receive a subpoena for his or her physician?

____

24. This question is presented for critical thinking. A patient comes into the office for treatment. He does not return, because he is dissatisified with Dr. Practon's treatment.

Is it necessary to keep his records when he obviously will not return? ________

Why? ____

____

____

ASSIGNMENT 2

1. Mrs. Merry M. Mclean is negligent about following Dr. Ulibarri's advice after she received surgery. Write an appropriate letter to Mrs. Mclean advising her of the doctor's withdrawal from the case. Dr. Ulibarri will sign the letter. Use a typewritten letterhead and modified block style as shown in *Handbook* Figure 2–7. Refer to Assignment 19 for information from the patient record. Type Mrs. Mclean's address on a number 10 envelope, referring to *Workbook* Figure 2–1. Send the letter by certified mail with return receipt requested.
2. Mr. Walter J. Stone telephones on June 3, sounding extremely upset and irrational. He says that he is unable to return to work on June 22 and that he does not want to be seen by Dr. Input again. Write a letter to confirm this discharge by the patient. Suggest that he contact the local medical society for the names of three internists for further care. Refer to Assignment 21 for information from the patient record. Use a typewritten letterhead and modified block style as shown in *Handbook* Figure 2–8. Type Mr. Stone's address on a number 10 envelope, referring to *Workbook* Figure 2–1. Send the letter by certified mail with return receipt requested.

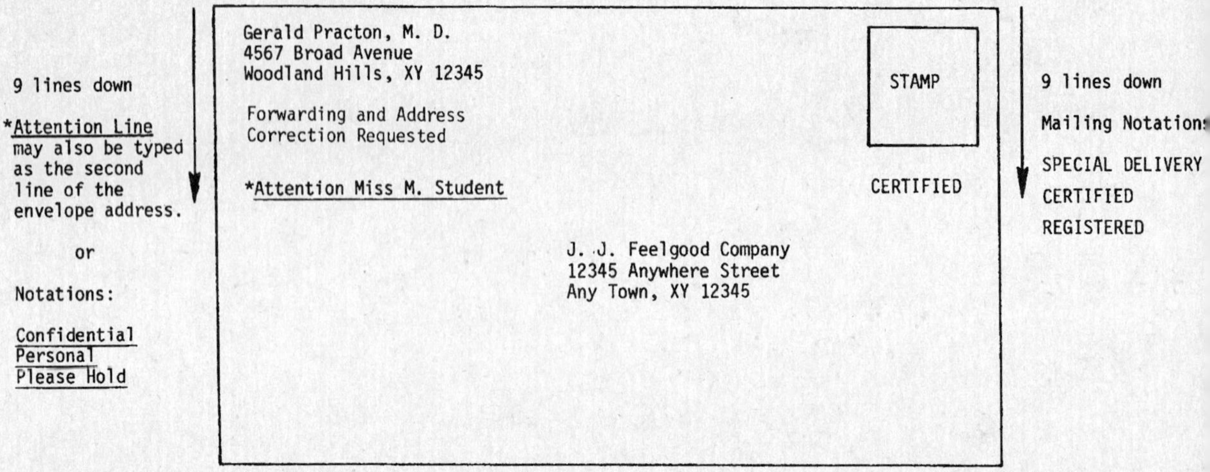

FIGURE 2–1.
An example of how to address a billing envelope correctly. Note the designation "Forwarding and Address Correction Requested," which tells the post office personnel that they are to trace a person who has moved and obtain a new address.

Remember that these letters must be prepared for the physician's signature, as they are legal documents.

CHAPTER 3

Basics of Health Insurance

Key Terms

Your instructor may wish to select some words pertinent to this chapter for a test. For definitions of the terms, further study, and/or reference, the words, phrases, and abbreviations may be found in the Glossary at the end of the textbook. Key terms for this chapter follow.

applicant
blanket contract
Blue Cross (BC)
Blue Shield (BS)
CHAMPUS
CHAMPVA
claim
coinsurance
Competitive medical plan (CMP)
conditionally renewable
contract
disability income insurance
exclusion
Exclusive provider organization (EPO)
Foundations for medical care (FMC)
guaranteed renewable
Health Maintenance Organization (HMO)
high risk
indemnity
Independent Practice Association (IPA)
insured
Maternal and Child Health Programs (MCHP)
Medicaid
Medicare (M)
member
noncancelable clause or policy
optionally renewable
personal insurance
preauthorization
precertification
predetermination
Preferred Provider Organization (PPO)
subscriber
Unemployment Compensation Disability (UCD) or State Disability
Veterans' Administration (VA) Outpatient Clinic
Workers' Compensation Insurance

Performance Objectives

The student will be able to

- Define and spell the key terms for this chapter, given the information from the textbook Glossary, within a reasonable period of time and with enough accuracy to obtain a satisfactory evaluation.
- Answer the review questions after reading the chapter with enough accuracy to obtain a satisfactory evaluation.
- Use critical thinking to list the basic steps in processing an insurance claim from submission to payment, given data from the textbook, within a reasonable period of time, and with enough accuracy to obtain a satisfactory evaluation.

Study Outline

INTRODUCTION
HISTORY
THE INSURANCE POLICY
 Policy Application
 Policy Provisions
 Coordination of Benefits
 General Policy Limitations
  Case Management Provisions
CHOICE OF HEALTH INSURANCE
 Group Contract
 Individual Contract
 Prepaid Health Plan
TYPES OF HEALTH INSURANCE COVERAGE
EXAMPLES OF INSURANCE BILLING
BASIC STEPS IN PROCESSING AN INSURANCE CLAIM
HANDLING INSURANCE CLAIMS
 First Visit: Patient Information Sheet
 Submitting and Tracing the Claim
 Insurance Claims Register
KEEPING UP-TO-DATE

Review Questions

Review the objectives, key terms, glossary definitions to key terms, chapter information, and figures before completing the following review questions.

1. A/an ______________________ is a legally enforceable agreement or contract.
2. List five health insurance policy renewal provisions.
   a. ______________________
   b. ______________________
   c. ______________________
   d. ______________________
   e. ______________________
3. Insurance reimbursement or payment is also called ______________________
4. Name two general health insurance policy limitations.
   a. ______________________
   b. ______________________
5. The act of finding out whether treatment is covered under an individual's health insurance policy is called ______________________

6. The procedure to obtain permission for a procedure before it is done to see whether the insurance program agrees it is medically necessary is termed ______________

7. Determining the maximum dollar amount the insurance company will pay for a procedure before it is done is known as ______________________________

8. Name three ways an individual may obtain health insurance.

a. ____

b. ____

c. ____

9. List four ways a physician's practice may use to submit insurance claims to insurance companies.

a. ____

b. ____

c. ____

d. ____

10. A patient service slip personalized to the practice of the physician and used as a communications/billing tool during routing of the patient is also known as a/an

a. ____

b. ____

c. ____

d. ____

11. Match the insurance terms in the first column with the definitions in the second column. Write the correct letters in the blanks.

adjuster ____

assignment ____

carrier ____

coordination of benefits ____

deductible ____

exclusions ____

indemnity ____

premium ____

subscriber ____

time limit ____

waiting period ____

a. An insurance company takes into account benefits payable by another carrier in determining its own liability.

b. Benefits paid by an insurance company to an insured person.

c. Transfer of one's right to collect an amount payable under an insurance contract.

d. Time that must elapse before an indemnity is paid.

e. Acts for insurance company or insured in settlement of claims.

f. Periodic payment to keep insurance policy in force.

g. Amount insured person must pay before policy will pay.

h. Period of time in which a claim must be filed.

i. Certain illnesses or injuries listed in a policy that the insurance company will not cover.

j. Insurance company that carries the insurance.

k. One who belongs to a group plan.

ASSIGNMENT 3

This assignment is given to enhance critical thinking skills. Write down the basic steps in processing an insurance claim from the physician's office, to the insurance company, and after payment is received.

CHAPTER 4

Procedural Coding

Key Terms

Your instructor may wish to select some words pertinent to this chapter for a test. For definitions of the terms, further study, and/or reference, the words, phrases, and abbreviations may be found in the Glossary at the end of the textbook. Key terms for this chapter follow.

actual charge
asterisk procedures
coding creep
conversion factor
crib sheet
Current Procedural Terminology (*CPT*)
customary charge
documentation
down coding
global fee
Health Care Financing Administration Common Procedure Coding System (HCPCS)
modifier
prevailing charges
procedure codes
relative value study (RVS)
SOAP
special report
unbundling
upcoding
usual, customary, and reasonable (UCR)

Performance Objectives

The student will be able to

- Define and spell the key terms for this chapter, given the information from the textbook Glossary, within a reasonable period of time and with enough accuracy to obtain satisfactory evaluation.
- Answer the review questions after reading the chapter with enough accuracy to obtain a satisfactory evaluation.
- Select the five-digit procedure code numbers, modifiers, and/or descriptors of each service, given a series of problems relating to various medical procedures and services and using the *Current Procedural Terminology* (CPT) code book or the Mock Fee Schedule in Appendix A of the *Workbook* with enough accuracy to obtain a satisfactory evaluation.
- Fill in the correct meaning of each abbreviation, given a list of common medical abbreviations and symbols that appear in chart notes, and with enough accuracy to obtain a satisfactory evaluation.

Study Outline

INTRODUCTION
CODING OF PROCEDURES
  Current Procedural Terminology (CPT)
  Relative value studies (RVS)
METHODS OF PAYMENT
  Fee schedule
  RVS
  Resource-based relative value scale (RBRVS)
  Usual, customary, and reasonable (UCR)
  Diagnosis-related groups (DRGs)
VOCABULARY USED IN CODING
EVALUATION AND MANAGEMENT SECTION
  Unlisted procedures
  Basic Life and/or Disability Evaluation Services
DOCUMENTATION
  Documentation Guidelines for Evaluation and Management Services
  General principles of medical record documentation
  Internal audit
SURGERY SECTION
HOW TO USE THE CPT CODE BOOK
  Code book symbols
  Code modifiers
  Multiple modifiers
HOW TO CODE EFFECTIVELY
CODING TIPS
  Bundled codes
  Down coding
  Upcoding
  Unbundling
  Code monitoring
  Office visits
  Consultations
  Drugs and injections
  Administrative or add-on codes
  Surgeries
  Concurrent care
  Follow-up days
  Surgical package
  Medicare global package
  Prolonged services, detention, or standby
  Critical care
  Emergency hospital care
  Emergency office visits
  All-inclusive codes
  Repair of lacerations
  Multiple lesions
RELATIVE VALUE SCALE OR SCHEDULE VARIANCES
  Determining RVS conversion factors
COMPREHENSIVE LIST OF MODIFIER CODES
  Current Procedural Terminology modifier codes
  Relative values for physicians' modifier codes
MEDICARE CODING
LABORATORY ABBREVIATIONS

Review Questions

Review the objectives, key terms, and chapter information before completing the following review questions.

1. The system for coding and billing diagnoses is found in a book entitled ______________________________

____

2. The coding system used for billing professional medical services and procedures is found in a book entitled ______________________________

____

3. For retrieving types of diagnoses related to pathology by an institution within an institution, the coding system is found in a book entitled ______________________________

____

4. The Medicare program uses a system of coding composed of three levels, and this is called ______________________________

5. Complications or special circumstances about a medical service or procedure may be shown by using a CPT code with a/an ______________________________

6. A relative value scale or schedule is a listing of procedure codes indicating the relative value of services performed, which is shown by ______________________________

7. Name four methods for basing payments adopted by insurance companies and state and federal programs.

   a. ______________________________

   b. ______________________________

   c. ______________________________

   d. ______________________________

8. List three programs or plans when a medical practice may elect to use more than one fee schedule.

   a. ______________________________

   b. ______________________________

   c. ______________________________

9. Define the following terms as far as billing is concerned.

   a. New patient ______________________________

   ____

   ____

b. Established patient ______________________________

____

____

10. Explain the difference between a consultation and a referral of a patient.

____

____

11. Briefly state four reasons why medical documentation is required.

a. ______________________________

b. ______________________________

c. ______________________________

d. ______________________________

12. Indicate whether these statements are true (T) or false (F).

a. To be sure correct procedural codes are used, the *Current Procedural Terminology* code book must be purchased annually. ______

b. Crib sheets withstand audits and may be used as documentation. ______

c. Simple lacerations involve the deep layers of the skin. ______

d. When billing surgery for a Medicare patient, the postoperative period can range anywhere from 0 to 90 days. ______

13. Name the six main sections of *CPT.*

a. ______________________________

b. ______________________________

c. ______________________________

d. ______________________________

e. ______________________________

f. ______________________________

14. Give eight reasons for using modifiers on insurance claims.

a. ______________________________

b. ______________________________

c. ______________________________

d. ______________________________

e. ______________________________

f. ______________________________

g. ____________________

h. ____________________

15. Explain when to use the -99 or 09999 modifier code.* ____________________

____

____

16. A code used on a claim that does not match the code system used by the insurance carrier and is converted to the closest code rendering less payment is termed ________

17. Intentional manipulation of procedural codes to generate increased reimbursement is called ____________________

18. Use of many procedural codes to identify procedures that may be described by one code is termed ____________________

19. What modifier is usually used when billing for an assistant surgeon? ________

20. A single fee, which may be seen in some Relative Value Schedules, encompassing services delivered, e.g., surgical procedure, pre- and postoperative care, is known as

____

ASSIGNMENT 4

INTRODUCTION AND EVALUATION AND MANAGEMENT SERVICES

1. To become acquainted with the sections of the *Current Procedural Terminology** code book, match the code number in the left column with the appropriate description in the right column by writing the letters in the blanks. Locate each code number in the *Current Procedural Terminology* code book. As you work through the assignment, the problems are easy at the beginning and get more difficult and complex as you progress.

99231	___	a. Chest x-ray
59400	___	b. Anesthesia for procedures on cervical spine and cord
71010	___	c. Subsequent hospital care
00600	___	d. Supplies and materials
85031	___	e. Routine OB care, ante- and postpartum
99070	___	f. CBC

2. Name the section of CPT where each of the following codes is located.

a. 65091 ____________________

b. 86038 ____________________

c. 92596 ____________________

d. 75982 ____________________

**Current Procedural Terminology* codes, descriptions, and two-digit numeric modifiers only are from CPT 96 copyright 1995 American Medical Association. All rights reserved.

e. 00600 ______________________________

f. 99321 ______________________________

3. Evaluation and Management (E/M) codes are used by physicians to report a significant portion of their services. Remember, it is the physician's responsibility to assign E/M codes and the exercises presented are only for familiarization purposes. The problems will acquaint you with terminology for this section of the CPT code book. Select the appropriate **new patient** office visit codes using the key components:

a. This is a Level 3 case: Detailed history ______________
Detailed examination
Low-complexity decision making

b. This is a Level 1 case: Problem-focused history ______________
Problem-focused examination
Straightforward decision making

c. This is a Level 5 case: Comprehensive history ______________
Comprehensive examination
High-complexity decision making

4. Select the appropriate **established patient** office visit codes using the key components. Coding these cases illustrates consideration of 2 out of 3 components.

a. This is a Level 4 case: Detailed history ______________
Detailed examination
Low-complexity decision making

b. This is a Level 5 case: Comprehensive history ______________
Comprehensive examination
Moderate-complexity decision making

c. This is a Level 5 case: Detailed history ______________
Comprehensive examination
High-complexity decision making

5. Evaluation and Management (E/M) codes **99201** to **99238** are used for services provided in the physician's office or in an outpatient or other ambulatory facility. Read the brief statement and then locate the code number in the *Current Procedural Terminology** code book.

a. Level 1: Office visit of a 20-year-old seen within the last 3 years for instruction in diabetes injection sites. ______________

b. Level 2: Office visit of a 30-year-old new patient with allergic rhinitis. ______________

c. Discussion of medication with the son of an 80-year-old patient with dementia on discharge from the *observation* unit. ______________

d. Admission to hospital of 60-year-old established patient in acute respiratory distress with bronchitis. ______________

e. Hospital visit of a 4-year-old boy, now stable, who will be discharged the next day. ______________

f. Level 5: New patient seen in the office for chest pain, congestive heart failure, and hypertension. ______________

**Current Procedural Terminology* codes, descriptions, and two-digit numeric modifiers only are from CPT 96 copyright 1995 American Medical Association. All rights reserved.

6. Evaluation and Management codes **99241** to **99275** are used for consultations provided in the physician's office or in an outpatient or other ambulatory facility. A consultation is a service provided by a physician whose *opinion* about a case is requested by another physician. Read the brief statement and then locate the code number in the *Current Procedural Terminology** code book.

   a. Level 2: Office consultation for a 30-year-old woman complaining of palpitations and chest pains. Her family physician described a mild systolic click. ________________

   b. Follow-up inpatient consultation for a 64-year-old woman who is now stable admitted 2 days ago for a bleeding ulcer. ________________

   c. Level 4: Office consultation for a 14-year-old boy with poor grades in school and suspected alcohol abuse. ________________

   d. Follow-up inpatient consultation for a 70-year-old man who is diabetic and is suffering with fever, chills, gangrenous heel ulcer, rhonchi, and dyspnea (difficulty breathing), an unstable condition. The patient appears lethargic and tachypneic (rapid breathing). ________________

   e. Level 5: Initial emergency room consultation for a senior who presents with thyrotoxicosis, exophthalmos, cardiac arrhythmia, and congestive heart failure. ________________

   f. Initial hospital consultation for a 30-year-old woman, postabdominal surgery, who is exhibiting a fever. ________________

7. Evaluation and Management codes **99281** to **99499** are used for emergency department, critical care, nursing facility, rest home, custodial care, home, prolonged, physician standby, and preventive medicine services. Read the brief statement and then locate the code number in the *Current Procedural Terminology** code book.

   a. First hour of critical care of a senior who, following major surgery, suffers a cardiac arrest from a pulmonary embolus. ________________

   b. A 40-year-old woman is admitted to the OB unit, and the primary care physician is requested by the Ob-Gyn physician to *stand by* for possible cesarean section and neonatal resuscitation. ________________

   c. A child is seen in the emergency department with a fever, diarrhea, abdominal cramps, and vomiting. ________________

   d. A patient is seen for an annual visit at a nursing facility. ________________

   e. Initial visit to a domiciliary care facility for a developmentally disabled individual with a mild rash on hands and face.

Current Procedural Terminology codes, descriptions, and two-digit numeric modifiers only are from CPT 96 copyright 1995 American Medical Association. All rights reserved.

f. A 50-year-old man with a history of asthma comes into the office with acute bronchospasm and moderate respiratory distress. Office treatment is initiated. The case requires intermittent physician face-to-face time with the patient for 1 hour and 15 minutes, prolonged services. ________________

ASSIGNMENT 5

ANESTHESIA CODING PROBLEMS

Anesthesia codes **00100** to **01999** may be used by anesthesiologists as well as physicians. Some plastic surgeons, other medical specialists, and large clinics may have a room set aside to perform surgical procedures that might be performed in a hospital outpatient surgical department. For Medicare claims some regions do not use the Anesthesia Section of *CPT* for billing but use a surgical code with a HCPCS modifier appended. Read the brief statement and then locate the code number in the *Current Procedural Terminology** code book. Special modifiers **P1** through **P6** may be needed when coding for this section, as well as code numbers for cases that have difficult circumstances. Definitions for abbreviations may be found in the introductory chapter.

a. Abdominal amniocentesis of normal healthy woman ________________

b. Reduction mammoplasty of a woman with mild systemic disease ________________

c. Total right hip replacement, 71-year-old patient ________________

____

d. Repair of cleft palate, critical newborn infant ________________

____

e. TURP, normal healthy male ________________

ASSIGNMENT 6

SURGERY CODING PROBLEMS

Surgery codes **10040** to **69979** are used for each anatomic part of the body. Read over each case carefully. It is preferable to use the *Current Procedural Terminology** code book, but if you do not have one then refer to the Mock Fee Schedule found in Appendix A of this *Workbook* to obtain the correct code number for each descriptor given. Full descriptors for services rendered have been omitted in some instances to give you practice in abstracting the correct descriptor from the available information. Indicate the correct two-digit modifier if necessary. The skill of critical thinking enters this section of the assignment, since you may have to use your own judgment to code as the cases do not contain full details. Definitions for abbreviations may be found in the introductory chapter. Remember to use the index at the back of the *CPT* code book.

**Current Procedural Terminology* codes, descriptions, and two-digit numeric modifiers only are from CPT 96 copyright 1995 American Medical Association. All rights reserved.

a. Suppose you work in an office that has an encounter form listing either code 36240 or 36250. Check your edition of *CPT* and see if you can locate either one or both of them. If the code(s) does not appear, what code number are you directed to use? ________________

Integumentary System 10040–19499

b. Removal of benign lesion from the back (1.0 cm) and left foot (0.5 cm) ________________

____

c. Drainage of deep breast abscess ________________

d. Laser destruction of two benign facial lesions ________________

____

Musculoskeletal System 20000–29909

e. Aspiration of fluid (arthrocentesis) from right knee joint, not infectious ________________

f. Deep tissue biopsy of left upper arm ________________

g. Fracture of the left tibia, closed treatment ________________

Does the procedural code include the application and removal of the first cast? ______

______________ If done as an office procedure, may supplies be coded? ____________

If so, what is the code number from the Medicine section? __________________ Does the procedural code include subsequent replacement of a cast for follow-up care?

______________ If not, list the code number for application of a walking short leg cast

____

Respiratory System 30000–32999

h. Partial parietal pleurectomy ________________

i. Removal of two nasal polyps, simple ________________

j. Diagnostic bronchoscopy with biopsy ________________

Cardiovascular System 33010–37799

k. Pacemaker insertion with transvenous electrode, atrial ________________

l. Thromboendarterectomy with patch graft ________________

m. Introduction of intracatheter and injection procedure for contrast venography ________________

Hemic/Lymphatic/Diaphragm 38100–39599

n. Repair, esophageal/diaphragmatic hernia ______

o. Partial splenectomy ______

p. Excision, two deep cervical nodes ______

Digestive System 40490–49999

q. T & A, 12-year-old boy ______

r. Balloon dilation of esophagus ______

Urinary System/Male and Female Genital 50010–55980

s. Removal of urethral diverticulum from female patient ______

t. Anastomosis of single ureter to bladder ______

Laparoscopy/Peritoneoscopy/Hysteroscopy/Female Genital/Maternity 56300–59899

u. Routine OB care, ante- and postpartum care ______

v. Therapeutic D & C, nonobstetric ______

ASSIGNMENT 7

CODING PROBLEMS FOR RADIOLOGY 70010-79999 AND PATHOLOGY 80002-89399

Radiologists as well as other physicians in many specialties perform these studies. A physician who interprets, dictates, and signs a report may not bill for the report separately as it is considered part of the radiology procedure.

Some medical practices perform basic laboratory tests under a waived test certificate that complies with the rules of the Clinical Laboratory Improvement Amendments (CLIA) of 1988, implemented in September 1992.

a. Upper GI x-ray study with films and KUB ______

b. Ultrasound, pregnant uterus after first trimester, multiple gestation ______

c. Routine urinalysis with microscopy, nonautomated ______

d. Hemoglobin (Hgb), electrophoretic method ______

ASSIGNMENT 8

MODIFIERS AND MEDICINE SECTION 90700–99199

This assignment will reinforce what you have already learned about procedural coding, since code numbers for the problems presented will be located in all the sections of the *CPT* code book. To further enhance your coding skill, insert two-digit modifiers if necessary and search for codes in the Medicine Section. The *CPT* list of modifiers may be found in the *Handbook.*

1. A new patient had five benign skin lesions on the right arm destroyed with surgical curettement. Complete the coding for the surgery.

Code Number	*Description*	
____________	Initial new pt ofice visit	$00.00
____________	Supplies and materials (itemized)	$00.00
____________	Destruction of benign skin lesion rt arm	$00.00
____________	Destruction of second lesion	$00.00
____________	Destruction of third, fourth, and fifth lesions	$00.00

Remember, always list the highest surgical dollar figure first when itemizing on an insurance claim.

2. Mrs. Stayman had four moles on her back. Dr. Davis excised the multiple nevi in one office visit. The information on the pathology report stated nonmalignant lesions measuring 2.2 cm, 1.5 cm, 1 cm, and 0.75 cm.

Code Number	*Description*	
____________	Initial OV	$00.00
____________	Excision, benign lesion 2.2 cm	$00.00
____________	Excision, benign lesion 1.5 cm	$00.00
____________	Excision, benign lesion 1 cm	$00.00
____________	Excision, benign lesion 0.75 cm	$00.00
____________	Supplies and materials (itemized surgical tray)	$00.00

In another case, if a patient required removal of a 1.0-cm lesion on the back and a 0.5-cm lesion on the neck, the procedural codes would be ____________ for the back lesion and ____________ for the neck lesion.

3. Dr. Davis stated on his operative report that Mr. Allen was suffering from a complex, complicated nasal fracture. Dr. Davis debrided the wound, since it was contaminated, and performed an open reduction with internal fixation in a complex and complicated procedure.

Code Number	*Description*	
99204 ________	Initial OV	$00.00
21330	Open tx nasal fracture complicated	$00.00
11044 ________	Debridement, skin, subcutaneous tissue, muscle, and bone	$00.00

4. An R. N., an established patient (est pt) aged 40 years, sees the doctor for an annual physical. A Pap (Papanicolaou) smear is taken and sent to an outside laboratory. The patient also has a furuncle on the right axilla at the time of the visit, which the doctor incises and drains (I & D). The doctor always gives this patient a professional discount for the annual physical but charges the usual and customary fees for other procedures.

Code Number	*Description*
________________	Periodic physical examination
________________	Collection of specimen
________________	I & D, furuncle, right axilla
________________	Sterile tray (itemized)
________________	5 ml penicillin inj IM

5. While making his rounds in the hospital during the noon hour, Dr. James sees a new patient in the ED (emergency department) for a laceration of the forehead, 5.0 cm long. Doctor does a work-up for possible concussion.

Code Number	*Description*
________________	ED care, expanded problem-focused history, expanded problem-focused exam, low complexity decision making
________________	Repair of laceration, simple

6. The doctor sees a new patient in the office with the same condition as the patient in Problem 5, with a dressing change 2 days later by the medical assistant and suture removal 4 days later by the physician.

Code Number	*Description*
________________	Initial new patient office visit
________________	Repair of laceration
________________	Sterile tray (itemized)
________________	Tet tox (tetanus toxoid) 0.5 cc
________________	Minimal service, OV, dressing change (2 days)-NC
________________	OV, suture removal (4 days)-NC
________________	Sterile tray, itemized (optional listing for some practices)

Note: Some fee schedules allow no follow-up days; Medicare fee schedule allows 10 follow-up days for the procedural code number for repair of laceration.

7. The doctor makes a house call on Bobby Jones (est pt) at 11 p.m. for acute otitis media; while there she checks Bobby's sister Mary, whom she has treated previously in the office for tonsillitis. Antibiotic injections are administered to both patients. The physician elects to bill Mary a reduced fee.

Code Number	*Description*
________________	HC (house call), problem-focused interval hx and exam
________________	5 ml penicillin inj IM (intramuscular)

_______________ HC problem-focused interval hx and exam (Mary)

_______________ 5 ml penicillin inj IM

8. A new patient, David Ramsey, age 15 years, was seen by Dr. Menter for lapses of memory and frequent headaches. The doctor performed an EEG (electroencephalogram) and some psychologic tests (including psychodiagnostic assessment of personality and psychopathology tests [Rorschach and MMPI]). Dr. Astro Parkinson was called in as consultant. All the tests were negative, and the patient was advised to come in for weekly psychotherapy.

Code Number *Description*

Dr. Menter's bill:

_______________ OV, comp hx & exam, mod complex decision making

_______________ EEG, extended monitoring (1 hr)

_______________ Psychologic tests (Rorschach and MMPI)

_______________ Psychotherapy (50 min)

Dr. Parkinson's bill:

_______________ Consultation, expanded problem-focused hx and exam, straightforward decision making

9. An est pt, age 70 years, requires repair of a bilateral inguinal hernia. The code for this procedure is _______________________

ASSIGNMENT 9

1. The doctor sees Horace Hart, a 60-year-old new patient, in the office for bronchial asthma, ASHD (arteriosclerotic heart disease), and hypertension. He performs an ECG (electrocardiogram) and UA (urinalysis) without microscopy, and takes x-rays. Seven profile (panel) tests and a CBC (complete blood count) are done by an outside laboratory.

Code Number *Description*

Physician's bill:

_______________ Initial OV, comp hx and exam, high-complexity decision making

_______________ EEG with interpret and report

_______________ UA, routine, nonautomated

_______________ Chest x-ray, 2 views

_______________ Routine venipuncture for collection of specimen

Laboratory's bill:

_______________ Automated multichannel tests: cholesterol, creatinine, glucose, urea nitrogen, calcium, uric acid, albumin

_______________ CBC, completely automated

If the doctor decides to have the chest x-rays interpreted by a radiologist, the procedural code billed by the radiologist would be ____________________.

2. Mr. Hart is seen again in the office on May 12. On May 25 he is seen at home at 2 a.m. with asthma exacerbation, possible myocardial infarct, and congestive heart failure. The doctor consulted with a thoracic cardiovascular surgeon by telephone. He also called to make arrangements for hospitalization. These services required 2 hours and 40 minutes to complete the patient care.

Code Number	*Description*
______________	OV, problem-focused hx and exam, straightforward decision making
______________	Home visit, detailed interval hx and exam, high-complexity decision making
______________	Detention time, prolonged (list time required)

3. On June 9, Horace Hart is seen again in the hospital. The thoracic cardiovascular surgeon who was called in for consultation examines him and says that surgery is necessary. The patient's doctor acts as assistant surgeon and visits the patient for his asthmatic condition. The surgeon does the follow-up care and assumes care in the case.

Code Number	*Description*
Assistant surgeon's bill:	
______________	Hospital visit, problem-focused hx and exam, low-complexity decision making
______________	Pericardiotomy
Thoracic cardiovascular surgeon's bill:	
______________	Consultation, comp hx and exam, moderate-complexity decision making
______________	Pericardiotomy

ASSIGNMENT 10

This is an assignment presented to assist in developing critical thinking skills. Read through this progress note on Roy A. Takashima. Next write down the codes you think this case would warrant and state the reasons for choosing the procedural code numbers that you decide are appropriate.

Takashima, Roy A.
October 5, 199X

Pt. has many things going on. First, he's had no difficulties following the feral cat attack, and the cat was normal on quarantine.

He seemed to be recovering from the flu with the above treatment but is plagued with a very persisting cough and pain down the center of his chest without fever or grossly discolored phlegm.

Physical exam shows expiratory rhonchi and gross exacerbation of his cough on forced expiration. Spirometry before and after bronchodilator was remarkably good, nonetheless it is improved and he is symptomatically improved with a Proventil inhaler which he is given as a sample. I don't think other antibiotics would help.

His reflux is under good control with proprietary antacids with a clear exam.
He has several areas of keratoses on his face and head that need attention.
Finally, in follow up of all the above, he needs a complete physical exam.
Diagnosis: Influenza and bronchitis.

____
Ting Cho, M. D.

mtf

ASSIGNMENT 11

To reinforce abbreviations you have learned, let's review some of the ones encountered during the *Workbook* assignments presented in this chapter. You should be able to decode these abbreviations without a reference. However, if you have difficulty with one or two, simply refer to the introductory chapter of the *Workbook.*

I & D	______________	CBC	______________
IM	______________	E/M	______________
Pap	______________	*CPT*	______________
ER	______________	Ob-Gyn	______________
EEG	______________	TURP	______________
DPT	______________	cm	______________
ECG	______________	T & A	______________
IUD	______________	KUB	______________
OB	______________	GI	______________
D & C	______________	Hgb	______________
OV	______________	new pt	______________
UA	______________	rt	______________
est pt	______________	ml	______________
ASHD	______________	inj	______________
tet. tox.	______________	hx	______________
		NC	______________

CHAPTER 5

Diagnostic Coding

Key Terms

Your instructor may wish to select some words pertinent to this chapter for a test. For definitions and further study of words, phrases, and abbreviations, refer to the Glossary at the end of the textbook. The words for this chapter follow.

combination code
complication
E codes
eponyms
etiology
International Classification of Diseases, Ninth Revision, Clinical Modification (ICD-9-CM)
italicized code
late effect
Not elsewhere classifiable (NEC)
Not otherwise specified (NOS)
primary diagnosis
principal diagnosis
slanted brackets
V codes

Performance Objectives

The student will be able to

- Define and spell the key terms for this chapter, given the information from the textbook Glossary, within a reasonable period of time and with enough accuracy to obtain a satisfactory evaluation.
- Answer the review questions after reading the chapter with enough accuracy to obtain a satisfactory evaluation.
- Assignment 12: Indicate main terms, subterms, subterms to subterms, and carry-over lines, given a section of a page from the *ICD-9-CM* code book, with enough accuracy to obtain a satisfactory evaluation.
- Assignment 13: Answer questions given a section of a page from the *ICD-9-CM* code book with enough accuracy to obtain a satisfactory evaluation.
- Assignment 14: Select the correct diagnostic code numbers, given a series of diagnoses using Volumes 1 and 2 of the *International Classification of Diseases, Ninth Revision, Clinical Modification* (*ICD-9-CM*) code book, with enough accuracy to obtain a satisfactory evaluation.
- Assignment 15: Select the correct procedural and diagnostic code numbers, given a series of diagnoses and procedures using Volumes 1 and 2 of the *ICD-9-CM* and *CPT* code books, with enough accuracy to obtain a satisfactory evaluation.
- Assignment 16: Select the correct code numbers and modifiers, write in the description, and underline the main terms in each diagnosis, given the problems using Volumes 1 and 2 of the *ICD-9-CM* and *CPT* code books, with enough accuracy to obtain a satisfactory evaluation.

Study Outline

INTRODUCTION
CODING OF DISEASES
- History
- ICD-9-CM
- ICD-10
- ICD-9-CM contents

HOW TO USE THE DIAGNOSTIC CODE BOOKS PROPERLY
- Coding instructions
- Basic steps in coding
- Handy hints in diagnostic coding
- E codes
- V codes
- Rules for coding signs, symptoms, and ill-defined conditions
- Rules for coding sterilization
- Rules for coding neoplasms
- Rules for coding circulatory system conditions
- Rules for coding diabetes mellitus
- Rules for coding pregnancy, delivery, or abortion
- Rules for coding admitting diagnoses
- Rules for coding burns
- Rules for coding injuries and late effects

DIAGNOSTIC CODING AND THE PHYSICIAN'S FEE PROFILE

Review Questions

Review the objectives, key terms, and chapter information before completing the following review questions.

1. The abbreviation *ICD-9-CM* means ____

   ____

2. The coding in *ICD-9-CM* varies from ________ to ________ characters.

3. Volume 1, Diseases, is a/an ____________________ listing of code numbers.

4. Volume 2, Diseases, is a/an ____________________ index or listing of code numbers.

5. The abbreviation NEC appearing in the *ICD-9-CM* code books means __________

____

6. To code using Volume 2, the Alphabetic Index, the ____________________ is looked up rather than the anatomic part.

7. E codes are a supplementary classification of coding for ______________ rather than disease and of coding for ______________________________

8. Why is it important that diagnostic *ICD-9-CM* coding become routinely used in the physician's office? ____

____

ASSIGNMENT 12

Abstracted sections from a page of the *International Classification of Diseases, 9th Revision, Clinical Modification,* Volume 2 are shown. Label the line indicated as either main term, subterm, subterm to subterm, or carry-over line. Refer to Chapter 5 in the textbook to the section, "Rules for Coding Diabetes Mellitus" and locate an unnumbered figure that graphically illustrates heading, section title, main term and subterms, subterms to subterms, and carryover lines.

1. ______________________	**Saccharomyces infection** (*see also*
2. ______________________	Candidiasis) 112.9
	Sacroilitis NEC 720.2
	Sacrum—*see* condition
	Saddle
3. ______________________	back 737.8
	embolus, aorta 444.0
4. ______________________	nose 738.0
	congenital 754.0
	due to syphilis 090.5
5. ______________________	**Salicylism**
	correct substance properly administered
	535.4
	Salmonella (aertrycke) (choleraesuis)
6. ______________________	(enteritidis) (gallinarum) (suipestifer)
	(typhimurium) (*see also* Infection,
7. ______________________	Salmonella) 003.9
	arthritis 003.23
	carrier (suspected) of V02.3

ASSIGNMENT 13

A section from a page of the *International Classification of Diseases, 9th Revision, Clinical Modification,* Volume 2, is shown. Answer the questions pertaining to Categories 320 and 321.

6. DISEASES OF THE NERVOUS SYSTEM AND SENSE ORGANS (320-389)

INFLAMMATORY DISEASES OF THE CENTRAL NERVOUS SYSTEM (320-326)

320 Bacterial meningitis

Includes: arachnoiditis, leptomeningitis, meningitis, meningoencephalitis } bacterial
meningomyelitis
pachymeningitis

320.0 Hemophilus meningitis

Meningitis due to Hemophilus influenzae [H. Influenzae]

320.1 Pneumococcal meningitis

320.2 Streptococcal meningitis

320.3 Staphylococcal meningitis

320.7 Meningitis in other bacterial diseases classified elsewhere

Code first underlying disease as:
actinomycosis (039.8)
listeriosis (027.0)
typhoid fever (002.0)
whooping cough (033.0-033.9)

Excludes: *meningitis (in):*
epidemic (036.0)
gonococcal (098.82)
meningococcal (036.0)
salmonellosis (003.21)
syphilis:
NOS (094.2)
congenital (090.42)
meningovascular (094.2)
secondary (091.81)
tuberculous (013.0)

320.8 Meningitis due to other specified bacteria

320.81 Anaerobic meningitis

Gram-negative anaerobes
Bacteroides (fragilis)

320.82 Meningitis due to gram-negative bacteria, not elsewhere classified

Aerobacter aerogenes
Escherichia coli [E. coli]
Friedländer bacillus
Klebsiella pneumoniae
Proteus morganii
Pseudomonas

Excludes: *gram-negative anaerobes (320.81)*

320.89 Meningitis due to other specified bacteria

Bacillus pyocyaneus

320.9 Meningitis due to unspecified bacterium

Meningitis:
bacterial NOS
purulent NOS

Meningitis:
pyogenic NOS
suppurative NOS

321 Meningitis due to other organisms

Includes: arachnoiditis, leptomeningitis, meningitis, pachymeningitis } due to organisms other than bacteria

321.0 Cryptococcal meningitis

Code first underlying disease (117.5)

1. Locate the section title ______________________________
____

2. Refer to the INCLUSION TERMS listed under category code 320, entitled "Bacterial meningitis." Place an "X" in front of each of the following diagnostic statements that are included in category 320.

____ purulent meningitis

____ bacterial meningomyelitis

____ meningitis

____ meningoencephalitis

____ pyogenic meningitis

____ meningococcal

3. Refer to the EXCLUSION TERMS located under code 320.7, entitled "Meningitis in other bacterial diseases classified elsewhere." Place an "X" in front of the following code number(s) which are excluded.

____ secondary syphilis 091.81

____ acquired syphilis 097.9

____ gonococcal meningitis 036.0

____ congenital syphilis 090.42

____ primary syphilis 091.2

____ gram-negative anaerobes 320.81

4. Place an "X" in front of each of the following diagnostic statements included in category code 320 and its subcategories.

____ leptomeningitis

____ meningitis due to E. coli

____ pyogenic meningitis

____ epidemic meningitis

____ tuberculous meningitis

5. Write the code numbers for category 320 that require fifth digits.

____

ASSIGNMENT 14

To locate the correct code numbers, use Volumes 1 and 2 of *ICD-9-CM.* Enter the appropriate code number(s) for the diagnoses. Locate the code in the Alphabetic List (Volume 2), and check the code number with the Tabular List (Volume 1). To assist you in locating the proper code, the key words appear in italics. These diagnoses appear on subsequent patient records in this *Workbook.*

Diagnosis	ICD-9-CM *Code Number(s)*	
1. Urinary *incontinence*	______	
2. Multiple vesicovaginal *fistulas* of bladder	______	
3. *Carcinoma* of prostate	______	
4. Prepyloric gastric *ulcer*	______	
5. *Hypertension,* benign essential	______	
6. *Cholecystitis* with *cholelithiasis*	______	
7. Inflammatory cystic *lesion* of scalp, 1.5 cm diameter	______	______
8. Severe *onychocryptosis,* both margins of left hallux	______	______
9. Recurrent *epistaxis* due to *hypertension*	______	______
10. *Infection* at base of nail of great left toe	______	
11. Internal and external *hemorrhoids*	______	______
12. Two infected rectal *polyps*	______	
13. Acute *tonsillitis*	______	
14. *Effusion* and ligament *strain,* left knee	______	______
15. Arteriosclerotic cardiovascular *disease, angina* pectoris	______	______
16. Acute *cephalgia*	______	
17. Nasal *laceration*	______	
18. *Deviated* septum	______	
19. Pulmonary *emphysema*	______	
20. Recurrent *pneumonitis* due to inhalation of oils and essences	______	
21. Exertional *dyspnea*	______	
22. Food and inhalant *allergy*	______	
23. Internal and external bleeding *hemorrhoids*	______	______
24. Anal *fistula*	______	
25. *Onychauxis* and *onychocryptosis*	______	______

26. Right *otitis* media, nonsuppurative ________

27. Suburethral *cyst* ________

28. Lung *abscess* ________

ASSIGNMENT 15

To locate the correct code numbers for this assignment, use Volumes 1 and 2 of *ICD-9-CM.* Enter the appropriate code number(s) for the diagnoses, watching carefully for the coding instructions. These questions require two code numbers.

Diagnosis	ICD-9-CM *Code Number(s)*
1. Acute gastritis with hemorrhage	________

Code the following diagnoses both alone and with the additional diagnoses or information provided.

Alone		*With Additional Information*	
2. Menorrhagia	________	in a 12-year-old person	________
3. Septic shock	________	postoperative	________
4. Hemiplegia	________	congenital	________
5. Papanicolaou smear	________	as part of gynecologic exam	________

Now bring your coding expertise to an advanced level and code the following questions using your *ICD-9-CM* code book to code the diagnoses and your *Current Procedural Terminology* (CPT) code book to code the procedures. Be sure to check that listed procedures are consistent with the diagnosis.

6. Corneal foreign body, right eye	ICD #	________
Removal of foreign body, slit lamp, cornea	CPT #	________
7. Spondylolysis (lumbosacral region)	ICD #	________
Chiropractic manipulation of LS area	CPT #	________
8. Bleeding duodenal ulcer	ICD #	________
Esophagogastroduodenoscopy (EGD)	CPT #	________
9. Bacterial meningitis (pneumococcal)	ICD #	________
Lumbar puncture	CPT #	________
10. Ingrown nail, right great toe, with infection	ICD #	________
Avulsion of nail plate	CPT #	________
11. Diabetes mellitus with polyneuropathy	ICD #	________
	ICD #	________
EMGs of all four extremities	CPT #	________

12. Fibrocystic disease of the breast ICD # ______

    Bilateral mammograms CPT # ______

13. Crohn's disease of colon ICD # ______

    Colonoscopy with biopsy CPT # ______

14. Acute arthropathy associated with infection (rheumatic fever) ICD # ______

    ICD # ______

    Aspiration of right knee joint CPT # ______

15. Trifascicular heart block ICD # ______

    Placement permanent pacemaker, AV sequential CPT # ______

ASSIGNMENT 16

Read over each case carefully. Use your *CPT* and *ICD-9-CM* code books to locate the correct code numbers. Then write in the appropriate descriptions. Full descriptions for services rendered have been omitted in some instances to give you practice in abstracting the correct descriptor from the available information. Indicate the correct modifiers for the procedures, if necessary. *Underline* the *main* term in each diagnosis. This is the term that you looked up first. Be sure to check that listed procedures are consistent with the diagnosis.

Case 1: A new patient is seen with a complaint of low back pain and lack of feeling in the lower back. The physician does a level III examination and orders x-ray films of the lumbosacral spine in AP, lateral, and flexed positions. A diagnosis of vertebrogenic lumbosacral radiculitis is made. The patient is referred to a facility for electromyography of the right extremity and related paraspinal areas. Code the visit, x-ray, EMG of paraspinal areas and 2 extremities (do not include a visit), and the diagnosis.

___ ______________________________

___ ______________________________

___ ______________________________

___ Dx: ______________________________

Case 2: Maria, an established patient, was seen by her gynecologist for a Level II visit. A conization of the cervix (cone) was done during this visit. A sterile tray was used during the procedure. The pathology report of the biopsy read squamous cell dysplasia of the cervix. Code the visit, biopsy, and diagnosis.

___ ______________________________

___ ______________________________

___ ______________________________

___ Dx: ______________________________

Case 3: The patient is seen by the family physician for a complaint of extreme loss of strength in her arms and legs. The physician has not seen the patient for almost 3 years, so he performs a Level V extended examination. The patient is referred to a neurologist for further study with a diagnosis of generalized muscle weakness. Code the visit and diagnosis.

____ ____

____ Dx: ____

Case 4: Mr. Smith is seen in the emergency department of a local hospital for an expanded problem-focused hx and exam and moderate decision making. He was a long-time patient of Dr. Jones. Dr. Jones took the patient's call, and, since he was going to be in the emergency room for another patient that afternoon, he asked Mr. Smith to meet him there. An anoplasty was done to repair the stricture lacerated by an enema tube, and an anoscopy was done for control of hemorrhage. The diagnosis on the medical record was lacerated anal sphincter. Code the ED visit, surgical procedures, and diagnosis. The hospital will bill separately for the room and sterile setup.

____ ____

____ ____

____ ____

____ Dx: ____

Case 5: A mother brings her 5-year-old child, who is an established patient, to the family physician for a Level II visit. The child has lesions on the face, which are diagnosed as chronic impetiginous eczema. Code the visit and diagnosis.

____ ____

____ Dx: ____

Case 6: A dermatologist is seeing a patient for a fungus infection. The patient now comes in with a new complaint. After a comprehensive hx and exam with high-complexity decision making, the new complaint is diagnosed as discoid lupus erythematosus. The patient is referred to an outside laboratory for studies. Code the visit and diagnosis.

____ ____

____ Dx: ____

Case 7: A patient is referred by her family physician after a diagnosis of malaria is reported by the lab. The specific diagnosis is falciparum malaria (Dx Code ________). She is quite ill and has a complication of *Klebsiella* pneumonia (Dx Code ________). Her hospital admis-sion is billed as initial comprehensive hx and exam with high-complexity decision making hosp care (Proc Code ________). The physician is charging her less because he is not using the consultation code since it is such an interesting case for him. A modifier is not necessary.

Case 8: A regular patient comes in for an office visit—expanded problem-focused hx and exam with low-complexity decision making—(Proc Code ________) with a diagnosis of influenza with laryngitis (Dx Code ________). She returns in 4 days for a minimal visit, at which time her antibiotic is changed (Proc Code ________).

Case 9: The last patient of the day was seen in follow up—expanded problem-focused hx and exam with low-complexity decision making— (Proc Code ________). The diagnosis for this visit is intra-abdominal abscess of the peritoneum (Dx Code ________). The original culture was diagnosed as staphylococcemia (staph septicemia) (Dx Code ________).

Case 10: An internist who specializes in infectious diseases sees a patient who has eye pain, a swollen forehead, and sores on his face. The patient is an established patient who has chronic obstructive pulmonary disease. His hospital admitting diagnoses are herpes ophthalmicus (zoster) (Dx Code ________) and COPD (Dx Code ________). Hospital services include (1) comprehensive H & P with moderately complex decision making, TX program (Proc Code ________) and (2) daily problem-focused interval hx and exam, low-complex decision making hosp visits X 11 (Proc Code ________). The patient is discharged after discussion of hospital stay and instructions for continuing care and preparation of hospital records (Proc Code ________). The patient is to appear at the physician's office daily for therapeutic IV injections of corticosteroids (problem-focused hx and exam with low-complex decision making). Code the injection–IV therapy and visit (Proc Codes ________ ________). The patient will have quantitative blood urea nitrogen (Proc Code ________) and blood creatinine (Proc Code ________) studies done periodically at the physician's lab. The added diagnoses of eye pain (Dx Code ________) and anorexia (Dx Code ________) are now in effect.

CHAPTER 6

The Health Insurance Claim Form

Key Terms

Your instructor may wish to select some specific words pertinent to this chapter for a test. For definitions of the terms, further study, and/or reference, words, phrases, and abbreviations may be found in the Glossary at the end of the textbook. *Key terms for this chapter follow.*

clean claim
digital fax claim
dingy claims
dirty claims
electronic claim
employer supplemental insurance
HCFA-1500 claim form
incomplete claim
intelligent character recognition (ICR)
invalid claim
Medigap policy
optical character recognition (OCR)
ordering physician
"other" claims
paper claim
pending claim
physically clean claim
referring physician
rejected claim

Performance Objectives

The student will be able to

- Define and spell the key terms for this chapter, given the information from the textbook Glossary, within a reasonable period of time and with enough accuracy to obtain a satisfactory evaluation.
- Answer the review questions after reading the chapter, with enough accuracy to obtain a satisfactory evaluation.
- Type a HCFA-1500 Health Insurance Claim Form and list the reasons why the claim was either rejected or delayed, given a handwritten HCFA-1500 Form, within a reasonable period of time and with enough accuracy to obtain a satisfactory evaluation.
- Complete each HCFA-1500 Health Insurance Claim Form for billing, given the patients' medical chart notes, ledger cards, encounter forms, and blank insurance claim forms, within a reasonable period of time and with enough accuracy to obtain a satisfactory evaluation.
- Correctly post payments, adjustments, and balances to the patients' ledger cards, using the Mock Fee Schedule in Appendix A, within a reasonable period of time and with enough accuracy to obtain a satisfactory evaluation.
- Fill in the correct meaning of each abbreviation, given a list of common medical abbreviations and symbols that appear in chart notes within a reasonable period of time and with enough accuracy to obtain a satisfactory evaluation.

Study Outline

INTRODUCTION
TYPES OF CLAIMS
ABSTRACTING FROM MEDICAL RECORDS
MEDICAL AND DIAGNOSTIC TERMINOLOGY
PROCEDURES FOR USE OF THE HEALTH INSURANCE CLAIM FORM—HCFA-1500
COMMON REASONS WHY CLAIMS ARE REJECTED OR DELAYED
COMPLETING AN OPTICALLY SCANNED FORM
  Optical Character Recognition
  Optical Character Recognition (OCR) or Intelligent Character Recognition (ICR) Guidelines
COMPLETING THE HEALTH INSURANCE CLAIM FORM—HCFA-1500 BLOCKS 1 THROUGH 33
EXPLANATION OF BENEFITS

Review Questions

Review the objectives, key terms, chapter information, glossary definitions to key terms, and figures before completing the following review questions.

1. Who developed the Standard or Uniform Form? ____________________

2. State the name of the insurance form adopted by the American Medical Association.

____

3. Does Medicare accept the HCFA-1500 claim form? ____________________

4. Match the word from the left column with its definition from the right column.

clean claim ______
paper claim ______
invalid claim ______
dirty claim ______
electronic claim ______

a. Insurance carrier is unable to process a claim for a certain service, and claim is held until system changes are made.

b. A phrase used when a claim is held back from payment.

c. Claim submitted and then optically scanned by the insurance carrier.

suspense claim	______	d.	Claim that needs manual processing because of errors or to solve a problem.
rejected claim	______	e.	Claim needing clarification and answers to questions.
dingy claim	______	f.	Claim submitted via telephone or fax.
		g.	Claim submitted within the time limit and correctly completed.
		h.	Medicare claim that contains complete, necessary information but is illogical or incorrect.

5. What is an eponym? ____

6. Match the following medical and diagnostic terms in the second column with the correct definitions in the first column. Write the correct letters in the blanks.

a bruise	______	a.	pertussis
stone	______	b.	epistaxis
mole	______	c.	otitis
nosebleed	______	d.	cachexia
inflammation of ear	______	e.	calculus
painful urination	______	f.	nevus
general ill health	______	g.	epigastrium
wart	______	h.	alopecia
over the stomach	______	i.	ecchymosis
loss of appetite	______	j.	anorexia
incision below ribs	______	k.	dysuria
headache	______	l.	verruca
pus	______	m.	hypogastrium
whooping cough	______	n.	purulent
baldness	______	o.	cephalgia
		p.	subcostal incision

7. What important document must you have before an insurance company can photocopy a patient's chart? ____

8. What is dual coverage? ______________________________

____

9. If a patient brings in a form for group insurance through his or her employer, where do you send the form after completion by the patient and by the physician? ____

____

10. If the patient brings in a private insurance form that is not group insurance, where do you send the form after completion? ______________________

11. What is the *usual* time frame for sending in an insurance claim form for an extended illness? ______________________________

12. In completing an insurance claim form, the patient can be either the __________ ______________ or the ______________________. However, as written in Chapter 3, the insured is also known as the ____________________ or ____________________.

13. Indicate whether the following statements are True (T) or False (F).

   a. A photocopy of a claim form may be optically scanned. _____

   b. Handwriting is permitted on optically scanned insurance claims. _____

   c. Do not fold or crease an insurance form that will be optically scanned. _____

   d. Never strike over errors when making a correction on a claim form that is to be optically scanned. _____

14. When preparing a claim that is to be optically scanned, birth dates are keyed in using ______________________ digits.

15. Define this abbreviation. MG/MCD ______________________________

16. A HCFA-assigned National Provider Identifier Number (NPI) consists of_______ __________ characters.

17. The employer I.D. number is also sometimes called ______________________ or ____________________________.

18. After an insurance claim is paid by the carrier, a document known as a/an ______________________________ is sent to the patient and to the physician.

ASSIGNMENT 17

To alleviate frustration and ease into completing a claim form for the first time, read the handwritten HCFA-1500 Health Insurance Claim Form (Fig. 6–1). Type the information on

PLEASE DO NOT STAPLE IN THIS AREA

APPROVED OMB-0938-0008

ASSIGNMENT 19

CARRIER

PICA

HEALTH INSURANCE CLAIM FORM

PICA

1. MEDICARE (Medicare #) ☐ MEDICAID (Medicaid #) ☐ CHAMPUS (Sponsor's SSN) ☐ CHAMPVA (VA File #) ☐ GROUP HEALTH PLAN (SSN or ID) ☐ FECA BLK LUNG (SSN) ☐ OTHER (ID) ☑

1a. INSURED'S I.D. NUMBER (FOR PROGRAM IN ITEM 1): PX 4278A

2. PATIENT'S NAME (Last Name, First Name, Middle Initial): Parkinson, Jamie B.

3. PATIENT'S BIRTH DATE MM DD YY: 04 06 83 SEX M ☒ F ☐

4. INSURED'S NAME (Last Name, First Name, Middle Initial): Parkinson, Jamie B.

5. PATIENT'S ADDRESS (No., Street): 4510 South A Street

CITY: Woodland Hills STATE: XY

ZIP CODE TELEPHONE (Include Area Code) ( )

6. PATIENT RELATIONSHIP TO INSURED: Self ☐ Spouse ☐ Child ☒ Other ☐

7. INSURED'S ADDRESS (No., Street): 4510 South A Street

CITY: Woodland Hills STATE: XY

ZIP CODE: 12345 TELEPHONE (INCLUDE AREA CODE): (013) 742-1560

8. PATIENT STATUS: Single ☒ Married ☐ Other ☐ Employed ☐ Full-Time Student ☒ Part-Time Student ☐

9. OTHER INSURED'S NAME (Last Name, First Name, Middle Initial)

a. OTHER INSURED'S POLICY OR GROUP NUMBER

b. OTHER INSURED'S DATE OF BIRTH MM DD YY SEX M ☐ F ☐

c. EMPLOYER'S NAME OR SCHOOL NAME

d. INSURANCE PLAN NAME OR PROGRAM NAME

10. IS PATIENT'S CONDITION RELATED TO:

a. EMPLOYMENT? (CURRENT OR PREVIOUS) ☐ YES ☒ NO

b. AUTO ACCIDENT? ☐ YES ☒ NO PLACE (State)

c. OTHER ACCIDENT? ☐ YES ☒ NO

10d. RESERVED FOR LOCAL USE

11. INSURED'S POLICY GROUP OR FECA NUMBER

a. INSURED'S DATE OF BIRTH MM DD YY SEX M ☐ F ☐

b. EMPLOYER'S NAME OR SCHOOL NAME

c. INSURANCE PLAN NAME OR PROGRAM NAME

d. IS THERE ANOTHER HEALTH BENEFIT PLAN? ☐ YES ☒ NO *If yes,* return to and complete item 9 a-d.

READ BACK OF FORM BEFORE COMPLETING & SIGNING THIS FORM.

12. PATIENT'S OR AUTHORIZED PERSON'S SIGNATURE I authorize the release of any medical or other information necessary to process this claim. I also request payment of government benefits either to myself or to the party who accepts assignment below.

SIGNED Jamie B. Parkinson DATE 7-14-9X

13. INSURED'S OR AUTHORIZED PERSON'S SIGNATURE I authorize payment of medical benefits to the undersigned physician or supplier for services described below.

SIGNED Jamie B. Parkinson

PATIENT AND INSURED INFORMATION

14. DATE OF CURRENT: MM DD YY 07 14 9X ◀ ILLNESS (First symptom) OR INJURY (Accident) OR PREGNANCY(LMP)

15. IF PATIENT HAS HAD SAME OR SIMILAR ILLNESS. GIVE FIRST DATE MM DD YY

16. DATES PATIENT UNABLE TO WORK IN CURRENT OCCUPATION FROM MM DD YY TO MM DD YY

17. NAME OF REFERRING PHYSICIAN OR OTHER SOURCE

17a. I.D. NUMBER OF REFERRING PHYSICIAN

18. HOSPITALIZATION DATES RELATED TO CURRENT SERVICES FROM MM DD YY TO MM DD YY

19. RESERVED FOR LOCAL USE

20. OUTSIDE LAB? ☐ YES ☒ NO $ CHARGES

21. DIAGNOSIS OR NATURE OF ILLNESS OR INJURY. (RELATE ITEMS 1,2,3 OR 4 TO ITEM 24E BY LINE)

1. ___ . ___ 3. ___ . ___

2. ___ . ___ 4. ___ . ___

22. MEDICAID RESUBMISSION CODE ORIGINAL REF. NO.

23. PRIOR AUTHORIZATION NUMBER

24. A DATE(S) OF SERVICE From MM DD YY	To MM DD YY	B Place of Service	C Type of Service	D PROCEDURES, SERVICES, OR SUPPLIES (Explain Unusual Circumstances) CPT/HCPCS	MODIFIER	E DIAGNOSIS CODE	F $ CHARGES	G DAYS OR UNITS	H EPSDT Family Plan	I EMG	J COB	K RESERVED FOR LOCAL USE
07 04 9X				99242		1	85 00					
07 14 9X				71020		1						

PHYSICIAN OR SUPPLIER INFORMATION

25. FEDERAL TAX I.D. NUMBER: 95-1234567 SSN ☐ EIN ☒

26. PATIENT'S ACCOUNT NO.

27. ACCEPT ASSIGNMENT? (For govt. claims, see back) ☒ YES ☐ NO

28. TOTAL CHARGE $ 165 00

29. AMOUNT PAID $

30. BALANCE DUE $ 165 00

31. SIGNATURE OF PHYSICIAN OR SUPPLIER INCLUDING DEGREES OR CREDENTIALS (I certify that the statements on the reverse apply to this bill and are made a part thereof.)

SIGNED DATE 7-14-9X

32. NAME AND ADDRESS OF FACILITY WHERE SERVICES WERE RENDERED (If other than home or office)

33. PHYSICIAN'S, SUPPLIER'S BILLING NAME, ADDRESS, ZIP CODE & PHONE #

JOHN DOE, M.D. 013/742-1002
1234 Main Street
Woodland Hills, XY 12345

PIN# GRP# 3664021 CC

(APPROVED BY AMA COUNCIL ON MEDICAL SERVICE 8/88)

PLEASE PRINT OR TYPE

FORM HCFA-1500 (U2) (12-90)
FORM OWCP-1500 FORM RRB-1500

mtf

FIGURE 6-1

the blank HCFA-1500 Form (Fig. 6–2). Then list the reasons why the claim may be either rejected or delayed according to the errors found. The name of the insurance carrier is ABC Insurance Company, 111 Main Street, Denver, Colorado 80210. Assume the patient's private insurance form is to be attached to this claim. Refer to *Insurance Handbook for the Medical Office*, Chapter 6, for instructions about how to complete the HCFA-1500 insurance claim form and see Figure 6-1 for visual placement of data. Remember to refer to the Workbook Introduction section, pp. 1-14.

ASSIGNMENT 18

1. Assume the *Health Insurance Claim Form** HCFA-1500 claim form is printed in red ink for processing by OCR or ICR. Complete the form using OCR or ICR guidelines and send the form to the Prudential Insurance Company for Mrs. Merry M. Mclean by referring to her E/M Code Slip (Fig. 6–3), patient record (Fig. 6–4), and ledger card (Fig. 6–5). Date the claim June 15. Refer to Appendix A to fill in the fees on the ledger card. Many physicians complete an E/M Code Slip for each patient encounter. This chapter's assignments feature examples of this form as a reference for part of each exercise to give you experience and to assist you with E/M *CPT* code selection. Be sure to type your initials at the lower left corner of the claim form (Fig. 6–6).
2. Use your *Current Procedural Terminology (CPT)* code book or Appendix A to determine the correct five-digit code number for each professional service rendered. Remember to include modifiers if necessary. Check the Mock Fee Schedule in Appendix A to see how many follow-up days are included for the surgical fee that would be listed as in-office documentation and would not receive a charge. Refer to the textbook for detailed discussion about follow-up days. Do not type *no charge* entries on the insurance claim, which may appear on the ledger card for documentation purposes.
3. Record on the ledger card when you have billed the insurance company.

Abbreviations pertinent to this record:

adm ______________	intermed ______________
CC ______________	init ______________
Cont ______________	IVP ______________
Cysto ______________	mo ______________
Disch ______________	NC ______________
Dx ______________	OC ______________
hosp ______________	Op ______________
HV ______________	PC ______________
$\bar{c}$ ______________	

Text continued on page 67

*See Chapter 6 for help in completing this form.

HEALTH INSURANCE CLAIM FORM

PICA

MEDICAID | CHAMPUS | CHAMPVA | GROUP HEALTH PLAN | FECA BLK LUNG | OTHER

) ☐ (Medicaid #) ☐ (Sponsor's SSN) ☐ (VA File #) ☐ (SSN or ID) ☐ (SSN) ☐ (ID)

1a. INSURED'S I.D. NUMBER (FOR PROGRAM IN ITEM 1)

AME (Last Name, First Name, Middle Initial)

3. PATIENT'S BIRTH DATE MM | DD | YY SEX M ☐ F ☐

4. INSURED'S NAME (Last Name, First Name, Middle Initial)

DDRESS (No., Street)

6. PATIENT RELATIONSHIP TO INSURED Self ☐ Spouse ☐ Child ☐ Other ☐

7. INSURED'S ADDRESS (No., Street)

STATE

8. PATIENT STATUS Single ☐ Married ☐ Other ☐

CITY | STATE

TELEPHONE (Include Area Code) ( )

Employed ☐ Full-Time Student ☐ Part-Time Student ☐

ZIP CODE | TELEPHONE (INCLUDE AREA CODE) ( )

RED'S NAME (Last Name, First Name, Middle Initial)

10. IS PATIENT'S CONDITION RELATED TO:

11. INSURED'S POLICY GROUP OR FECA NUMBER

RED'S POLICY OR GROUP NUMBER

a. EMPLOYMENT? (CURRENT OR PREVIOUS) ☐ YES ☐ NO

a. INSURED'S DATE OF BIRTH MM | DD | YY SEX M ☐ F ☐

RED'S DATE OF BIRTH YY SEX M ☐ F ☐

b. AUTO ACCIDENT? ☐ YES ☐ NO PLACE (State)

b. EMPLOYER'S NAME OR SCHOOL NAME

S NAME OR SCHOOL NAME

c. OTHER ACCIDENT? ☐ YES ☐ NO

c. INSURANCE PLAN NAME OR PROGRAM NAME

PLAN NAME OR PROGRAM NAME

10d. RESERVED FOR LOCAL USE

d. IS THERE ANOTHER HEALTH BENEFIT PLAN? ☐ YES ☐ NO *If yes*, return to and complete item 9 a-d.

READ BACK OF FORM BEFORE COMPLETING & SIGNING THIS FORM.

OR AUTHORIZED PERSON'S SIGNATURE I authorize the release of any medical or other information necessary nis claim. I also request payment of government benefits either to myself or to the party who accepts assignment

DATE

13. INSURED'S OR AUTHORIZED PERSON'S SIGNATURE I authorize payment of medical benefits to the undersigned physician or supplier for services described below.

SIGNED

PATIENT AND INSURED INFORMATION

URRENT: YY ◀ ILLNESS (First symptom) OR INJURY (Accident) OR PREGNANCY(LMP)

15. IF PATIENT HAS HAD SAME OR SIMILAR ILLNESS. GIVE FIRST DATE MM | DD | YY

16. DATES PATIENT UNABLE TO WORK IN CURRENT OCCUPATION FROM MM | DD | YY TO MM | DD | YY

EFERRING PHYSICIAN OR OTHER SOURCE

17a. I.D. NUMBER OF REFERRING PHYSICIAN

18. HOSPITALIZATION DATES RELATED TO CURRENT SERVICES FROM MM | DD | YY TO MM | DD | YY

FOR LOCAL USE

20. OUTSIDE LAB? ☐ YES ☐ NO $ CHARGES

OR NATURE OF ILLNESS OR INJURY. (RELATE ITEMS 1,2,3 OR 4 TO ITEM 24E BY LINE)

3. ___ . ___

4. ___ . ___

22. MEDICAID RESUBMISSION CODE | ORIGINAL REF. NO.

23. PRIOR AUTHORIZATION NUMBER

	B	C	D	E	F	G	H	I	J	K
E(S) OF SERVICE To YY MM DD YY	Place of Service	Type of Service	PROCEDURES, SERVICES, OR SUPPLIES (Explain Unusual Circumstances) CPT/HCPCS | MODIFIER	DIAGNOSIS CODE	$ CHARGES	DAYS OR UNITS	EPSDT Family Plan	EMG	COB	RESERVED FOR LOCAL USE

AX I.D. NUMBER SSN EIN ☐ ☐

26. PATIENT'S ACCOUNT NO.

27. ACCEPT ASSIGNMENT? (For govt. claims, see back) ☐ YES ☐ NO

28. TOTAL CHARGE $

29. AMOUNT PAID $

30. BALANCE DUE $

OF PHYSICIAN OR SUPPLIER DEGREES OR CREDENTIALS the statements on the reverse bill and are made a part thereof.)

DATE

32. NAME AND ADDRESS OF FACILITY WHERE SERVICES WERE RENDERED (If other than home or office)

33. PHYSICIAN'S, SUPPLIER'S BILLING NAME, ADDRESS, ZIP CODE & PHONE #

PIN# | GRP#

PHYSICIAN OR SUPPLIER INFORMATION

D BY AMA COUNCIL ON MEDICAL SERVICE 8/88)

PLEASE PRINT OR TYPE

FORM HCFA-1500 (U2) (12-90)
FORM OWCP-1500 FORM RRB-1500

FIGURE 6-2

E/M Code Slip

Patient *Mclean, Merry M.*

Date *5-6-9X*
CPT Code________
Dx Code________

HISTORY

☐ Problem Focused
Chief complaint; Brief history of present illness

☐ Expanded Problem Focused
Chief complaint; Brief history of present illness;
Problem pertinent system review

☑ Detailed
Chief complaint; Extended history of present illness;
Extended system review; Pertinent past family, social history

☐ Comprehensive
Chief complaint; Extended history of present illness;
Complete system review; Complete past family, social history

EXAMINATION

☐ Problem Focused
Exam limited to affected body area or organ system

☐ Expanded Problem Focused
Exam extended to other symptomatic or related organ systems

☑ Detailed
Extended exam of affected area(s) and other symptomatic or related systems

☐ Comprehensive
Complete single system specialty exam or complete multi-system exam

MEDICAL DECISION MAKING

	Medical Decision	Number of Dx Options	Amount of Data	Risk M & M
☐	Straightforward	minimal 1 dx	minimal	minimal
☑	Low Complexity	limited 1-2 dx	limited	low
☐	Moderate Complexity	multiple 1-2 dx	moderate	moderate
☐	High Complexity	extensive 2-3 dx	extensive	high

☐ Counseling Time________________
☐ Consult Referring Dr.________________

Diagnosis *see Pt Record*

FIGURE 6-3

PATIENT RECORD

LAST NAME	FIRST NAME	MIDDLE NAME	BIRTH DATE	SEX	HOME PHONE
Mclean,	Merry	M.	2-2-28	F	013/486-1859

ADDRESS	CITY	STATE	ZIP CODE
4919 Dolphin Way,	Woodland Hills,	XY	12345

PATIENT'S OCCUPATION: secretary
NAME OF COMPANY: Porter Company

ADDRESS OF EMPLOYER: 5490 Wilshire Blvd., Merck, XY 12346
PHONE: 013/466-7781

SPOUSE OR PARENT: Harry L. Mclean (insured)
OCCUPATION: computer programmer

EMPLOYER: IBM Corp. 5616 Wilshire Blvd.,
ADDRESS: Merck, XY 12346
PHONE: 013/664-9023

NAME OF INSURANCE GROUP: Prudential Ins. Co. 5621 Wilshire Blvd., Merck, XY 12346
SUBSCRIBER:

Policy # 459-62-9989
GROUP NO.: 8832
CURRENT COVERAGE NO.:
EFFECTIVE DATE: 6-2-80

MEDICARE NO.:
MEDICAID NO.:
EFFECTIVE DATE:
SOC. SEC. NO.: 459-62-9989

REFERRED BY:

Emdee Fine, M.D. 5000 Wilshire Blvd., Merck, XY 12346 UPIN # 730271

DATE	PROGRESS
5-6-9X	BEGAN ABOUT JUNE 1990 C̄ CONSTANT DRIBBLING, WETTING AT NIGHT, USE 15 PADS/DAY. UA SP GR 1.0, FEW BACTERIA, FEW URATES. DX URINARY INCONTINENCE. PTR 4 DAYS FOR DIAGNOSTIC TESTS. Gene Ulibarri M.D.
5-10-9X	IVP ? CYSTO REVEALED MULTIPLE FISTULA OF BLADDER C̄ 2 OPENINGS INTO URINARY BLADDER AND COPIOUS LEAKAGE INTO VAGINA, CONT TO WORK. Gene Ulibarri M.D.
5-16-9X	ADM TO HOSP. DX: MULTIPLE VESICOVAGINAL FISTULAE G.U.
5-17-9X	OP: REPAIR OF VESICOVAGINAL FISTULAE G. Ulibarri M.D.
5-18-9X	THRU 5-31-9X. HV BRIEF DISCH 5-31 TO BE SEEN IN 1 MO. Gene Ulibarri M.D.
6-10-9X	RECOVERING RAPIDLY, NO PAIN. NO PC. MAY RETN TO WORK 6-20-9X Gene Ulibarri M.D.

FIGURE 6-4

STATEMENT

College Clinic
4567 Broad Avenue
Woodland Hills, XY 12345-0001
Telephone: 013-486-9002
Fax: 013-487-8976

Mrs. Merry M. Mclean
4919 Dolphin Way
Woodland Hills, XY 12345-0001

DATE	PROFESSIONAL SERVICE DESCRIPTION	CHARGE	CREDITS		CURRENT BALANCE
			PAYMENTS	ADJUSTMENTS	
	Balance forward				25 --
-6-9x	OC				
-6-9x	Lab, UA dipstick, nonautomated, complete microscopic				
-10-9x	Cystourethroscopy				
-16-9x	Initial hospital care, C hx/exam LC decision making				
-17-9x	Closure of vesicovaginal fistula abdominal approach				
-18-9x	thru 5-31-9x HV, brief				
-10-9x	OC, PF hx/exam, SF decision making				

ue and payable within 10 days. **Pay last amount in balance column** ⇧

ey: PF: Problem-focused
EPF: Expanded problem-focused
D: Detailed
C: Comprehensive
SF: Straightforward
LC: Low complexity
MC: Moderate complexity
HC: High complexity
CON: Consultation
CPX: Complete Phys Exam
E: Emergency
ER: Emergency Dept.
HCD: House Call (Day)
HCN: House Call (Night)
HV: Hospital visit
OV: Office Visit

FIGURE 6-5

PICA

HEALTH INSURANCE CLAIM FORM

PI

1. MEDICARE (Medicare #) MEDICAID (Medicaid #) CHAMPUS (Sponsor's SSN) CHAMPVA (VA File #) GROUP HEALTH PLAN (SSN or ID) FECA BLK LUNG (SSN) OTHER (ID)

1a. INSURED'S I.D. NUMBER (FOR PROGRAM IN

2. PATIENT'S NAME (Last Name, First Name, Middle Initial)

3. PATIENT'S BIRTH DATE MM DD YY SEX M F

4. INSURED'S NAME (Last Name, First Name, Middle Initial)

5. PATIENT'S ADDRESS (No., Street)

6. PATIENT RELATIONSHIP TO INSURED Self Spouse Child Other

7. INSURED'S ADDRESS (No., Street)

CITY STATE

8. PATIENT STATUS Single Married Other

CITY ST

ZIP CODE TELEPHONE (Include Area Code) ( )

Employed Full-Time Student Part-Time Student

ZIP CODE TELEPHONE (INCLUDE AREA ( )

9. OTHER INSURED'S NAME (Last Name, First Name, Middle Initial)

10. IS PATIENT'S CONDITION RELATED TO:

11. INSURED'S POLICY GROUP OR FECA NUMBER

a. OTHER INSURED'S POLICY OR GROUP NUMBER

a. EMPLOYMENT? (CURRENT OR PREVIOUS) YES NO

a. INSURED'S DATE OF BIRTH MM DD YY SEX M F

b. OTHER INSURED'S DATE OF BIRTH MM DD YY SEX M F

b. AUTO ACCIDENT? PLACE (State) YES NO

b. EMPLOYER'S NAME OR SCHOOL NAME

c. EMPLOYER'S NAME OR SCHOOL NAME

c. OTHER ACCIDENT? YES NO

c. INSURANCE PLAN NAME OR PROGRAM NAME

d. INSURANCE PLAN NAME OR PROGRAM NAME

10d. RESERVED FOR LOCAL USE

d. IS THERE ANOTHER HEALTH BENEFIT PLAN? YES NO ***If yes***, return to and complete item

READ BACK OF FORM BEFORE COMPLETING & SIGNING THIS FORM.

12. PATIENT'S OR AUTHORIZED PERSON'S SIGNATURE I authorize the release of any medical or other information necessary to process this claim. I also request payment of government benefits either to myself or to the party who accepts assignment below.

SIGNED DATE

13. INSURED'S OR AUTHORIZED PERSON'S SIGNATURE I auth payment of medical benefits to the undersigned physician or su services described below.

SIGNED

14. DATE OF CURRENT: MM DD YY ILLNESS (First symptom) OR INJURY (Accident) OR PREGNANCY(LMP)

15. IF PATIENT HAS HAD SAME OR SIMILAR ILLNESS. GIVE FIRST DATE MM DD YY

16. DATES PATIENT UNABLE TO WORK IN CURRENT OCCUPA FROM MM DD YY TO MM DD Y

17. NAME OF REFERRING PHYSICIAN OR OTHER SOURCE

17a. I.D. NUMBER OF REFERRING PHYSICIAN

18. HOSPITALIZATION DATES RELATED TO CURRENT SERVIC FROM MM DD YY TO MM DD Y

19. RESERVED FOR LOCAL USE

20. OUTSIDE LAB? YES NO $ CHARGES

21. DIAGNOSIS OR NATURE OF ILLNESS OR INJURY. (RELATE ITEMS 1,2,3 OR 4 TO ITEM 24E BY LINE)

1. ___ . __ 3. ___ . __

2. ___ . __ 4. ___ . __

22. MEDICAID RESUBMISSION CODE ORIGINAL REF. NO.

23. PRIOR AUTHORIZATION NUMBER

24. A DATE(S) OF SERVICE From MM DD YY To MM DD YY	B Place of Service	C Type of Service	D PROCEDURES, SERVICES, OR SUPPLIES (Explain Unusual Circumstances) CPT/HCPCS MODIFIER	E DIAGNOSIS CODE	F $ CHARGES	G DAYS OR UNITS	H EPSDT Family Plan	I EMG	J COB	K RESERV LOCAL
1										
2										
3										
4										
5										
6										

25. FEDERAL TAX I.D. NUMBER SSN EIN

26. PATIENT'S ACCOUNT NO.

27. ACCEPT ASSIGNMENT? (For govt. claims, see back) YES NO

28. TOTAL CHARGE $

29. AMOUNT PAID $

30. BALAN $

31. SIGNATURE OF PHYSICIAN OR SUPPLIER INCLUDING DEGREES OR CREDENTIALS (I certify that the statements on the reverse apply to this bill and are made a part thereof.)

SIGNED DATE

32. NAME AND ADDRESS OF FACILITY WHERE SERVICES WERE RENDERED (If other than home or office)

33. PHYSICIAN'S, SUPPLIER'S BILLING NAME, ADDRESS, ZIP C & PHONE #

PIN# GRP#

(APPROVED BY AMA COUNCIL ON MEDICAL SERVICE 8/88)

PLEASE PRINT OR TYPE

FORM HCFA-1500 (U2) (12-90)
FORM OWCP-1500 FORM

FIGURE 6-6

ASSIGNMENT 19

1. Complete the *Health Insurance Claim Form** to Aetna Life and Casualty Company on Mr. Billy S. Rubin by referring to his E/M Code Slip (Fig. 6–7), patient record (Fig. 6–8), and ledger card (Fig. 6–9). Date the claim August 30. Refer to Appendix A to fill in the fees on the ledger card. Use OCR guidelines.
2. Use your *CPT* code book or Appendix A to determine the correct five-digit code number and modifiers for each professional service rendered. Do not type no charge entries on the claim form (Fig. 6–10).
3. Record when you have billed the insurance company on the ledger card.
4. On September 1, Mr. Rubin sends you check No. 421 in the amount of $200 to apply to his account. Post this entry and show the balance due.

Abbreviations pertinent to this record:

adm	______________	hist	______________
CA	______________	hosp	______________
CC	______________	HV	______________
Comp	______________	hx	______________
Disch	______________	mo	______________
est	______________	NC	______________
exam	______________	OC	______________

Text continued on page 71

E/M Code Slip

Patient Rubin, Billy S.

Date 8 7 /4
CPT Code________
Dx Code________

HISTORY

- ☑ Problem Focused — Chief complaint; Brief history of present illness
- ☐ Expanded Problem Focused — Chief complaint; Brief history of present illness; Problem pertinent system review
- ☐ Detailed — Chief complaint; Extended history of present illness; Extended system review; Pertinent past family, social history
- ☐ Comprehensive — Chief complaint; Extended history of present illness; Complete system review; Complete past family, social history

EXAMINATION

- ☑ Problem Focused — Exam limited to affected body area or organ system
- ☐ Expanded Problem Focused — Exam extended to other symptomatic or related organ systems
- ☐ Detailed — Extended exam of affected area(s) and other symptomatic or related systems
- ☐ Comprehensive — Complete single system specialty exam or complete multi-system exam

MEDICAL DECISION MAKING

	Medical Decision	Number of Dx Options	Amount of Data	Risk M & M
☐	Straightforward	minimal 1 dx	minimal	minimal
☑	Low Complexity	limited 1-2 dx	limited	low
☐	Moderate Complexity	multiple 1-2 dx	moderate	moderate
☐	High Complexity	extensive 2-3 dx	extensive	high

☐ Counseling Time________
☐ Consult Referring Dr.________
Diagnosis________

FIGURE 6-7

*See Chapter 6 for help in completing this form.

PATIENT RECORD

LAST NAME	FIRST NAME	MIDDLE NAME	BIRTH DATE	SEX	HOME PHONE
Rubin,	Billy	S.	11-9-33	M	013/893-5770

ADDRESS / CITY / STATE / ZIP CODE: 547 North Oliver Road, Woodland Hills, XY 12345

PATIENT'S OCCUPATION: salesman

NAME OF COMPANY: Nate's Clothiers

ADDRESS OF EMPLOYER: 7786 East Chabner Blvd., Dorland, XY 12347

PHONE: 013/349-6605

SPOUSE OR PARENT: Lydia B. Rubin (wife)

OCCUPATION:

EMPLOYER:

ADDRESS:

PHONE:

NAME OF INSURANCE GROUP: Aetna Life and Casualty Ins. Co. 3055 Wilshire Blvd., Merck, XY 12346

SUBSCRIBER:

BLUE SHIELD OR BLUE CROSS CERT. NO.: Subscriber: Billy S. Rubin

GROUP NO.: 2641

CURRENT COVERAGE NO.:

EFFECTIVE DATE: 3-5-80

MEDICARE NO.:

MEDICAID NO.:

EFFECTIVE DATE:

SOC. SEC. NO.: 505-12-1159

REFERRED BY: U.R. Wright, M.D. 5010 Wrong Road, Torres, XY 12349 UPIN # 273855 013/907-5440

DATE	PROGRESS
8-7-9x	Office exam est pt CC: urinary hesitancy, frequency & post-urinary dribbling since July 15 of this year. Exam revealed hard nodule in prostate. Silverman needle biopsy of prostate performed in office. *Gene Ulibarri, MD*
8-14-9x	Office exam. Biopsy report positive for Ca of prostate in situ. Advised patient that an operation was necessary and explained surgery to pt. Arranged for adm to hosp. *Gene Ulibarri, MD*
8-22-9x	Adm to hosp. Pt last worked 8-21-9x. *Gene Ulibarri, MD*
8-23-9x	Surg: Bilateral orchiectomy (scrotal), TURP. Est disability 6 wks Pt to be kept under observation for 2 mo & will retn to wk 12-3-9x. *Gene Ulibarri, MD*
8-28-9x	Disch from hosp. Confined at home for 1 wk at which time patient will be seen in office. *Gene Ulibarri, MD*

FIGURE 6-8

STATEMENT

College Clinic
4567 Broad Avenue
Woodland Hills, XY 12345-0001
Telephone: 013-486-9002
Fax: 013-487-8976

Mr. Billy S. Rubin
547 North Oliver Road
Woodland Hills, XY 12345-0001

DATE	PROFESSIONAL SERVICE DESCRIPTION	CHARGE	CREDITS PAYMENTS	CREDITS ADJUSTMENTS	CURRENT BALANCE
	Balance forward				10 --
-7-9x	OC				
-7-9x	Biopsy, prostate				
-14-9x	OC				
-22-9x	Adm hosp, comp hx/exam, HC decision making				
-23-9x	Bilateral orchiectomy, simple (scrotal)				
-23-9x	TURP, complete				
-24-9x	to 8-28-9x HV, PF hx/exam LC decision making				

and payable within 10 days. Pay last amount in balance column ⇧

y: **PF:** Problem-focused **SF:** Straightforward **CON:** Consultation **HCD:** House Call (Day)
EPF: Expanded problem-focused **LC:** Low complexity **CPX:** Complete Phys Exam **HCN:** House Call (Night)
D: Detailed **MC:** Moderate complexity **E:** Emergency **HV:** Hospital visit
C: Comprehensive **HC:** High complexity **ER:** Emergency Dept. **OV:** Office Visit

FIGURE 6-9

PICA

HEALTH INSURANCE CLAIM FORM

1. MEDICARE (Medicare #) MEDICAID (Medicaid #) CHAMPUS (Sponsor's SSN) CHAMPVA (VA File #) GROUP HEALTH PLAN (SSN or ID) FECA BLK LUNG (SSN) OTHER (ID)

1a. INSURED'S I.D. NUMBER (FOR PROGRAM

2. PATIENT'S NAME (Last Name, First Name, Middle Initial)

3. PATIENT'S BIRTH DATE MM | DD | YY SEX M F

4. INSURED'S NAME (Last Name, First Name, Middle Initial)

5. PATIENT'S ADDRESS (No., Street)

6. PATIENT RELATIONSHIP TO INSURED Self Spouse Child Other

7. INSURED'S ADDRESS (No., Street)

CITY STATE

8. PATIENT STATUS Single Married Other

CITY S

ZIP CODE TELEPHONE (Include Area Code) ( )

Employed Full-Time Student Part-Time Student

ZIP CODE TELEPHONE (INCLUDE ARE ( )

9. OTHER INSURED'S NAME (Last Name, First Name, Middle Initial)

10. IS PATIENT'S CONDITION RELATED TO:

11. INSURED'S POLICY GROUP OR FECA NUMBER

a. OTHER INSURED'S POLICY OR GROUP NUMBER

a. EMPLOYMENT? (CURRENT OR PREVIOUS) YES NO

a. INSURED'S DATE OF BIRTH MM | DD | YY SEX M F

b. OTHER INSURED'S DATE OF BIRTH MM | DD | YY SEX M F

b. AUTO ACCIDENT? YES NO PLACE (State)

b. EMPLOYER'S NAME OR SCHOOL NAME

c. EMPLOYER'S NAME OR SCHOOL NAME

c. OTHER ACCIDENT? YES NO

c. INSURANCE PLAN NAME OR PROGRAM NAME

d. INSURANCE PLAN NAME OR PROGRAM NAME

10d. RESERVED FOR LOCAL USE

d. IS THERE ANOTHER HEALTH BENEFIT PLAN? YES NO ***If yes***, return to and complete ite

READ BACK OF FORM BEFORE COMPLETING & SIGNING THIS FORM.

12. PATIENT'S OR AUTHORIZED PERSON'S SIGNATURE I authorize the release of any medical or other information necessary to process this claim. I also request payment of government benefits either to myself or to the party who accepts assignment below.

SIGNED ______________________ DATE ________

13. INSURED'S OR AUTHORIZED PERSON'S SIGNATURE I aut payment of medical benefits to the undersigned physician or su services described below.

SIGNED ________

14. DATE OF CURRENT: MM | DD | YY ◀ ILLNESS (First symptom) OR INJURY (Accident) OR PREGNANCY(LMP)

15. IF PATIENT HAS HAD SAME OR SIMILAR ILLNESS. GIVE FIRST DATE MM | DD | YY

16. DATES PATIENT UNABLE TO WORK IN CURRENT OCCUP FROM MM | DD | YY TO MM | DD |

17. NAME OF REFERRING PHYSICIAN OR OTHER SOURCE

17a. I.D. NUMBER OF REFERRING PHYSICIAN

18. HOSPITALIZATION DATES RELATED TO CURRENT SERVI FROM MM | DD | YY TO MM | DD |

19. RESERVED FOR LOCAL USE

20. OUTSIDE LAB? YES NO $ CHARGES

21. DIAGNOSIS OR NATURE OF ILLNESS OR INJURY. (RELATE ITEMS 1,2,3 OR 4 TO ITEM 24E BY LINE)

1. ____ . __

3. ____ . __

2. ____ . __

4. ____ . __

22. MEDICAID RESUBMISSION CODE ORIGINAL REF. NO.

23. PRIOR AUTHORIZATION NUMBER

24. A DATE(S) OF SERVICE From MM DD YY To MM DD YY	B Place of Service	C Type of Service	D PROCEDURES, SERVICES, OR SUPPLIES (Explain Unusual Circumstances) CPT/HCPCS | MODIFIER	E DIAGNOSIS CODE	F $ CHARGES	G DAYS OR UNITS	H EPSDT Family Plan	I EMG	J COB	K RESERV LOCA
1										
2										
3										
4										
5										
6										

25. FEDERAL TAX I.D. NUMBER SSN EIN

26. PATIENT'S ACCOUNT NO.

27. ACCEPT ASSIGNMENT? (For govt. claims, see back) YES NO

28. TOTAL CHARGE $

29. AMOUNT PAID $

30. BALAN $

31. SIGNATURE OF PHYSICIAN OR SUPPLIER INCLUDING DEGREES OR CREDENTIALS (I certify that the statements on the reverse apply to this bill and are made a part thereof.)

SIGNED DATE

32. NAME AND ADDRESS OF FACILITY WHERE SERVICES WERE RENDERED (If other than home or office)

33. PHYSICIAN'S, SUPPLIER'S BILLING NAME, ADDRESS, ZIP C & PHONE #

PIN# GRP#

(APPROVED BY AMA COUNCIL ON MEDICAL SERVICE 8/88)

PLEASE PRINT OR TYPE

FORM HCFA-1500 (U2) (12-90)
FORM OWCP-1500 FORM

FIGURE 6-10

phys ____________________ TURP ____________________

Pt ____________________ wk ____________________

retn ____________________ wks ____________________

surg ____________________

ASSIGNMENT 20

1. Complete two *Health Insurance Claim Forms** to Travelers Insurance Company on Mr. Walter J. Stone by referring to his E/M Code Slip (Fig. 6–11), patient record (Fig. 6–12), and ledger card (Fig. 6–13). Date the claims June 1 and make a photocopy of this form to use as thesecond claim form (Fig. 6–14). Refer to Appendix A to fill in the fees on the ledger card. Use OCR guidelines.
2. Use your *CPT* code book or Appendix A to determine the correct five-digit code number and modifiers for each professional service rendered. The surgeon, Dr. Cutler, is charging $937.74 for the cholecystectomy. You are submitting a claim for the assistant surgeon, Dr. Input, and using a standard 20% of the surgeon's fee.
3. On May 14, the insurance company sends the physician check Number 48572 for $25. Post this entry.

Text continued on p. 75

E/M Code Slip

Patient Stone, Walter J. — Date 5-21-9X

CPT Code ________

Dx Code ________

HISTORY

- [x] Problem Focused
  Chief complaint; Brief history of present illness
- [ ] Expanded Problem Focused
  Chief complaint; Brief history of present illness; Problem pertinent system review
- [ ] Detailed
  Chief complaint; Extended history of present illness; Extended system review; Pertinent past family, social history
- [ ] Comprehensive
  Chief complaint; Extended history of present illness; Complete system review; Complete past family, social history

EXAMINATION

- [x] Problem Focused
  Exam limited to affected body area or organ system
- [ ] Expanded Problem Focused
  Exam extended to other symptomatic or related organ systems
- [ ] Detailed
  Extended exam of affected area(s) and other symptomatic or related systems
- [ ] Comprehensive
  Complete single system specialty exam or complete multi-system exam

MEDICAL DECISION MAKING

Medical Decision	Number of Dx Options	Amount of Data	Risk M & M
[ ] Straightforward	minimal 1 dx	minimal	minimal
[x] Low Complexity	limited 1-2 dx	limited	low
[ ] Moderate Complexity	multiple 1-2 dx	moderate	moderate
[ ] High Complexity	extensive 2-3 dx	extensive	high

- [ ] Counseling Time ____________
- [ ] Consult Referring Dr. ____________

Diagnosis ____________

FIGURE 6-11

*See Chapter 6 of the *Handbook* for help in completing this form.

PATIENT RECORD

Stone,	Walter	J.	3-14-39	M	013/345-0776
LAST NAME	FIRST NAME	MIDDLE NAME	BIRTH DATE	SEX	HOME PHONE

2008 Converse Street,	Woodland Hills,	XY	12345
ADDRESS	CITY	STATE	ZIP CODE

advertising agent	R.V. Black and Associates
PATIENT'S OCCUPATION	NAME OF COMPANY
1267 Broad Street, Woodland Hills, XY 12345	013/345-6012
ADDRESS OF EMPLOYER	PHONE
widow	
SPOUSE OR PARENT	OCCUPATION

EMPLOYER	ADDRESS	PHONE

Travelers Ins. Co. 5460 Olympic Blvd., Woodland Hills, XY 12345	
NAME OF INSURANCE GROUP	SUBSCRIBER

Subscriber: Walter J. Stone Policy #6754			6-1-81
BLUE SHIELD OR BLUE CROSS CERT. NO.	GROUP NO.	CURRENT COVERAGE NO.	EFFECTIVE DATE
			456-65-9989
MEDICARE NO.	MEDICAID NO.	EFFECTIVE DATE	SOC. SEC. NO.

REFERRED BY:

brother: John B. Stone (former patient of Dr. Input)

DATE	PROGRESS
5-3-9x	Sun 2 a.m. Est pt had sudden onset of profuse rectal bleeding with nausea & severe abdominal pains; called from home to ER. Consulted with Dr. Cutler who recommended pt be admitted for further evaluation & diagnostic treatment. Disabled from wk. BP 180/100. Pt admitted to hosp. Gaston Input (signature) Gaston Input, MD
5-4-9x	Pt symptoms have subsided somewhat. GB series showed prepyloric gastric ulcer, inflam of gb & gallstones present. Gaston Input (signature) Gaston Input, MD
5-5-9x	Discharged to home. To be seen in ofc in 1 wk. Gaston Input (signature) Gaston Input, MD
5-21-9x	Pt complains of GI distress. BP 180/100 shows a concern for hypertension. Adv to see Dr. Cutler for further evaluation & possible surgery. Dx: Acute prepyloric gastric ulcer with hemorrhage, cholecystitis with cholelithiasis, hypertension. Gaston Input (signature) Gaston Input, MD
5-26-9x	Adm to hosp by Dr. Input. Gaston Input (signature) Gaston Input, MD
5-27-9x	Cholecystectomy, acted as asst surgeon to Dr. Cutler. Pt will resume wk abt 6-22-9x. Gaston Input (signature) Gaston Input, MD

FIGURE 6-12

STATEMENT

College Clinic
4567 Broad Avenue
Woodland Hills, XY 12345-0001
Telephone: 013-486-9002
Fax: 013-487-8976

Mr. Walter J. Stone
2008 Converse Street
Woodland Hills, XY 12345-0001

DATE	PROFESSIONAL SERVICE DESCRIPTION	CHARGE	CREDITS		CURRENT BALANCE
			PAYMENTS	ADJUSTMENTS	
-3-9x	OV	75 --			75 --
-15-9x	Billed Travelers Insurance Company				
-2-9x	ROA ins ck		60 --		15 --
-3-9x	OV	50 --			65 --
-3-9x	Billed Travelers Insurance Company				
-3-9x	E service, PF hx/exam, SF decision making				
-4-9x	HV, PF hx./exam, LC decision making				
-5-9x	Hosp. discharge				
-21-9x	OC, EPF hx/exam, LC decision making				
-26-9x	Hosp. admit				
-27-9x	Cholecystectomy asst.				

ue and payable within 10 days. **Pay last amount in balance column** ⇧

ey: PF: Problem-focused	**SF:** Straightforward	**CON:** Consultation	**HCD:** House Call (Day)
EPF: Expanded problem-focused	**LC:** Low complexity	**CPX:** Complete Phys Exam	**HCN:** House Call (Night)
D: Detailed	**MC:** Moderate complexity	**E:** Emergency	**HV:** Hospital visit
C: Comprehensive	**HC:** High complexity	**ER:** Emergency Dept.	**OV:** Office Visit

FIGURE 6-13

PICA

HEALTH INSURANCE CLAIM FORM

PIC

1. MEDICARE (Medicare #) MEDICAID (Medicaid #) CHAMPUS (Sponsor's SSN) CHAMPVA (VA File #) GROUP HEALTH PLAN (SSN or ID) FECA BLK LUNG (SSN) OTHER (ID)

1a. INSURED'S I.D. NUMBER (FOR PROGRAM IN

2. PATIENT'S NAME (Last Name, First Name, Middle Initial)

3. PATIENT'S BIRTH DATE MM DD YY SEX M F

4. INSURED'S NAME (Last Name, First Name, Middle Initial)

5. PATIENT'S ADDRESS (No., Street)

6. PATIENT RELATIONSHIP TO INSURED Self Spouse Child Other

7. INSURED'S ADDRESS (No., Street)

CITY STATE

8. PATIENT STATUS Single Married Other

CITY ST

ZIP CODE TELEPHONE (Include Area Code) ( )

Employed Full-Time Student Part-Time Student

ZIP CODE TELEPHONE (INCLUDE AREA ( )

9. OTHER INSURED'S NAME (Last Name, First Name, Middle Initial)

10. IS PATIENT'S CONDITION RELATED TO:

11. INSURED'S POLICY GROUP OR FECA NUMBER

a. OTHER INSURED'S POLICY OR GROUP NUMBER

a. EMPLOYMENT? (CURRENT OR PREVIOUS) YES NO

a. INSURED'S DATE OF BIRTH MM DD YY SEX M F

b. OTHER INSURED'S DATE OF BIRTH MM DD YY SEX M F

b. AUTO ACCIDENT? YES NO PLACE (State)

b. EMPLOYER'S NAME OR SCHOOL NAME

c. EMPLOYER'S NAME OR SCHOOL NAME

c. OTHER ACCIDENT? YES NO

c. INSURANCE PLAN NAME OR PROGRAM NAME

d. INSURANCE PLAN NAME OR PROGRAM NAME

10d. RESERVED FOR LOCAL USE

d. IS THERE ANOTHER HEALTH BENEFIT PLAN? YES NO *If yes*, return to and complete item

READ BACK OF FORM BEFORE COMPLETING & SIGNING THIS FORM.

12. PATIENT'S OR AUTHORIZED PERSON'S SIGNATURE I authorize the release of any medical or other information necessary to process this claim. I also request payment of government benefits either to myself or to the party who accepts assignment below.

SIGNED ______ DATE ______

13. INSURED'S OR AUTHORIZED PERSON'S SIGNATURE I auth payment of medical benefits to the undersigned physician or sup services described below.

SIGNED ______

14. DATE OF CURRENT: MM DD YY ILLNESS (First symptom) OR INJURY (Accident) OR PREGNANCY(LMP)

15. IF PATIENT HAS HAD SAME OR SIMILAR ILLNESS. GIVE FIRST DATE MM DD YY

16. DATES PATIENT UNABLE TO WORK IN CURRENT OCCUPA FROM MM DD YY TO MM DD Y

17. NAME OF REFERRING PHYSICIAN OR OTHER SOURCE

17a. I.D. NUMBER OF REFERRING PHYSICIAN

18. HOSPITALIZATION DATES RELATED TO CURRENT SERVIC FROM MM DD YY TO MM DD Y

19. RESERVED FOR LOCAL USE

20. OUTSIDE LAB? YES NO $ CHARGES

21. DIAGNOSIS OR NATURE OF ILLNESS OR INJURY. (RELATE ITEMS 1,2,3 OR 4 TO ITEM 24E BY LINE)

1. ____ . __ 3. ____ . __

2. ____ . __ 4. ____ . __

22. MEDICAID RESUBMISSION CODE ORIGINAL REF. NO.

23. PRIOR AUTHORIZATION NUMBER

24. A DATE(S) OF SERVICE From MM DD YY To MM DD YY	B Place of Service	C Type of Service	D PROCEDURES, SERVICES, OR SUPPLIES (Explain Unusual Circumstances) CPT/HCPCS MODIFIER	E DIAGNOSIS CODE	F $ CHARGES	G DAYS OR UNITS	H EPSDT Family Plan	I EMG	J COB	K RESERVE LOCAL
1										
2										
3										
4										
5										
6										

25. FEDERAL TAX I.D. NUMBER SSN EIN

26. PATIENT'S ACCOUNT NO.

27. ACCEPT ASSIGNMENT? (For govt. claims, see back) YES NO

28. TOTAL CHARGE $

29. AMOUNT PAID $

30. BALAN $

31. SIGNATURE OF PHYSICIAN OR SUPPLIER INCLUDING DEGREES OR CREDENTIALS (I certify that the statements on the reverse apply to this bill and are made a part thereof.)

SIGNED DATE

32. NAME AND ADDRESS OF FACILITY WHERE SERVICES WERE RENDERED (If other than home or office)

33. PHYSICIAN'S, SUPPLIER'S BILLING NAME, ADDRESS, ZIP C & PHONE #

PIN# GRP#

(APPROVED BY AMA COUNCIL ON MEDICAL SERVICE 8/88)

PLEASE PRINT OR TYPE

FORM HCFA-1500 (U2) (12-90)
FORM OWCP-1500 FORM

FIGURE 6-14

4. Record on the ledger card when you have billed the insurance company.

Abbreviations pertinent to this record:

abt ________	GB ________
adm ________	hosp ________
asst ________	inflam ________
BP ________	intermed ________
E ________	OC ________
ER ________	ofc ________
Dx ________	pt ________
est ________	wk ________

ASSIGNMENT 21

After completing all the patient records in the *Workbook* pertinent to this chapter, you will be able to answer the next two questions.

1. What do these abbreviations mean?

a. PTR ________	f. Dx ________
b. TURP ________	g. BP ________
c. HX ________	h. CC ________
d. IVP ________	i. UA ________
e. c̄ ________	j. PE ________

2. Give the abbreviations for the following terms.

a. return ________

b. cancer, carcinoma ________

c. patient ________

d. established ________

e. discharged ________

f. gallbladder ________

g. initial ________

CHAPTER 7

Electronic Data Interchange (EDI)

Key Terms

Your instructor may wish to select some specific words pertinent to this chapter for a test. For definitions of the terms, further study, and/or reference, the words, phrases, and abbreviations may be found in the Glossary at the end of the textbook. *Key terms for this chapter follow.*

audit trail
back up
batch
bit
bug
byte
carrier-direct system
central processing unit (CPU)
clearinghouse system
data base
debug
disk
down time
electronic claims professional (ECP)
electronic claims submission (ECS)
electronic data interchange (EDI)
encounter form
file
format
hard copy
hardware
input
interactive transactions
interface
K
keypad
memory
modem
network
on-line system
output
program
prompts
RAM
retrieve
ROM
soft copy
software
terminal
time-sharing
video display terminal (VDT)
virus

Performance Objectives

The student will be able to

- Define and spell the key terms for this chapter, given the information from the textbook Glossary, within a reasonable period of time and with enough accuracy to obtain a satisfactory evaluation.
- Answer the review questions after reading the chapter, with enough accuracy to obtain a satisfactory evaluation.
- Locate errors, given computer-generated insurance forms, within a reasonable period of time and with enough accuracy to obtain a satisfactory evaluation.
- Fill in the correct meaning of each abbreviation, given a list of common medical abbreviations and symbols that appear in chart notes, with enough accuracy to obtain a satisfactory evaluation.

Study Outline

BACKGROUND
COMPUTER
COMPUTER CLAIM SYSTEMS
- Carrier-direct
- Clearinghouse
- Electronic claims processor

ELECTRONIC DATA INTERCHANGE
- Carrier agreements
- Signature requirements
  - Physician
  - Patient
- Workers' compensation
- Encounter forms
- Crib sheets
- Eligibility verification
  - Smart and swipe cards
  - Computer verification
- Keying insurance data
- Electronically completing the claim
  - Coding
  - Computer electronic transmission
  - Facsimile communication transmission
- Electronic inquiry or claims status review

REMITTANCE ADVICE
- Explanation of benefits
- Statements

COMPUTER CONFIDENTIALITY
- Confidentiality statement
- Prevention measures

RECORDS MANAGEMENT
- Data storage

Review Questions

Review the objectives, key terms, glossary definitions to key terms, chapter information, and figures before completing the following review questions.

1. The process by which understandable data items are sent back and forth via computer linkages between two or more entities functioning as sender and receiver is known as

   ____.

2. Insurance claims prepared on a computer and submitted via modem (telephone lines) to the insurance carrier's computer system is known as ____________________.

3. Match the terms below with the definitions that follow:

a. batch	f. ROM	k. network	p. hard copy
b. software	g. CPU	l. keypad	q. modem
c. clearinghouse	h. smart card	m. soft copy	r. memory
d. hardware	i. swipe card	n. input	s. disk
e. RAM	j. back up	o. file	

_____ Memory into which the user can enter information and instructions and from which the user can call up data.

_____ A device that contains keys to control mathematical functions.

_____ A printout.

_____ Two or more interconnected computers.

_____ The brains of a computer device controlling the internal memory, which directs the flow and processing of information.

_____ A duplicate data file.

_____ Data that go into a computer memory bank.

_____ A single, stored unit of information assigned a file name.

_____ A device that converts data into signals for telephone transmission and then (at the receiving end) back again into data.

_____ That which is displayed on a CRT screen.

_____ A magnetic storage device made of either rigid material or flexible plastic.

_____ Storage in a computer.

_____ Instructions required to make hardware perform a certain task.

_____ Physical components of a computer system.

_____ Group of claims for many patients submitted in one computer transmission from one office.

_____ Computer memory permanently programmed with a group of frequently used instructions.

_____ Card containing a computer chip allowing storage of a variety of information.

_____ Third-party administrator who receives transmission of claims, separates them, and sends each one to the correct insurance payer.

_____ Card with a magnetic stripe containing a small capacity microchip that holds small amounts of information.

4. Two types of computer claim systems that may be used when transmitting insurance claims via modem to insurance carriers are __________________ and __________________.
5. When electronically transmitting a claim directly to an insurance carrier, insurance billing specialists may be made aware of errors immediately and can make corrections using a process called ____ .

6. An individual who converts insurance claims to standardized electronic formats and transmits them to the insurance carrier is known as a/an ________________.
7. For electronic insurance claims, an assignment of benefits agreement requires that each patient's signature be ________________ or ________________.
8. Forms used for verifying data regarding services rendered to each patient during a visit are called ________________.
9. Mrs. James comes in for an office visit to see Dr. Doe on March 12. She returns again on March 14, 15, and 16. Abbreviated routing slips for E & M procedural codes used by Dr. Doe's office are called ________________.
10. Codes required when electronically transmitting claims are:
    a. ________________
    b. ________________
    c. ________________
11. After receiving a faxed insurance claim, some insurance carriers send a ________ report.
12. State the definition of an electronic remittance notice.

    ____
13. Various limiting conditions and guidelines that tell the computer to deny, review, or pay transmitted insurance claims are known as ________________.
14. To maintain confidentiality and enhance security, ________________ or ________________ should be developed and changed at regular intervals.
15. To prevent computer and data file damage caused by electric power spikes, computer equipment may be plugged into a/an ________________.

ASSIGNMENT 22

On the following pages are two different insurance forms as output from the computer (Figs. 7-1 and 7-2). Locate the areas on each form that need completion before submission to the insurance company. Circle in red any errors you discover on the computer-generated insurance claim. In regard to Brad E. Diehl and Evert I. Strain, refer to their patient records if you need any pertinent information for the insurance claims (Figs. 7–3 and 7–4). Mr. Strain did not pay anything on his account.

Text continued on page 85

HEALTH INSURANCE CLAIM FORM

PICA

E | MEDICAID | CHAMPUS | CHAMPVA | GROUP HEALTH PLAN | FECA BLK LUNG | OTHER

#) [ ] (Medicaid #) [ ] (Sponsor's SSN) [ ] (VA File #) [ ] (SSN or ID) [ ] (SSN) [X] (ID)

1a. INSURED'S I.D. NUMBER (FOR PROGRAM IN ITEM 1): 403119

NAME (Last Name, First Name, Middle Initial): BRAD E

3. PATIENT'S BIRTH DATE MM DD YY: 09 21 46 — SEX M [ ] F [ ]

4. INSURED'S NAME (Last Name, First Name, Middle Initial): SAME

ADDRESS (No., Street): HILLS ROAD

6. PATIENT RELATIONSHIP TO INSURED: Self [ ] Spouse [ ] Child [ ] Other [ ]

7. INSURED'S ADDRESS (No., Street): SAME

STATE: XY — AND HILLS

8. PATIENT STATUS: Single [ ] Married [X] Other [ ]; Employed [X] Full-Time Student [ ] Part-Time Student [ ]

CITY | STATE

-0001 — TELEPHONE (Include Area Code): (013) 222-0123

ZIP CODE | TELEPHONE (INCLUDE AREA CODE) ( )

SURED'S NAME (Last Name, First Name, Middle Initial)

10. IS PATIENT'S CONDITION RELATED TO:

11. INSURED'S POLICY GROUP OR FECA NUMBER

SURED'S POLICY OR GROUP NUMBER

a. EMPLOYMENT? (CURRENT OR PREVIOUS) [ ] YES [X] NO

a. INSURED'S DATE OF BIRTH MM DD YY — SEX M [ ] F [ ]

SURED'S DATE OF BIRTH YY — SEX M [ ] F [ ]

b. AUTO ACCIDENT? [ ] YES [X] NO — PLACE (State)

b. EMPLOYER'S NAME OR SCHOOL NAME

'S NAME OR SCHOOL NAME

c. OTHER ACCIDENT? [ ] YES [X] NO

c. INSURANCE PLAN NAME OR PROGRAM NAME

E PLAN NAME OR PROGRAM NAME

10d. RESERVED FOR LOCAL USE

d. IS THERE ANOTHER HEALTH BENEFIT PLAN? [ ] YES [X] NO *If yes*, return to and complete item 9 a-d.

READ BACK OF FORM BEFORE COMPLETING & SIGNING THIS FORM.

S OR AUTHORIZED PERSON'S SIGNATURE I authorize the release of any medical or other information necessary this claim. I also request payment of government benefits either to myself or to the party who accepts assignment

DATE

13. INSURED'S OR AUTHORIZED PERSON'S SIGNATURE I authorize payment of medical benefits to the undersigned physician or supplier for services described below.

SIGNED

CURRENT: YY — ILLNESS (First symptom) OR INJURY (Accident) OR PREGNANCY(LMP)

15. IF PATIENT HAS HAD SAME OR SIMILAR ILLNESS. GIVE FIRST DATE MM DD YY

16. DATES PATIENT UNABLE TO WORK IN CURRENT OCCUPATION FROM MM DD YY TO MM DD YY

REFERRING PHYSICIAN OR OTHER SOURCE

17a. I.D. NUMBER OF REFERRING PHYSICIAN

18. HOSPITALIZATION DATES RELATED TO CURRENT SERVICES FROM MM DD YY TO MM DD YY

D FOR LOCAL USE

20. OUTSIDE LAB? [ ] YES [ ] NO — $ CHARGES

S OR NATURE OF ILLNESS OR INJURY. (RELATE ITEMS 1,2,3 OR 4 TO ITEM 24E BY LINE)

3. ___ . ___

4. ___ . ___

22. MEDICAID RESUBMISSION CODE — ORIGINAL REF. NO.

23. PRIOR AUTHORIZATION NUMBER

TE(S) OF SERVICE YY	To MM	DD	YY	B Place of Service	C Type of Service	D PROCEDURES, SERVICES, OR SUPPLIES (Explain Unusual Circumstances) CPT/HCPCS	MODIFIER	E DIAGNOSIS CODE	F $ CHARGES	G DAYS OR UNITS	H EPSDT Family Plan	I EMG	J COB	K RESERVED FOR LOCAL USE
9X				11		99203			50 00					
9X				11		93000			50 00					
9X				11		71020			80 00					
9X				11		99213			25 00					
9X				11		85025			25 00					
9X				11					175 00					

TAX I.D. NUMBER — SSN EIN [ ] [ ]

26. PATIENT'S ACCOUNT NO.

27. ACCEPT ASSIGNMENT? (For govt. claims, see back) [ ] YES [ ] NO

28. TOTAL CHARGE $ | 29. AMOUNT PAID $ | 30. BALANCE DUE $

E OF PHYSICIAN OR SUPPLIER S DEGREES OR CREDENTIALS t the statements on the reverse bill and are made a part thereof.)

01-25-9X
DATE

32. NAME AND ADDRESS OF FACILITY WHERE SERVICES WERE RENDERED (If other than home or office)

33. PHYSICIAN'S, SUPPLIER'S BILLING NAME, ADDRESS, ZIP CODE & PHONE # 013-486-9002
COLLEGE CLINIC
4567 BROAD AVENUE
WOODLAND HILLS XY 12345

PIN# — GRP# 3664021CC

ITIALS

ED BY AMA COUNCIL ON MEDICAL SERVICE 8/88)

PLEASE PRINT OR TYPE

FORM HCFA-1500 (U2) (12-90)
FORM OWCP-1500 FORM RRB-1500

PATIENT AND INSURED INFORMATION

PHYSICIAN OR SUPPLIER INFORMATION

FIGURE 7-1

PICA

HEALTH INSURANCE CLAIM FORM

1. MEDICARE (Medicare #) | MEDICAID (Medicaid #) | CHAMPUS (Sponsor's SSN) | CHAMPVA (VA File #) | GROUP HEALTH PLAN (SSN or ID) [X] | FECA BLK LUNG (SSN) | OTHER (ID)

1a. INSURED'S I.D. NUMBER (FOR PROGRAM I...): 453-32-4739 96476A

2. PATIENT'S NAME (Last Name, First Name, Middle Initial): STRAIN EVERT I

3. PATIENT'S BIRTH DATE MM DD YY — SEX M [ ] F [ ]

4. INSURED'S NAME (Last Name, First Name, Middle Initial): SAME

5. PATIENT'S ADDRESS (No., Street): 7650 NONE SUCH ROAD

6. PATIENT RELATIONSHIP TO INSURED: Self [ ] Spouse [ ] Child [ ] Other [ ]

7. INSURED'S ADDRESS (No., Street): SAME

CITY: WOODLAND HILLS — STATE: XY

8. PATIENT STATUS: Single [ ] Married [X] Other [ ]; Employed [X] Full-Time Student [ ] Part-Time Student [ ]

CITY — S...

ZIP CODE — TELEPHONE (Include Area Code) ( )

ZIP CODE — TELEPHONE (INCLUDE ARE...) ( )

9. OTHER INSURED'S NAME (Last Name, First Name, Middle Initial)

10. IS PATIENT'S CONDITION RELATED TO:

11. INSURED'S POLICY GROUP OR FECA NUMBER

a. OTHER INSURED'S POLICY OR GROUP NUMBER

a. EMPLOYMENT? (CURRENT OR PREVIOUS) [ ] YES [X] NO

a. INSURED'S DATE OF BIRTH MM DD YY — SEX M [ ] F

b. OTHER INSURED'S DATE OF BIRTH MM DD YY — SEX M [ ] F [ ]

b. AUTO ACCIDENT? [ ] YES [X] NO — PLACE (State)

b. EMPLOYER'S NAME OR SCHOOL NAME

c. EMPLOYER'S NAME OR SCHOOL NAME

c. OTHER ACCIDENT? [ ] YES [X] NO

c. INSURANCE PLAN NAME OR PROGRAM NAME

d. INSURANCE PLAN NAME OR PROGRAM NAME

10d. RESERVED FOR LOCAL USE

d. IS THERE ANOTHER HEALTH BENEFIT PLAN? [ ] YES [ ] NO *If yes,* return to and complete ite...

READ BACK OF FORM BEFORE COMPLETING & SIGNING THIS FORM.

12. PATIENT'S OR AUTHORIZED PERSON'S SIGNATURE I authorize the release of any medical or other information necessary to process this claim. I also request payment of government benefits either to myself or to the party who accepts assignment below.

SIGNED ____ DATE ____

13. INSURED'S OR AUTHORIZED PERSON'S SIGNATURE I aut... payment of medical benefits to the undersigned physician or s... services described below.

SIGNED ____

14. DATE OF CURRENT: ILLNESS (First symptom) OR INJURY (Accident) OR PREGNANCY(LMP) — MM 01 DD YY 9X

15. IF PATIENT HAS HAD SAME OR SIMILAR ILLNESS. GIVE FIRST DATE MM DD YY

16. DATES PATIENT UNABLE TO WORK IN CURRENT OCCUP... FROM MM DD YY TO MM DD

17. NAME OF REFERRING PHYSICIAN OR OTHER SOURCE: GERALD C JONES MD

17a. I.D. NUMBER OF REFERRING PHYSICIAN: 690235

18. HOSPITALIZATION DATES RELATED TO CURRENT SERVI... FROM 01 09 9X TO 01 11

19. RESERVED FOR LOCAL USE

20. OUTSIDE LAB? [ ] YES [X] NO — $ CHARGES

21. DIAGNOSIS OR NATURE OF ILLNESS OR INJURY. (RELATE ITEMS 1,2,3 OR 4 TO ITEM 24E BY LINE)

1. ___ . ___
2. ___ . ___
3. ___ . ___
4. ___ . ___

22. MEDICAID RESUBMISSION CODE — ORIGINAL REF. NO.

23. PRIOR AUTHORIZATION NUMBER

24.	A From MM	DD	YY	To MM	DD	YY	B Place of Service	C Type of Service	D CPT/HCPCS	MODIFIER	E DIAGNOSIS CODE	F $ CHARGES	G DAYS OR UNITS	H EPSDT Family Plan	I EMG	J COB	K RESERV... LOCA...
1	01	08	9X				11		99215			75 00					
2	01	08	9X				11		93000			50 00					
3	01	09	9X				21		99222			100 00					
4	01	10	9X				21		99231			30 00					
5	01	11	9X				21		99231			30 00					
6																	

25. FEDERAL TAX I.D. NUMBER: 70-3459766 — SSN [ ] EIN [X]

26. PATIENT'S ACCOUNT NO.

27. ACCEPT ASSIGNMENT? (For govt. claims, see back) [ ] YES [ ] NO

28. TOTAL CHARGE $ 285 00

29. AMOUNT PAID $

30. BALA... $

31. SIGNATURE OF PHYSICIAN OR SUPPLIER INCLUDING DEGREES OR CREDENTIALS (I certify that the statements on the reverse apply to this bill and are made a part thereof.)

SIGNED — DATE 01-25-9X

32. NAME AND ADDRESS OF FACILITY WHERE SERVICES WERE RENDERED (If other than home or office)

33. PHYSICIAN'S, SUPPLIER'S BILLING NAME, ADDRESS, ZIP & PHONE #
013-486-9002
COLLEGE CLINIC
4567 BROAD AVENUE
WOODLAND HILLS XY 123...

PIN# — GRP# 3664021C...

REF. INITIALS

(APPROVED BY AMA COUNCIL ON MEDICAL SERVICE 8/88)

PLEASE PRINT OR TYPE

FORM HCFA-1500 (U2) (12-90)
FORM OWCP-1500 — FOR...

FIGURE 7-2

PATIENT RECORD

LAST NAME	FIRST NAME	MIDDLE NAME	BIRTH DATE	SEX	HOME PHONE
Diehl,	Brad	E.	09/21/46	M	013/222/0123

ADDRESS	CITY	STATE	ZIP CODE
3975 Hills Road,	Woodland Hills,	XY	12345

PATIENT'S OCCUPATION: radio advertising salesman
NAME OF COMPANY: KACY Radio

ADDRESS OF EMPLOYER: 4071 Mills Road, Woodland Hills, XY 12345
PHONE: 013/201-6666

SPOUSE OR PARENT: Tak E. Diehl (birthdate 4-7-45)
OCCUPATION: legal secretary

EMPLOYER: Attys. Dilman,Forewise, & Gilson
ADDRESS: 12 W. Dix St., Woodland Hills. XY 12345
PHONE: Tel. 013/222/6432

NAME OF INSURANCE GROUP: Aetna Insurance Co. 2412 Main St., Woodland Hills, XY 12345 Brad E. Diehl Subscriber

BLUE SHIELD OR BLUE CROSS CERT. NO.: Policy #403119
GROUP NO.:
CURRENT COVERAGE NO.:
EFFECTIVE DATE: 3-2-80

MEDICARE NO.:
MEDICAID NO.:
EFFECTIVE DATE:
SOC. SEC. NO.: 561-02-1501

REFERRED BY: Raymond Skelton, M D

DATE	PROGRESS
1-5-9x	Pt. comes in complaining of coughing & sneezing. Some difficulty in breathing. Dizziness occasionally & stomach pain c̄ cramping of 6 mo duration. EKG essentially neg. AP & lat chest x-rays neg. Pt brought in bone marrow aspiration report done by Dr. Skelton. BP 180/100. Pt to have oral cholecystography & CBC. Dx: irritable colon (ICD-9-CM diagnosis code no. 5641) and hypertension (ICD-9-CM diagnosis code no. 4011) No disability at this time.
	Gaston Input, MD
1-20-9x	Oral cholecystography reveals a single 1.5 cm in maximal diameter radiolucent calculus within the cholecyst. WBC 10,000 DX: cholecystitis with cholelithiasis (ICD-9-CM diagnosis code no. 574.10). Adv. cholecystectomy as soon as possible.
	Gaston Input, MD

FIGURE 7-3

PATIENT RECORD

LAST NAME	FIRST NAME	MIDDLE NAME	BIRTH DATE	SEX	HOME PHONE
Strain,	Evert	I.	09-11-46	M	013/678-0211

ADDRESS	CITY	STATE	ZIP CODE
7650 None Such Road,	Woodland Hills,	XY	12345

PATIENT'S OCCUPATION	NAME OF COMPANY
mechanical engineer	R and R Company

ADDRESS OF EMPLOYER	PHONE
2400 Davon Road, Woodland Hills, XY 12345	013/520-8977

SPOUSE OR PARENT	OCCUPATION
Esther I. Strain (wife)	Administrative Assistant

EMPLOYER	ADDRESS	PHONE
University College	4021 Book Road, Woodland Hills, XY 12345	013/450-9908

NAME OF INSURANCE GROUP	SUBSCRIBER
Blue Cross/Blue Shield	Evert I. Strain

BLUE SHIELD OR BLUE CROSS CERT. NO.	GROUP NO.	CURRENT COVERAGE NO.	EFFECTIVE DATE
453-32-4739	96476A		1-1-80

MEDICARE NO.	MEDICAID NO.	EFFECTIVE DATE	SOC. SEC. NO.
			453-32-4739

REFERRED BY: Gerald C. Jones, M D. 1403 Haven St., Woodland Hills, XY 12345

DATE	PROGRESS
1-8-9x	Est pt comes in complaining of frequency in urination, headaches, polyphagia, unable to remember current events. These problems have been present for almost a year. PE: BP 160/110. Lab work done at an Urgent Care center showed SGOT, cholesterol elevated. blood sugar glucose extremely high range. DX: diabetes mellitus. (ICD-9-CM Code No. 2500), ASHD (ICD-9-CM Code No. 4140), hypertension (ICD-9-CM Code No. 4011). Adv hospitalization at College Hospital on 1-9. Disability 1-9 thru 1-31. Gerald Practon MD
1-9-9x	Adm H & P. Hosp visit Gerald Practon MD
1-10-9x	Hosp visit Pt doing well on special diet. Pt to remain in hosp for one more day. BP 130/85. Gerald Practon, MD
1-11-9x	DC from hosp. Pt to be seen in one month. Gerald Practon, MD

FIGURE 7-4

ASSIGNMENT 23

After completing the assignments in this chapter, you will be able to define the abbreviations shown here.

Abbreviations pertinent to the record of Brad E. Diehl:

abt ______________________ AP ______________________

adv ______________________ BP ______________________

CBC ______________________ neg ______________________

cm ______________________ Pt ______________________

Dx ______________________ WBC ______________________

EKG ______________________ WNL ______________________

hr ______________________ wk ______________________

lat ______________________ c̄ ______________________

mo ______________________

Abbreviations pertinent to the record of Evert I. Strain:

adv ______________________ hosp ______________________

ASHD ______________________ ltd ______________________

BP ______________________ PE ______________________

DC ______________________ pt ______________________

Dx ______________________ SGOT* ______________________

est ______________________

*See laboratory abbreviations in Chapter 4 of the *Handbook*.

CHAPTER 8

Tracing Delinquent Claims and Insurance Problem Solving

Key Terms

Your instructor may wish to select some specific words pertinent to this chapter for a test. For definitions of the terms, further study, and/or reference, the words, phrases, and abbreviations may be found in the Glossary at the end of the textbook. *Key terms for this chapter follow.*

appeal
delinquent claim
denied claim
inquiry
lost claim
overpayment
payments
peer review
rebill
rejected claim
review
tracer

Performance Objectives

The student will be able to

- Define and spell the key terms for this chapter, given the information from the textbook Glossary, within a reasonable period of time and with enough accuracy to obtain a satisfactory evaluation.
- Answer the review questions after reading the chapter with enough accuracy to obtain a satisfactory evaluation.
- Complete the insurance claim tracer form, given a request for an insurance claim trace and the patient's insurance claim, within a reasonable period of time and with enough accuracy to obtain a satisfactory evaluation.
- Locate the errors on each claim, given three returned insurance claims, within a reasonable period of time and with enough accuracy to obtain a satisfactory evaluation.
- Complete a form, given form HCFA-1965, Request for Hearing, Part B, Medicare Claim, within a reasonable period of time and with enough accuracy to obtain a satisfactory evaluation.

Study Outline

CLAIMS PROVISIONS
STATE INSURANCE COMMISSIONER
  Commission objectives
  Types of problems
  Commission inquiries
CLAIM MANAGEMENT TECHNIQUES
  Insurance claims register
  Insurance company payment history
  Tickler file
PROBLEM CLAIMS
  Types of problems
  Delinquent, pending, or suspense
  Lost claims
  Rejected claims
  Denied claims
  Down coding
  Partial payment
  Payment paid to patient
  Two-party check
  Overpayment
REBILLING
  Claim inquiries
REVIEW AND APPEAL PROCESS
  Blue Cross and Blue Shield review and appeal process
  CHAMPUS review and appeal process
    Reconsideration
    Formal review
    Hearing
  Medicare review and appeal process
    Inquiry
    Review
    Fair hearing
    Administrative law judge hearing
    Appeals council review
    Federal district court hearing
    HCFA regional offices
  Medigap

Review Questions

Review the objectives, key terms, and chapter information before completing the following review questions.

1. Name provisions seen in health insurance policies

a. ____

____

b. ____

____

____

c. ____

____

____

2. At the time of his first office visit, Mr. Doi signed an Assignment of Benefits, and Dr. James' office submitted a claim to ABC Insurance Company. Mr. Doi received, in error, a check from the insurance company and cashed it. What step(s) should be taken by Dr.

James' office after this error is discovered? ________________________

____

3. State insurance commissions' responsibilities are directed to what individuals? __

____

4. To locate quickly delinquent insurance claims on an insurance claims register, which

column should be looked at first? ________________________

Would it appear blank or completed? ________________________

5. When no payment has been received from an insurance company, what follow-up should

take place? ________________________

6. Name some of the principal procedures that should be followed in good bookkeeping and record keeping practice when a payment has been received from an insurance company.

____

____

____

7. In good office management, to track submitted pending or resubmitted insurance

claims, a/an ________________________ is used.

8. When a copy of a submitted insurance claim remains in the suspense file beyond the

time for response from the insurance carrier, the action to take is ____________

____

9. An insurance claim becomes delinquent when ________________________

____

10. It is reasonable to assume that a Blue Cross/Blue Shield claim would become delinquent

after _________ weeks and a CHAMPUS claim after _________ weeks.

11. Two categories of claim denials are ________________________

and ________________________.

12. State the solution if a claim has been denied because the professional service rendered was for an injury that is being considered as compensable under workers' compensation.

____

____

____

____

13. The best solution to prevent down coding is to _______________

____

____

____

14. This question is presented to enhance your skill of critical thinking. Using your diagnostic code book, look up the *ICD-9-CM* diagnostic code for a patient being treated for a perforated and hemorrhaging gastric ulcer with no mention of whether it was acute or chronic. To code such a case, what would you do and why? _______________

____

15. You receive a Medicare EOB and notice an excessive reduction in the allowed payment. What step(s) would you take? _______________

____

16. When making an inquiry about a claim by telephone, efficient secretarial procedure would be to _______________

_______________.

17. A CHAMPUS explanation of benefits is received stating that the allowable charge for Mrs. Dayton's office visit is $30.00. Is it possible to appeal this for additional payment?

____

18. Name the six levels for appealing a Medicare claim.

a. _______________

b. _______________

c. _______________

d. _______________

e. _______________

f. _______________

19. Medicare reviews by the insurance carrier are usually completed within _______________ days.

20. A Medicare patient has insurance with United American (a Medigap policy), and payment has not been received from the Medigap insurer within a reasonable length of time. State the action to take in this case ________________________________

____.

ASSIGNMENT 24

You discover that the Medicare claim you submitted to Medicare Blue Shield, 146 Main Street, Woodland Hills, XY 12345 on Bill Hutch 3 months ago was never paid. Complete an insurance claim tracer form (Fig. 8–1). Make a photocopy of textbook Figure 6–8 in Chapter 6 to attach to the tracer form. Mr. Hutch is retired. Place your name on the tracer form as the person to contact at Dr. Doe's office.

INSURANCE CLAIM TRACER

INSURANCE COMPANY NAME: ______________________ DATE: ______________

ADDRESS: ______________________________

PATIENT NAME: ______________________________ INSURED: ______________

POLICY/CERTIFICATE NUMBER: ______________________ GROUP NAME/NUMBER: ________

EMPLOYER NAME AND ADDRESS: ______________________________________

DATE OF INITIAL CLAIM SUBMISSION: ______________ AMOUNT: ______________

An inordinate amount of time has passed since submission of our original claim as described above. We have not received a request for additional information and still await payment of this assigned claim. Please review the attached duplicate and process for payment within seven (7) days.

If there is any difficulty with this claim, please check one of these below and return this letter to our office.

Claim pending because: ______________________________________

Payment of claim in process: ______________________________________

Payment made on claim: Date: ______________ To Whom: ______________

Claim denied: (Reason) ______________________________________

Patient notified: Yes _____ No _____

Remarks: ______________________________________

____

Thank you for your assistance in this important matter. Please contact ______________________ in our office if you have any questions regarding this claim.

Office of: ______________________ M. D.

Address: ______________________________________

______________________ TELEPHONE NUMBER: ______________

FIGURE 8-1

ASSIGNMENT 25

Insurance claims were returned by Medicare (Fig. 8–2), a Blue Plan (Fig. 8–3), and a private insurance carrier (Fig. 8–4). Highlight the blocks on the form where errors are discovered. On a separate sheet of paper, number the elements from 1 to 33 and either insert the correction if data is available to fix the error or write “need” or “missing.”

Blue Cross/Blue Shield of Woodland Hills
509 Main Street
Woodland Hills, XY 12345

APPROVED OMB-0938-0008

ASE- NOT PLE HIS A

CARRIER

PICA

HEALTH INSURANCE CLAIM FORM

PICA

EDICARE (Medicare #) [ ] MEDICAID (Medicaid #) [ ] CHAMPUS (Sponsor's SSN) [ ] CHAMPVA (VA File #) [ ] GROUP HEALTH PLAN (SSN or ID) [ ] FECA BLK LUNG (SSN) [ ] OTHER (ID) [X]

1a. INSURED'S I.D. NUMBER (FOR PROGRAM IN ITEM 1)

TIENT'S NAME (Last Name, First Name, Middle Initial): ARY T. AVERY

3. PATIENT'S BIRTH DATE MM DD YY — SEX M [ ] F [ ]

4. INSURED'S NAME (Last Name, First Name, Middle Initial): SAME

TIENT'S ADDRESS (No., Street): 309 MAIN STREET

6. PATIENT RELATIONSHIP TO INSURED: Self [X] Spouse [ ] Child [ ] Other [ ]

7. INSURED'S ADDRESS (No., Street): SAME

CITY: OODLAND HILLS — STATE: XY

8. PATIENT STATUS: Single [ ] Married [ ] Other [ ]; Employed [ ] Full-Time Student [ ] Part-Time Student [ ]

CITY — STATE

ODE: 2345 — TELEPHONE (Include Area Code): (013) 450-9899

ZIP CODE — TELEPHONE (INCLUDE AREA CODE) ( )

HER INSURED'S NAME (Last Name, First Name, Middle Initial)

10. IS PATIENT'S CONDITION RELATED TO:

11. INSURED'S POLICY GROUP OR FECA NUMBER

HER INSURED'S POLICY OR GROUP NUMBER

a. EMPLOYMENT? (CURRENT OR PREVIOUS) [ ] YES [X] NO

a. INSURED'S DATE OF BIRTH MM DD YY — SEX M [ ] F [ ]

HER INSURED'S DATE OF BIRTH DD YY — SEX M [ ] F [ ]

b. AUTO ACCIDENT? [ ] YES [X] NO — PLACE (State)

b. EMPLOYER'S NAME OR SCHOOL NAME

PLOYER'S NAME OR SCHOOL NAME

c. OTHER ACCIDENT? [ ] YES [X] NO

c. INSURANCE PLAN NAME OR PROGRAM NAME

SURANCE PLAN NAME OR PROGRAM NAME

10d. RESERVED FOR LOCAL USE

d. IS THERE ANOTHER HEALTH BENEFIT PLAN? [ ] YES [ ] NO *If yes*, return to and complete item 9 a-d.

READ BACK OF FORM BEFORE COMPLETING & SIGNING THIS FORM.

ATIENT'S OR AUTHORIZED PERSON'S SIGNATURE I authorize the release of any medical or other information necessary to process this claim. I also request payment of government benefits either to myself or to the party who accepts assignment below.

GNED *Mary T. Avery* DATE 11-10-9X

13. INSURED'S OR AUTHORIZED PERSON'S SIGNATURE I authorize payment of medical benefits to the undersigned physician or supplier for services described below.

SIGNED

PATIENT AND INSURED INFORMATION

ATE OF CURRENT: MM DD YY — ILLNESS (First symptom) OR INJURY (Accident) OR PREGNANCY(LMP)

15. IF PATIENT HAS HAD SAME OR SIMILAR ILLNESS. GIVE FIRST DATE MM DD YY

16. DATES PATIENT UNABLE TO WORK IN CURRENT OCCUPATION FROM MM DD YY TO MM DD YY

AME OF REFERRING PHYSICIAN OR OTHER SOURCE: GERALD PRICE MD

17a. I.D. NUMBER OF REFERRING PHYSICIAN

18. HOSPITALIZATION DATES RELATED TO CURRENT SERVICES FROM 11 11 9X TO 11 12 9X

ESERVED FOR LOCAL USE

20. OUTSIDE LAB? [ ] YES [X] NO — $ CHARGES

IAGNOSIS OR NATURE OF ILLNESS OR INJURY. (RELATE ITEMS 1,2,3 OR 4 TO ITEM 24E BY LINE)

1. 463 .
3. .
4. .

22. MEDICAID RESUBMISSION CODE — ORIGINAL REF. NO.

23. PRIOR AUTHORIZATION NUMBER

A DATE(S) OF SERVICE From DD	YY	To MM	DD	YY	B Place of Service	C Type of Service	D CPT/HCPCS	MODIFIER	E DIAGNOSIS CODE	F $ CHARGES	G DAYS OR UNITS	H EPSDT Family Plan	I EMG	J COB	K RESERVED FOR LOCAL USE
10	9X				11		99203		1	50 00					
11	9X				21		99222		1	100 00					
11	9X				21		42821		1	500 00					
12	9X				21		99231		1	20 00					

EDERAL TAX I.D. NUMBER: 71-5737291 — SSN [ ] EIN [X]

26. PATIENT'S ACCOUNT NO.

27. ACCEPT ASSIGNMENT? (For govt. claims, see back) [ ] YES [ ] NO

28. TOTAL CHARGE $

29. AMOUNT PAID $

30. BALANCE DUE $

IGNATURE OF PHYSICIAN OR SUPPLIER INCLUDING DEGREES OR CREDENTIALS (I certify that the statements on the reverse apply to this bill and are made a part thereof.)

ED *Clarence Cutler MD* DATE 11-15-9X

32. NAME AND ADDRESS OF FACILITY WHERE SERVICES WERE RENDERED (If other than home or office)
COLLEGE HOSPITAL
4500 BROAD AVENUE
WOODLAND HILLS, XY 12345

33. PHYSICIAN'S, SUPPLIER'S BILLING NAME, ADDRESS, ZIP CODE & PHONE # 013-486-9002
COLLEGE CLINIC
4567 BROAD AVENUE
WOODLAND HILLS, XY 12345
PIN# GRP# 3664021 CC

PHYSICIAN OR SUPPLIER INFORMATION

APPROVED BY AMA COUNCIL ON MEDICAL SERVICE 8/88)

PLEASE PRINT OR TYPE

FORM HCFA-1500 (U2) (12-90)
FORM OWCP-1500 FORM RRB-1500

FIGURE 8-2

PLEASE DO NOT STAPLE IN THIS AREA

APPROVED OMB-0938-0008

PICA

HEALTH INSURANCE CLAIM FORM

PICA

1. MEDICARE [X] (Medicare #) MEDICAID [ ] (Medicaid #) CHAMPUS [ ] (Sponsor's SSN) CHAMPVA [ ] (VA File #) GROUP HEALTH PLAN [ ] (SSN or ID) FECA BLK LUNG [ ] (SSN) OTHER [ ] (ID)

1a. INSURED'S I.D. NUMBER (FOR PROGRAM IN ITEM: 433-12-9870A

2. PATIENT'S NAME (Last Name, First Name, Middle Initial): DUGAN, CHARLES C

3. PATIENT'S BIRTH DATE MM DD YY: 12 24 18 SEX M [X] F [ ]

4. INSURED'S NAME (Last Name, First Name, Middle Initial): SAME

5. PATIENT'S ADDRESS (No., Street): 5900 ELM STREET

6. PATIENT RELATIONSHIP TO INSURED: Self [X] Spouse [ ] Child [ ] Other [ ]

7. INSURED'S ADDRESS (No., Street): SAME

CITY: WOODLAND HILLS STATE: XY

8. PATIENT STATUS: Single [ ] Married [X] Other [ ]

CITY STATE

ZIP CODE: 12345 TELEPHONE (Include Area Code): (013) 559-3300

Employed [ ] Full-Time Student [ ] Part-Time Student [ ]

ZIP CODE TELEPHONE (INCLUDE AREA CODE) ( )

9. OTHER INSURED'S NAME (Last Name, First Name, Middle Initial)

10. IS PATIENT'S CONDITION RELATED TO:

11. INSURED'S POLICY GROUP OR FECA NUMBER

a. OTHER INSURED'S POLICY OR GROUP NUMBER: 2340

a. EMPLOYMENT? (CURRENT OR PREVIOUS) [ ] YES [X] NO

a. INSURED'S DATE OF BIRTH MM DD YY SEX M [ ] F [ ]

b. OTHER INSURED'S DATE OF BIRTH MM DD YY SEX M [ ] F [ ]

b. AUTO ACCIDENT? [ ] YES [X] NO PLACE (State)

b. EMPLOYER'S NAME OR SCHOOL NAME

c. EMPLOYER'S NAME OR SCHOOL NAME

c. OTHER ACCIDENT? [ ] YES [X] NO

c. INSURANCE PLAN NAME OR PROGRAM NAME

d. INSURANCE PLAN NAME OR PROGRAM NAME: AETNA INSURANCE COMPANY

10d. RESERVED FOR LOCAL USE

d. IS THERE ANOTHER HEALTH BENEFIT PLAN? [X] YES [ ] NO *If yes*, return to and complete item 9 a-

READ BACK OF FORM BEFORE COMPLETING & SIGNING THIS FORM.

12. PATIENT'S OR AUTHORIZED PERSON'S SIGNATURE I authorize the release of any medical or other information necessary to process this claim. I also request payment of government benefits either to myself or to the party who accepts assignment below.

SIGNED ______ DATE ______

13. INSURED'S OR AUTHORIZED PERSON'S SIGNATURE I authorize payment of medical benefits to the undersigned physician or supplier services described below.

SIGNED ______

14. DATE OF CURRENT: MM DD YY ILLNESS (First symptom) OR INJURY (Accident) OR PREGNANCY(LMP)

15. IF PATIENT HAS HAD SAME OR SIMILAR ILLNESS. GIVE FIRST DATE MM DD YY

16. DATES PATIENT UNABLE TO WORK IN CURRENT OCCUPATION FROM MM DD YY TO MM DD YY

17. NAME OF REFERRING PHYSICIAN OR OTHER SOURCE: PERRY CARDI, MD

17a. I.D. NUMBER OF REFERRING PHYSICIAN

18. HOSPITALIZATION DATES RELATED TO CURRENT SERVICES FROM MM DD YY TO MM DD YY

19. RESERVED FOR LOCAL USE

20. OUTSIDE LAB? [ ] YES [X] NO $ CHARGES

21. DIAGNOSIS OR NATURE OF ILLNESS OR INJURY. (RELATE ITEMS 1,2,3 OR 4 TO ITEM 24E BY LINE)

1. 239 . 9
2. ___ . __
3. ___ . __
4. ___ . __

22. MEDICAID RESUBMISSION CODE ORIGINAL REF. NO.

23. PRIOR AUTHORIZATION NUMBER

24.	A DATE(S) OF SERVICE From MM DD YY	To MM DD YY	B Place of Service	C Type of Service	D PROCEDURES, SERVICES, OR SUPPLIES (Explain Unusual Circumstances) CPT/HCPCS MODIFIER	E DIAGNOSIS CODE	F $ CHARGES	G DAYS OR UNITS	H EPSDT Family Plan	I EMG	J COB	K RESERVED FOR LOCAL USE
1	09 55 9X		11		99203	1	50 00					
2	09 25 9X		11		12001	1						
3												
4												
5												
6												

25. FEDERAL TAX I.D. NUMBER SSN [ ] EIN [X]

26. PATIENT'S ACCOUNT NO.

27. ACCEPT ASSIGNMENT? (For govt. claims, see back) [X] YES [ ] NO

28. TOTAL CHARGE $

29. AMOUNT PAID $

30. BALANCE DUE $

31. SIGNATURE OF PHYSICIAN OR SUPPLIER INCLUDING DEGREES OR CREDENTIALS (I certify that the statements on the reverse apply to this bill and are made a part thereof.)

SIGNED Gerald Practon MD DATE 9-30-9X

32. NAME AND ADDRESS OF FACILITY WHERE SERVICES WERE RENDERED (If other than home or office)

33. PHYSICIAN'S, SUPPLIER'S BILLING NAME, ADDRESS, ZIP CODE & PHONE # 013-486-9002
COLLEGE CLINIC
4567 BROAD AVENUE
WOODLAND HILLS, XY 12345
PIN# GRP# 3664021 CC

(APPROVED BY AMA COUNCIL ON MEDICAL SERVICE 8/88)

PLEASE PRINT OR TYPE

FORM HCFA-1500 (U2) (12-90)
FORM OWCP-1500 FORM RRB

FIGURE 8-3

PRUDENTIAL INSURANCE COMPANY
500 SOUTH BEND STREET
WOODLAND HILLS XY 12345

APPROVED OMB-0938-0008

CARRIER

HEALTH INSURANCE CLAIM FORM

PICA

E MEDICAID CHAMPUS CHAMPVA GROUP HEALTH PLAN FECA BLK LUNG OTHER
#) (Medicaid #) (Sponsor's SSN) (VA File #) (SSN or ID) (SSN) [X] (ID)

1a. INSURED'S I.D. NUMBER (FOR PROGRAM IN ITEM 1)

NAME (Last Name, First Name, Middle Initial): NSON EMILY B

3. PATIENT'S BIRTH DATE MM DD YY: 02 12 63 — SEX M [ ] F [ ]

4. INSURED'S NAME (Last Name, First Name, Middle Initial): JOHNSON ERRON T

ADDRESS (No., Street): 1 EVERETT STREET

6. PATIENT RELATIONSHIP TO INSURED: Self [ ] Spouse [X] Child [ ] Other [ ]

7. INSURED'S ADDRESS (No., Street): SAME

STATE: XY — OLAND HILLS

8. PATIENT STATUS: Single [ ] Married [X] Other [ ]; Employed [ ] Full-Time Student [ ] Part-Time Student [ ]

CITY — STATE

45 — TELEPHONE (Include Area Code) ( )

ZIP CODE — TELEPHONE (INCLUDE AREA CODE) ( )

SURED'S NAME (Last Name, First Name, Middle Initial)

10. IS PATIENT'S CONDITION RELATED TO:

11. INSURED'S POLICY GROUP OR FECA NUMBER

SURED'S POLICY OR GROUP NUMBER

a. EMPLOYMENT? (CURRENT OR PREVIOUS) [ ] YES [ ] NO

a. INSURED'S DATE OF BIRTH MM DD YY — SEX M [ ] F [ ]

SURED'S DATE OF BIRTH YY — SEX M [ ] F [ ]

b. AUTO ACCIDENT? [ ] YES [ ] NO — PLACE (State)

b. EMPLOYER'S NAME OR SCHOOL NAME

R'S NAME OR SCHOOL NAME

c. OTHER ACCIDENT? [ ] YES [ ] NO

c. INSURANCE PLAN NAME OR PROGRAM NAME

E PLAN NAME OR PROGRAM NAME

10d. RESERVED FOR LOCAL USE

d. IS THERE ANOTHER HEALTH BENEFIT PLAN? [ ] YES [ ] NO *If yes*, return to and complete item 9 a-d.

READ BACK OF FORM BEFORE COMPLETING & SIGNING THIS FORM.

'S OR AUTHORIZED PERSON'S SIGNATURE I authorize the release of any medical or other information necessary s this claim. I also request payment of government benefits either to myself or to the party who accepts assignment

Emily B. Johnson DATE 1-4-9X

13. INSURED'S OR AUTHORIZED PERSON'S SIGNATURE I authorize payment of medical benefits to the undersigned physician or supplier for services described below.

SIGNED Emily B Johnson

PATIENT AND INSURED INFORMATION

CURRENT: ILLNESS (First symptom) OR INJURY (Accident) OR PREGNANCY(LMP)

15. IF PATIENT HAS HAD SAME OR SIMILAR ILLNESS. GIVE FIRST DATE MM DD YY

16. DATES PATIENT UNABLE TO WORK IN CURRENT OCCUPATION FROM MM DD YY TO MM DD YY

REFERRING PHYSICIAN OR OTHER SOURCE: LD PRACTON MD

17a. I.D. NUMBER OF REFERRING PHYSICIAN

18. HOSPITALIZATION DATES RELATED TO CURRENT SERVICES FROM MM DD YY TO MM DD YY

ED FOR LOCAL USE

20. OUTSIDE LAB? [ ] YES [X] NO — $ CHARGES

IS OR NATURE OF ILLNESS OR INJURY. (RELATE ITEMS 1,2,3 OR 4 TO ITEM 24E BY LINE)

3. ___ . ___

4. ___ . ___

22. MEDICAID RESUBMISSION CODE — ORIGINAL REF. NO.

23. PRIOR AUTHORIZATION NUMBER

ATE(S) OF SERVICE To YY MM DD YY	B Place of Service	C Type of Service	D PROCEDURES, SERVICES, OR SUPPLIES (Explain Unusual Circumstances) CPT/HCPCS | MODIFIER	E DIAGNOSIS CODE	F $ CHARGES	G DAYS OR UNITS	H EPSDT Family Plan	I EMG	J COB	K RESERVED FOR LOCAL USE
9X	11		99213	1	25 00					
9X	11		99213	1	25 00					

TAX I.D. NUMBER SSN EIN [ ] [X]

26. PATIENT'S ACCOUNT NO.

27. ACCEPT ASSIGNMENT? (For govt. claims, see back) [ ] YES [ ] NO

28. TOTAL CHARGE $

29. AMOUNT PAID $

30. BALANCE DUE $

RE OF PHYSICIAN OR SUPPLIER G DEGREES OR CREDENTIALS at the statements on the reverse is bill and are made a part thereof.)

a Cutis, M.D. 1-6-9X DATE

32. NAME AND ADDRESS OF FACILITY WHERE SERVICES WERE RENDERED (If other than home or office)

33. PHYSICIAN'S, SUPPLIER'S BILLING NAME, ADDRESS, ZIP CODE & PHONE # 013-486-9002
COLLEGE CLINIC
4567 BROAD AVENUE
WOODLAND HILLS, XY 12345
PIN# — GRP# 3664021 CC

PHYSICIAN OR SUPPLIER INFORMATION

VED BY AMA COUNCIL ON MEDICAL SERVICE 8/88)

PLEASE PRINT OR TYPE

FORM HCFA-1500 (U2) (12-90)
FORM OWCP-1500 FORM RRB-1500

FIGURE 8-4

ASSIGNMENT 26

After Medicare processes the insurance claim tracer on Bill Hutch, you receive a Medicare EOB and payment check but the amount is incorrect due to an excessive reduction in the allowed payment. An appeal was made in September and denied; Dr. John Doe feels a mistake has been made and wishes to request a hearing.

Complete the HCFA-1965 Request for Hearing, Part B, Medicare Claim form for this case (Fig. 8–5) by referring to the tracer form completed for Assignment 24 (Fig. 8–1) and textbook Figure 6–8 in Chapter 6. As you will learn in the chapter on Medicare, the Health Insurance Claim Number is the patient's Medicare identification number as shown in Figure 6–7, Block 1a. No additional evidence is to be presented and the doctor does not wish to appear for the hearing. Date the form December 5, 199X.

EPARTMENT OF HEALTH AND HUMAN SERVICES
EALTH CARE FINANCING ADMINISTRATION

Form Approved
OMB No. 0938-0034

REQUEST FOR HEARING - PART B MEDICARE CLAIM

Medical Insurance Benefits - Social Security Act

OTICE—Anyone who misrepresents or falsifies essential information requested by this form may upon conviction be subject to fine and imprisonment under Federal Law.

Carrier's Name and Address	1 Name of Patient
	2 Health Insurance Claim Number

3 I disagree with the review determination on my claim, and request a hearing before a hearing officer of the insurance carrier named above.

MY REASONS ARE: *(Attach a copy of the Review Notice. NOTE.—If the review decision was made more than 6 months ago include your reason for not making this request earlier)*

____

____

____

____

4 Check one of the Following:

☐ I have additional evidence to submit. *(Attach such evidence to this form or forward it to the carrier within 10 days.)*

☐ I do not have additional evidence.

Check Only One of the Statements Below:

☐ I wish to appear in person before the Hearing Officer.

☐ I do not wish to appear and hereby request a decision on the evidence before the Hearing Officer.

5 **EITHER THE CLAIMANT OR REPRESENTATIVE SHOULD SIGN IN THE APPROPRIATE SPACE BELOW:**

Signature or Name of Claimant's Representative ➔		Claimant's Signature ➔	
Address		Address	
City, State, and ZIP Code		City, State, and ZIP Code	
Telephone Number	Date	Telephone Number	Date

(Claimant should not write below this line)

ACKNOWLEDGMENT OF REQUEST FOR HEARING

Your request for a hearing was received on ______________________. You will be notified of the time and place of the hearing at least 10 days before the date of the hearing.

Signed	Date

Form **HCFA-1965** (8-79)

CARRIER COPY

FIGURE 8-5

CHAPTER 9

Managed Care Systems and Special Plans

Key Terms

Your instructor may wish to select some specific words pertinent to this chapter for a test. For definitions of the terms, further study, and/or reference, the words, phrases, and abbreviations may be found in the Glossary at the end of the textbook. *Key terms for this chapter follow.*

ancillary services
buffing
capitated payment
capitation
churning
claims-review type of foundation
closed panel program
comprehensive type of foundation
copayment (copay)
cost containment
deductible
disenrollment
employer mandate
encounter record
encounters
fee for service
foundations for medical care
gatekeeper
gatekeeper system
group model
health care center
health maintenance organization (HMO)
in-area
individual or independent practice association (IPA)
individual responsibility program (IRP)
managed care organization (MCO)
managed care system (MCS)
medical capitation plan
National Health Board (NHB)
optometric service plan
out-of-area
participating doctor
physician provider group (PPG)
point-of-service (POS) plan
preferred provider organization (PPO)
prepaid group practice plan
prepaid health plan (PHP)
primary-care physician (PCP)
quality assurance
regional health alliance
service area
single-payer health care system
staff model
standard benefits package
stop-loss
tertiary care
turfing
universal access
universal coverage
utilization review (UR)
withhold

Performance Objectives

The student will be able to

- Define and spell the key terms for this chapter, given the information from the textbook Glossary, within a reasonable period of time and with enough accuracy to obtain a satisfactory evaluation.
- Answer the review questions after reading the chapter, with enough accuracy to obtain a satisfactory evaluation.
- Complete treatment authorization forms fo managed care plans, given completed new patient information forms, within a reasonable period of time and with enough accuracy to obtain a satisfactory evaluation.

Study Outline

HISTORY
- Prepaid group practice health plans
  - Health Maintenance Organization Act of 1973
- Health care reform

MANAGED CARE SYSTEMS
- Health Maintenance Oreganizations (HMOs)
  - Prepaid group practice model
  - Staff model
  - Independent practice association
  - Network HMO
- Individual or independent practice association (IPA)
- Preferred provider organizations
  - Blue Cross/Blue Shield and managed care programs
  - Medicare Blue USA
  - Point of service programs
- CHAMPUS and managed care programs
  - TRICARE Prime
  - TRICARE Extra
  - CHAMPUS and HMO coverage
- Medicare and managed care programs
- Medicaid and managed care programs
- Point of service plans
- Physician provider groups
- Triple option health plan
- Foundations for medical care

MEDICAL REVIEW
- Professional review organizations (PROs)
- Utilization review or management

MANAGEMENT OF PLANS
- Contracts
- Precertification or prior authorization
- Laboratory and x-ray
- Managed care guide
- Plan administration
  - Copayments
  - Deductibles
  - Identification card
  - Patient information letter

FINANCIAL MANAGEMENT
- Statement of remittance
- Accounting
- Fee for service
- Capitation and year-end evaluation

BANKRUPTCY

SPECIAL PLANS
- Individual responsibility plan
- Optometric service plans

Review Questions

Review the objectives, key terms, glossary definitions to key terms, figures, and chapter information before completing the following review questions.

1. A prepaid group practice plan means the patient pays ______________________
   and health services are rendered by ______________________.
2. When a prepaid group practice plan limits the patient's choice of personal physicians, this is termed a/an ______________________ program.

3. Systems that allow for better negotiations for contracts with large employers are

   a. ______

   b. ______

   c. ______

4. The most popular of the prepaid health plans is ______

   ______.

5. In a managed care setting, a physician who controls patient access to specialists is known as a/an ______.

6. Name four types of HMOs.

   a. ______

   b. ______

   c. ______

   d. ______

7. When a certain percentage of the premium fund is set aside to operate an individual practice association, this is known as a/an ______.

8. A health benefit program in which enrollees may choose any physician or hospital for services but obtain a higher level of benefits if preferred providers are used is known as a/an ______.

9. In California and Hawaii as well as some other states, two CHAMPUS managed care programs are known as ______ and ______, and CHAMPUS standard coverage is known as ______.

10. Two kinds of Medicare Part B health maintenance organization contracts are ______ and ______.

11. If a physician or hospital in a managed care plan is paid a fixed, per capita amount for each patient enrolled regardless of the type and number of services rendered, this is a payment system known as ______.

12. HMOs and PPOs that consist of a network of physicians and hospitals that provide an insurance company or employer with discounts on their services are referred to as a/an ______.

13. What is a foundation for medical care? ______

    ______

    ______

    ______

14. Name two types of operations used by foundations for medical care and explain the main feature of each.

    a. ____

    ____

    b. ____

    ____

15. Professional review organizations are established to determine ______________

    ______________ and ______________.

16. Name the three duties of the PROs.

    a. ____

    b. ____

    c. ____

17. To control health care costs, the process of reviewing and establishing medical necessity for services and providers' use of medical care resources is termed______________.

18. Explain the meaning of a "stop loss" provision that might appear in a managed care contract. ____

    ____

19. Mark the following statements as true or false.

a.	An HMO can be sponsored and operated by a foundation.	T	F
b.	Peer review determines the quality and operation of health care.	T	F
c.	An employer may offer the services of an HMO clinic if he or she has five or more employees.	T	F
d.	Medicare and Medicaid beneficiaries may not join an HMO.	T	F
e.	Managed care withhold amounts should be shown as a write-off in an accounts journal.	T	F

ASSIGNMENT 27

Meriweather B. Cohn's primary physician, Gerald Practon, M.D., took her clinical history. Physical examination revealed a normal blood pressure and was basically negative except for diagnosis of a heart murmur. Dr. Practon decides to make a semi-urgent request to refer Mrs. Cohn for an office consultation (other service) to Victor M. Salazar, M.D., 20 Excalibur Street, Woodland Hills, XY 12345, telephone 013-625-7344. Dr. Salazar is a cardiologist and will evaluate Mrs. Cohn's heart murmur; diagnosis code 785.2. Dr. Salazar will take a detailed history, perform a detailed examination, and medical decision making will be of low complexity. Complete a treatment authorization form (Fig. 9–1) for Mrs. Cohn's managed care plan to obtain permission for the office consultation, dating it August 2. Refer to the New Patient Information form completed by Mrs. Cohn when she came into the office for her visit with Dr. Practon (Fig. 9–2). Dr. Practon's FHP is CC 4602.

HP® IPA TREATMENT AUTHORIZATION FORM
LTH CARE

____ Referral
____ Participating
____ Non-Participating
____ Commercial
____ Senior

For Billing Instructions, Patient and Non-Affiliated Providers, and Consultants please see reverse side for instructions

THIS PORTION COMPLETED BY PHYSICIAN

ent Name________________________________ Date____/____/____
______ F______ Age______ FHP #______________ Home Phone______________
ress____
ary Care MD____________________ Primary Care MD's FHP #____________________
erring MD____________________ Referring MD's FHP #____________________
erred To____________________ Address____________________
Office Phone____________________
of service: ☐ In-Patient ☐ Out-Patient Services ☐ Initital Visit ☐ Return Visit ☐ Other
ical History and Findings____

gnosis____
ICD-9-CM CODE
luation and Treatment to Date____

cedure____
RVS/CPT-4 CODE
son for Referral/Consultation/Procedure____

ident: ☐ Yes ☐ No Where Occurred: ☐ Home ☐ Work ☐ Auto ☐ Other
☐ Urgent ☐ Semi-Urgent ☐ Elective
ility To Be Used:____________________ Estimated Length of Stay____________________
☐ Office ☐ Out-Patient ☐ In-Patient

THIS PORTION COMPLETED BY FHP UR

THIS AUTHORIZATION GOOD FOR 60 DAYS ONLY

e of Contract: ☐ Capitation ☐ Fee For Service ☐ Per Diem
jected Cost of Procedure____________________ Projected Cost of Facility____________________
O Verification: Effective____________________ Group #____________________
nefits: Co-Pay Per Visit____________________ Hospital____________________
itations:____
___ Authorized Date______ Initials______ Reason______ Authorization #______
___ Deferred Date______ Initials______ Reason______
___ Denied Date______ Initials______ Reason______
___ Modified Date______ Initials______ Reason______

WHITE UR Copy CANARY - Hospital Copy PINK - Physician Copy GOLDENROD - Claims Copy

FIGURE 9-1

Welcome To Our Office NEW PATIENT INFORMATION DATE 8-2-9X

PATIENT'S NAME (PLEASE PRINT)	S.S. #	MARITAL STATUS	SEX	BIRTH DATE	AGE	RELIG
Meriweather B. Cohn	430-17-0261	S [X] W D SEP	M [X]	11-14-65		
STREET ADDRESS PERMANENT TEMPORARY	CITY AND STATE			ZIP CODE	HOME PHON	
267 Blake Street	Woodland Hills		XY	12345	013-263	
PATIENT'S OR PARENT'S EMPLOYER	OCCUPATION (INDICATE IF STUDENT)			HOW LONG EMPLOYED	BUS. PHONE	
SUN corporation	sales representative			5 yrs	013-263	
EMPLOYER'S STREET ADDRESS	CITY AND STATE				ZIP CODE	
74 Rain street	Woodland Hills		XY		1234	
DRUG ALLERGIES, IF ANY						
Penicillin						
SPOUSE OR PARENT'S NAME	S.S. #	BIRTHDATE				
Starkweather L. Cohn	273-05-9961	7-9-63				
SPOUSE OR PARENT'S EMPLOYER	OCCUPATION (INDICATE IF STUDENT)			HOW LONG EMPLOYED	BUS. PHONE	
B + L Stormdrain Co.	accountant			10 yrs	013-421	
EMPLOYER'S STREET ADDRESS	CITY AND STATE				ZIP CODE	
20 South Wind Road	Woodland Hills		XY		1234	
*SPOUSE'S STREET ADDRESS, IF DIVORCED OR SEPARATED	CITY AND STATE			ZIP CODE	HOME PHON	

PLEASE READ: ALL CHARGES ARE DUE AT THE TIME OF SERVICES. IF HOSPITALIZATION IS INDICATED, THE PATIENT IS RESPONSIBLE FOR FUR INSURANCE CLAIM FORMS TO THE OFFICE PRIOR TO HOSPITALIZATION.

PERSON RESPONSIBLE FOR PAYMENT, IF NOT ABOVE	STREET ADDRESS, CITY, STATE		ZIP CODE	HOME PHONE #
BLUE SHIELD (GIVE NAME OF POLICYHOLDER) ☐	EFFECTIVE DATE	CERTIFICATE #	GROUP #	COVERAGE CODE
OTHER (WRITE IN NAME OF INSURANCE COMPANY) ☐ FHP Healthcare	EFFECTIVE DATE 1-1-8X		POLICY # FHP # A4932	
OTHER (WRITE IN NAME OF INSURANCE COMPANY) ☐	EFFECTIVE DATE		POLICY #	

MEDICARE (PLEASE GIVE NUMBER) ☐			RAILROAD RETIREMENT (PLEASE GIVE NUMBER) ☐	
MEDICAID ☐	EFFECTIVE DATE	PROGRAM #	COUNTY #	CASE # / ACCOUNT #
INDUSTRIAL ☐	WERE YOU INJURED ON THE JOB? ☐ YES [X] NO	DATE OF INJURY	INDUSTRIAL CLAIM #	
ACCIDENT ☐	WAS AN AUTOMOBILE INVOLVED? ☐ YES [X] NO	DATE OF ACCIDENT	NAME OF ATTORNEY	
WERE X-RAYS TAKEN OF THIS INJURY OR PROBLEM? ☐ YES [X] NO		IF YES, WHERE WERE X-RAYS TAKEN? (HOSPITAL, ETC.)		DATE X-RAYS

HAS ANY MEMBER OF YOUR IMMEDIATE FAMILY BEEN TREATED BY OUR PHYSICIAN(S) BEFORE? INCLUDE NAME OF PHYSICIAN AND FAMILY MEMBER.
No

REFERRED BY	STREET ADDRESS, CITY, STATE	ZIP CODE	PHONE #
Breezie N. Cloud	521 N. Wind Rd. Woodland Hills, XY	12345	013-721-9

ALL PROFESSIONAL SERVICES RENDERED ARE CHARGED TO THE PATIENT. NECESSARY FORMS WILL BE COMPLETED TO HELP EXPEDITE INS CARRIER PAYMENTS. HOWEVER, THE PATIENT IS RESPONSIBLE FOR ALL FEES, REGARDLESS OF INSURANCE COVERAGE. IT IS ALSO CUSTOMARY FOR SERVICES WHEN RENDERED UNLESS OTHER ARRANGEMENTS HAVE BEEN MADE IN ADVANCE WITH OUR OFFICE BOOKKEEPER.

INSURANCE AUTHORIZATION AND ASSIGNMENT

Name of Policy Holder Meriweather B. Cohn HIC Number

I request that payment of authorized Medicare/Other Insurance company benefits be made either to me or on my behalf to College Clinic for any services furnished me by that party who accepts assignment/physician. Regulations pertaining to Medicare assignment of benefits apply.

I authorize any holder of medical or other information about me to release to the Social Security Administration and Health Care Financing Administrati intermediaries or carrier or any other insurance company any information needed for this or a related Medicare/Other Insurance company claim.

I understand my signature requests that payment be made and authorizes release of medical information necessary to pay the claim. If item 9 of the HCFA-15 form is completed, my signature authorizes releasing of the information to the insurer or agency shown. In Medicare/Other Insurance company assigned ca physician or supplier agrees to accept the charge determination of the Medicare/Other Insurance company as the full charge, and the patient is responsible on deductible, coinsurance, and noncovered services. Coinsurance and the deductible are based upon the charge determination of the Medicare/Other Insurance co

Signature Meriweather B. Cohn Date 8-2-9X

NEW PATIENT INFORMATION

Form #F200-2 Rev. 8/92 Professional Filing Systems, Inc. To Order Call 1-800-477-7374, In Atlanta 404/396-4994

FIGURE 9-2

ASSIGNMENT 28

Mrs. Rosario Jimenez comes into Dr. Gerald Practon's office complaining of neck pain. He is the primary care physician for the managed care program, Healthnet, of which Mrs. Jimenez is a member. Mrs. Jimenez lives at 350 South Carib Street, Woodland Hills, XY 12340-0329, telephone number 013-450-9987. Her plan identification number is JIM40896 and she was born April 6, 1960. After taking a history, completing a physical examination, and taking x-rays and reviewing them, Dr. Practon makes a diagnosis of cervical radiculitis, diagnosis code 723.4. He gives her a prescription for some medication and says it is necessary to order outpatient physical therapy 2 X a week for 6 weeks at College Hospital. Authorization must be obtained for this treatment. The procedure number for physical therapy treatment is 97110.

Complete the managed care authorization form for this patient (Figure 9-3), date it July 7 of current year, and submit it to the managed care plan. Refer to textbook Figure 9-1 for visual guidance.

MANAGED CARE PLAN
TREATMENT AUTHORIZATION REQUEST

TO BE COMPLETED BY PRIMARY CARE PHYSICIAN OR OUTSIDE PROVIDER

Health Net	☐	Met Life	☐
Pacificare	☐	Travelers	☐
Secure Horizons	☐	Pru Care	☐

Patient Name:________________________________Date:____________________

M____ F____ Birthdate________________ Home telephone number________________

Address____

Primary Care Physician__________________________Member ID#________________

Referring Physician____________________________Member ID#________________

Referred to__________________________ Address______________________________

__________________________________ Office telephone no.____________________

Diagnosis Code__________ Diagnosis____

Diagnosis Code__________ Diagnosis____

Treatment Plan:____

Authorization requested for procedures/tests/visits:

Procedure Code__________ Description____

Procedure Code__________ Description____

Facility to be used:__________________________Estimated length of stay______________

Office ☐ Outpatient ☐ Inpatient ☐ Other ☐

List of potential consultants (i.e., anesthetists, assistants, or medical/surgical):

____

Physician's signature____

TO BE COMPLETED BY PRIMARY CARE PHYSICIAN

PCP Recommendations:______________________________________PCP Initials________

Eligibility checked__________________Effective date______________________________

TO BE COMPLETED BY UTILIZATION MANAGEMENT

Authorized____________________________ Not authorized__________________________

Deferred______________________________ Modified______________________________

Authorization Request #____

Comments:____

FIGURE 9-3

ASSIGNMENT 29

Daniel Chan comes into Dr. Raymond Skelton's office complaining of pain, swelling and crepitus of the right knee. The patient is having difficulty walking but indicates no recent injury to the knee. Dr. Skelton is the orthopedic surgeon and was referred by the primary care physician, Dr. Gerald Practon, for the managed care program, Met Life, of which this patient is a member. Mr. Chan lives at 226 West Olive Avenue, Woodland Hills, XY 12340-0329, thelephone number is 013-540-6700. His plan identification number is FTW90876 and he was born February 23, 1971. After taking a history, completing a physical examination, and taking x-rays and reviewing them, Dr. Skelton decides to send Mr. Chan for a diagnostic arthroscopy to determine the cause of the symptoms as he suspects the patient has a tear of the medial meniscus (ICD-9-CM code no. 836.0) and may require debridement of articular cartilage. This procedure will be done as an outpatient at College Hospital. Authorization must be obtained for the arthroscopy with debridement (CPT code no. 29877). Dr. Skelton's Met Life identification number is 98-261.

Complete the managed care authorization form for this patient (Figure 9-4), date it August 12 of current year, and submit it to the managed care plan. Refer to textbook Figure 9-1 for visual guidance.

MANAGED CARE PLAN
TREATMENT AUTHORIZATION REQUEST

TO BE COMPLETED BY PRIMARY CARE PHYSICIAN OR OUTSIDE PROVIDER

Health Net	☐	Met Life	☐
Pacificare	☐	Travelers	☐
Secure Horizons	☐	Pru Care	☐

Patient Name:________________________________ Date:____________________

M____ F____ Birthdate________________ Home telephone number__________________

Address____

Primary Care Physician__________________________Member ID#________________

Referring Physician____________________________Member ID#________________

Referred to_________________________ Address______________________________

_________________________________ Office telephone no.____________________

Diagnosis Code__________ Diagnosis____

Diagnosis Code__________ Diagnosis____

Treatment Plan:____

Authorization requested for procedures/tests/visits:

Procedure Code__________ Description_______________________________________

Procedure Code__________ Description_______________________________________

Facility to be used:_________________________Estimated length of stay______________

Office ☐ Outpatient ☐ Inpatient ☐ Other ☐

List of potential consultants (i.e., anesthetists, assistants, or medical/surgical):

____

Physician's signature____

TO BE COMPLETED BY PRIMARY CARE PHYSICIAN

PCP Recommendations:____________________________________PCP Initials________

Eligibility checked___________________Effective date___________________________

TO BE COMPLETED BY UTILIZATION MANAGEMENT

Authorized____________________________ Not authorized__________________________

Deferred______________________________ Modified_______________________________

Authorization Request #____

Comments:____

FIGURE 9-4

CHAPTER 10

Blue Cross and Blue Shield

Key Terms

Your instructor may wish to select some specific words pertinent to this chapter for a test. For definitions of the terms, further study, and/or reference, the words, phrases, and abbreviations may be found in the Glossary at the end of the textbook. *Key terms for this chapter follow.*

adjustments
assignment of benefits
BlueCard Program
Blue Cross and Blue Shield Association (BCBSA)
Blue Cross and Blue Shield Plans
carrier
certificate number
complementary benefits
control plan
direct payment
explanation of benefits (EOB)
Federal Employee Health Benefits Program (FEHBP)
Federal Employee Program (FEP)
Federal Tax Identification Number
indemnity benefit contract
itemized bill
medical record number
member
national account
participating physician
Point of service (POS) product
service benefit contract
subscriber
third-party payer

Performance Objectives

The student will be able to

- Define and spell the key terms for this chapter, given the information from the textbook Glossary, within a reasonable period of time and with enough accuracy to obtain a satisfactory evaluation.
- Answer the review questions after reading the chapter, with enough accuracy to obtain a satisfactory evaluation.
- Fill in the correct meaning of each abbreviation, given a list of common medical abbreviations and symbols that appear in chart notes, within a reasonable period of time and with enough accuracy to obtain a satisfactory evaluation.
- Complete each HCFA-1500 health insurance claim form for billing, given the patients' medical chart notes, ledger cards, encounter forms, and blank insurance claim forms, within a reasonable period of time and with enough accuracy to obtain a satisfactory evaluation.
- Correctly post payments, adjustments, and balances on the patients' ledger cards, using the Mock Fee Schedule in Appendix A, within a reasonable period of time and with enough accuracy to obtain a satisfactory evaluation.

Study Outline

INTRODUCTION
HISTORY AND PURPOSE
SPECIAL CLAUSES AND BENEFITS
TYPES OF BLUE CROSS AND BLUE SHIELD CONTRACTS
  Service benefit contracts
  Indemnity benefit contracts
METHODS OF PAYMENT
  Usual, customary, and reasonable (UCR) payment program
  Payments under UCR
  Fee schedules
    Relative value studies
PHYSICIAN PARTICIPATION CONCEPT
BLUECARD PROGRAM
CENTRAL CERTIFICATION AND CENTRAL SITE PROCESSING
IDENTIFYING INFORMATION
BLUE CROSS/BLUE SHIELD AND MEDICARE CLAIMS
  Local Blue Shield plan is Medicare Part B carrier
MANAGED CARE
  Preferred Provider Organizations (PPOs)
  Health Maintenance Organizations (HMOs)
  Point of Service (POS) programs
MEDICAL NECESSITY PROGRAM
TECHNOLOGY ASSESSMENT
PREADMISSION TESTING, AMBULATORY SURGERY, AND SECOND OPINIONS
STANDARD BLUE PLANS CLAIMS PROCEDURE
  Manual completion of HCFA-1500 claim form
  Electronic claims submission
  Following up on delinquent claims
  Blue Cross/Blue Shield state insurance addresses
  Reference books
EXPLANATION OF BENEFITS (EOB)
PROVIDER NUMBER
FEDERAL EMPLOYEE HEALTH BENEFITS PROGRAM
  Nonbenefits
  Identification card
  Claims procedure
  Time limit
  Explanation of benefits

Review Questions

Review the objectives, key terms, glossary definitions to key terms, chapter information, and figures before completing the following review questions.

1. Because individuals prepay for health care services under Blue Cross and Blue Shield, the programs are known as ____

____.

2. A contract holder who enters into a Blue Cross/Blue Shield Plan is called a

_____________________, not a policy holder, and retains a _____________________, not a policy.

3 If a Medicare fiscal intermediary is a Blue Cross and Blue Shield Plan, the

_____________________________ within the Plan handles Medicare Part A and the

_____________________________ within the plan handles Medicare Part B.

4. Name four special clauses or benefits that may be present in Blue Cross and Blue Shield contracts.

a. ____

b. ____

c. ____

d. ____

5. Name two types of Blue Shield contracts.

a. ____

b. ____

6. Explain the terms *usual, customary,* and *reasonable* as they pertain to a Blue Plan UCR payment program.

a. Usual means ____

____

____

b. Customary means ____

____

____

c. Reasonable means ____

____

____

7. If a physician is a participating member physician of a Blue Plan, what fee is he or she

entitled to? ____

____

8. If a physician is a nonparticipating physician of a Blue Plan, what fee is he or she entitled to? ______________________________

____

9. A Blue Cross/Blue Shield Plan subscriber who lives and works in New York goes to New Jersey for a vacation, where he suffers an injury and seeks medical care. What is the name of the program that handles this type of case, and how do you handle the bill?

____

____

10. Claim processing arrangements used to administer benefits of a Blue Plan corporate account with employees in several states are ______________________________ and ______________________________.

11. Name three practices commonly used for reducing surgical costs, hospital stays, and surgical procedures.

a. ______________________________

b. ______________________________

c. ______________________________

12. State important information to obtain from the patient's Blue Cross/Blue Shield card.

a. ______________________________

b. ______________________________

13. Usual time limit for submitting a Blue Cross/Blue Shield insurance claim is ______________________________.

14. If a patient is a union worker and has Blue Cross and Blue Shield coverage, what is important to remember in regard to eligibility for benefits? ______________________________

____

15. To validate that a provider holds a state license, Blue Cross/Blue Shield issues a/an ______________________________.

16. If an individual is employed by the federal government and is under a Blue Plan, the program is entitled ______________________________

______________________________.

17. How do you identify federal (national) account numbers? ______________________________

____

18. State the time limit for submitting a claim for a federal employee with a Blue Plan contract. ______________________________

____

19. Define these abbreviations.

UCR ______________ DRG ______________

EOB ______________ ITS ______________

FEHBP ______________ TEC ______________

ASSIGNMENT 30

1. Assume the *Health Insurance Claim Form* HCFA-1500 is printed in red ink for processing by OCR or ICR (Fig. 10–3). Complete the form using OCR or ICR guidelines, and send the form to Blue Cross for David M. Cash. See Chapter 10 of the *Handbook* for help in completing this form. Refer to his patient record (Fig. 10–1) and ledger card. Date the claim February 27. You have had Mr. Cash sign the release of information portion of the form as well as the assignment of benefits. Refer to Appendix A to fill in the fees on the ledger card (Fig. 10–2). When finishing the form, be sure to type your initials at the bottom lower left corner. The local Blue Cross/Blue Shield addresses for each state may be found at the end of the *Handbook* in Appendix A.
2. Use your *Current Procedural Terminology* (CPT) code book or Appendix A of this *Workbook* to determine the correct five-digit code number for each professional service rendered. Remember to include modifiers if necessary. Check the Mock Fee Schedule in Appendix A to check for surgical follow-up days. No-charge entries are for documentation purposes and do not have to be typed on the insurance claim form.
3. Record on the ledger card when you have billed Blue Cross.

Abbreviations pertinent to this record:

adv ______________ neg ______________

dia ______________ OC ______________

exc ______________ PRN ______________

imp ______________ PT ______________

N ______________ RTO ______________

slt ______________ wk ______________

Tr ______________ c̄ ______________

PATIENT RECORD

LAST NAME	FIRST NAME	MIDDLE NAME	BIRTH DATE	SEX	HOME PHONE
Cash,	David	M.	03-15-40	M	013/666-8901

ADDRESS	CITY	STATE	ZIP CODE
5729 Redwood Avenue	Woodland Hills	XY	12345

PATIENT'S OCCUPATION	NAME OF COMPANY
teacher	City Unified School District

ADDRESS OF EMPLOYER	PHONE
301 West Third Street, Dorland, XY 12347	013/667-9018

SPOUSE OR PARENT	OCCUPATION
unmarried	

EMPLOYER	ADDRESS	PHONE
Century High School,	2031 W. Olympic Blvd., Dorland, XY 12347	013/678-0176

NAME OF INSURANCE GROUP		SUBSCRIBER
Blue Cross	Union Local #2	David M. Cash

BLUE SHIELD OR BLUE CROSS CERT. NO.	GROUP NO.	CURRENT COVERAGE NO.	EFFECTIVE DATE
XEA298-34-6754	82099A	2716	1-9-9x

MEDICARE NO.	MEDICAID NO.	EFFECTIVE DATE	SOC. SEC. NO.
			298-34-6754

REFERRED BY:
Hugh R. Foot, M D 2010 Main Street, Woodland Hills, XY 12345 UPIN #612509

DATE	PROGRESS
1-4-9x	Pt comes in complaining of slt pain in parietal area of skull which began earlier today. Exam N. Some slt redness of parietal area of scalp. Retn in 1 wk for observation. Imp: head pain undetermined. No disability from work. Clarence Cutler, MD
1-11-9x	Some slt elevation of skin in parietal area of scalp. Otherwise essentially neg. No warmth over area. Slt pain on pressure. CC
2-3-9x	Elevation of skin still persisting. Imp: inflammatory cystic lesion of scalp 1.5 cm. Tr: excision of inflammatory cystic lesion of skin 1.5 cm dia on parietal scalp area. Removed cyst under procaine block; knife dissection; closure of wound c̄ six #000 black silk sutures. Adv to retn in 5 days for removal of sutures. CC
2-9-9x	Sutures removed & dressed. To retn in 1 wk. Clarence Cutler, MD
2-15-9x	Parietal area well healed. RTO prn. C Cutler, MD

FIGURE 10-1

STATEMENT

College Clinic
4567 Broad Avenue
Woodland Hills, XY 12345-0001
Telephone: 013-486-9002
Fax: 013-487-8976

Mr. David M. Cash
5729 Redwood Avenue
Woodland Hills, XY 12345-0001

DATE	PROFESSIONAL SERVICE DESCRIPTION	CHARGE	CREDITS		CURRENT BALANCE
			PAYMENTS	ADJUSTMENTS	
1-4-9x	OC, EPF hx & exam, SF decision making				
1-11-9x	OC, PF hx/exam, LC decision making				
2-3-9x	OC, EPF hx/exam, LC decision making				
2-3-9x	Exc inflammatory cystic lesion scalp 1.5 cm dia				
2-3-9x	Sterile tray				
2-9-9x	OC, minimal (5 min)				
2-15-9x	OC, minimal (5 min)				

Due and payable within 10 days. **Pay last amount in balance column** ⇧

Key:
PF: Problem-focused
EPF: Expanded problem-focused
D: Detailed
C: Comprehensive
SF: Straightforward
LC: Low complexity
MC: Moderate complexity
HC: High complexity
CON: Consultation
CPX: Complete Phys Exam
E: Emergency
ER: Emergency Dept.
HCD: House Call (Day)
HCN: House Call (Night)
HV: Hospital visit
OV: Office Visit

FIGURE 10-2

PICA

HEALTH INSURANCE CLAIM FORM

P

1. MEDICARE (Medicare #) MEDICAID (Medicaid #) CHAMPUS (Sponsor's SSN) CHAMPVA (VA File #) GROUP HEALTH PLAN (SSN or ID) FECA BLK LUNG (SSN) OTHER (ID)

1a. INSURED'S I.D. NUMBER (FOR PROGRAM I

2. PATIENT'S NAME (Last Name, First Name, Middle Initial)

3. PATIENT'S BIRTH DATE MM DD YY SEX M F

4. INSURED'S NAME (Last Name, First Name, Middle Initial)

5. PATIENT'S ADDRESS (No., Street)

6. PATIENT RELATIONSHIP TO INSURED Self Spouse Child Other

7. INSURED'S ADDRESS (No., Street)

CITY STATE

8. PATIENT STATUS Single Married Other

CITY S

ZIP CODE TELEPHONE (Include Area Code) ( )

Employed Full-Time Student Part-Time Student

ZIP CODE TELEPHONE (INCLUDE AREA ( )

9. OTHER INSURED'S NAME (Last Name, First Name, Middle Initial)

10. IS PATIENT'S CONDITION RELATED TO:

11. INSURED'S POLICY GROUP OR FECA NUMBER

a. OTHER INSURED'S POLICY OR GROUP NUMBER

a. EMPLOYMENT? (CURRENT OR PREVIOUS) YES NO

a. INSURED'S DATE OF BIRTH MM DD YY SEX M F

b. OTHER INSURED'S DATE OF BIRTH MM DD YY SEX M F

b. AUTO ACCIDENT? PLACE (State) YES NO

b. EMPLOYER'S NAME OR SCHOOL NAME

c. EMPLOYER'S NAME OR SCHOOL NAME

c. OTHER ACCIDENT? YES NO

c. INSURANCE PLAN NAME OR PROGRAM NAME

d. INSURANCE PLAN NAME OR PROGRAM NAME

10d. RESERVED FOR LOCAL USE

d. IS THERE ANOTHER HEALTH BENEFIT PLAN? YES NO *If yes*, return to and complete ite

READ BACK OF FORM BEFORE COMPLETING & SIGNING THIS FORM.

12. PATIENT'S OR AUTHORIZED PERSON'S SIGNATURE I authorize the release of any medical or other information necessary to process this claim. I also request payment of government benefits either to myself or to the party who accepts assignment below.

SIGNED ______ DATE ______

13. INSURED'S OR AUTHORIZED PERSON'S SIGNATURE I aut payment of medical benefits to the undersigned physician or su services described below.

SIGNED ______

14. DATE OF CURRENT: MM DD YY ILLNESS (First symptom) OR INJURY (Accident) OR PREGNANCY(LMP)

15. IF PATIENT HAS HAD SAME OR SIMILAR ILLNESS. GIVE FIRST DATE MM DD YY

16. DATES PATIENT UNABLE TO WORK IN CURRENT OCCUP FROM MM DD YY TO MM DD

17. NAME OF REFERRING PHYSICIAN OR OTHER SOURCE

17a. I.D. NUMBER OF REFERRING PHYSICIAN

18. HOSPITALIZATION DATES RELATED TO CURRENT SERVI FROM MM DD YY TO MM DD

19. RESERVED FOR LOCAL USE

20. OUTSIDE LAB? YES NO $ CHARGES

21. DIAGNOSIS OR NATURE OF ILLNESS OR INJURY. (RELATE ITEMS 1,2,3 OR 4 TO ITEM 24E BY LINE)

1. ___ . __

3. ___ . __

2. ___ . __

4. ___ . __

22. MEDICAID RESUBMISSION CODE ORIGINAL REF. NO.

23. PRIOR AUTHORIZATION NUMBER

24. A DATE(S) OF SERVICE From MM DD YY To MM DD YY	B Place of Service	C Type of Service	D PROCEDURES, SERVICES, OR SUPPLIES (Explain Unusual Circumstances) CPT/HCPCS MODIFIER	E DIAGNOSIS CODE	F $ CHARGES	G DAYS OR UNITS	H EPSDT Family Plan	I EMG	J COB	K RESERV LOCA
1										
2										
3										
4										
5										
6										

25. FEDERAL TAX I.D. NUMBER SSN EIN

26. PATIENT'S ACCOUNT NO.

27. ACCEPT ASSIGNMENT? (For govt. claims, see back) YES NO

28. TOTAL CHARGE $

29. AMOUNT PAID $

30. BALA $

31. SIGNATURE OF PHYSICIAN OR SUPPLIER INCLUDING DEGREES OR CREDENTIALS (I certify that the statements on the reverse apply to this bill and are made a part thereof.)

SIGNED DATE

32. NAME AND ADDRESS OF FACILITY WHERE SERVICES WERE RENDERED (If other than home or office)

33. PHYSICIAN'S, SUPPLIER'S BILLING NAME, ADDRESS, ZIP & PHONE #

PIN# GRP#

(APPROVED BY AMA COUNCIL ON MEDICAL SERVICE 8/88)

PLEASE PRINT OR TYPE

FORM HCFA-1500 (U2) (12-90)
FORM OWCP-1500 FORI

FIGURE 10-3

ASSIGNMENT 31

1. Complete the *Health Insurance Claim Form* (Fig. 10–6) to Blue Cross using OCR guidelines for Mrs. Frances F. Foote by referring to her patient record (Fig. 10–4) and ledger card (Fig. 10–5). See Chapter 10 of the *Handbook* for help in completing this form. Date the claim October 31. You have had Mrs. Foote sign the release of information portion of the form, but no assignment has been taken on this claim. Refer to Appendix A to fill in the fees on the ledger card.
2. Use your *CPT Code Book* or Appendix A to determine the correct five-digit code number and modifiers for each professional service rendered.
3. Record on the ledger card when you have billed the insurance company.

Abbreviations pertinent to this record:

adv ______________________________

AP ______________________________

CC ______________________________

compl ______________________________

D.P.M. ______________________________

Dx ______________________________

exam ______________________________

interpret ______________________________

lat ______________________________

lt ______________________________

neg ______________________________

OC ______________________________

OP ______________________________

Op ______________________________

PO ______________________________

re ch ______________________________

RTC ______________________________

wk ______________________________

PATIENT RECORD

Foote,	Frances	F.	8-10-52	F	013/678/0943
LAST NAME	FIRST NAME	MIDDLE NAME	BIRTH DATE	SEX	HOME PHONE

984 North A Street,	Woodland Hills,	XY	12345
ADDRESS	CITY	STATE	ZIP CODE

legal secretary	
PATIENT'S OCCUPATION	NAME OF COMPANY
ADDRESS OF EMPLOYER	PHONE
Harry L. Foote	roofer
SPOUSE OR PARENT	OCCUPATION

BDO Construction Co.	340 N. 6th St., Woodland Hills, XY 12345	013/478-9083
EMPLOYER	ADDRESS	PHONE

Blue Cross	Frances F. Fonte
NAME OF INSURANCE GROUP	SUBSCRIBER

XEA 548-78-8924	16524A	8126	1-1-80
BLUE SHIELD OR BLUE CROSS CERT. NO.	GROUP NO.	CURRENT COVERAGE NO.	EFFECTIVE DATE
			588-90-8701
MEDICARE NO.	MEDICAID NO.	EFFECTIVE DATE	SOC. SEC. NO.

REFERRED BY:

UPIN #342166

G.U. Curette, M D 4780 Main St., Ehrlich, XY 12350 tel: 013-430-8788

DATE	PROGRESS
10-11-9x	CC: Discomfort around lt toe. Exam: severe overgrowth of nail into surrounding tissues. X-rays taken & interp shows lt foot essentially neg. No gout or arthritis seen. Dx: severe onychocryptosis both margins of lt hallux. Adv to retn as OP to hosp for surgery on lt hallux. No disability from work. *Nick Pedro*
10-13-9x	Op: Complete wedge resection for repair of ingrown nails. Retn 1 wk for PO re ch. Pt may continue to work. No disability. *N Pedro*
10-20-9x	Lt hallux healing well. RTC as necessary. *Nick Pedro, DPM*

FIGURE 10-4

STATEMENT

College Clinic
4567 Broad Avenue
Woodland Hills, XY 12345-0001
Telephone: 013-486-9002
Fax: 013-487-8976

Mrs. Frances F. Foote
984 North A Street
Woodland Hills, XY 12345-0001

DATE	PROFESSIONAL SERVICE DESCRIPTION	CHARGE	CREDITS		CURRENT BALANCE
			PAYMENTS	ADJUSTMENTS	
10-11-9x	OC, PF hx/exam, SF decision making				
10-11-9x	AP & lat x-rays lt foot with interpret.				
10-13-9x	Exc nail & nail matrix, compl				
10-20-9x	OC, PF hx/exam, SF decision making				

Due and payable within 10 days. **Pay last amount in balance column** ⇧

Key: PF: Problem-focused
EPF: Expanded problem-focused
D: Detailed
C: Comprehensive
SF: Straightforward
LC: Low complexity
MC: Moderate complexity
HC: High complexity
CON: Consultation
CPX: Complete Phys Exam
E: Emergency
ER: Emergency Dept.
HCD: House Call (Day)
HCN: House Call (Night)
HV: Hospital visit
OV: Office Visit

FIGURE 10-5

PICA

HEALTH INSURANCE CLAIM FORM

1. MEDICARE (Medicare #) | MEDICAID (Medicaid #) | CHAMPUS (Sponsor's SSN) | CHAMPVA (VA File #) | GROUP HEALTH PLAN (SSN or ID) | FECA BLK LUNG (SSN) | OTHER (ID)

1a. INSURED'S I.D. NUMBER (FOR PROGRAM

2. PATIENT'S NAME (Last Name, First Name, Middle Initial)

3. PATIENT'S BIRTH DATE MM DD YY SEX M F

4. INSURED'S NAME (Last Name, First Name, Middle Initial)

5. PATIENT'S ADDRESS (No., Street)

6. PATIENT RELATIONSHIP TO INSURED Self Spouse Child Other

7. INSURED'S ADDRESS (No., Street)

CITY STATE

8. PATIENT STATUS Single Married Other

CITY S

ZIP CODE TELEPHONE (Include Area Code) ( )

Employed Full-Time Student Part-Time Student

ZIP CODE TELEPHONE (INCLUDE ARE ( )

9. OTHER INSURED'S NAME (Last Name, First Name, Middle Initial)

10. IS PATIENT'S CONDITION RELATED TO:

11. INSURED'S POLICY GROUP OR FECA NUMBER

a. OTHER INSURED'S POLICY OR GROUP NUMBER

a. EMPLOYMENT? (CURRENT OR PREVIOUS) YES NO

a. INSURED'S DATE OF BIRTH MM DD YY SEX M F

b. OTHER INSURED'S DATE OF BIRTH MM DD YY SEX M F

b. AUTO ACCIDENT? YES NO PLACE (State)

b. EMPLOYER'S NAME OR SCHOOL NAME

c. EMPLOYER'S NAME OR SCHOOL NAME

c. OTHER ACCIDENT? YES NO

c. INSURANCE PLAN NAME OR PROGRAM NAME

d. INSURANCE PLAN NAME OR PROGRAM NAME

10d. RESERVED FOR LOCAL USE

d. IS THERE ANOTHER HEALTH BENEFIT PLAN? YES NO *If yes*, return to and complete ite

READ BACK OF FORM BEFORE COMPLETING & SIGNING THIS FORM.

12. PATIENT'S OR AUTHORIZED PERSON'S SIGNATURE I authorize the release of any medical or other information necessary to process this claim. I also request payment of government benefits either to myself or to the party who accepts assignment below.

SIGNED ______ DATE ______

13. INSURED'S OR AUTHORIZED PERSON'S SIGNATURE I au payment of medical benefits to the undersigned physician or s services described below.

SIGNED

14. DATE OF CURRENT: MM DD YY ILLNESS (First symptom) OR INJURY (Accident) OR PREGNANCY(LMP)

15. IF PATIENT HAS HAD SAME OR SIMILAR ILLNESS. GIVE FIRST DATE MM DD YY

16. DATES PATIENT UNABLE TO WORK IN CURRENT OCCUF FROM MM DD YY TO MM DD

17. NAME OF REFERRING PHYSICIAN OR OTHER SOURCE

17a. I.D. NUMBER OF REFERRING PHYSICIAN

18. HOSPITALIZATION DATES RELATED TO CURRENT SERV FROM MM DD YY TO MM DD

19. RESERVED FOR LOCAL USE

20. OUTSIDE LAB? YES NO $ CHARGES

21. DIAGNOSIS OR NATURE OF ILLNESS OR INJURY. (RELATE ITEMS 1,2,3 OR 4 TO ITEM 24E BY LINE)

1. ___ . ___ 3. ___ . ___

2. ___ . ___ 4. ___ . ___

22. MEDICAID RESUBMISSION CODE ORIGINAL REF. NO.

23. PRIOR AUTHORIZATION NUMBER

24. A DATE(S) OF SERVICE From MM DD YY To MM DD YY	B Place of Service	C Type of Service	D PROCEDURES, SERVICES, OR SUPPLIES (Explain Unusual Circumstances) CPT/HCPCS MODIFIER	E DIAGNOSIS CODE	F $ CHARGES	G DAYS OR UNITS	H EPSDT Family Plan	I EMG	J COB	RESER LOC
1										
2										
3										
4										
5										
6										

25. FEDERAL TAX I.D. NUMBER SSN EIN

26. PATIENT'S ACCOUNT NO.

27. ACCEPT ASSIGNMENT? (For govt. claims, see back) YES NO

28. TOTAL CHARGE $

29. AMOUNT PAID $

30. BALA $

31. SIGNATURE OF PHYSICIAN OR SUPPLIER INCLUDING DEGREES OR CREDENTIALS (I certify that the statements on the reverse apply to this bill and are made a part thereof.)

SIGNED DATE

32. NAME AND ADDRESS OF FACILITY WHERE SERVICES WERE RENDERED (If other than home or office)

33. PHYSICIAN'S, SUPPLIER'S BILLING NAME, ADDRESS, ZIP & PHONE #

PIN# GRP#

(APPROVED BY AMA COUNCIL ON MEDICAL SERVICE 8/88) ***PLEASE PRINT OR TYPE*** FORM HCFA-1500 (U2) (12-90 FORM OWCP-1500 FOR

FIGURE 10-6

ASSIGNMENT 32

1. Complete the *Health Insurance Claim Form* (Fig. 10–9) to Blue Cross using OCR guidelines for Charles B. Kamb by referring to his patient record (Fig. 10–7) and ledger card (Fig. 10–8). See Chapter 10 of the *Handbook* for help in completing this form. Date the claim June 30. You have had Mr. Kamb sign the release of information portion of the form, but no assignment has been taken on this claim. Refer to Appendix A to fill in the fees on the ledger card. Since all the June entries do not fit on the HCFA-1500 claim form, make two copies of the blank form. This assignment requires three claim forms, so make two photocopies of the HCFA-1500 claim form.
2. Use your *CPT Code Book* or Appendix A to determine the correct five-digit code number and modifiers for each professional service rendered.
3. Record on the ledger card when you have billed insurance company.

Abbreviations pertinent to this record:

adv	______	med	______
ant	______	mg	______
BP	______	mo	______
cc	______	OV	______
D	______	PH	______
Dr	______	post	______
exam	______	Pt	______
HBP	______	retn	______
inj	______	rev	______
intermed	______	W	______
int	______	c̄	______
ltd	______	♂	______

PATIENT RECORD

Kamb,	Charles	B.	01-26-27	M	013/467-2601
LAST NAME	FIRST NAME	MIDDLE NAME	BIRTH DATE	SEX	HOME PHONE

2600 West Nautilus Street,	Woodland Hills,	XY	12345
ADDRESS	CITY	STATE	ZIP CODE

TV actor	Amer. Federation of TV & Radio Artists (AFTRA)
PATIENT'S OCCUPATION	NAME OF COMPANY

30077 Ventura Blvd., Woodland Hills, XY 12345	013/466-3331
ADDRESS OF EMPLOYER	PHONE

Jane C. Kamb	homemaker
SPOUSE OR PARENT	OCCUPATION

EMPLOYER	ADDRESS	PHONE

Blue Cross	Charles B. Kamb
NAME OF INSURANCE GROUP	SUBSCRIBER

ABC 246-31-2201	26071 Union Local TV-303	#4133	1-30-80
BLUE SHIELD OR BLUE CROSS CERT. NO.	GROUP NO.	CURRENT COVERAGE NO.	EFFECTIVE DATE

			246-31-2201
MEDICARE NO.	MEDICAID NO.	EFFECTIVE DATE	SOC. SEC. NO.

REFERRED BY:
Mrs. O.S. Tomy (friend)

DATE	PROGRESS
6-1-9x	New pt W ♂ comes in complaining of nasal bleeding for 2½ mo c̄ headaches + nasal congestion. PH pt has had HBP for 1 yr. Taking med Serpasil prescribed by dr in Ohio. Coagulation time + platelet count done in ofc - normal. Exam revealed nasal hemorrhage. BP 200/120. Gave inj IM Adrenosem Salicylate 5mg/1cc, used cautery, ant + post nasal packs. Adv retn tomorrow. Ordered previous med records from dr in Ohio. D: recurrent epistaxis due to hypertension. No disability from work. D Proctor MD
6-2-9x	Removed nasal packs, replaced post nasal pack. Inj IM 5mg/1cc adrenosem Salicylate. BP 180/100 adv retn in 3 days D Proctor MD
6-5-9x	Removed post pack + replaced BP 200/100 adv retn in 4 days for recheck Gerald Proctor MD
6-9-9x	Removed post pack BP 180/120 adv retn 3 days D Proctor MD
6-12-9x	Rev previous med records Pt referred to Dr Perry Cardi (int) for future care re. HBP. No dis from work Gerald Proctor MD

FIGURE 10-7

STATEMENT

College Clinic
4567 Broad Avenue
Woodland Hills, XY 12345-0001
Telephone: 013-486-9002
Fax: 013-487-8976

Mr. Charles B. Kamb
2600 West Nautilus Street
Woodland Hills, XY 12345-0001

DATE	PROFESSIONAL SERVICE DESCRIPTION	CHARGE	CREDITS		CURRENT BALANCE
			PAYMENTS	ADJUSTMENTS	
6-1-9x	Initial OV new pt				
6-1-9x	Coagulation time/Lee & White				
6-1-9x	Platelet count manual				
6-1-9x	Inj 5 mg/1 cc Adrenosem Salicylate				
6-1-9x	Sterile tray (nasal packs, syringe, med.)				
6-1-9x	Post nasal packs with cauterization & ant packs				
6-2-9x	Sterile tray				
6-2-9x	Subsequent post packing				
6-2-9x	Inj 5 mg/1 cc Adrenosem Salicylate				
6-5-9x	Sterile tray				
6-5-9x	Subsequent post packing				
6-9-9x	OC, PF hx/exam, LC decision making removal post packs				
6-12-9x	OC, D hx/exam, MC decision making				

Due and payable within 10 days. **Pay last amount in balance column** ⇧

Key:
PF: Problem-focused
EPF: Expanded problem-focused
D: Detailed
C: Comprehensive
SF: Straightforward
LC: Low complexity
MC: Moderate complexity
HC: High complexity
CON: Consultation
CPX: Complete Phys Exam
E: Emergency
ER: Emergency Dept.
HCD: House Call (Day)
HCN: House Call (Night)
HV: Hospital visit
OV: Office Visit

FIGURE 10-8

PICA

HEALTH INSURANCE CLAIM FORM

1. MEDICARE (Medicare #) MEDICAID (Medicaid #) CHAMPUS (Sponsor's SSN) CHAMPVA (VA File #) GROUP HEALTH PLAN (SSN or ID) FECA BLK LUNG (SSN) OTHER (ID)

1a. INSURED'S I.D. NUMBER (FOR PROGRAM

2. PATIENT'S NAME (Last Name, First Name, Middle Initial)

3. PATIENT'S BIRTH DATE MM DD YY SEX M F

4. INSURED'S NAME (Last Name, First Name, Middle Initial)

5. PATIENT'S ADDRESS (No., Street)

6. PATIENT RELATIONSHIP TO INSURED Self Spouse Child Other

7. INSURED'S ADDRESS (No., Street)

CITY STATE

8. PATIENT STATUS Single Married Other

CITY S

ZIP CODE TELEPHONE (Include Area Code) ( )

Employed Full-Time Student Part-Time Student

ZIP CODE TELEPHONE (INCLUDE ARE ( )

9. OTHER INSURED'S NAME (Last Name, First Name, Middle Initial)

10. IS PATIENT'S CONDITION RELATED TO:

11. INSURED'S POLICY GROUP OR FECA NUMBER

a. OTHER INSURED'S POLICY OR GROUP NUMBER

a. EMPLOYMENT? (CURRENT OR PREVIOUS) YES NO

a. INSURED'S DATE OF BIRTH MM DD YY SEX M F

b. OTHER INSURED'S DATE OF BIRTH MM DD YY SEX M F

b. AUTO ACCIDENT? PLACE (State) YES NO

b. EMPLOYER'S NAME OR SCHOOL NAME

c. EMPLOYER'S NAME OR SCHOOL NAME

c. OTHER ACCIDENT? YES NO

c. INSURANCE PLAN NAME OR PROGRAM NAME

d. INSURANCE PLAN NAME OR PROGRAM NAME

10d. RESERVED FOR LOCAL USE

d. IS THERE ANOTHER HEALTH BENEFIT PLAN? YES NO ***If yes***, return to and complete ite

READ BACK OF FORM BEFORE COMPLETING & SIGNING THIS FORM.

12. PATIENT'S OR AUTHORIZED PERSON'S SIGNATURE I authorize the release of any medical or other information necessary to process this claim. I also request payment of government benefits either to myself or to the party who accepts assignment below.

SIGNED ______ DATE ______

13. INSURED'S OR AUTHORIZED PERSON'S SIGNATURE I au payment of medical benefits to the undersigned physician or s services described below.

SIGNED ______

14. DATE OF CURRENT: MM DD YY ILLNESS (First symptom) OR INJURY (Accident) OR PREGNANCY(LMP)

15. IF PATIENT HAS HAD SAME OR SIMILAR ILLNESS. GIVE FIRST DATE MM DD YY

16. DATES PATIENT UNABLE TO WORK IN CURRENT OCCUP FROM MM DD YY TO MM DD

17. NAME OF REFERRING PHYSICIAN OR OTHER SOURCE

17a. I.D. NUMBER OF REFERRING PHYSICIAN

18. HOSPITALIZATION DATES RELATED TO CURRENT SERV FROM MM DD YY TO MM DD

19. RESERVED FOR LOCAL USE

20. OUTSIDE LAB? YES NO $ CHARGES

21. DIAGNOSIS OR NATURE OF ILLNESS OR INJURY. (RELATE ITEMS 1,2,3 OR 4 TO ITEM 24E BY LINE)

1. ___ . ___ 3. ___ . ___

2. ___ . ___ 4. ___ . ___

22. MEDICAID RESUBMISSION CODE ORIGINAL REF. NO.

23. PRIOR AUTHORIZATION NUMBER

24. A DATE(S) OF SERVICE From MM DD YY To MM DD YY	B Place of Service	C Type of Service	D PROCEDURES, SERVICES, OR SUPPLIES (Explain Unusual Circumstances) CPT/HCPCS MODIFIER	E DIAGNOSIS CODE	F $ CHARGES	G DAYS OR UNITS	H EPSDT Family Plan	I EMG	J COB	RESER LOC
1										
2										
3										
4										
5										
6										

25. FEDERAL TAX I.D. NUMBER SSN EIN

26. PATIENT'S ACCOUNT NO.

27. ACCEPT ASSIGNMENT? (For govt. claims, see back) YES NO

28. TOTAL CHARGE $

29. AMOUNT PAID $

30. BALA $

31. SIGNATURE OF PHYSICIAN OR SUPPLIER INCLUDING DEGREES OR CREDENTIALS (I certify that the statements on the reverse apply to this bill and are made a part thereof.)

SIGNED DATE

32. NAME AND ADDRESS OF FACILITY WHERE SERVICES WERE RENDERED (If other than home or office)

33. PHYSICIAN'S, SUPPLIER'S BILLING NAME, ADDRESS, ZIP & PHONE #

PIN# GRP#

(APPROVED BY AMA COUNCIL ON MEDICAL SERVICE 8/88) ***PLEASE PRINT OR TYPE*** FORM HCFA-1500 (U2) (12-90) FORM OWCP-1500 FOR

FIGURE 10-9

ASSIGNMENT 33

1. Complete the *Blue Shield form* (Fig. 10–12) for Mrs. Hortense N. Hope using OCR guidelines by referring to her patient record (Fig. 10–10) and ledger card (Fig. 10–11).See Chapter 10 of the *Handbook* for help in completing this form. Assume Dr. Practon is a participating physician of Blue Shield. Date the claim July 31. Refer to Appendix A to fill in the fees on the ledger card.
2. Use your *CPT Code Book* or Appendix A to determine the correct five-digit code number and modifiers for each professional service rendered.
3. Record on the ledger card when the insurance company has been billed.

Abbreviations pertinent to this record:

adv	____________	PRN	____________
Drs	____________	Pt	____________
exam	____________	PTR	____________
lt	____________	retn	____________
NC	____________	♀	____________
OC	____________		

PATIENT RECORD

LAST NAME	FIRST NAME	MIDDLE NAME	BIRTH DATE	SEX	HOME PHONE
Hope,	Hortense	N.	4-12-46	F	013/666-7821

ADDRESS	CITY	STATE	ZIP CODE
247 Lantern Pike, Woodland Hills, XY 12345			

PATIENT'S OCCUPATION	NAME OF COMPANY
clerk typist	R and S Manufacturing Company

ADDRESS OF EMPLOYER	PHONE
2271 West 74 Street, Torres, XY 12349	013/466-5890

SPOUSE OR PARENT	OCCUPATION
Harry J. Hope	carpenter

EMPLOYER	ADDRESS	PHONE
Jesse Construction Co.	3861 S. Orange St., Torres, XY 12349	013/765-2318

NAME OF INSURANCE GROUP	SUBSCRIBER
Blue Shield	Hortense N. Hope

BLUE SHIELD OR BLUE CROSS CERT. NO.	GROUP NO.	CURRENT COVERAGE NO.	EFFECTIVE DATE
ATC 32145 8809	T8471811A		

MEDICARE NO.	MEDICAID NO.	EFFECTIVE DATE	SOC. SEC. NO.
			321-45-8809

REFERRED BY:
husband

DATE	PROGRESS
7-1-9x	New ♀ pt comes in complaining of lt great toe. Exam reveals slight infection of lt great toe. Drained and cleaned nail lt great toe. Adv to retn in 2 days. *Gerald Preston, M.D.*
7-3-9x	Excised entire lt great toenail under total toe procaine block. Drs applied. PTR in 5 days for checkup. *G Preston, MD*
7-7-9x	Nail bed healing well. Retn PRN. *Gerald Preston, MD*

FIGURE 10-10

STATEMENT

College Clinic
4567 Broad Avenue
Woodland Hills, XY 12345-0001
Telephone: 013-486-9002
Fax: 013-487-8976

Mrs. Hortense N. Hope
247 Lantern Pike
Woodland Hills, XY 12345-0001

DATE	PROFESSIONAL SERVICE DESCRIPTION	CHARGE	CREDITS		CURRENT BALANCE
			PAYMENTS	ADJUSTMENTS	
7-1-9x	OC, initial new pt				
7-1-9x	Sterile tray (itemized)				
7-1-9x	Drainage lt great toenail				
7-3-9x	Excision entire lt great toenail under total toe procaine block				
7-3-9x	Sterile tray (itemized)				
7-7-9x	OC, PF hx/exam, SF decision making				

Due and payable within 10 days. **Pay last amount in balance column** ⇧

Key:
PF: Problem-focused
EPF: Expanded problem-focused
D: Detailed
C: Comprehensive
SF: Straightforward
LC: Low complexity
MC: Moderate complexity
HC: High complexity
CON: Consultation
CPX: Complete Phys Exam
E: Emergency
ER: Emergency Dept.
HCD: House Call (Day)
HCN: House Call (Night)
HV: Hospital visit
OV: Office Visit

FIGURE 10-11

HEALTH INSURANCE CLAIM FORM

PICA

1. MEDICARE (Medicare #) | MEDICAID (Medicaid #) | CHAMPUS (Sponsor's SSN) | CHAMPVA (VA File #) | GROUP HEALTH PLAN (SSN or ID) | FECA BLK LUNG (SSN) | OTHER (ID)

1a. INSURED'S I.D. NUMBER (FOR PROGRAM

2. PATIENT'S NAME (Last Name, First Name, Middle Initial)

3. PATIENT'S BIRTH DATE MM DD YY SEX M F

4. INSURED'S NAME (Last Name, First Name, Middle Initial)

5. PATIENT'S ADDRESS (No., Street)

6. PATIENT RELATIONSHIP TO INSURED Self Spouse Child Other

7. INSURED'S ADDRESS (No., Street)

CITY STATE

8. PATIENT STATUS Single Married Other

Employed Full-Time Student Part-Time Student

CITY S

ZIP CODE TELEPHONE (Include Area Code) ( )

ZIP CODE TELEPHONE (INCLUDE ARE ( )

9. OTHER INSURED'S NAME (Last Name, First Name, Middle Initial)

10. IS PATIENT'S CONDITION RELATED TO:

11. INSURED'S POLICY GROUP OR FECA NUMBER

a. OTHER INSURED'S POLICY OR GROUP NUMBER

a. EMPLOYMENT? (CURRENT OR PREVIOUS) YES NO

a. INSURED'S DATE OF BIRTH MM DD YY SEX M F

b. OTHER INSURED'S DATE OF BIRTH MM DD YY SEX M F

b. AUTO ACCIDENT? PLACE (State) YES NO

b. EMPLOYER'S NAME OR SCHOOL NAME

c. EMPLOYER'S NAME OR SCHOOL NAME

c. OTHER ACCIDENT? YES NO

c. INSURANCE PLAN NAME OR PROGRAM NAME

d. INSURANCE PLAN NAME OR PROGRAM NAME

10d. RESERVED FOR LOCAL USE

d. IS THERE ANOTHER HEALTH BENEFIT PLAN? YES NO *If yes*, return to and complete ite

READ BACK OF FORM BEFORE COMPLETING & SIGNING THIS FORM.

12. PATIENT'S OR AUTHORIZED PERSON'S SIGNATURE I authorize the release of any medical or other information necessary to process this claim. I also request payment of government benefits either to myself or to the party who accepts assignment below.

SIGNED ______________________ DATE ______________

13. INSURED'S OR AUTHORIZED PERSON'S SIGNATURE I au payment of medical benefits to the undersigned physician or s services described below.

SIGNED ______________

14. DATE OF CURRENT: MM DD YY ◀ ILLNESS (First symptom) OR INJURY (Accident) OR PREGNANCY(LMP)

15. IF PATIENT HAS HAD SAME OR SIMILAR ILLNESS. GIVE FIRST DATE MM DD YY

16. DATES PATIENT UNABLE TO WORK IN CURRENT OCCUP FROM MM DD YY TO MM DD

17. NAME OF REFERRING PHYSICIAN OR OTHER SOURCE

17a. I.D. NUMBER OF REFERRING PHYSICIAN

18. HOSPITALIZATION DATES RELATED TO CURRENT SERVI FROM MM DD YY TO MM DD

19. RESERVED FOR LOCAL USE

20. OUTSIDE LAB? $ CHARGES YES NO

21. DIAGNOSIS OR NATURE OF ILLNESS OR INJURY. (RELATE ITEMS 1,2,3 OR 4 TO ITEM 24E BY LINE)

1. ___ . __ 3. ___ . __

2. ___ . __ 4. ___ . __

22. MEDICAID RESUBMISSION CODE ORIGINAL REF. NO.

23. PRIOR AUTHORIZATION NUMBER

24. A DATE(S) OF SERVICE From MM DD YY	To MM DD YY	B Place of Service	C Type of Service	D PROCEDURES, SERVICES, OR SUPPLIES (Explain Unusual Circumstances) CPT/HCPCS	MODIFIER	E DIAGNOSIS CODE	F $ CHARGES	G DAYS OR UNITS	H EPSDT Family Plan	I EMG	J COB	RESER LOCA
1												
2												
3												
4												
5												
6												

25. FEDERAL TAX I.D. NUMBER SSN EIN

26. PATIENT'S ACCOUNT NO.

27. ACCEPT ASSIGNMENT? (For govt. claims, see back) YES NO

28. TOTAL CHARGE $

29. AMOUNT PAID $

30. BALA $

31. SIGNATURE OF PHYSICIAN OR SUPPLIER INCLUDING DEGREES OR CREDENTIALS (I certify that the statements on the reverse apply to this bill and are made a part thereof.)

SIGNED DATE

32. NAME AND ADDRESS OF FACILITY WHERE SERVICES WERE RENDERED (If other than home or office)

33. PHYSICIAN'S, SUPPLIER'S BILLING NAME, ADDRESS, ZIP & PHONE #

PIN# GRP#

(APPROVED BY AMA COUNCIL ON MEDICAL SERVICE 8/88)

PLEASE PRINT OR TYPE

FORM HCFA-1500 (U2) (12-90) FORM OWCP-1500 FOR

FIGURE 10-12

ASSIGNMENT 34

1. Complete the *Blue Shield Form* (Fig. 10–15) using OCR guidelines for Mrs. Louise K. Herman by referring to her patient record (Fig. 10–13) and ledger card (Fig. 10–14).See Chapter 10 of the *Handbook* for help in completing this form. Date the claim May 31. Refer to Appendix A to fill in the fees on the ledger card.
2. Use your *CPT Code Book* or Appendix A to determine the correct five-digit code number and modifiers for each professional service rendered.
3. Record on the ledger cardwhen the insurance company has been billed.
4. Enter a payment from the insurance company of $350, 40 days after claim submission.

Abbreviations pertinent to this record:

adv	______	int	______
cc	______	OC	______
diag	______	ofc	______
DNS	______	perf	______
Dx	______	pre-op	______
exam	______	PRN	______
exc	______	pt	______
ext	______	retn	______
init	______	wk	______

COMPUTER EXERCISE

CASE 1 BLUE CROSS/BLUE SHIELD

Before proceeding, you may want to do an exercise based on the concepts you have learned. Additional practice material is on your computer diskette.

Directions: Insert the diskette into the computer and follow the instructions on the screen for Computer Exercise Case 1.

PATIENT RECORD

LAST NAME	FIRST NAME	MIDDLE NAME	BIRTH DATE	SEX	HOME PHONE
Herman,	Louise	K.	11-04-36	F	013/266-9085

ADDRESS	CITY	STATE	ZIP CODE
13453 Burbank Boulevard,	Woodland Hills,	XY	12345

PATIENT'S OCCUPATION: budget analyst
NAME OF COMPANY: City Unified School District

ADDRESS OF EMPLOYER: 900 North 9th Street, Saunders, XY 12348
PHONE: 013/666-0985

SPOUSE OR PARENT: Harold D. Herman
OCCUPATION: salesman

EMPLOYER: V. X. Paint Supply Co.
ADDRESS: 335 Burbank Blvd.,Woodland Hills,XY 12345
PHONE: 013/457-8009

NAME OF INSURANCE GROUP: Blue Shield
SUBSCRIBER: Louise K. Herman

BLUE SHIELD OR BLUE CROSS CERT. NO.	GROUP NO.	CURRENT COVERAGE NO.	EFFECTIVE DATE
BCD 519-36-0018	T2097700C		1-1-80

MEDICARE NO.	MEDICAID NO.	EFFECTIVE DATE	SOC. SEC. NO.
			519-36-0018

REFERRED BY:
Raymond Skelton, M.D.

DATE	PROGRESS
5-6-9x	PT REFERRED BY DR. SKELTON CC BLEEDING HEMORRHOIDS
	ANOSCOPY EXAM REVEALED DX INT + EXT HEMORRHOIDS
	& 2 INFECTED RECTAL POLYPS. ADV. RETN 2 DAYS FOR
	REMOVAL OF HEMORRHOIDS + POLYPS. Rex Rumsey M.D.
5-8-9x	IN OFC PERF INT + EXT HEMORRHOIDECTOMY;
	PROCTOSIGMOIDOSCOPY THEN PERF FOR REMOVAL
	OF POLYPS. ADV SITZ BATHS DAILY. PT ADV
	TO RETN 1 WK WILL BE OFF WK FROM 5-8
	THRU 5-14- Rex Rumsey M.D.
5-15-9x	D.N.S.
5-17-9x	PROGRESSING WELL W/O PAIN, NO DISCOMFORT.
	RETN PRN. Rex Rumsey M.D.

FIGURE 10-13

STATEMENT

College Clinic
4567 Broad Avenue
Woodland Hills, XY 12345-0001
Telephone: 013-486-9002
Fax: 013-487-8976

Mrs. Louise K. Herman
13453 Burbank Boulevard
Woodland Hills, XY 12345-0001

DATE	PROFESSIONAL SERVICE DESCRIPTION	CHARGE	CREDITS PAYMENTS	ADJUSTMENTS	CURRENT BALANCE
5-6-9x	C hx/exam, HC decision making				
5-6-9x	Anoscopy, diag				
5-8-9x	Int & ext hemorrhoidectomy				
5-8-9x	Proctosigmoidoscopy exc rectal polyps, complicated				
5-17-9x	PO follow-up visit				

Due and payable within 10 days. **Pay last amount in balance column** ⇧

Key:

PF: Problem-focused	**SF:** Straightforward	**CON:** Consultation	**HCD:** House Call (Day)
EPF: Expanded problem-focused	**LC:** Low complexity	**CPX:** Complete Phys Exam	**HCN:** House Call (Night)
D: Detailed	**MC:** Moderate complexity	**E:** Emergency	**HV:** Hospital visit
C: Comprehensive	**HC:** High complexity	**ER:** Emergency Dept.	**OV:** Office Visit

FIGURE 10-14

PICA

HEALTH INSURANCE CLAIM FORM

1. MEDICARE (Medicare #) MEDICAID (Medicaid #) CHAMPUS (Sponsor's SSN) CHAMPVA (VA File #) GROUP HEALTH PLAN (SSN or ID) FECA BLK LUNG (SSN) OTHER (ID)

1a. INSURED'S I.D. NUMBER (FOR PROGRAM

2. PATIENT'S NAME (Last Name, First Name, Middle Initial)

3. PATIENT'S BIRTH DATE MM DD YY SEX M F

4. INSURED'S NAME (Last Name, First Name, Middle Initial)

5. PATIENT'S ADDRESS (No., Street)

6. PATIENT RELATIONSHIP TO INSURED Self Spouse Child Other

7. INSURED'S ADDRESS (No., Street)

CITY STATE

8. PATIENT STATUS Single Married Other

CITY S

ZIP CODE TELEPHONE (Include Area Code) ( )

Employed Full-Time Student Part-Time Student

ZIP CODE TELEPHONE (INCLUDE ARE ( )

9. OTHER INSURED'S NAME (Last Name, First Name, Middle Initial)

10. IS PATIENT'S CONDITION RELATED TO:

11. INSURED'S POLICY GROUP OR FECA NUMBER

a. OTHER INSURED'S POLICY OR GROUP NUMBER

a. EMPLOYMENT? (CURRENT OR PREVIOUS) YES NO

a. INSURED'S DATE OF BIRTH MM DD YY SEX M F

b. OTHER INSURED'S DATE OF BIRTH MM DD YY SEX M F

b. AUTO ACCIDENT? YES NO PLACE (State)

b. EMPLOYER'S NAME OR SCHOOL NAME

c. EMPLOYER'S NAME OR SCHOOL NAME

c. OTHER ACCIDENT? YES NO

c. INSURANCE PLAN NAME OR PROGRAM NAME

d. INSURANCE PLAN NAME OR PROGRAM NAME

10d. RESERVED FOR LOCAL USE

d. IS THERE ANOTHER HEALTH BENEFIT PLAN? YES NO *If yes*, return to and complete ite

READ BACK OF FORM BEFORE COMPLETING & SIGNING THIS FORM.

12. PATIENT'S OR AUTHORIZED PERSON'S SIGNATURE I authorize the release of any medical or other information necessary to process this claim. I also request payment of government benefits either to myself or to the party who accepts assignment below.

SIGNED ______ DATE ______

13. INSURED'S OR AUTHORIZED PERSON'S SIGNATURE I au payment of medical benefits to the undersigned physician or s services described below.

SIGNED ______

14. DATE OF CURRENT: MM DD YY ILLNESS (First symptom) OR INJURY (Accident) OR PREGNANCY(LMP)

15. IF PATIENT HAS HAD SAME OR SIMILAR ILLNESS. GIVE FIRST DATE MM DD YY

16. DATES PATIENT UNABLE TO WORK IN CURRENT OCCUP FROM MM DD YY TO MM DD

17. NAME OF REFERRING PHYSICIAN OR OTHER SOURCE

17a. I.D. NUMBER OF REFERRING PHYSICIAN

18. HOSPITALIZATION DATES RELATED TO CURRENT SERVI FROM MM DD YY TO MM DD

19. RESERVED FOR LOCAL USE

20. OUTSIDE LAB? YES NO $ CHARGES

21. DIAGNOSIS OR NATURE OF ILLNESS OR INJURY. (RELATE ITEMS 1,2,3 OR 4 TO ITEM 24E BY LINE)

1. ___ . __ 3. ___ . __

2. ___ . __ 4. ___ . __

22. MEDICAID RESUBMISSION CODE ORIGINAL REF. NO.

23. PRIOR AUTHORIZATION NUMBER

24. A DATE(S) OF SERVICE From MM DD YY To MM DD YY	B Place of Service	C Type of Service	D PROCEDURES, SERVICES, OR SUPPLIES (Explain Unusual Circumstances) CPT/HCPCS MODIFIER	E DIAGNOSIS CODE	F $ CHARGES	G DAYS OR UNITS	H EPSDT Family Plan	I EMG	J COB	K RESERV LOCA
1										
2										
3										
4										
5										
6										

25. FEDERAL TAX I.D. NUMBER SSN EIN

26. PATIENT'S ACCOUNT NO.

27. ACCEPT ASSIGNMENT? (For govt. claims, see back) YES NO

28. TOTAL CHARGE $

29. AMOUNT PAID $

30. BALA $

31. SIGNATURE OF PHYSICIAN OR SUPPLIER INCLUDING DEGREES OR CREDENTIALS (I certify that the statements on the reverse apply to this bill and are made a part thereof.)

SIGNED DATE

32. NAME AND ADDRESS OF FACILITY WHERE SERVICES WERE RENDERED (If other than home or office)

33. PHYSICIAN'S, SUPPLIER'S BILLING NAME, ADDRESS, ZIP & PHONE #

PIN# GRP#

(APPROVED BY AMA COUNCIL ON MEDICAL SERVICE 8/88)

PLEASE PRINT OR TYPE

FORM HCFA-1500 (U2) (12-90)
FORM OWCP-1500 FORM

FIGURE 10-15

CHAPTER 11

Medicaid and Other State Programs

Key Terms

Your instructor may wish to select some specific words pertinent to this chapter for a test. For definitions of the terms, further study, and/or reference, the words, phrases, and abbreviations may be found in the Glossary at the end of the textbook. Key terms for this chapter follow:

aid category
capitation(fee)
categorically needy
covered services
Early and Periodic Screening, Diagnosis, and Treatment (EPSDT)
emergency
family planning services
fiscal agent
fiscal year
Maternal and Child Health Programs (MCHP)
Medicaid
Medi-Cal
medically needy
prior approval
recipient
remittance advice (RA)
share of cost
Supplemental Security Income (SSI)

Performance Objectives

The student will be able to

- Define and spell the key terms for this chapter, given the information from the textbook Glossary, within a reasonable period of time and with enough accuracy to obtain a satisfactory evaluation.
- Answer the review questions after reading the chapter, with enough accuracy to obtain a satisfactory evaluation.
- Fill in the correct meaning of each abbreviation, given a list of common medical abbreviations and symbols that appear in chart notes, within a reasonable period of time and with enough accuracy to obtain a satisfactory evaluation.
- Complete each HCFA-1500 Health Insurance Claim Form for billing, given the patients' medical chart notes, ledger cards, and blank insurance claim forms, within a reasonable period of time and with enough accuracy to obtain a satisfactory evaluation.
- Correctly post payments, adjustments, and balances on the patients' ledger cards, using the Mock Fee Schedule in Appendix A, within a reasonable period of time and with enough accuracy to obtain a satisfactory evaluation.

Study Outline

HISTORY
- Medicaid qualified Medicare beneficiaries program
- Medicaid reform

MEDICAID ELIGIBILITY
- Benefits

CLAIM PROCEDURE
- Identification card
- Copayment
- Prior approval
- Time limit
- Reciprocity
- Claim form
- Explanation of benefits
- Appeals
- Third-party liability
- Medicaid and HMOs
- Medicaid and CHAMPUS/CHAMPVA
- Medicaid and Medicare
- Medicaid and aliens

HANDY HINTS

MATERNAL AND CHILD HEALTH PROGRAM (MCHP)
- Eligibility
- Claims procedure

Review Questions*

Review the objcctives, key terms, glossary definitions to key terms, chapter information, and figures before completing the following review questions.

1. Medicaid is admininistered by ______________ with partial ______________ funding.
2. Medicaid is not an insurance program. It is a/an ______________________ program.
3. In all other states the program is known as Medicaid but in California the program is called ______________________________________.
4. Because the federal government sets minimum requirements, states are free to enhance the Medicaid program. Name three ways Medicaid programs vary from state to state.

   a. ______________________________________

   b. ______________________________________

   c. ______________________________________

* Review questions for Medi-Cal are provided in this Workbook in Appendix C.

5. What people might be eligible for Medicaid?

a. ______________________________

b. ______________________________

c. ______________________________

d. ______________________________

e. ______________________________

f. ______________________________

6. Name two broad classifications of people eligible for Medicaid assistance.

a. ______________________________

b. ______________________________

7. The name of the program for the prevention, early detection, and treatment of conditions of welfare children is known as ______________________________ ______________. It is abbreviated as ______________.

8. When professional services are rendered, the Medicaid identification card or electronic verification must show eligibility for (circle one):

a. day of service
b. year of service
c. month of service
d. week of service

9. Mrs. Ho suddenly experiences a pain in her right lower abdominal area and rushes to a local hospital for emergency care. Laboratory work verifies that she has a ruptured appendix and immediate surgery is recommended. Is prior authorization required in a bona fide emergency situation like this ______________________________?
What two blocks on the HCFA-1500 claim form need to be completed for emergency services? ______________________________

10. Your Medicaid patient seen today needs hemodialysis services. You telephone for authorization to get verbal approval. Four important items to obtain are:

a. ______________________________

b. ______________________________

c. ______________________________

d. ______________________________

11. The time limit for submitting a Medicaid claim varies from ______________ to ______________ from the date the service is rendered. In your state, the time limit is ______________________________.

12. The insurance claim form for submitting Medicaid claims in all states is ______________________________.

13. Five categories of adjudicated claims that may appear on a Medicaid Remittance Advice document are

 a. ______

 b. ______

 c. ______

 d. ______

 e. ______

14. Name three levels of Medicaid appeals.

 a. ______

 b. ______

 c. ______

15. When a Medicaid patient is injured in an automobile accident and the car has liability insurance, the insurance claim is sent to the (circle one):
 a. patient
 b. automobile insurance carrier
 c. Medicaid fiscal agent

16. Your Medicaid patient also has CHAMPUS. What procedure do you follow? Be exact in your steps for a dependent of an active military person.

 a. ______

 b. ______

17. Define these abbreviations.

 a. EPSDT ______ c. AFDC ______

 b. SSI ______ d. MI ______

18. MCHP means ______, and covers children of what age group?

ASSIGNMENT 35

1. Complete the *Health Insurance Claim Form* (Fig. 11–3) to Medicaid using OCR guidelines for Rose Clarkson by referring to her patient record (Fig. 11–1) and ledger card (Fig. 11–2). Date the claim September 6. Refer to Appendix A to fill in the fees on the ledger card. Obtain the address of your Medicaid fiscal agent by referring to Appendix A in the *Handbook*. See page 6 of this Workbook for Medicaid information. To complete the HCPA-1500 claim form for the Medi-Cal program, see Appendix C.
2. Refer to Chapter 6 of the text for instructions on how to complete this claim form.
3. Refer to your *Current Procedural Terminology* code book to find the correct five-digit code number and modifiers for each professional service rendered.

PATIENT RECORD

Clarkson,	Rose	-	3-9-44	F	013/487-2209
LAST NAME	FIRST NAME	MIDDLE NAME	BIRTH DATE	SEX	HOME PHONE

3408 Jackston Street,	Hempstead,	XY	11551-0300
ADDRESS	CITY	STATE	ZIP CODE

PATIENT'S OCCUPATION: unemployed
NAME OF COMPANY:

ADDRESS OF EMPLOYER:
PHONE:

SPOUSE OR PARENT:
OCCUPATION:

EMPLOYER:
ADDRESS:
PHONE:

NAME OF INSURANCE GROUP: Medicaid
SUBSCRIBER:

BLUE SHIELD OR BLUE CROSS CERT. NO.:
GROUP NO.:
CURRENT COVERAGE NO.:
EFFECTIVE DATE:

MEDICARE NO.:
MEDICAID NO.: CC99756E **
EFFECTIVE DATE:
SOC. SEC. NO.: 030-87-9543

REFERRED BY:
James Jackson, M.D. 100 N. Main Street, Hempstead, NY 11551 UPIN #B72011

DATE	PROGRESS
9-4-9x	Pt complains of cough & SOB. After an EKG and chest x-rays (2 views) the primary diagnosis was congestive heart disease (ICD-9-CM Code No. 4280). Pt to return in 2 wks for further observation. Perry Cardi, MD
	** In some states, the Medicaid number may be as many as 14 digits in length.

FIGURE 11-1

STATEMENT

College Clinic
4567 Broad Avenue
Woodland Hills, XY 12345-0001
Telephone: 013-486-9002
Fax: 013-487-8976

Miss Rose Clarkson
3408 Jackson Street
Hempstead, XY 11551-0300

DATE	PROFESSIONAL SERVICE DESCRIPTION	CHARGE	CREDITS		CURRENT BALANCE
			PAYMENTS	ADJUSTMENTS	
9-4-9x	OC, D hx/exam, LC decision making				
9-4-9x	EKG				
9-4-9x	Chest x-rays (2 views)				

Due and payable within 10 days. **Pay last amount in balance column** ⇧

Key:

PF: Problem-focused	**SF:** Straightforward	**CON:** Consultation	**HCD:** House Call (Day)
EPF: Expanded problem-focused	**LC:** Low complexity	**CPX:** Complete Phys Exam	**HCN:** House Call (Night)
D: Detailed	**MC:** Moderate complexity	**E:** Emergency	**HV:** Hospital visit
C: Comprehensive	**HC:** High complexity	**ER:** Emergency Dept.	**OV:** Office Visit

FIGURE 11-2

HEALTH INSURANCE CLAIM FORM

PICA

MEDICAID (Medicaid #) | CHAMPUS (Sponsor's SSN) | CHAMPVA (VA File #) | GROUP HEALTH PLAN (SSN or ID) | FECA BLK LUNG (SSN) | OTHER (ID)

1a. INSURED'S I.D. NUMBER (FOR PROGRAM IN ITEM 1)

AME (Last Name, First Name, Middle Initial)

3. PATIENT'S BIRTH DATE MM DD YY SEX M F

4. INSURED'S NAME (Last Name, First Name, Middle Initial)

DDRESS (No., Street)

6. PATIENT RELATIONSHIP TO INSURED Self Spouse Child Other

7. INSURED'S ADDRESS (No., Street)

STATE

8. PATIENT STATUS Single Married Other

CITY STATE

TELEPHONE (Include Area Code) ( )

Employed Full-Time Student Part-Time Student

ZIP CODE TELEPHONE (INCLUDE AREA CODE) ( )

RED'S NAME (Last Name, First Name, Middle Initial)

10. IS PATIENT'S CONDITION RELATED TO:

11. INSURED'S POLICY GROUP OR FECA NUMBER

RED'S POLICY OR GROUP NUMBER

a. EMPLOYMENT? (CURRENT OR PREVIOUS) YES NO

a. INSURED'S DATE OF BIRTH MM DD YY SEX M F

RED'S DATE OF BIRTH YY SEX M F

b. AUTO ACCIDENT? YES NO PLACE (State)

b. EMPLOYER'S NAME OR SCHOOL NAME

NAME OR SCHOOL NAME

c. OTHER ACCIDENT? YES NO

c. INSURANCE PLAN NAME OR PROGRAM NAME

PLAN NAME OR PROGRAM NAME

10d. RESERVED FOR LOCAL USE

d. IS THERE ANOTHER HEALTH BENEFIT PLAN? YES NO ***If yes***, return to and complete item 9 a-d.

READ BACK OF FORM BEFORE COMPLETING & SIGNING THIS FORM.

OR AUTHORIZED PERSON'S SIGNATURE I authorize the release of any medical or other information necessary
is claim. I also request payment of government benefits either to myself or to the party who accepts assignment

DATE

13. INSURED'S OR AUTHORIZED PERSON'S SIGNATURE I authorize payment of medical benefits to the undersigned physician or supplier for services described below.

SIGNED

PATIENT AND INSURED INFORMATION

URRENT: YY ILLNESS (First symptom) OR INJURY (Accident) OR PREGNANCY(LMP)

15. IF PATIENT HAS HAD SAME OR SIMILAR ILLNESS. GIVE FIRST DATE MM DD YY

16. DATES PATIENT UNABLE TO WORK IN CURRENT OCCUPATION FROM MM DD YY TO MM DD YY

EFERRING PHYSICIAN OR OTHER SOURCE

17a. I.D. NUMBER OF REFERRING PHYSICIAN

18. HOSPITALIZATION DATES RELATED TO CURRENT SERVICES FROM MM DD YY TO MM DD YY

FOR LOCAL USE

20. OUTSIDE LAB? YES NO $ CHARGES

OR NATURE OF ILLNESS OR INJURY. (RELATE ITEMS 1,2,3 OR 4 TO ITEM 24E BY LINE)

22. MEDICAID RESUBMISSION CODE ORIGINAL REF. NO.

3. ___ . ___

23. PRIOR AUTHORIZATION NUMBER

4. ___ . ___

	B	C	D		E	F	G	H	I	J	K
E(S) OF SERVICE To YY MM DD YY	Place of Service	Type of Service	PROCEDURES, SERVICES, OR SUPPLIES (Explain Unusual Circumstances) CPT/HCPCS	MODIFIER	DIAGNOSIS CODE	$ CHARGES	DAYS OR UNITS	EPSDT Family Plan	EMG	COB	RESERVED FOR LOCAL USE

AX I.D. NUMBER SSN EIN

26. PATIENT'S ACCOUNT NO.

27. ACCEPT ASSIGNMENT? (For govt. claims, see back) YES NO

28. TOTAL CHARGE $

29. AMOUNT PAID $

30. BALANCE DUE $

E OF PHYSICIAN OR SUPPLIER DEGREES OR CREDENTIALS the statements on the reverse bill and are made a part thereof.)

DATE

32. NAME AND ADDRESS OF FACILITY WHERE SERVICES WERE RENDERED (If other than home or office)

33. PHYSICIAN'S, SUPPLIER'S BILLING NAME, ADDRESS, ZIP CODE & PHONE #

PIN# GRP#

PHYSICIAN OR SUPPLIER INFORMATION

D BY AMA COUNCIL ON MEDICAL SERVICE 8/88)

PLEASE PRINT OR TYPE

FORM HCFA-1500 (U2) (12-90)
FORM OWCP-1500 FORM RRB-1500

FIGURE 11-3

4. Record on the ledger card when you have billed Medicaid.

Abbreviations pertinent to this record:

EKG ______________________ SOB ______________________

Pt ______________________ wks ______________________

ASSIGNMENT 36

1. Assume you have completed a *Medicaid treatment authorization request* form for Stephen M. Drake's hospital admission, and the prior authorization number is 45042. Complete the Medicaid form (Fig. 11–6) for Stephen M. Drake by referring to his patient record (Fig. 11–4) and ledger card (Fig. 11–5). Refer to Appendix A to fill in the fees on the ledger card. Date the claim May 26. See page 6 of this Workbook for Medicaid information. To complete the HCFA-1500 claim form for the Medi-Cal program. see Appendix C.

   Physicians' offices usually bill showing itemization of charges, such as for an office visit or admission to the hospital and the name of the surgery. However, many Medicaid programs do not pay for the office call or hospital admission. This is considered to be included in the surgical *global* fee when payment is issued to the attending physician.

   No charges (NC) do not necessarily have to be shown on the claim. However, postoperative follow-up visits may be listed using a code number in the CPT medicine section. See if you can locate it.

   Remember the physician must ALWAYS sign all forms on Medicaid cases: stamped signatures are not allowed.
2. Use your *Current Procedural Terminology* (CPT) and *International Classification of Disease, 9th Revision, Clinical Modification* (*ICD-9-CM*) code books to determine the diagnostic codes and the correct five-digit code number and modifiers for each professional service rendered. If you do not have access to the *CPT Code Book*, refer to Appendix A of this *Workbook*.
3. Record on the ledger card when Medicaid has been billed.
4. Refer to page 6 of this *Workbook* for the clinical and hospital provider numbers that are needed when completing Medicaid forms.
5. On July 1, Medicaid paid $200 on this claim. Post this payment (voucher no. 76L504) to the patient's ledger card and adjust off the balance.

Abbreviations pertinent to this record:

adm ______________________ imp ______________________

adv ______________________ inflam ______________________

cc ______________________ NC ______________________

comp ______________________ phys ______________________

exam ______________________ Pt ______________________

hosp ______________________ temp ______________________

HV ______________________ wk ______________________

IM ______________________

PATIENT RECORD

LAST NAME	FIRST NAME	MIDDLE NAME	BIRTH DATE	SEX	HOME PHONE
Drake,	Stephen	M.	04-03-81	M	013/277-5831

ADDRESS	CITY	STATE	ZIP CODE
2317 Charnwood Avenue,	Woodland Hills,	XY	12345

PATIENT'S OCCUPATION	NAME OF COMPANY
student full time	

ADDRESS OF EMPLOYER	PHONE

SPOUSE OR PARENT	OCCUPATION
Mrs. Virginia B. Drake (mother)	None - family on welfare

EMPLOYER	ADDRESS	PHONE

NAME OF INSURANCE GROUP	SUBSCRIBER

BLUE SHIELD OR BLUE CROSS CERT. NO.	GROUP NO.	CURRENT COVERAGE NO.	EFFECTIVE DATE

MEDICARE NO.	MEDICAID NO.	EFFECTIVE DATE	SOC. SEC. NO.
	19-37-1524033-1-62		566-09-0081

REFERRED BY: Provider No. A12345
James B. Jeffers, M.D., 100 S. Broadway, Woodland Hills, XY 12345

DATE	PROGRESS
5-1-9x	Pt comes in complaining of severe sore throat since April 4. Exam shows much enlargement & inflam of tonsils. Temp 101.2 Did complete phys exam. Gave penicillin 5 cc IM. Imp: Acute tonsillitis (ICD-9-CM diagnostic code no. 463). G. Practon, M.D.
5-6-9x	Pt comes in again with severe sore throat. Mother states Stephen has had bouts of tonsillitis since age 6. Adv. tonsillectomy. Phoned for prior authorization 3 p.m., Log #102, authorized by Mrs. Jane Michaels. Pt admitted to hosp for 2 days stay during which time surgery will be performed. G. Practon, M.D.
5-7-9x	Tonsillectomy and hospital visit. Pt doing well. G. Practon, M.D.
5-8-9x	Brief hospital visit made and pt discharged. To be seen in office in 10 days. Gerald Practon, M.D.
5-18-9x	No complaints. Temp 98.1. Return if necessary. Gerald Practon, M.D.

FIGURE 11-4

STATEMENT

College Clinic
4567 Broad Avenue
Woodland Hills, XY 12345-0001
Telephone: 013-486-9002
Fax: 013-487-8976

Mrs. Virginia B. Drake
2317 Charnwood Avenue
Woodland Hills, XY 12345-0001

rofessional Services - Stephen M. Drake

	PROFESSIONAL SERVICE DESCRIPTION	CHARGE	CREDITS		CURRENT BALANCE
			PAYMENTS	ADJUSTMENTS	
	OC, comp hx/exam, HC decision making				
	Penicillin inj				
	OC				
	Adm to hosp, C hx/exam initial hospital care, LC decision making				
	Tonsillectomy				
	HV				
)x	OC				

d payable within 10 days. Pay last amount in balance column

F: Problem-focused
F: Expanded problem-focused
D: Detailed
C: Comprehensive
SF: Straightforward
LC: Low complexity
MC: Moderate complexity
HC: High complexity
CON: Consultation
CPX: Complete Phys Exam
E: Emergency
ER: Emergency Dept.
HCD: House Call (Day)
HCN: House Call (Night)
HV: Hospital visit
OV: Office Visit

FIGURE 11-5

PICA

HEALTH INSURANCE CLAIM FORM

1. MEDICARE (Medicare #) MEDICAID (Medicaid #) CHAMPUS (Sponsor's SSN) CHAMPVA (VA File #) GROUP HEALTH PLAN (SSN or ID) FECA BLK LUNG (SSN) OTHER (ID)

1a. INSURED'S I.D. NUMBER (FOR PROGRAM I

2. PATIENT'S NAME (Last Name, First Name, Middle Initial)

3. PATIENT'S BIRTH DATE MM DD YY SEX M F

4. INSURED'S NAME (Last Name, First Name, Middle Initial)

5. PATIENT'S ADDRESS (No., Street)

6. PATIENT RELATIONSHIP TO INSURED Self Spouse Child Other

7. INSURED'S ADDRESS (No., Street)

CITY STATE

8. PATIENT STATUS Single Married Other

CITY S

ZIP CODE TELEPHONE (Include Area Code) ( )

Employed Full-Time Student Part-Time Student

ZIP CODE TELEPHONE (INCLUDE ARE ( )

9. OTHER INSURED'S NAME (Last Name, First Name, Middle Initial)

10. IS PATIENT'S CONDITION RELATED TO:

11. INSURED'S POLICY GROUP OR FECA NUMBER

a. OTHER INSURED'S POLICY OR GROUP NUMBER

a. EMPLOYMENT? (CURRENT OR PREVIOUS) YES NO

a. INSURED'S DATE OF BIRTH MM DD YY SEX M F

b. OTHER INSURED'S DATE OF BIRTH MM DD YY SEX M F

b. AUTO ACCIDENT? PLACE (State) YES NO

b. EMPLOYER'S NAME OR SCHOOL NAME

c. EMPLOYER'S NAME OR SCHOOL NAME

c. OTHER ACCIDENT? YES NO

c. INSURANCE PLAN NAME OR PROGRAM NAME

d. INSURANCE PLAN NAME OR PROGRAM NAME

10d. RESERVED FOR LOCAL USE

d. IS THERE ANOTHER HEALTH BENEFIT PLAN? YES NO ***If yes***, return to and complete ite

READ BACK OF FORM BEFORE COMPLETING & SIGNING THIS FORM.

12. PATIENT'S OR AUTHORIZED PERSON'S SIGNATURE I authorize the release of any medical or other information necessary to process this claim. I also request payment of government benefits either to myself or to the party who accepts assignment below.

SIGNED ______ DATE ______

13. INSURED'S OR AUTHORIZED PERSON'S SIGNATURE I au payment of medical benefits to the undersigned physician or s services described below.

SIGNED ______

14. DATE OF CURRENT: MM DD YY ◀ ILLNESS (First symptom) OR INJURY (Accident) OR PREGNANCY(LMP)

15. IF PATIENT HAS HAD SAME OR SIMILAR ILLNESS. GIVE FIRST DATE MM DD YY

16. DATES PATIENT UNABLE TO WORK IN CURRENT OCCUP FROM MM DD YY TO MM DD

17. NAME OF REFERRING PHYSICIAN OR OTHER SOURCE

17a. I.D. NUMBER OF REFERRING PHYSICIAN

18. HOSPITALIZATION DATES RELATED TO CURRENT SERV FROM MM DD YY TO MM DD

19. RESERVED FOR LOCAL USE

20. OUTSIDE LAB? YES NO $ CHARGES

21. DIAGNOSIS OR NATURE OF ILLNESS OR INJURY. (RELATE ITEMS 1,2,3 OR 4 TO ITEM 24E BY LINE)

1. ___ . __ 3. ___ . __

2. ___ . __ 4. ___ . __

22. MEDICAID RESUBMISSION CODE ORIGINAL REF. NO.

23. PRIOR AUTHORIZATION NUMBER

24. A DATE(S) OF SERVICE From MM DD YY To MM DD YY	B Place of Service	C Type of Service	D PROCEDURES, SERVICES, OR SUPPLIES (Explain Unusual Circumstances) CPT/HCPCS MODIFIER	E DIAGNOSIS CODE	F $ CHARGES	G DAYS OR UNITS	H EPSDT Family Plan	I EMG	J COB	RESER LOCA
1										
2										
3										
4										
5										
6										

25. FEDERAL TAX I.D. NUMBER SSN EIN

26. PATIENT'S ACCOUNT NO.

27. ACCEPT ASSIGNMENT? (For govt. claims, see back) YES NO

28. TOTAL CHARGE $

29. AMOUNT PAID $

30. BALA $

31. SIGNATURE OF PHYSICIAN OR SUPPLIER INCLUDING DEGREES OR CREDENTIALS (I certify that the statements on the reverse apply to this bill and are made a part thereof.)

SIGNED DATE

32. NAME AND ADDRESS OF FACILITY WHERE SERVICES WERE RENDERED (If other than home or office)

33. PHYSICIAN'S, SUPPLIER'S BILLING NAME, ADDRESS, ZIP & PHONE #

PIN# GRP#

(APPROVED BY AMA COUNCIL ON MEDICAL SERVICE 8/88)

PLEASE PRINT OR TYPE

FORM HCFA-1500 (U2) (12-90)
FORM OWCP-1500 FOR

FIGURE 11-6

ASSIGNMENT 37

1. Complete the Medicaid form (Fig. 11–9) for Barry L. Brook by referring to his patient record (Fig. 11–7) and ledger card (Fig. 11–8). Refer to Appendix A to fill in the fees on the ledger card. Date the claim May 31. See page 6 of this Workbook for Medicaid information. To complete the HCFA-1500 claim form for the Medi-Cal program. see Appendix C.
2. Use your *CPT* and *ICD-9-CM* code books to determine the diagnostic codes and the correct five-digit code number and modifiers for each professional service rendered. If you do not have access to the *CPT Code Book*, refer to Appendix A.
3. Record on the ledger card when you have billed Medicaid.
4. Refer to page 6 of this *Workbook* for the facility provider number that is needed when completing Medicaid forms.
5. On July 1, Medicaid paid $75 (Voucher No. 32M670) on this claim. Post this payment to the patient's ledger card and adjust off the balance.

Abbreviations pertinent to this record:

cc ______________________ L ______________________

ER ______________________ lt ______________________

Fx ______________________ N ______________________

hosp ______________________ pt ______________________

hist ______________________ wks ______________________

imp ______________________ TX ______________________

COMPUTER EXERCISE

CASE 2 MEDICAID

Before proceeding, you may want to do an exercise based on the concepts you have learned. Additional practice material is on your computer diskette.

Directions: Insert the diskette into the computer and follow the instructions on the screen for Computer Exercise Case 2.

PATIENT RECORD

LAST NAME	FIRST NAME	MIDDLE NAME	BIRTH DATE	SEX	HOME PHONE
Brook,	Barry	I.	02-03-85	M	013/487-9770

ADDRESS	CITY	STATE	ZIP CODE
3821 Ocean Drive,	Woodland Hills,	XY	12345-0001

PATIENT'S OCCUPATION	NAME OF COMPANY
child full-time student	

ADDRESS OF EMPLOYER	PHONE

SPOUSE OR PARENT	OCCUPATION
Robert D. Brook (father)	None - family on welfare (father totally disabled)

EMPLOYER	ADDRESS	PHONE

NAME OF INSURANCE GROUP	SUBSCRIBER

BLUE SHIELD OR BLUE CROSS CERT. NO.	GROUP NO.	CURRENT COVERAGE NO.	EFFECTIVE DATE

MEDICARE NO.	MEDICAID NO.	EFFECTIVE DATE	SOC. SEC. NO.
	54-32-7681533-1-03		776-09-1931

REFERRED BY:
Virginia B. Drake (friend)

DATE	PROGRESS
5-28-9x	11:30 PM Sunday new pt seen in ER at hosp. Pt twisted Ⓛ knee while playing baseball at Grove Playground. X-rays were ordered - N for Fx. Imp: effusion + ligament strain lt knee. Tx: aspirated lt knee + removed 5cc bloody fluid. Applied long leg cylinder walking cast. Pt to be seen in office in 2 wks. Raymond Skelton, MD
	NOTE: ICD-9-CM diagnostic code numbers for this case are 719.06 and 844.9

FIGURE 11-7

STATEMENT

College Clinic
4567 Broad Avenue
Woodland Hills, XY 12345-0001
Telephone: 013-486-9002
Fax: 013-487-8976

Mr. Robert D. Brook
3821 Ocean Drive
Woodland Hills, XY 12345-0001

Re: Professional Services - Barry L. Brook

DATE	PROFESSIONAL SERVICE DESCRIPTION	CHARGE	CREDITS		CURRENT BALANCE
			PAYMENTS	ADJUSTMENTS	
5-28-9x	ER init, D hx/exam, MC decision making				
5-28-9x	Aspiration lt knee				
5-28-9x	Application long leg cylinder cast, lt leg, walker				

Due and payable within 10 days. **Pay last amount in balance column** ⇧

Key: PF: Problem-focused	**SF:** Straightforward	**CON:** Consultation	**HCD:** House Call (Day)
EPF: Expanded problem-focused	**LC:** Low complexity	**CPX:** Complete Phys Exam	**HCN:** House Call (Night)
D: Detailed	**MC:** Moderate complexity	**E:** Emergency	**HV:** Hospital visit
C: Comprehensive	**HC:** High complexity	**ER:** Emergency Dept.	**OV:** Office Visit

FIGURE 11-8

PICA

HEALTH INSURANCE CLAIM FORM

P

1. MEDICARE (Medicare #) | MEDICAID (Medicaid #) | CHAMPUS (Sponsor's SSN) | CHAMPVA (VA File #) | GROUP HEALTH PLAN (SSN or ID) | FECA BLK LUNG (SSN) | OTHER (ID)

1a. INSURED'S I.D. NUMBER (FOR PROGRAM I

2. PATIENT'S NAME (Last Name, First Name, Middle Initial)

3. PATIENT'S BIRTH DATE MM DD YY — SEX M F

4. INSURED'S NAME (Last Name, First Name, Middle Initial)

5. PATIENT'S ADDRESS (No., Street)

6. PATIENT RELATIONSHIP TO INSURED — Self Spouse Child Other

7. INSURED'S ADDRESS (No., Street)

CITY | STATE

8. PATIENT STATUS — Single Married Other; Employed, Full-Time Student, Part-Time Student

CITY | S

ZIP CODE | TELEPHONE (Include Area Code) ( )

ZIP CODE | TELEPHONE (INCLUDE AREA ( )

9. OTHER INSURED'S NAME (Last Name, First Name, Middle Initial)

10. IS PATIENT'S CONDITION RELATED TO:

11. INSURED'S POLICY GROUP OR FECA NUMBER

a. OTHER INSURED'S POLICY OR GROUP NUMBER

a. EMPLOYMENT? (CURRENT OR PREVIOUS) YES NO

a. INSURED'S DATE OF BIRTH MM DD YY — SEX M F

b. OTHER INSURED'S DATE OF BIRTH MM DD YY — SEX M F

b. AUTO ACCIDENT? YES NO — PLACE (State)

b. EMPLOYER'S NAME OR SCHOOL NAME

c. EMPLOYER'S NAME OR SCHOOL NAME

c. OTHER ACCIDENT? YES NO

c. INSURANCE PLAN NAME OR PROGRAM NAME

d. INSURANCE PLAN NAME OR PROGRAM NAME

10d. RESERVED FOR LOCAL USE

d. IS THERE ANOTHER HEALTH BENEFIT PLAN? YES NO ***If yes***, return to and complete ite

READ BACK OF FORM BEFORE COMPLETING & SIGNING THIS FORM.

12. PATIENT'S OR AUTHORIZED PERSON'S SIGNATURE I authorize the release of any medical or other information necessary to process this claim. I also request payment of government benefits either to myself or to the party who accepts assignment below.

SIGNED ______________________ DATE ______________

13. INSURED'S OR AUTHORIZED PERSON'S SIGNATURE I au payment of medical benefits to the undersigned physician or s services described below.

SIGNED ______________

14. DATE OF CURRENT: MM DD YY — ILLNESS (First symptom) OR INJURY (Accident) OR PREGNANCY(LMP)

15. IF PATIENT HAS HAD SAME OR SIMILAR ILLNESS. GIVE FIRST DATE MM DD YY

16. DATES PATIENT UNABLE TO WORK IN CURRENT OCCUP — FROM MM DD YY TO MM DD

17. NAME OF REFERRING PHYSICIAN OR OTHER SOURCE

17a. I.D. NUMBER OF REFERRING PHYSICIAN

18. HOSPITALIZATION DATES RELATED TO CURRENT SERVI — FROM MM DD YY TO MM DD

19. RESERVED FOR LOCAL USE

20. OUTSIDE LAB? YES NO — $ CHARGES

21. DIAGNOSIS OR NATURE OF ILLNESS OR INJURY. (RELATE ITEMS 1,2,3 OR 4 TO ITEM 24E BY LINE)

1. ____ . __   3. ____ . __

2. ____ . __   4. ____ . __

22. MEDICAID RESUBMISSION CODE — ORIGINAL REF. NO.

23. PRIOR AUTHORIZATION NUMBER

24. A						B	C	D		E	F	G	H	I	J	K
DATE(S) OF SERVICE From MM	DD	YY	To MM	DD	YY	Place of Service	Type of Service	PROCEDURES, SERVICES, OR SUPPLIES (Explain Unusual Circumstances) CPT/HCPCS	MODIFIER	DIAGNOSIS CODE	$ CHARGES	DAYS OR UNITS	EPSDT Family Plan	EMG	COB	RESER LOCA
1																
2																
3																
4																
5																
6																

25. FEDERAL TAX I.D. NUMBER — SSN EIN

26. PATIENT'S ACCOUNT NO.

27. ACCEPT ASSIGNMENT? (For govt. claims, see back) YES NO

28. TOTAL CHARGE $

29. AMOUNT PAID $

30. BALA $

31. SIGNATURE OF PHYSICIAN OR SUPPLIER INCLUDING DEGREES OR CREDENTIALS (I certify that the statements on the reverse apply to this bill and are made a part thereof.)

SIGNED DATE

32. NAME AND ADDRESS OF FACILITY WHERE SERVICES WERE RENDERED (If other than home or office)

33. PHYSICIAN'S, SUPPLIER'S BILLING NAME, ADDRESS, ZIP & PHONE #

PIN# GRP#

(APPROVED BY AMA COUNCIL ON MEDICAL SERVICE 8/88) ***PLEASE PRINT OR TYPE***

FORM HCFA-1500 (U2) (12-90)
FORM OWCP-1500 FOR

FIGURE 11-9

CHAPTER 12

Medicare

Key Terms

Your instructor may wish to select some specific words pertinent to this chapter for a test. For definitions of the terms, further study, and/or reference, the words, phrases, and abbreviations may be found in the Glossary at the end of the textbook. Key terms for this chapter follow:

allowed amount
assignment
benefit period
crossover claim
diagnostic cost groups (DCGs)
disabled
employer group health plan (EGHP)
end-stage renal disease (ESRD)
fiscal intermediary
Health Care Financing Administration (HCFA)
home health agency
hospice
hospital insurance
intermediate care facility
internal control number
limiting charge
medical necessity
Medicare
Medicare/Medicaid (Medi-Medi)
Medigap (MG)
national codes
nursing facility (NF)
participating physician program
peer review organizations (PRO)
premium
primary payer
prospective payment system (PPS)
reasonable fee
relative value unit (RVU)
Remittance Advice (RA)
resource based relative value scale (RBRVS)
respite care
secondary payer
short-stay hospital
supplemental insurer
Supplemental Security Income (SSI)
supplementary medical insurance (SMI)
volume performance standard (VPS)

Performance Objectives

The student will be able to

- Define and spell the key terms for this chapter, given the information from the textbook Glossary, within a reasonable period of time and with enough accuracy to obtain a satisfactory evaluation.
- Answer the review questions after reading the chapter, with enough accuracy to obtain a satisfactory evaluation.
- Fill in the correct meaning of each abbreviation, given a list of common medical abbreviations and symbols that appear in chart notes, within a reasonable period of time and with enough accuracy to obtain a satisfactory evaluation.
- Complete each HCFA-1500 Health Insurance Claim Form for billing, given the patients' medical chart notes, ledger cards, and blank insurance claim forms, within a reasonable period of time and with enough accuracy to obtain a satisfactory evaluation.
- Post payments, adjustments, and balances on the patient's ledger cards, using the Medicare Mock Fee Schedule in Appendix A, within a reasonable period of time and with enough accuracy to obtain a satisfactory evaluation.
- Compute mathematic calculations, given Medicare problem situations, within a reasonable period of time and with enough accuracy to obtain a satisfactory evaluation.
- Select the HCPCS and/or procedural code numbers, given a series of medical services, procedures, or supplies, using the *Current Procedural Terminology* (CPT) code book or the Mock Fee Schedule in Appendix A and the HCPCS list of codes in Appendix B, within a reasonable period of time and with enough accuracy to obtain a satisfactory evaluation.

Study Outline

INTRODUCTION

MEDICARE PROGRAM
  Eligibility requirements
  Fiscal intermediaries and fiscal agents
    Medicare Part A
    Medicare Part B
  Aliens on Medicare
  Beneficiary representative/representative payee
MEDICARE PAYMENTS
  Civil Monetary Penalties Law
  Medicare health insurance card
COVERAGE
  Hospital benefits
  Medical benefits
  Railroad retirement benefits
  Physician Self Referrals
  Employed elderly health care coverage
    Physician identification numbers
MEDICARE SUPPLEMENTAL INSURANCE
  Medigap
  Medicare secondary payer (MSP)
  Medigap and MSP guidelines
  Medigap and MSP claims
MEDICARE AND PREPAYMENT PLANS
  Health Maintenance Organizations
  Carrier-dealing prepayment organization
AUTOMOBILE OR LIABILITY INSURANCE COVERAGE
BILLING FOR A DECEASED PATIENT
MEDICARE/MEDICAID (MEDI-MEDI)
  Benefits
  Claim procedure
UTILIZATION AND QUALITY CONTROL
  Peer review organization program
PRIOR AUTHORIZATION OR PRECERTIFICATION
MEDICARE CODING TIPS
  Medicare and Medicaid coverage data bank
  Medicare claim form
  Electronic claims submission
  Medicare fraud and abuse
  Medicare review and appeal process
  Posting Medicare payments

Review Questions

Review the objectives, key terms, and glossary definitions to key terms, chapter information, and figures before completing the following review questions.

1. An individual becomes eligible for Medicare Parts A and B at age ____________ .

2. Medicare Part A is __________________________ coverage and Medicare Part B is

   ________________________ coverage.

3. Organizations or claims processors under contract to the federal government that handle insurance claims and payments for hospitals under Medicare Part A are known

   as ________________________________, and those that process claims for physicians

   and other suppliers of services under Medicare Part B are called______________ .

4. Funding for the Medicare Part A program is obtained from __________________

   ____

   and for the Medicare Part B program is obtained equally from ________________

   ____ .

5. Define a Medicare Part A hospital benefit period.

   ____

   ____

6. A program designed to provide pain relief, symptom management, and supportive

   services to terminally ill individuals and their families is known as_____________ .

7. Short-term inpatient medical care for terminally ill individuals to give temporary relief

   to the caregiver is known as ____ .

8. An agreement in which the patient transfers to the physician the right to receive payment

   from the Medicare fiscal intermediary or agent is known as a/an ____________ .
   Under this agreement, the physician must agree to accept the Medicare payment as

   payment in full except for ____

   ____ .

9. If circumstances make it impossible to obtain a signature on an insurance claim from

   a Medicare patient, physicians may obtain a/an ___________________________ .

10. The time limit for sending in a Medicare insurance claim is_________________

    ____ .

11. An eligibility requirement for aliens to receive Medicare benefits is that a/an____

    ____ .

12. A Medicare insurance claim form showed a number, J0540, for an injection of 600,000 units of penicillin G. This number is referred to as a/an ______________________ .
13. When a Medicare claim form is shown with a number, W0730, this code number is referred to as a/an ____ .
14. The frequency of Pap tests for Medicare patients is ___________________________ and for mammograms, ____ .
15. Philip Lenz is seen by Dr. Doe, who schedules an operative procedure in one month. This type of surgery is known as ______________________________________ , since it does not have to be performed immediately.
16. An HCFA-assigned provider identification number is known as a/an __________ ____________________ .

    Physicians who supply durable medical equipment must have a/an __________ number.
17. Name two types of policies for Medicare supplemental insurance.

    a. ____

    b. ____
18. Policies offered by third-party payers that fall under guidelines issued by the Federal government and cover Medicare deductibles and copayments are known as ____________________ insurance policies.
19. If an individual is 65 years of age and a Medicare beneficiary but is working and has a group insurance policy, where is the insurance claim form sent initially? ______ ____
20. If a person on Medicare is injured in an automobile accident, the physician submits the claim form to ____ .
21. Mrs. Davis, a Medi-Medi patient, has a cholecystectomy. In completing the insurance claim form, the assignment portion is left blank in error. What will happen in this case?

    ____

    ____
22. Jeremy Conrad, a patient on Medicare, received two vitamin B_{12} injections in April. Will Medicare pay on these services and why or why not? ______________________ ____

23. Criteria for Medicare payments are established using a fee schedule based on

a. ____________________

b. ____________________

c. ____________________

ASSIGNMENT 38

MATHEMATIC PROBLEMS

Submitting insurance claims, particularly Medicare claims, involves a bit of arithmetic. Several problems will be given here so you will gain experience with situations encountered daily in your work. The Medicare deductible is always subtracted from the allowed amount first before continuing mathematic computations.

Problem 1: Mr. Doolittle has Medicare Part B coverage. He was well during the entire past year. It is now January 1 and Mr. Doolittle is rushed to the hospital, where Dr. Input performs an emergency gastric resection. Medicare is billed for $450, and the doctor agrees to accept an assignment. The patient has not paid any deductible. Complete the following statements by putting in the correct amounts.

Original bill ____________________

A. Medicare allows $400. Medicare payment ____________________

B. Patient owes Dr. Input ____________________

C. Dr. Input's courtesy adjustment ____________________

Mathematic computations:

Problem 2: Mrs. James has Medicare Part B coverage. She met her deductible when she was ill in March of this year. It is now November 1 and Dr. Caesar performs a bilateral salpingo-oophorectomy, for which he bills her $300 and agrees to accept a Medicare assignment.

Original bill ____________________

A. Medicare allows $275. Medicare payment ____________________

B. Patient owes Dr. Caesar ____________________

C. Dr. Caesar's courtesy adjustment ____________________

The assistant surgeon charged Mrs. James $60 and does not accept an assignment. After receiving her check from Medicare, Mrs. James sends the surgeon his $60. Medicare has allowed $55 for the fee. How much of the money was from Mrs. James' private funds?

$______________ How much did Medicare pay? $______________

Mathematic computations for assistant surgeon:

Problem 3: You work for Dr. Coccidioides. He does not accept assignment. He is treating Mr. Robinson for allergies. Mr. Robinson has Medicare Part A. You send in a bill to Medicare for the $135 that Mr. Robinson owes you. What portion of the bill will Medicare pay?

____

Problem 4: Mr. Fay was not sick until November of last year, when he had an illness resulting in $57 worth of medical bills. Since he was not eligible for any reimbursement from Medicare, he paid your bill himself. In June of the new year, he has a new illness that incurs $89 in medical bills. He asks you to bill Medicare, and the physician does not accept assignment. He has paid the deductible at another physician's office. Assuming that Medicare allows the entire amount of your fees, the Medicare check to the patient is $______________ (which comes to you). The patient's part of the bill to you is $______________ .

Mathematic computations:

Problem 5: Mr. Iba, a Medicare patient with a Medigap insurance policy, is seen for an office visit and the fee is $80. The Medicare-approved amount is $54.44. The patient has met his deductible for the year. The Medicare payment check is $__________________
After submitting the claim to the Medigap insurance, the Medigap payment check is

$__________________

Note: Chapter 12 gives details on Medigap coverage guidelines. To zero out the balance, the Medicare courtesy adjustment is $__________________

Mathematic computations:

Problem 6: Mrs. Smith, a Medicare patient, had surgery, and the physician's fee is $1250. This patient is working part-time, and the patient's employer group health plan allowed $1100, applied $500 to the deductible, and paid 80% of $600.

Amount paid by this plan $__________________

The spouse's employer group health plan is billed for the balance, which is $__________________, and this program also has a $500 deductible. This plan pays 100% of the fee billed less the deductible. The spouse's employer group plan makes a payment of $__________________. You send copies of RAs from the two group health plans and submit a claim to Medicare for $1250, but the balance at this point is $__________________.

Mathematic computations:

Problem 7: In the late 1980s Medicare's Resource-Based Relative Value System (RBRVS) became the way payment was determined each year. However, since the early 1990s, annual fee schedules are supplied by local fiscal intermediaries so the RBRVS has become more useful in determining practice cost to convert patients to capitation when negotiating managed care contracts. Because physicians may request determination of fees for certain procedures to discover actual cost and what compensation ratios should be, it is important to know how Medicare fees are determined. Each year the *Federal Register* publishes geographic practice cost indices by Medicare carrier and locality as well as relative value units and related information. This assignment will give you some mathematic practice using figures for annual conversion factors* to determine fees for given procedures in various regions of the United States. Refer to Figures 12–1 and 12–2, which are pages of the *Federal Register*.

a. HCPCS Code 47600 Removal of gallbladder. The medical practice is located in Phoenix, Arizona.

	Work	*Overhead*	*Malpractice*
RVUs	________	________	________
GPCI	x ________	x ________	x ________

________ + ________ + ________ = Total adj. RVUs ________

1997 Conversion factor* $40.9603 x Total adj. RVUs ________ = allowed amount $ ________

b. HCPCS Code 47715 Excision of bile duct cyst. The medical practice is located in Arkansas.

	Work	*Overhead*	*Malpractice*
RVUs	________	________	________
GPCI	x ________	x ________	x ________

________ + ________ + ________ = Total adj. RVUs ________

1997 Conversion factor* $40.9603 x Total adj. RVUs ________ = allowed amount $ ________

* 1996 conversion factors are: $33.8454 for non-surgical services, $35.7617 for primary care services, and $40.9603 for surgical services. The anesthesia conversion factor is $16.68.

c. HCPCS Code 48146 Pancreatectomy. The medical practice is located in Fresno, California.

	Work	*Overhead*	*Malpractice*
RVUs	________	________	________
GPCI	x ________	x ________	x ________

________ + ________ + ________ = Total adj. RVUs ________

1997 Conversion factor* $40.9603 x Total adj. RVUs ____________ = allowed

amount $ ________________

ADDENDUM D.—GEOGRAPHIC PRACTICE COST INDICES BY MEDICARE CARRIER AND LOCALITY

Carrier number	Locality number	Locality name	Work	Practice expense	Mal-practice
510	5	Birmingham, AL	0.981	0.913	0.824
510	4	Mobile, AL	0.964	0.911	0.824
510	2	North Central AL	0.970	0.867	0.824
510	1	Northwest AL	0.985	0.869	0.824
510	6	Rest of AL	0.975	0.851	0.824
510	3	Southeast AL	0.972	0.869	0.824
1020	1	Alaska	1.106	1.255	1.042
1030	5	Flagstaff (city), AZ	0.983	0.911	1.255
1030	1	Phoenix, AZ	1.003	1.016	1.255
1030	7	Prescott (city), AZ	0.983	0.911	1.255
1030	99	Rest of Arizona	0.987	0.943	1.255
1030	2	Tucson (city), AZ	0.987	0.989	1.255
1030	8	Yuma (city), AZ	0.983	0.911	1.255
520	13	Arkansas	0.960	0.856	0.302
2050	26	Anaheim-Santa Ana, CA	1.046	1.220	1.370
542	14	Bakersfield, CA	1.028	1.050	1.370
542	11	Fresno/Madera, CA	1.006	1.009	1.370
542	13	Kings/Tulare, CA	0.999	1.001	1.370
2050	18	Los Angeles, CA (1st of 8)	1.060	1.196	1.370
2050	19	Los Angeles, CA (2nd of 8)	1.060	1.196	1.370

FIGURE 12-1

Addendum D. Geographic practice cost indices by Medicare carrier and locality. Federal Register, Rules and Regulations, Vol. 58, No. 230. Washington, D.C., Superintendent of Documents, U.S. Government Printing Office, December 2, 1993, page 63848.

Addendum B.—Relative Value Units (RVUs) and Related Information

HCPCS[1]	MOD	Status	Description	Work RVUs	Practice expense RVUs[2]	Mal-practice RVUs	Total	Global period	Update
47399	....	C	Liver surgery procedure	0.00	0.00	0.00	0.00	YYY	S
47400	....	A	Incision of liver duct	19.11	8.62	1.38	29.11	090	S
47420	....	A	Incision of bile duct	15.48	9.59	2.01	27.08	090	S
47425	....	A	Incision of bile duct	14.95	11.84	2.48	29.27	090	S
47440	....	A	Incision of bile duct	18.51	10.61	2.23	31.35	090	S
47460	....	A	Incise bile duct sphincter	14.57	15.71	1.84	32.12	090	N
47480	....	A	Incision of gallbladder	8.14	7.68	1.61	17.43	090	S
47490	....	A	Incision of gallbladder	6.11	3.61	0.38	10.10	090	N
47500	....	A	Injection for liver x-rays	1.98	1.53	0.14	3.65	000	N
47505	....	A	Injection for liver x-rays	0.77	1.34	0.14	2.25	000	N
47510	....	A	Insert catheter, bile duct	7.47	2.90	0.25	10.62	090	N
47511	....	A	Insert bile duct drain	10.02	2.90	0.25	13.17	090	N
47525	....	A	Change bile duct catheter	5.47	1.61	0.16	7.24	010	N
47530	....	A	Revise, reinsert bile tube	5.47	1.53	0.19	7.19	090	N
47550	....	A	Bile duct endoscopy	3.05	1.58	0.35	4.98	000	S
47552	....	A	Biliary endoscopy, thru skin	6.11	1.38	0.21	7.70	000	S
47553	....	A	Biliary endoscopy, thru skin	6.42	3.84	0.63	10.89	000	N
47554	....	A	Biliary endoscopy, thru skin	9.16	3.97	0.68	13.81	000	S
47555	....	A	Biliary endoscopy, thru skin	7.64	2.66	0.30	10.60	000	N
47556	....	A	Biliary endoscopy, thru skin	8.66	2.66	0.30	11.62	000	N
47600	....	A	Removal of gallbladder	10.80	7.61	1.60	20.01	090	S
47605	....	A	Removal of gallbladder	11.66	8.23	1.77	21.66	090	S
47610	....	A	Removal of gallbladder	14.01	9.47	2.02	25.50	090	S
47612	....	A	Removal of gallbladder	14.91	14.39	3.08	32.38	090	S
47620	....	A	Removal of gallbladder	15.97	11.35	2.39	29.71	090	S
47630	....	A	Remove bile duct stone	8.40	3.79	0.40	12.59	090	N
47700	....	A	Exploration of bile ducts	13.90	7.71	1.60	23.21	090	S
47701	....	A	Bile duct revision	26.87	8.30	1.92	37.09	090	S
47710	....	A	Excision of bile duct tumor	18.64	12.19	2.49	33.32	090	S
47715	....	A	Excision of bile duct cyst	14.66	8.31	1.73	24.70	090	S
47716	....	A	Fusion of bile duct cyst	12.67	6.63	1.55	20.85	090	S
47720	....	A	Fuse gallbladder & bowel	12.03	9.26	1.95	23.24	090	S
47721	....	A	Fuse upper gi structures	14.57	11.55	2.50	28.62	090	S
47740	....	A	Fuse gallbladder & bowel	14.08	10.32	2.16	26.56	090	S
47760	....	A	Fuse bile ducts and bowel	20.15	11.74	2.56	34.45	090	S
47765	....	A	Fuse liver ducts & bowel	19.25	14.77	3.00	37.02	090	S
47780	....	A	Fuse bile ducts and bowel	20.63	13.22	2.76	36.61	090	S
47800	....	A	Reconstruction of bile ducts	17.91	13.37	2.46	33.74	090	S
47801	....	A	Placement, bile duct support	11.41	5.54	0.82	17.77	090	S
47802	....	A	Fuse liver duct & intestine	16.19	10.38	1.77	28.34	090	S
47999	....	C	Bile tract surgery procedure	0.00	0.00	0.00	0.00	YYY	S
48000	....	A	Drainage of abdomen	13.25	7.13	1.42	21.80	090	S
48001	....	A	Placement of drain, pancreas	15.71	8.22	1.91	25.84	090	S
48005	....	A	Resect/debride pancreas	17.77	9.29	2.16	29.22	090	S
48020	....	A	Removal of pancreatic stone	13.12	6.86	1.59	21.57	090	S
48100	....	A	Biopsy of pancreas	10.30	4.26	0.80	15.36	090	S
48102	....	A	Needle biopsy, pancreas	4.48	2.44	0.25	7.17	010	N
48120	....	A	Removal of pancreas lesion	12.93	9.83	2.09	24.85	090	S
48140	....	A	Partial removal of pancreas	18.47	13.44	2.86	34.77	090	S
48145	....	A	Partial removal of pancreas	19.30	15.88	3.20	38.38	090	S
48146	....	A	Pancreatectomy	21.97	16.67	1.94	40.58	090	S
48148	....	A	Removal of pancreatic duct	14.57	8.32	1.70	24.59	090	S
48150	....	A	Partial removal of pancreas	34.55	22.79	4.80	62.14	090	S
48151	....	D	Partial removal of pancreas	0.00	0.00	0.00	0.00	090	0
48152	....	A	Pancreatectomy	31.33	22.79	4.80	58.92	090	S
48153	....	A	Pancreatectomy	34.55	22.79	4.80	62.14	090	S
48154	....	A	Pancreatectomy	31.33	22.79	4.80	58.92	090	S
48155	....	A	Removal of pancreas	19.65	20.63	4.31	44.59	090	S
48160	....	N	Pancreas removal, transplant	0.00	0.00	0.00	0.00	XXX	0
48180	....	A	Fuse pancreas and bowel	21.11	12.74	2.66	36.51	090	S
48400	....	A	Injection, intraoperative	1.97	1.04	0.24	3.25	ZZZ	S
48500	....	A	Surgery of pancreas cyst	12.17	8.62	1.68	22.47	090	S
48510	....	A	Drain pancreatic pseudocyst	11.34	7.62	1.46	20.42	090	S
48520	....	A	Fuse pancreas cyst and bowel	13.11	11.43	2.46	27.00	090	S
48540	....	A	Fuse pancreas cyst and bowel	15.95	12.80	2.68	31.43	090	S
48545	....	A	Pancreatorrhaphy	14.81	7.75	1.81	24.37	090	S
48547	....	A	Duodenal exclusion	21.42	11.20	2.61	35.23	090	S

[1] All numeric CPT HCPCS Copyright 1993 American Medical Association.

[2] * Indicates reduction of Practice Expense RVUs as a result of OBRA 1993.

FIGURE 12-2

Addendum B. Relative Value Units (RVUs) and related information. The insurance carrier uses this data to do calculations and then annually prints out physician's regional Medicare fee schedules. Abbreviations may be defined as follows: Status indicator. A = active code, B = bundled service—no payment, C = carrier priced code, X = excluded code by law, Global period. XXX = no modifier needed no global concept, YYY = carrier determines global period, ZZZ included as part of another service, 010 = 10 days global period, 090 = 90 days global period; Update indicator. N = nonsurgical service, S = surgical service Federal Register, Rules and Regulations, Vol. 58, No. 230. Washington, D.C., Superintendent of Documents, U.S. Government Printing Office, December 2, 1993, page 63738. CPT codes,

ASSIGNMENT 39

HCPCS ALPHA/NUMERIC CODING PROBLEMS

As you have learned from the *Handbook*, it is necessary to use three levels of codes (CPT, HCPCS, and regional codes) when submitting Medicare claims. Refer to Appendix B to complete this HCPCS coding exercise for Medicare claims.

In addition to referring to Appendix B for HCPCS codes and modifiers, you will also need to refer to your *CPT Code Book* or Appendix A to complete these Medicare problems.

1. cellular therapy ____________

2. Injection amygdalin ____________

3. Laboratory handling charge ____________

4. Xylocaine (lidocaine) injection for local anesthetic ____________

5. Splint, wrist ____________

6. Crutches ____________

7. Cervical head harness ____________

8. 1 ml gamma globulin ____________

9. Coumadin (warfarin sodium) injection ____________

10. Contraceptives (unclassified drugs) ____________

11. Anesthesia for UGI endoscopy, furnished by anesthesiologist, simple exam ____________

12. Anesthesia for tibial osteotomy, bilateral, direction of own employees ____________

13. Second surgical opinion, detailed hx/exam, low-complexity decision making ____________

14. Penicillin injection ____________

    When sending in a claim on a non-Medicare patient, what code would be used for a penicillin injection? ____________

15. Chiropractic manipulation of spine, acute treatment ____________

16. Biopsy, excisional, superficial lesion of sternum (bone) ____________

    Surgical tray ____________

INSURANCE CLAIM ASSIGNMENTS

Assignments presented in this section are to give you hands-on experience in completing a variety of Medicare insurance cases using the HCFA-1500 claim form. Periodically, bulletins are issued by Medicare fiscal carriers relaying new federal policies and guidelines. This may mean lower reimbursement or denial of reimbursement for a particular code number. Cases shown do not necessarily indicate that the provider may get paid for the service, as this depends on federal guidelines at the time of submission of the claim. The cases presented in this section are

Assignment 40	Medicare
Assignment 41	Third party payer—liability insurance/medicare
Assignment 42	Medicare/Medigap
Assignment 43	Medicare railroad retiree
Assignments 44 and 45	Medicare/Medicaid (Medi-Medi)

ASSIGNMENT 40

1. Complete the *Medicare Form** (Fig. 12–5) using OCR guidelines, directing it to your local fiscal intermediary. Refer to Elsa M. Mooney's patient record (Fig. 12–3) and ledger card for information (Fig. 12–4). Refer to Appendix A to fill in the fees on the ledger card. Date the claim December 21. Dr. Cardi is accepting assignment in this particular case. Mrs. Mooney has already met her deductible for the year, owing to previous medical expenses from another physician.
2. Use your *CPT Code Book* or Appendix A to determine the correct five-digit code number and modifiers for each professional service rendered. Refer to Appendix B for HCPCS procedure codes and modifiers.
3. Record on the ledger card when you have billed Medicare.
4. On February 12, Medicare allowed $75 on this claim. Post 80% of this payment from Medicare check No. 115620 to the patient's ledger card. Post the courtesy adjustment and show the balance due from the patient.

Abbreviations pertinent to this record:

ASCVD ______________________ N ______________________

EKG ______________________ OC ______________________

exam ______________________ Pt ______________________

interpret ______________________ ret ______________________

init ______________________ Rx ______________________

mo ______________________ c̄ ______________________

Here are three questions suggested for critical thinking and class discussion after completion of the Medicare health insurance claim form. Refer to the Mock Fee Schedule shown in Appendix A.

1. If Dr. Cardi is **participating**, how much will he receive from Medicare for the **office** visit and EKG? $______________

2. If Dr. Cardi is **not participating**, how much will he receive for the EKG?

   $______________

*See Chapter 6 of the *Handbook* for help in completing this form and refer to Figure 6-7.

PATIENT RECORD

LAST NAME	FIRST NAME	MIDDLE NAME	BIRTH DATE	SEX	HOME PHONE
Mooney,	Elsa	M.	02-06-10	F	013/452-4968

ADDRESS	CITY	STATE	ZIP CODE
5750 Canyon Road,	Woodland Hills,	XY	12345

PATIENT'S OCCUPATION: retired secretary

NAME OF COMPANY:

ADDRESS OF EMPLOYER:

PHONE:

SPOUSE OR PARENT: husband deceased

OCCUPATION:

EMPLOYER:

ADDRESS:

PHONE:

NAME OF INSURANCE GROUP: Medicare

SUBSCRIBER:

BLUE SHIELD OR BLUE CROSS CERT. NO.	GROUP NO.	CURRENT COVERAGE NO.	EFFECTIVE DATE

MEDICARE NO.	MEDICAID NO.	EFFECTIVE DATE	SOC. SEC. NO.
321-10-2653B			321-10-2653

REFERRED BY: UPIN # 402131

George Gentle, M.D. 1000 N. Main Street, Woodland Hills, XY 12345

DATE	PROGRESS
12-15-9x	New pt comes in complaining of chest pain +
	shortness of breath
	Exam essentially N
	EKG done to rule out myocardial infarction
	Imp: ASCVD - angina pectoris
	Given Rx + advised to ret in 1 mo.
	Perry Cardi M.D.

FIGURE 12-3

STATEMENT

College Clinic
4567 Broad Avenue
Woodland Hills, XY 12345-0001
Telephone: 013-486-9002
Fax: 013-487-8976

Mrs. Elsa M. Mooney
5750 Canyon Road
Woodland Hills, XY 12345-0001

DATE	PROFESSIONAL SERVICE DESCRIPTION	CHARGE	CREDITS PAYMENTS	CREDITS ADJUSTMENTS	CURRENT BALANCE
12-15-9x	Init OC, D hx/exam, LC decision making				
12-15-9x	EKG c̄ interpret & report				

Due and payable within 10 days. **Pay last amount in balance column** ⇧

Key: PF: Problem-focused **SF:** Straightforward **CON:** Consultation **HCD:** House Call (Day)
EPF: Expanded problem-focused **LC:** Low complexity **CPX:** Complete Phys Exam **HCN:** House Call (Night)
D: Detailed **MC:** Moderate complexity **E:** Emergency **HV:** Hospital visit
C: Comprehensive **HC:** High complexity **ER:** Emergency Dept. **OV:** Office Visit

FIGURE 12-4

HEALTH INSURANCE CLAIM FORM

PICA

E MEDICAID CHAMPUS CHAMPVA GROUP HEALTH PLAN FECA BLK LUNG OTHER

#) (Medicaid #) (Sponsor's SSN) (VA File #) (SSN or ID) (SSN) (ID)

1a. INSURED'S I.D. NUMBER (FOR PROGRAM IN ITEM 1)

NAME (Last Name, First Name, Middle Initial)

3. PATIENT'S BIRTH DATE MM DD YY SEX M F

4. INSURED'S NAME (Last Name, First Name, Middle Initial)

ADDRESS (No., Street)

6. PATIENT RELATIONSHIP TO INSURED Self Spouse Child Other

7. INSURED'S ADDRESS (No., Street)

STATE

8. PATIENT STATUS Single Married Other

Employed Full-Time Student Part-Time Student

CITY STATE

TELEPHONE (Include Area Code) ( )

ZIP CODE

TELEPHONE (INCLUDE AREA CODE) ( )

URED'S NAME (Last Name, First Name, Middle Initial)

10. IS PATIENT'S CONDITION RELATED TO:

11. INSURED'S POLICY GROUP OR FECA NUMBER

URED'S POLICY OR GROUP NUMBER

a. EMPLOYMENT? (CURRENT OR PREVIOUS) YES NO

a. INSURED'S DATE OF BIRTH MM DD YY SEX M F

URED'S DATE OF BIRTH YY SEX M F

b. AUTO ACCIDENT? PLACE (State) YES NO

b. EMPLOYER'S NAME OR SCHOOL NAME

'S NAME OR SCHOOL NAME

c. OTHER ACCIDENT? YES NO

c. INSURANCE PLAN NAME OR PROGRAM NAME

E PLAN NAME OR PROGRAM NAME

10d. RESERVED FOR LOCAL USE

d. IS THERE ANOTHER HEALTH BENEFIT PLAN? YES NO ***If yes***, return to and complete item 9 a-d.

READ BACK OF FORM BEFORE COMPLETING & SIGNING THIS FORM.

S OR AUTHORIZED PERSON'S SIGNATURE I authorize the release of any medical or other information necessary this claim. I also request payment of government benefits either to myself or to the party who accepts assignment

DATE

13. INSURED'S OR AUTHORIZED PERSON'S SIGNATURE I authorize payment of medical benefits to the undersigned physician or supplier for services described below.

SIGNED

PATIENT AND INSURED INFORMATION

CURRENT:) YY ILLNESS (First symptom) OR INJURY (Accident) OR PREGNANCY(LMP)

15. IF PATIENT HAS HAD SAME OR SIMILAR ILLNESS. GIVE FIRST DATE MM DD YY

16. DATES PATIENT UNABLE TO WORK IN CURRENT OCCUPATION FROM MM DD YY TO MM DD YY

REFERRING PHYSICIAN OR OTHER SOURCE

17a. I.D. NUMBER OF REFERRING PHYSICIAN

18. HOSPITALIZATION DATES RELATED TO CURRENT SERVICES FROM MM DD YY TO MM DD YY

D FOR LOCAL USE

20. OUTSIDE LAB? YES NO $ CHARGES

IS OR NATURE OF ILLNESS OR INJURY. (RELATE ITEMS 1,2,3 OR 4 TO ITEM 24E BY LINE)

22. MEDICAID RESUBMISSION CODE ORIGINAL REF. NO.

. — 3. ___ . ___

23. PRIOR AUTHORIZATION NUMBER

. — 4. ___ . ___

TE(S) OF SERVICE YY	MM	To DD	YY	B Place of Service	C Type of Service	D PROCEDURES, SERVICES, OR SUPPLIES (Explain Unusual Circumstances) CPT/HCPCS | MODIFIER	E DIAGNOSIS CODE	F $ CHARGES	G DAYS OR UNITS	H EPSDT Family Plan	I EMG	J COB	K RESERVED FOR LOCAL USE

TAX I.D. NUMBER SSN EIN

26. PATIENT'S ACCOUNT NO.

27. ACCEPT ASSIGNMENT? (For govt. claims, see back) YES NO

28. TOTAL CHARGE $

29. AMOUNT PAID $

30. BALANCE DUE $

RE OF PHYSICIAN OR SUPPLIER G DEGREES OR CREDENTIALS at the statements on the reverse is bill and are made a part thereof.)

DATE

32. NAME AND ADDRESS OF FACILITY WHERE SERVICES WERE RENDERED (If other than home or office)

33. PHYSICIAN'S, SUPPLIER'S BILLING NAME, ADDRESS, ZIP CODE & PHONE #

PIN# GRP#

PHYSICIAN OR SUPPLIER INFORMATION

VED BY AMA COUNCIL ON MEDICAL SERVICE 8/88)

PLEASE PRINT OR TYPE

FORM HCFA-1500 (U2) (12-90)
FORM OWCP-1500 FORM RRB-1500

FIGURE 12-5

3. If Dr. Cardi is a **nonparticipating** physician in the Medicare program, what is the maximum (limiting charge) he can bill for the **office visit**? $________________

ASSIGNMENT 41

1. Complete the *HCFA-1500 Form* (Fig. 12–8) using OCR guidelines, directing it to the primary insurance carrier. This assignment requires two claim forms, so make a photocopy of the HCFA-1500 claim form. See Chapter 6 of the *Handbook* for help in completing these forms. Refer to Peter F. Donlon's patient record (Fig. 12–6) and ledger card (Fig. 12–7) for information. Refer to Appendix A to fill in the fees on the ledger card. Date the claim May 14. Dr. Antrum is not accepting assignment in this case. For a nonparticipating physician, use the limiting charge column of the mock fee schedule.
2. Use your *CPT Code Book* or Appendix A to determine the correct five-digit code number and modifiers for each professional service rendered. Refer to Appendix B for HCPCS procedure codes and modifiers.
3. Record on the ledger card when you have billed the primary insurance carrier.
4. On July 3, the insurance carrier paid $400 (check No. 45632) on this claim. Post this payment to the patient's ledger card. *Note:* The EOB from the insurance carrier would be sent with a completed HCFA 1500 claim form to Medicare.

Abbreviations pertinent to this record:

adm ________________	NC ________________
a.m. ________________	OC ________________
auto ________________	PO ________________
ER ________________	postop ________________
est ________________	Pt ________________
hosp ________________	surg ________________
hrs ________________	c̄ ________________
imp ________________	

PATIENT RECORD

Donlon, — Peter — F. — 08-09-24 — M — 013/762-3580
LAST NAME — FIRST NAME — MIDDLE NAME — BIRTH DATE — SEX — HOME PHONE

1840 East Chevy Chase Drive, — Woodland Hills, — XY — 12345
ADDRESS — CITY — STATE — ZIP CODE

retired chef
PATIENT'S OCCUPATION — NAME OF COMPANY

ADDRESS OF EMPLOYER — PHONE

wife deceased
SPOUSE OR PARENT — OCCUPATION

EMPLOYER — ADDRESS — PHONE

Medicare
NAME OF INSURANCE GROUP — SUBSCRIBER — Policy #34276

Farmers Insurance Co. (auto ins) 10 N. Main St., Woodland Hills, XY 12345
BLUE SHIELD OR BLUE CROSS CERT. NO. — GROUP NO. — CURRENT COVERAGE NO. — EFFECTIVE DATE

987-65-4321A — 987-65-4321
MEDICARE NO. — MEDICAID NO. — EFFECTIVE DATE — SOC. SEC. NO.

REFERRED BY: — PIN # 271[illegible]
Martha Frederick, MD 1000 N. Main Street, Woodland Hills, XY 12345

DATE	PROGRESS
5-1-9x	Est pt injured in auto accident. Dr. called to ER (Sunday) from outside hosp at 3 a.m. Pt complains of acute headache & 2.0 cm laceration of nose. Request ER consult c̄ neurologist, Dr. Parkinson, who rec pt be adm to hosp. Sutured 2.0 cm laceration of nose. Pt admit. Imp: Acute cephalgia, nasal laceration, deviated septum.
5-2 & 5-3-9x	Hosp visits *Concha Antrum, MD*
5-4-9x	Discharged from hosp. See hosp records for daily notes. *C Antrum*
5-7-9x	Sutures removed. Recommended to have septoplasty surg. *C Antrum*
5-9-9x	Adm to hosp *C Antrum*
5-10-9x	Septoplasty. Pt doing well after surg. *C Antrum*
5-11-9x	Hosp visit. Pt seems to be improving. No hemorrhaging. Discharge *Concha Antrum, MD*
5-12-9x	Postop anterior nasal hemorrhage & cauterization of rt side. *C Antrum*

FIGURE 12-6

STATEMENT

College Clinic
4567 Broad Avenue
Woodland Hills, XY 12345-0001
Telephone: 013-486-9002
Fax: 013-487-8976

Mr. Peter F. Donlon
1840 East Chevy Chase Drive
Woodland Hills, XY 12345-0001

DATE	PROFESSIONAL SERVICE DESCRIPTION	CHARGE	CREDITS PAYMENTS	CREDITS ADJUSTMENTS	CURRENT BALANCE
5-1-9x	ER, D hx/exam, MC decision making				
5-1-9x	Suture 2.0 cm laceration of nose				
5-2-9x	HV, PF hx/exam, LC decision making				
5-3-9x	HV, PF hx/exam, LC decision making				
5-4-9x	Hospital discharge				
5-7-9x	OC, D hx/exam, MC decision making				
5-9-9x	Hosp. adm, D hx/exam, LC decision making				
5-10-9x	Septoplasty				
5-11-9x	Hospital discharge				
5-12-9x	OV, PO nasal hemorrhage				

Due and payable within 10 days. **Pay last amount in balance column** ⇧

Key: **PF:** Problem-focused; **EPF:** Expanded problem-focused; **D:** Detailed; **C:** Comprehensive; **SF:** Straightforward; **LC:** Low complexity; **MC:** Moderate complexity; **HC:** High complexity; **CON:** Consultation; **CPX:** Complete Phys Exam; **E:** Emergency; **ER:** Emergency Dept.; **HCD:** House Call (Day); **HCN:** House Call (Night); **HV:** Hospital visit; **OV:** Office Visit

FIGURE 12-7

PICA

HEALTH INSURANCE CLAIM FORM

1. MEDICARE (Medicare #) MEDICAID (Medicaid #) CHAMPUS (Sponsor's SSN) CHAMPVA (VA File #) GROUP HEALTH PLAN (SSN or ID) FECA BLK LUNG (SSN) OTHER (ID)

1a. INSURED'S I.D. NUMBER (FOR PROGRAM

2. PATIENT'S NAME (Last Name, First Name, Middle Initial)

3. PATIENT'S BIRTH DATE MM DD YY SEX M F

4. INSURED'S NAME (Last Name, First Name, Middle Initial)

5. PATIENT'S ADDRESS (No., Street)

6. PATIENT RELATIONSHIP TO INSURED Self Spouse Child Other

7. INSURED'S ADDRESS (No., Street)

CITY STATE

8. PATIENT STATUS Single Married Other

CITY S

ZIP CODE TELEPHONE (Include Area Code) ( )

Employed Full-Time Student Part-Time Student

ZIP CODE TELEPHONE (INCLUDE ARE ( )

9. OTHER INSURED'S NAME (Last Name, First Name, Middle Initial)

10. IS PATIENT'S CONDITION RELATED TO:

11. INSURED'S POLICY GROUP OR FECA NUMBER

a. OTHER INSURED'S POLICY OR GROUP NUMBER

a. EMPLOYMENT? (CURRENT OR PREVIOUS) YES NO

a. INSURED'S DATE OF BIRTH MM DD YY SEX M F

b. OTHER INSURED'S DATE OF BIRTH MM DD YY SEX M F

b. AUTO ACCIDENT? PLACE (State) YES NO

b. EMPLOYER'S NAME OR SCHOOL NAME

c. EMPLOYER'S NAME OR SCHOOL NAME

c. OTHER ACCIDENT? YES NO

c. INSURANCE PLAN NAME OR PROGRAM NAME

d. INSURANCE PLAN NAME OR PROGRAM NAME

10d. RESERVED FOR LOCAL USE

d. IS THERE ANOTHER HEALTH BENEFIT PLAN? YES NO ***If yes***, return to and complete ite

READ BACK OF FORM BEFORE COMPLETING & SIGNING THIS FORM.

12. PATIENT'S OR AUTHORIZED PERSON'S SIGNATURE I authorize the release of any medical or other information necessary to process this claim. I also request payment of government benefits either to myself or to the party who accepts assignment below.

SIGNED ______________________ DATE ______________

13. INSURED'S OR AUTHORIZED PERSON'S SIGNATURE I au payment of medical benefits to the undersigned physician or s services described below.

SIGNED ______________________

14. DATE OF CURRENT: MM DD YY ◀ ILLNESS (First symptom) OR INJURY (Accident) OR PREGNANCY(LMP)

15. IF PATIENT HAS HAD SAME OR SIMILAR ILLNESS. GIVE FIRST DATE MM DD YY

16. DATES PATIENT UNABLE TO WORK IN CURRENT OCCUP FROM MM DD YY TO MM DD

17. NAME OF REFERRING PHYSICIAN OR OTHER SOURCE

17a. I.D. NUMBER OF REFERRING PHYSICIAN

18. HOSPITALIZATION DATES RELATED TO CURRENT SERV FROM MM DD YY TO MM DD

19. RESERVED FOR LOCAL USE

20. OUTSIDE LAB? YES NO $ CHARGES

21. DIAGNOSIS OR NATURE OF ILLNESS OR INJURY. (RELATE ITEMS 1,2,3 OR 4 TO ITEM 24E BY LINE)

1. ____ . __

2. ____ . __

3. ____ . __

4. ____ . __

22. MEDICAID RESUBMISSION CODE ORIGINAL REF. NO.

23. PRIOR AUTHORIZATION NUMBER

24. A DATE(S) OF SERVICE From MM DD YY To MM DD YY	B Place of Service	C Type of Service	D PROCEDURES, SERVICES, OR SUPPLIES (Explain Unusual Circumstances) CPT/HCPCS MODIFIER	E DIAGNOSIS CODE	F $ CHARGES	G DAYS OR UNITS	H EPSDT Family Plan	I EMG	J COB	RESER LOCA
1										
2										
3										
4										
5										
6										

25. FEDERAL TAX I.D. NUMBER SSN EIN

26. PATIENT'S ACCOUNT NO.

27. ACCEPT ASSIGNMENT? (For govt. claims, see back) YES NO

28. TOTAL CHARGE $

29. AMOUNT PAID $

30. BALA $

31. SIGNATURE OF PHYSICIAN OR SUPPLIER INCLUDING DEGREES OR CREDENTIALS (I certify that the statements on the reverse apply to this bill and are made a part thereof.)

SIGNED DATE

32. NAME AND ADDRESS OF FACILITY WHERE SERVICES WERE RENDERED (If other than home or office)

33. PHYSICIAN'S, SUPPLIER'S BILLING NAME, ADDRESS, ZIP & PHONE #

PIN# GRP#

(APPROVED BY AMA COUNCIL ON MEDICAL SERVICE 8/88)

PLEASE PRINT OR TYPE

FORM HCFA-1500 (U2) (12-90)
FORM OWCP-1500 FOR

FIGURE 12-8

ASSIGNMENT 42

1. Complete the *Medicare Form* (Fig. 12–11) using OCR guidelines. This case involves a patient who has a Medigap supplemental policy that is secondary payer. Refer to Chapters 6 and 12 and Figure 12–11 for instructions on how to complete the HCFA-1500 claim form. Refer to Jeremiah W. Diffenderffer's patient record (Fig. 12–9) and ledger card (Fig. 12–10) for information. See Appendix A to fill in the fees on the ledger card. Date the claim June 13. Dr. Coccidioides is accepting assignment in this case. Mr. Diffenderffer has met his deductible for the year, owing to previous care by Dr. Coccidioides in March. (This part of the case has been omitted from the patient record for the sake of brevity.)
2. Use your *CPT Code Book* or Appendix A to determine the correct five-digit code number and modifiers for each professional service rendered. In this case the doctor is billing for the x-rays and bronchogram. Refer to Appendix B for HCPCS procedure codes and modifiers.
3. Record on the ledger card the proper information when you have billed Medicare.
4. On August 3, Medicare paid $240 (Check No. 654821) on this claim. Post this payment to the patient's ledger card. Medicare allowed $300 on this claim. Post the balance due from the patient.

Abbreviations pertinent to this record:

adv ____________________

AP ____________________

CPX ____________________

est ____________________

exam ____________________

HCN ____________________

imp ____________________

lat ____________________

phys ____________________

pt ____________________

re-exam ____________________

t.i.d. ____________________

wk ____________________

PATIENT RECORD

LAST NAME	FIRST NAME	MIDDLE NAME	BIRTH DATE	SEX	HOME PHONE
Diffenderffer,	Jeremiah	W.	08-24-31	M	013/471-9930

ADDRESS	CITY	STATE	ZIP CODE
120 Elm Street,	Woodland Hills,	XY	12345

PATIENT'S OCCUPATION	NAME OF COMPANY
retired painter	

ADDRESS OF EMPLOYER	PHONE

SPOUSE OR PARENT	OCCUPATION
deceased	

EMPLOYER	ADDRESS	PHONE

NAME OF INSURANCE GROUP	SUBSCRIBER
Medicare	

BLUE SHIELD OR BLUE CROSS CERT. NO.	GROUP NO.	CURRENT COVERAGE NO.	EFFECTIVE DATE
United American Insurance Co., P.O. Box 810, Dallas, TX 75221 214/328-2841			

MEDICARE NO.	MEDICAID NO.	EFFECTIVE DATE	SOC. SEC. NO.
731-32-7401T Other insurance Policy #007559715			731-32-7401

United American carrier's unique ED# 7211

REFERRED BY:
John M. Diffenderffer (brother)

DATE	PROGRESS
6-1-9x	Est pt phoned, Dr, ordered chest x-rays to be taken in office this p.m. as well as bilateral bronchogram. *B Coccidioides*
6-2-9x	Ap & lat chest x-rays showed pulmonary emphysema. Bilateral bronchogram showed pulmonary emphysema. Adv put to come in for PE *BC*
6-5-9x	Pt given comprehensive physical re-exam. Imp: bronchitis and pneumonitis due to inhalation of fumes and vapors at home. Adv. bed rest. *Brady Coccidioides MD*
6-12-9x	HCN 8 p.m., exam, administered medication (Coramine 1.5 ml two ampules IV). Imp: recurrent bronchitis and pneumonitis, exertional dyspnea. Adv. bed rest. To be seen in 1 wk. *Brady Coccidioides MD*

FIGURE 12-9

STATEMENT

College Clinic
4567 Broad Avenue
Woodland Hills, XY 12345-0001
Telephone: 013-486-9002
Fax: 013-487-8976

Mr. Jeremiah W. Diffenderffer
120 Elm Street
Woodland Hills, XY 12345-0001

DATE	PROFESSIONAL SERVICE DESCRIPTION	CHARGE	CREDITS PAYMENTS	CREDITS ADJUSTMENTS	CURRENT BALANCE
	Balance forward				20 00
6-1-9x	Chest x-rays (2 views)				
6-1-9x	Bilateral bronchogram				
6-5-9x	C hx/exam, HC decision making				
6-12-9x	HCN, PF hx/exam, MC decision making				
6-12-9x	Coramine IV (nikethamide) Pt seen at 8 p.m.	25 00			

Due and payable within 10 days. **Pay last amount in balance column** ⇧

Key: **PF:** Problem-focused **EPF:** Expanded problem-focused **D:** Detailed **C:** Comprehensive **SF:** Straightforward **LC:** Low complexity **MC:** Moderate complexity **HC:** High complexity **CON:** Consultation **CPX:** Complete Phys Exam **E:** Emergency **ER:** Emergency Dept. **HCD:** House Call (Day) **HCN:** House Call (Night) **HV:** Hospital visit **OV:** Office Visit

FIGURE 12-10

PICA

HEALTH INSURANCE CLAIM FORM

1. MEDICARE (Medicare #) MEDICAID (Medicaid #) CHAMPUS (Sponsor's SSN) CHAMPVA (VA File #) GROUP HEALTH PLAN (SSN or ID) FECA BLK LUNG (SSN) OTHER (ID)

1a. INSURED'S I.D. NUMBER (FOR PROGRAM

2. PATIENT'S NAME (Last Name, First Name, Middle Initial)

3. PATIENT'S BIRTH DATE MM DD YY SEX M F

4. INSURED'S NAME (Last Name, First Name, Middle Initial)

5. PATIENT'S ADDRESS (No., Street)

6. PATIENT RELATIONSHIP TO INSURED Self Spouse Child Other

7. INSURED'S ADDRESS (No., Street)

CITY STATE

8. PATIENT STATUS Single Married Other

CITY S

ZIP CODE TELEPHONE (Include Area Code) ( )

Employed Full-Time Student Part-Time Student

ZIP CODE TELEPHONE (INCLUDE ARE ( )

9. OTHER INSURED'S NAME (Last Name, First Name, Middle Initial)

10. IS PATIENT'S CONDITION RELATED TO:

11. INSURED'S POLICY GROUP OR FECA NUMBER

a. OTHER INSURED'S POLICY OR GROUP NUMBER

a. EMPLOYMENT? (CURRENT OR PREVIOUS) YES NO

a. INSURED'S DATE OF BIRTH MM DD YY SEX M F

b. OTHER INSURED'S DATE OF BIRTH MM DD YY SEX M F

b. AUTO ACCIDENT? PLACE (State) YES NO

b. EMPLOYER'S NAME OR SCHOOL NAME

c. EMPLOYER'S NAME OR SCHOOL NAME

c. OTHER ACCIDENT? YES NO

c. INSURANCE PLAN NAME OR PROGRAM NAME

d. INSURANCE PLAN NAME OR PROGRAM NAME

10d. RESERVED FOR LOCAL USE

d. IS THERE ANOTHER HEALTH BENEFIT PLAN? YES NO ***If yes***, return to and complete ite

READ BACK OF FORM BEFORE COMPLETING & SIGNING THIS FORM.

12. PATIENT'S OR AUTHORIZED PERSON'S SIGNATURE I authorize the release of any medical or other information necessary to process this claim. I also request payment of government benefits either to myself or to the party who accepts assignment below.

SIGNED ____________ DATE ____________

13. INSURED'S OR AUTHORIZED PERSON'S SIGNATURE I au payment of medical benefits to the undersigned physician or s services described below.

SIGNED ____________

14. DATE OF CURRENT: MM DD YY ◀ ILLNESS (First symptom) OR INJURY (Accident) OR PREGNANCY(LMP)

15. IF PATIENT HAS HAD SAME OR SIMILAR ILLNESS. GIVE FIRST DATE MM DD YY

16. DATES PATIENT UNABLE TO WORK IN CURRENT OCCUP FROM MM DD YY TO MM DD

17. NAME OF REFERRING PHYSICIAN OR OTHER SOURCE

17a. I.D. NUMBER OF REFERRING PHYSICIAN

18. HOSPITALIZATION DATES RELATED TO CURRENT SERVI FROM MM DD YY TO MM DD

19. RESERVED FOR LOCAL USE

20. OUTSIDE LAB? YES NO $ CHARGES

21. DIAGNOSIS OR NATURE OF ILLNESS OR INJURY. (RELATE ITEMS 1,2,3 OR 4 TO ITEM 24E BY LINE)

1. ____ . __ 3. ____ . __

2. ____ . __ 4. ____ . __

22. MEDICAID RESUBMISSION CODE ORIGINAL REF. NO.

23. PRIOR AUTHORIZATION NUMBER

24. A DATE(S) OF SERVICE From MM DD YY	To MM DD YY	B Place of Service	C Type of Service	D PROCEDURES, SERVICES, OR SUPPLIES (Explain Unusual Circumstances) CPT/HCPCS MODIFIER	E DIAGNOSIS CODE	F $ CHARGES	G DAYS OR UNITS	H EPSDT Family Plan	I EMG	J COB	RESER LOCA
1											
2											
3											
4											
5											
6											

25. FEDERAL TAX I.D. NUMBER SSN EIN

26. PATIENT'S ACCOUNT NO.

27. ACCEPT ASSIGNMENT? (For govt. claims, see back) YES NO

28. TOTAL CHARGE $

29. AMOUNT PAID $

30. BALA $

31. SIGNATURE OF PHYSICIAN OR SUPPLIER INCLUDING DEGREES OR CREDENTIALS (I certify that the statements on the reverse apply to this bill and are made a part thereof.)

SIGNED DATE

32. NAME AND ADDRESS OF FACILITY WHERE SERVICES WERE RENDERED (If other than home or office)

33. PHYSICIAN'S, SUPPLIER'S BILLING NAME, ADDRESS, ZIP & PHONE #

PIN# GRP#

(APPROVED BY AMA COUNCIL ON MEDICAL SERVICE 8/88)

PLEASE PRINT OR TYPE

FORM HCFA-1500 (U2) (12-90)
FORM OWCP-1500 FOR

FIGURE 12-11

ASSIGNMENT 43

1. Complete the *Medicare Form** (Fig. 12–14) using OCR guidelines, directing it to your local fiscal intermediary. This assignment requires two claim forms, so make a photocopy of the HCFA-1500 claim form. Refer to Raymond D. Fay's patient record (Fig. 12–12) and ledger card (Fig. 12–13) for information. Refer to Appendix A to fill in the fees on the ledger card. Date the claim December 31. Dr. Antrum is accepting assignment in this case. Mr. Fay has met his deductible for the year, owing to previous care by another physician.
2. One of the services is disallowed by Medicare. For this reason, complete the waiver agreement form (Figure 12-15)
3. Use your *CPT Code Book* or Appendix A to determine the correct five-digit code number and modifiers for each professional service rendered. Refer to Appendix B for HCPCS procedure codes and modifiers.
4. Record on the ledger card the proper information when you have billed Medicare.
5. On February 4, Medicare paid $360 (check No. 438911) on this claim. Post this payment to the patient's ledger card. Medicare allowed $450 on this claim. Post the courtesy adjustment. Post the balance due from the patient.

Abbreviations pertinent to this record:

exam ______________________ OV ______________________

imp ______________________ Pt ______________________

inj ______________________ retn ______________________

N ______________________ X ______________________

OC ______________________

*See Chapter 6 of the *Handbook* for help in completing this form and refer to Figure 6-7.

PATIENT RECORD

Fay,	Raymond		02-03-02	M	013/788-9090
LAST NAME	FIRST NAME	MIDDLE NAME	BIRTH DATE	SEX	HOME PHONE

333 North Pencil Avenue,	Woodland Hills,	XY	12345
ADDRESS	CITY	STATE	ZIP CODE

retired railroad engineer	Santa Fe Railroad
PATIENT'S OCCUPATION	NAME OF COMPANY

ADDRESS OF EMPLOYER	PHONE

Marilyn B. Fay	homemaker
SPOUSE OR PARENT	OCCUPATION

EMPLOYER	ADDRESS	PHONE

Medicare	
NAME OF INSURANCE GROUP	SUBSCRIBER

BLUE SHIELD OR BLUE CROSS CERT. NO.	GROUP NO.	CURRENT COVERAGE NO.	EFFECTIVE DATE

WA 887-66-1235			887-66-1235
MEDICARE NO.	MEDICAID NO.	EFFECTIVE DATE	SOC. SEC. NO.

REFERRED BY: UPIN # 402131

George Gentle, M.D. 1000 N. Main Street, Woodland Hills, XY 12345

DATE	PROGRESS
10-31-9x	New pt complains of dizziness for 3 days. Exam essentially N
	Imp: food & inhalant allergy. Retn in 4 days for tests C. Antrum, MD
11-4-9x	Audiometric hearing tests (air, bone, and speech) - N.
	Spontaneous nystagmus, including gaze test - N.
	10 intradermal allergy tests C. Antrum, MD
11-10-9x	Bilateral mastoid X
	OV ltd. Pt to retn daily for desensitization inj. C. Antrum, MD
11-11-9x	OC minimal desensitization inj
thru	" " " "
12-11-9x	Improved & discharged (31) C. Antrum, M.D.

FIGURE 12-12

STATEMENT

College Clinic
4567 Broad Avenue
Woodland Hills, XY 12345-0001
Telephone: 013-486-9002
Fax: 013-487-8976

Mr. Raymond D. Fay
333 North Pencil Avenue
Woodland Hills, XY 12345-0001

DATE	PROFESSIONAL SERVICE DESCRIPTION	CHARGE	CREDITS		CURRENT BALANCE
			PAYMENTS	ADJUSTMENTS	
10-31-9x	OC, D hx/exam, LC decision making				
11-4-9x	Audiometric comp. hearing test (air, bone, and speech)				
11-4-9x	Nystagmus, spontaneous test				
11-4-9x	10 intradermal allergy tests allergenic extracts				
11-10-9x	Mastoid x-rays complete				
11-10-9x	OC, EPF hx/exam, LC decision making				
11-11-9x to 12-11-9x	Desensitization injections (31) @ $15 each				

Due and payable within 10 days. **Pay last amount in balance column** ⇧

Key:
- **PF:** Problem-focused
- **EPF:** Expanded problem-focused
- **D:** Detailed
- **C:** Comprehensive
- **SF:** Straightforward
- **LC:** Low complexity
- **MC:** Moderate complexity
- **HC:** High complexity
- **CON:** Consultation
- **CPX:** Complete Phys Exam
- **E:** Emergency
- **ER:** Emergency Dept.
- **HCD:** House Call (Day)
- **HCN:** House Call (Night)
- **HV:** Hospital visit
- **OV:** Office Visit

FIGURE 12-13

PICA

HEALTH INSURANCE CLAIM FORM

P

1. MEDICARE (Medicare #) | MEDICAID (Medicaid #) | CHAMPUS (Sponsor's SSN) | CHAMPVA (VA File #) | GROUP HEALTH PLAN (SSN or ID) | FECA BLK LUNG (SSN) | OTHER (ID)

1a. INSURED'S I.D. NUMBER (FOR PROGRAM I

2. PATIENT'S NAME (Last Name, First Name, Middle Initial)

3. PATIENT'S BIRTH DATE MM | DD | YY SEX M ☐ F ☐

4. INSURED'S NAME (Last Name, First Name, Middle Initial)

5. PATIENT'S ADDRESS (No., Street)

6. PATIENT RELATIONSHIP TO INSURED Self ☐ Spouse ☐ Child ☐ Other ☐

7. INSURED'S ADDRESS (No., Street)

CITY | STATE

8. PATIENT STATUS Single ☐ Married ☐ Other ☐ Employed ☐ Full-Time Student ☐ Part-Time Student ☐

CITY | S

ZIP CODE | TELEPHONE (Include Area Code) ( )

ZIP CODE | TELEPHONE (INCLUDE AREA ( )

9. OTHER INSURED'S NAME (Last Name, First Name, Middle Initial)

10. IS PATIENT'S CONDITION RELATED TO:

11. INSURED'S POLICY GROUP OR FECA NUMBER

a. OTHER INSURED'S POLICY OR GROUP NUMBER

a. EMPLOYMENT? (CURRENT OR PREVIOUS) ☐ YES ☐ NO

a. INSURED'S DATE OF BIRTH MM | DD | YY SEX M ☐ F

b. OTHER INSURED'S DATE OF BIRTH MM | DD | YY SEX M ☐ F ☐

b. AUTO ACCIDENT? ☐ YES ☐ NO PLACE (State)

b. EMPLOYER'S NAME OR SCHOOL NAME

c. EMPLOYER'S NAME OR SCHOOL NAME

c. OTHER ACCIDENT? ☐ YES ☐ NO

c. INSURANCE PLAN NAME OR PROGRAM NAME

d. INSURANCE PLAN NAME OR PROGRAM NAME

10d. RESERVED FOR LOCAL USE

d. IS THERE ANOTHER HEALTH BENEFIT PLAN? ☐ YES ☐ NO *If yes*, return to and complete ite

READ BACK OF FORM BEFORE COMPLETING & SIGNING THIS FORM.

12. PATIENT'S OR AUTHORIZED PERSON'S SIGNATURE I authorize the release of any medical or other information necessary to process this claim. I also request payment of government benefits either to myself or to the party who accepts assignment below.

SIGNED ______________ DATE ______________

13. INSURED'S OR AUTHORIZED PERSON'S SIGNATURE I au payment of medical benefits to the undersigned physician or s services described below.

SIGNED ______________

14. DATE OF CURRENT: MM | DD | YY ◀ ILLNESS (First symptom) OR INJURY (Accident) OR PREGNANCY(LMP)

15. IF PATIENT HAS HAD SAME OR SIMILAR ILLNESS. GIVE FIRST DATE MM | DD | YY

16. DATES PATIENT UNABLE TO WORK IN CURRENT OCCUP FROM MM | DD | YY TO MM | DD

17. NAME OF REFERRING PHYSICIAN OR OTHER SOURCE

17a. I.D. NUMBER OF REFERRING PHYSICIAN

18. HOSPITALIZATION DATES RELATED TO CURRENT SERV FROM MM | DD | YY TO MM | DD

19. RESERVED FOR LOCAL USE

20. OUTSIDE LAB? ☐ YES ☐ NO $ CHARGES

21. DIAGNOSIS OR NATURE OF ILLNESS OR INJURY. (RELATE ITEMS 1,2,3 OR 4 TO ITEM 24E BY LINE)

1. ___ . __
2. ___ . __
3. ___ . __
4. ___ . __

22. MEDICAID RESUBMISSION CODE | ORIGINAL REF. NO.

23. PRIOR AUTHORIZATION NUMBER

24. A DATE(S) OF SERVICE From MM DD YY	To MM DD YY	B Place of Service	C Type of Service	D PROCEDURES, SERVICES, OR SUPPLIES (Explain Unusual Circumstances) CPT/HCPCS | MODIFIER	E DIAGNOSIS CODE	F $ CHARGES	G DAYS OR UNITS	H EPSDT Family Plan	I EMG	J COB	RESER LOCA
1											
2											
3											
4											
5											
6											

25. FEDERAL TAX I.D. NUMBER SSN EIN ☐ ☐

26. PATIENT'S ACCOUNT NO.

27. ACCEPT ASSIGNMENT? (For govt. claims, see back) ☐ YES ☐ NO

28. TOTAL CHARGE $

29. AMOUNT PAID $

30. BALA $

31. SIGNATURE OF PHYSICIAN OR SUPPLIER INCLUDING DEGREES OR CREDENTIALS (I certify that the statements on the reverse apply to this bill and are made a part thereof.)

SIGNED DATE

32. NAME AND ADDRESS OF FACILITY WHERE SERVICES WERE RENDERED (If other than home or office)

33. PHYSICIAN'S, SUPPLIER'S BILLING NAME, ADDRESS, ZIP & PHONE #

PIN# GRP#

(APPROVED BY AMA COUNCIL ON MEDICAL SERVICE 8/88)

PLEASE PRINT OR TYPE

FORM HCFA-1500 (U2) (12-90)
FORM OWCP-1500 FOR

FIGURE 12-14

College Clinic
4567 Broad Avenue
Woodland Hills, XY 12345-0001

ADVANCE NOTICE MEDICARE BENEFICIARY AGREEMENT

If Medicare determines that a particular service, although it would be otherwise covered, is not reasonable and necessary under Medicare program standards, Medicare will deny payment for that service. In your case, Medicare might deny payment for:

1.____
2____

for the following reasons:

Medicare does not usually pay for this:
__________many visits or treatments
__________service or this many services within this period of time
__________injection or this many injections
__________because it is a treatment that is yet to be proved effective
__________office visit unless it was needed because of an emergency
__________same services by more than one doctor during the same time period
__________equipment
__________laboratory test
__________visit since it is more than one visit per day
__________extensive procedure
__________same service by more than one doctor of the same specialty
__________nursing home visit since only one is allowed per month

Beneficiary Agreement

I have been notified by my physician that, in my case, Medicare might deny payment for the service(s) checked above. If Medicare denies payment, I agree to be personally and fully responsible for payment.

Raymond Foy________________ November 4, 199x__________
Beneficiary's Signature Date Signed

FIGURE 12-15

ASSIGNMENT 44

1. Complete the *Medicare Form* (Fig. 12–18) using OCR guidelines, directing it to your local Medicare fiscal intermediary. Refer to Chapter 12 and Figure 12-15 for instructions on how to complete the HCFA-1500 claim form. Refer to Mrs. Helen P. Nolan's patient record (Fig. 12–16) and ledger card (Fig. 12–17) for information. Refer to Appendix A to fill in the fees on the ledger card. Date the claim May 31.
2. Use your *CPT Code Book* or Appendix A to determine the correct five-digit code number and modifiers for each professional service rendered. Refer to Appendix B for HCPCS procedure codes and modifiers.
3. Record on the ledger card the proper information when you have billed Medicare/Medicaid. On July 1 you receive a check (No. 107621) from Medicare for $500, and on July 15 you receive a voucher # 3571 from Medicaid for $150. Record these payments on the ledger and show the courtesy adjustment.

Abbreviations pertinent to this record:

adm ______________	OC ______________
adv ______________	phys ______________
BP ______________	prep ______________
Dx ______________	PRN ______________
exam ______________	Pt ______________
ext ______________	Rx ______________
hosp ______________	slt ______________
int ______________	wk ______________
NC ______________	c̄ ______________

PATIENT RECORD

LAST NAME	FIRST NAME	MIDDLE NAME	BIRTH DATE	SEX	HOME PHONE
Nolan,	Helen	P.	05-10-07	F	013/660-9878

ADDRESS	CITY	STATE	ZIP CODE
2588 Cedar Street,	Woodland Hills,	XY	12345

PATIENT'S OCCUPATION	NAME OF COMPANY
homemaker	

ADDRESS OF EMPLOYER	PHONE

SPOUSE OR PARENT	OCCUPATION
James J. Nolan	retired journalist

EMPLOYER	ADDRESS	PHONE

NAME OF INSURANCE GROUP	SUBSCRIBER
Medicare/Medicaid (Medi-Cal)	

BLUE SHIELD OR BLUE CROSS CERT. NO.	GROUP NO.	CURRENT COVERAGE NO.	EFFECTIVE DATE

MEDICARE NO.	MEDICAID NO.	EFFECTIVE DATE	SOC. SEC. NO.
732-32-1573A	19-60-2358490-1-01		732-32-1573

REFERRED BY: James B. Jeffers, M.D., 100 S. Broadway, Woodland Hills, XY 12345 UPIN # 621074

DATE	PROGRESS
5-1-9x	This new pt comes in complaining of constipation & some rectal
	bleeding & pain. Exam reveals int & ext hemorrhoids. BP 120/80.
	Dx: hemorrhoids; int & ext bleeding; anal fistula
	Rx: Adv hospitalization for removal of hemorrhoids. R Rumsey, MD
5-7-9x	Adm to hosp - phys exam & prep hosp records R Rumsey MD
5-8-9x	Hemorrhoidectomy c̄ fistulectomy R Rumsey, MD
5-9-9x	Hosp visit, brief. Pt comfortable, slt pain. R Rumsey MD
5-10-9x	Hosp visit, no pain. Rex Rumsey MD
5-11-9x	Hosp visit. Discharged. To be seen in office in 1 wk. R Rumsey
5-17-9x	Well healed, no pain, return prn. Rex Rumsey, MD.

FIGURE 12-16

STATEMENT

College Clinic
4567 Broad Avenue
Woodland Hills, XY 12345-0001
Telephone: 013-486-9002
Fax: 013-487-8976

Mrs. Helen P. Nolan
2588 Cedar Street
Woodland Hills, XY 12345-0001

DATE	PROFESSIONAL SERVICE DESCRIPTION	CHARGE	CREDITS		CURRENT BALANCE
			PAYMENTS	ADJUSTMENTS	
5-1-9x	OC, D hx/exam, LC decision making				
5-7-9x	Initial HV, C hx/exam, MC decision making				
5-8-9x	Hemorrhoidectomy with fistulectomy				
5-9-9x	HV				
5-10-9x	HV				
5-11-9x	HV				
5-17-9x	OC				

Due and payable within 10 days. **Pay last amount in balance column** ⇧

Key: PF: Problem-focused
EPF: Expanded problem-focused
D: Detailed
C: Comprehensive
SF: Straightforward
LC: Low complexity
MC: Moderate complexity
HC: High complexity
CON: Consultation
CPX: Complete Phys Exam
E: Emergency
ER: Emergency Dept.
HCD: House Call (Day)
HCN: House Call (Night)
HV: Hospital visit
OV: Office Visit

FIGURE 12-17

HEALTH INSURANCE CLAIM FORM

PICA

MEDICAID (Medicaid #) | CHAMPUS (Sponsor's SSN) | CHAMPVA (VA File #) | GROUP HEALTH PLAN (SSN or ID) | FECA BLK LUNG (SSN) | OTHER (ID)

1a. INSURED'S I.D. NUMBER (FOR PROGRAM IN ITEM 1)

AME (Last Name, First Name, Middle Initial)

3. PATIENT'S BIRTH DATE MM DD YY SEX M F

4. INSURED'S NAME (Last Name, First Name, Middle Initial)

DDRESS (No., Street)

6. PATIENT RELATIONSHIP TO INSURED Self Spouse Child Other

7. INSURED'S ADDRESS (No., Street)

STATE

8. PATIENT STATUS Single Married Other

CITY STATE

TELEPHONE (Include Area Code) ( )

Employed Full-Time Student Part-Time Student

ZIP CODE TELEPHONE (INCLUDE AREA CODE) ( )

RED'S NAME (Last Name, First Name, Middle Initial)

10. IS PATIENT'S CONDITION RELATED TO:

11. INSURED'S POLICY GROUP OR FECA NUMBER

RED'S POLICY OR GROUP NUMBER

a. EMPLOYMENT? (CURRENT OR PREVIOUS) YES NO

a. INSURED'S DATE OF BIRTH MM DD YY SEX M F

RED'S DATE OF BIRTH YY SEX M F

b. AUTO ACCIDENT? PLACE (State) YES NO

b. EMPLOYER'S NAME OR SCHOOL NAME

NAME OR SCHOOL NAME

c. OTHER ACCIDENT? YES NO

c. INSURANCE PLAN NAME OR PROGRAM NAME

PLAN NAME OR PROGRAM NAME

10d. RESERVED FOR LOCAL USE

d. IS THERE ANOTHER HEALTH BENEFIT PLAN? YES NO *If yes*, return to and complete item 9 a-d.

READ BACK OF FORM BEFORE COMPLETING & SIGNING THIS FORM.

OR AUTHORIZED PERSON'S SIGNATURE I authorize the release of any medical or other information necessary his claim. I also request payment of government benefits either to myself or to the party who accepts assignment

DATE

13. INSURED'S OR AUTHORIZED PERSON'S SIGNATURE I authorize payment of medical benefits to the undersigned physician or supplier for services described below.

SIGNED

PATIENT AND INSURED INFORMATION

URRENT: YY ILLNESS (First symptom) OR INJURY (Accident) OR PREGNANCY(LMP)

15. IF PATIENT HAS HAD SAME OR SIMILAR ILLNESS. GIVE FIRST DATE MM DD YY

16. DATES PATIENT UNABLE TO WORK IN CURRENT OCCUPATION FROM MM DD YY TO MM DD YY

EFERRING PHYSICIAN OR OTHER SOURCE

17a. I.D. NUMBER OF REFERRING PHYSICIAN

18. HOSPITALIZATION DATES RELATED TO CURRENT SERVICES FROM MM DD YY TO MM DD YY

FOR LOCAL USE

20. OUTSIDE LAB? YES NO $ CHARGES

OR NATURE OF ILLNESS OR INJURY. (RELATE ITEMS 1,2,3 OR 4 TO ITEM 24E BY LINE)

3.

4.

22. MEDICAID RESUBMISSION CODE ORIGINAL REF. NO.

23. PRIOR AUTHORIZATION NUMBER

	B	C	D	E	F	G	H	I	J	K
E(S) OF SERVICE To YY MM DD YY	Place of Service	Type of Service	PROCEDURES, SERVICES, OR SUPPLIES (Explain Unusual Circumstances) CPT/HCPCS MODIFIER	DIAGNOSIS CODE	$ CHARGES	DAYS OR UNITS	EPSDT Family Plan	EMG	COB	RESERVED FOR LOCAL USE

AX I.D. NUMBER SSN EIN

26. PATIENT'S ACCOUNT NO.

27. ACCEPT ASSIGNMENT? (For govt. claims, see back) YES NO

28. TOTAL CHARGE $

29. AMOUNT PAID $

30. BALANCE DUE $

E OF PHYSICIAN OR SUPPLIER DEGREES OR CREDENTIALS the statements on the reverse bill and are made a part thereof.)

DATE

32. NAME AND ADDRESS OF FACILITY WHERE SERVICES WERE RENDERED (If other than home or office)

33. PHYSICIAN'S, SUPPLIER'S BILLING NAME, ADDRESS, ZIP CODE & PHONE #

PIN# GRP#

PHYSICIAN OR SUPPLIER INFORMATION

D BY AMA COUNCIL ON MEDICAL SERVICE 8/88)

PLEASE PRINT OR TYPE

FORM HCFA-1500 (U2) (12-90)
FORM OWCP-1500 FORM RRB-1500

FIGURE 12-18

ASSIGNMENT 45

1. Complete the *Medicare Form* (Fig. 12–21) using OCR guidelines, directing it to your local Medicare fiscal intermediary. Refer to Chapter 12 and Figure 12-15 for instructions on how to complete the HCFA-1500 claim form.Refer to Mr. Harris Fremont's patient record (Fig. 12–19) and ledger card (Fig. 12–20) for information. Refer to Appendix A to fill in the fees on the ledger card. Date the claim October 31.
2. Use your *CPT Code Book* or Appendix A to determine the correct five-digit code number and modifiers for each professional service rendered. Refer to Appendix B for HCPCS procedure codes and modifiers.
3. Record on the ledger card the proper information when you have billed Medicare/ Medicaid.
4. On December 12, Medicare paid $125 (check No. 281362) on this claim. Post this payment to the patient's ledger card. On December 29 you receive a voucher # 7234 from Medicaid for $45. Post this payment to the patient's ledger card and show the courtesy adjustment.

Abbreviations pertinent to this record:

adv ______________________	mo ______________________
AP ______________________	N ______________________
D.P.M. ______________________	OC ______________________
exam ______________________	Pt ______________________
ft ______________________	retn ______________________
imp ______________________	rt ______________________
lat ______________________	Rx ______________________
lt ______________________	

COMPUTER EXERCISE

CASE 3 MEDICARE

Before proceeding, you may want to do an exercise based on the concepts you have learned. Additional practice material is on your computer diskette and will give you a mock experience of electronically transmitting a Medicare claim.

Directions: Insert the diskette into the computer and follow the instructions on the screen for Computer Exercise Case 3.

PATIENT RECORD

LAST NAME	FIRST NAME	MIDDLE NAME	BIRTH DATE	SEX	HOME PHONE
Fremont,	Harris	-	07-10-23	M	013/899-0109

ADDRESS	CITY	STATE	ZIP CODE
735 North Center Street,	Woodland Hills,	XY	12345

PATIENT'S OCCUPATION	NAME OF COMPANY
retired baseball coach	

ADDRESS OF EMPLOYER	PHONE

SPOUSE OR PARENT	OCCUPATION
Emily B. Fremont	homemaker

EMPLOYER	ADDRESS	PHONE

NAME OF INSURANCE GROUP	SUBSCRIBER
Medicare/Medicaid (Medi-Cal)	

BLUE SHIELD OR BLUE CROSS CERT. NO.	GROUP NO.	CURRENT COVERAGE NO.	EFFECTIVE DATE

MEDICARE NO.	MEDICAID NO.	EFFECTIVE DATE	SOC. SEC. NO.
454-01-9569A	56-10-0020205-0-00		454-01-9569

REFERRED BY:

Raymond Skelton, MD

DATE	PROGRESS
10-2-9x	Pt referred by Dr. Skelton. Pt has gout. He comes in complaining
	of discomfort around toes of both feet. Exam shows overgrowth &
	hooking & curving of nails of great & little toes. X-rays of rt
	& lt feet essentially N Gout seen. Rx electrically trimmed away
	overgrowth & adv to retn for further care in 3 days.
	Imp: Onychocryptosis *Nick Pedro DPM*
10-5-9x	Manual debridement of great & little toes. Treated rt & lt feet,
	more thorough trimming of overgrowth & callus formation. To retn
	in 1 mo. *Nick Pedro DPM*

FIGURE 12-19

STATEMENT

College Clinic
4567 Broad Avenue
Woodland Hills, XY 12345-0001
Telephone: 013-486-9002
Fax: 013-487-8976

Mr. Harris Fremont
735 North Center Street
Woodland Hills, XY 12345-0001

DATE	PROFESSIONAL SERVICE DESCRIPTION	CHARGE	CREDITS		CURRENT BALANCE
			PAYMENTS	ADJUSTMENTS	
10-2-9x	OC, D hx/exam, MC decision making				
10-2-9x	AP & lat x-rays R/L feet				
10-2-9x	Debridement nails, elect.				
10-5-9x	OC, PF hx/exam, LC decision making				
10-5-9x	Debridement nails, manual				

Due and payable within 10 days. **Pay last amount in balance column**

Key: **PF:** Problem-focused; **EPF:** Expanded problem-focused; **D:** Detailed; **C:** Comprehensive; **SF:** Straightforward; **LC:** Low complexity; **MC:** Moderate complexity; **HC:** High complexity; **CON:** Consultation; **CPX:** Complete Phys Exam; **E:** Emergency; **ER:** Emergency Dept.; **HCD:** House Call (Day); **HCN:** House Call (Night); **HV:** Hospital visit; **OV:** Office Visit

FIGURE 12-20

PICA

HEALTH INSURANCE CLAIM FORM

1. MEDICARE (Medicare #) MEDICAID (Medicaid #) CHAMPUS (Sponsor's SSN) CHAMPVA (VA File #) GROUP HEALTH PLAN (SSN or ID) FECA BLK LUNG (SSN) OTHER (ID)

1a. INSURED'S I.D. NUMBER (FOR PROGRAM I

2. PATIENT'S NAME (Last Name, First Name, Middle Initial)

3. PATIENT'S BIRTH DATE MM DD YY SEX M F

4. INSURED'S NAME (Last Name, First Name, Middle Initial)

5. PATIENT'S ADDRESS (No., Street)

6. PATIENT RELATIONSHIP TO INSURED Self Spouse Child Other

7. INSURED'S ADDRESS (No., Street)

CITY STATE

8. PATIENT STATUS Single Married Other

CITY S

ZIP CODE TELEPHONE (Include Area Code) ( )

Employed Full-Time Student Part-Time Student

ZIP CODE TELEPHONE (INCLUDE AREA ( )

9. OTHER INSURED'S NAME (Last Name, First Name, Middle Initial)

10. IS PATIENT'S CONDITION RELATED TO:

11. INSURED'S POLICY GROUP OR FECA NUMBER

a. OTHER INSURED'S POLICY OR GROUP NUMBER

a. EMPLOYMENT? (CURRENT OR PREVIOUS) YES NO

a. INSURED'S DATE OF BIRTH MM DD YY SEX M F

b. OTHER INSURED'S DATE OF BIRTH MM DD YY SEX M F

b. AUTO ACCIDENT? PLACE (State) YES NO

b. EMPLOYER'S NAME OR SCHOOL NAME

c. EMPLOYER'S NAME OR SCHOOL NAME

c. OTHER ACCIDENT? YES NO

c. INSURANCE PLAN NAME OR PROGRAM NAME

d. INSURANCE PLAN NAME OR PROGRAM NAME

10d. RESERVED FOR LOCAL USE

d. IS THERE ANOTHER HEALTH BENEFIT PLAN? YES NO *If yes*, return to and complete ite

READ BACK OF FORM BEFORE COMPLETING & SIGNING THIS FORM.

12. PATIENT'S OR AUTHORIZED PERSON'S SIGNATURE I authorize the release of any medical or other information necessary to process this claim. I also request payment of government benefits either to myself or to the party who accepts assignment below.

SIGNED ______ DATE ______

13. INSURED'S OR AUTHORIZED PERSON'S SIGNATURE I au payment of medical benefits to the undersigned physician or s services described below.

SIGNED ______

14. DATE OF CURRENT: MM DD YY ◀ ILLNESS (First symptom) OR INJURY (Accident) OR PREGNANCY(LMP)

15. IF PATIENT HAS HAD SAME OR SIMILAR ILLNESS. GIVE FIRST DATE MM DD YY

16. DATES PATIENT UNABLE TO WORK IN CURRENT OCCUP FROM MM DD YY TO MM DD

17. NAME OF REFERRING PHYSICIAN OR OTHER SOURCE

17a. I.D. NUMBER OF REFERRING PHYSICIAN

18. HOSPITALIZATION DATES RELATED TO CURRENT SERV FROM MM DD YY TO MM DD

19. RESERVED FOR LOCAL USE

20. OUTSIDE LAB? YES NO $ CHARGES

21. DIAGNOSIS OR NATURE OF ILLNESS OR INJURY. (RELATE ITEMS 1,2,3 OR 4 TO ITEM 24E BY LINE)

1. ___ . __ 3. ___ . __

2. ___ . __ 4. ___ . __

22. MEDICAID RESUBMISSION CODE ORIGINAL REF. NO.

23. PRIOR AUTHORIZATION NUMBER

24. A DATE(S) OF SERVICE From MM DD YY To MM DD YY	B Place of Service	C Type of Service	D PROCEDURES, SERVICES, OR SUPPLIES (Explain Unusual Circumstances) CPT/HCPCS MODIFIER	E DIAGNOSIS CODE	F $ CHARGES	G DAYS OR UNITS	H EPSDT Family Plan	I EMG	J COB	RESER LOCA
1										
2										
3										
4										
5										
6										

25. FEDERAL TAX I.D. NUMBER SSN EIN

26. PATIENT'S ACCOUNT NO.

27. ACCEPT ASSIGNMENT? (For govt. claims, see back) YES NO

28. TOTAL CHARGE $

29. AMOUNT PAID $

30. BALA $

31. SIGNATURE OF PHYSICIAN OR SUPPLIER INCLUDING DEGREES OR CREDENTIALS (I certify that the statements on the reverse apply to this bill and are made a part thereof.)

SIGNED DATE

32. NAME AND ADDRESS OF FACILITY WHERE SERVICES WERE RENDERED (If other than home or office)

33. PHYSICIAN'S, SUPPLIER'S BILLING NAME, ADDRESS, ZIP & PHONE #

PIN# GRP#

(APPROVED BY AMA COUNCIL ON MEDICAL SERVICE 8/88)

PLEASE PRINT OR TYPE

FORM HCFA-1500 (U2) (12-90)
FORM OWCP-1500 FOR

FIGURE 12-21

CHAPTER 13

CHAMPUS, CHAMPVA, and TRICARE

Key Terms

Your instructor may wish to select some specific words pertinent to this chapter for a test. For definitions of the terms, further study, and/or reference, the words, phrases, and abbreviations may be found in the Glossary at the end of the textbook. Key terms for this chapter follow:

allowable charge
authorized provider
CHAMPUS
CHAMPUS supplemental insurance
CHAMPUS/TRICARE
CHAMPVA
claims processor
cooperative care
coordination of benefits
cost-share
Defense Enrollment Eligibility Reporting System (DEERS)
fiscal intermediary (FI)
health benefits advisor (HBA)
Inpatient Nonavailability Statement (INAS)
medically (or psychologically) necessary
military treatment facility (MTF)
Nonavailability Statement (NAS)
nonparticipating provider
other health insurance (OHI)
Outpatient Nonavailability Statement (ONAS)
participating provider
partnership program
provider
sponsor
Summary Payment Voucher
uniformed services hospitals

Performance Objectives

The student will be able to

- Define and spell the key terms for this chapter, given the information from the textbook Glossary, within a reasonable period of time and with enough accuracy to obtain a satisfactory evaluation.
- Answer the review questions after reading the chapter, with enough accuracy to obtain a satisfactory evaluation.
- Fill in the correct meaning of each abbreviation, given a list of common medical abbreviations and symbols that appear in chart notes, within a reasonable period of time and with enough accuracy to obtain a satisfactory evaluation.
- Complete each HCFA-1500 Health Insurance Claim Form for billing, given the patients' medical chart notes, ledger cards, and blank insurance claim forms, within a reasonable period of time and with enough accuracy to obtain a satisfactory evaluation.
- Correctly post payments, adjustments, and balances on the patients' ledger cards, using the Mock Fee Schedule in Appendix A, within a reasonable period of time and with enough accuracy to obtain a satisfactory evaluation.
- Compute mathematic calculations, given CHAMPUS problem situations, within a reasonable period of time and with enough accuracy to obtain a satisfactory evaluation.

Study Outline

BACKGROUND
- CHAMPUS
- CHAMPVA

CHAMPUS PROGRAM
- Eligibility
- Defense Enrollment Eligibility Reporting System
- Providers of health care
- CHAMPUS and CHAMPVA identification cards
- Inpatient and outpatient benefits and coverage

CHAMPVA PROGRAM
- Eligibility
- Preauthorization

PRIVACY ACT OF 1974

NONAVAILABILITY STATEMENT

CLAIMS PROCEDURE
- CHAMPUS/CHAMPVA
- Claims offices
- Participating providers
- Nonparticipating providers
- CHAMPUS
- CHAMPVA
  - Instructions for completing a CHAMPVA
- Claim form
- Summary Payment Voucher
- CHAMPUS/CHAMPVA and other insurance
- Claim submission
- Dual or double coverage
- Medicaid or Medigap
- CHAMPUS and Medicare
- CHAMPVA and Medicare
- Third-party liability
- Workers' compensation
- Claims inquiries and appeals

CHAMPUS/TRICARE MANAGED CARE PROGRAMS
- TRICARE Prime
- Benefits
- Enrollment
- Identification Cards
- Primary care manager
- Copayments

TRICARE EXTRA
- Identification Card
- Copayments
- Network provider
- Referrals and precertification
- TRICARE Prime/TRICARE Extra nonavailability statements
- Quality assurance
- Claims procedure
  - TRICARD Standard

Review Questions

Review the objectives, key terms, glossary definitions to key terms, chapter information, and figures before completing the following review questions.

1. CHAMPUS is the acronym for ____

______________________, and CHAMPVA is the acronym for ______________________

____.

2. An active duty service member is known as a/an __________________; once retired, this former member is called a/an ____.
3. Those individuals who serve in the United States armed forces, finish their service, and are honorably discharged are known as a/an ________________________________.
4. CHAMPUS and CHAMPVA are not insurance programs but are considered as ____________________________ programs.
5. An organization that contracts with the government to process CHAMPUS and CHAMPVA health insurance claims is known as a/an __________________________.
6. Name those individuals entitled to CHAMPUS medical benefits.

a. ____

b. ____

c. ____

d. ____

____

e. ____

____

7. Programs that allow CHAMPUS beneficiaries to receive treatment, services, or supplies from civilian providers are called ______________________ and ____________________.
8. A system for verifying an individual's CHAMPUS eligibility is called _____________

____.

9. CHAMPUS and CHAMPVA beneficiary identification cards are issued to _____________

______________________ and ______________________. Information must be obtained from ______________________ and ______________________ of the card and placed on the health insurance claim form.

10. The CHAMPUS deductible for outpatient care is how much per patient?________

Per family? ____

11. What percentage does CHAMPUS pay on outpatient services after the deductible has been met for dependents of active duty members? ____________________ For retired members or their dependents? ________________________________

12. For retired members or their dependents on CHAMPUS, what is their responsibility for outpatient services? ________________________________

13. Name those individuals entitled to CHAMPVA medical benefits.

a. ____

____

b. ____

____

____

c. ____

____

____

14. The public law establishing a person's right to review and contest inaccuracies in personal medical records is known as ________________________________.

15. Mrs. Hancock, a CHAMPUS beneficiary, lives two miles from a Uniformed Services Medical Treatment Facility and wishes to be hospitalized for surgery at Orlando Medical Center, a civilian hospital. What type of authorization does she require? _______

____

16. A CHAMPUS patient may go to an emergency room, private physician, or private hospital for medical care in the following situations.

a. ____

b. ____

c. ____

d. ____

17. The time limit for submitting a CHAMPUS/CHAMPVA claim for

outpatients is ____

inpatients is ____

18. If a patient has other insurance besides CHAMPUS and is the dependent of an active military person, whom do you bill first? ____________________

19. If Jason Williams, a CHAMPUS beneficiary who became disabled at age 10 years and is also receiving Medicare Part A benefits, is seen for a consultation, whom do you bill first?

____

20. A patient is seen as an emergency in the office who is a CHAMPVA and Medicaid beneficiary. Whom do you bill first? ____________________

ASSIGNMENT 46

MATHEMATIC PROBLEMS

Problem 1: It is October 1. In consultation, your physician sees the wife of a Navy man who is stationed at Port Hueneme. Dr. Caesar orders her to the hospital with a suspected ectopic pregnancy. She has a laparotomy and salpingectomy. Here are her bills. Indicate what CHAMPUS will pay.

Dr. Caesar bills:		*CHAMPUS*	
Consultation	$25	______	Patient owes Dr. Caesar $ ______
Salpingectomy	$300	______	
Hospital bill:			
5-day stay, drugs, lab, OR	$1500	______	Patient owes hospital $ ______
Assistant surgeon bill:	$60	______	
Anesthesiologist bill:	$120	______	

Mathematic computation:

Problem 2: Same situation as Problem 1, except that the patient is the wife of a retired military man.

Dr. Caesar bills:		*CHAMPUS*	
Consultation	$25	______	Patient owes Dr. Caesar $ ______
Salpingectomy	$300	______	
Hospital bill:			
5-day stay, drugs, lab, OR	$1500	______	Patient owes hospital $ ______
Assistant surgeon bill:	$60	______	
Anesthesiologist bill:	$120	______	

Mathematic computation:

Problem 3: Your CHAMPUS patient asks you to accept an assignment on her medical care and Dr. Caesar agrees. She has not met her deductible. She is the wife of an active duty man.

Your bill		
Consultation	$ 25	Allowable:$ 25
CBC	10	10
Urinalysis	5	5
Blood serology and complement fixation	17	15
PA & Lt Lat chest x-ray	15	15
EKG	10	10
Spirometry	100	95
TOTAL	$182	$175

How much is your check from CHAMPUS? $______________________

The patient owes the doctor $______________. Doctor Caesar's courtesy adjustment is $______________________.

ASSIGNMENT 47

1. Complete the CHAMPUS Claim Form (Fig. 13–3) using OCR guidelines directing it to your local CHAMPUS fiscal intermediary. Refer to Miss Rosa A. Sandoval's patient record (Fig. 13–1) and ledger card (Fig. 13–2) for information. Refer to Appendix A to fill in the fees on the ledger card. Date the claim May 31. Let us assume the patient's mother brings in a hard copy of a signed Nonavailability Statement DD Form 1251, which shows approval of the physician to treat the patient. Dr. Atrics is not accepting assignment but is completing the claim for the patient's convenience. The family of this patient has not previously met its deductible. See Chapter 6 of the *Handbook* for help in completing the HCFA-1500 claim form and refer to Chapter 13, Figure 13-7..
2. Use your *CPT Code Book* or Appendix A to determine the correct five-digit code number and modifiers for each professional service rendered.
3. On May 11 Mrs. Sandoval makes a partial payment by check (No. 4013) of $90. Record the proper information on the ledger card for the payment, and note when you have billed CHAMPUS (May 31).

Abbreviations pertinent to this record:

adv ______________ HV ______________

a.m. ______________ imp ______________

ER ______________ OC ______________

exam ______________ ofc ______________

FU ______________ PRN ______________

pt ______________ T ______________

retn ______________ temp ______________

rt ______________ wk ______________

surg ______________ $\bar{c}$ ______________

PATIENT RECORD

Sandoval,	Rosa	M	11-01-91	F	013/456-3322
LAST NAME	FIRST NAME	MIDDLE NAME	BIRTH DATE	SEX	HOME PHONE

209 West Maple Street	Woodland Hills,	XY	12345
ADDRESS	CITY	STATE	ZIP CODE

child full-time student
PATIENT'S OCCUPATION — NAME OF COMPANY

ADDRESS OF EMPLOYER — PHONE

Maria B. Sandoval (mother) homemaker
SPOUSE OR PARENT — OCCUPATION

Hernan J. Sandoval (father) Army Staff Sargeant, Active Status 2-10-60
EMPLOYER — ADDRESS — PHONE — Birthdate

Service # 886-91-0999 Soc.Sec. # 886-91-0999, HHC, 3rd Batt., 25th Infantry
NAME OF INSURANCE GROUP — SUBSCRIBER

Grade 9, A.P.O., New York, New York 10030
BLUE SHIELD OR BLUE CROSS CERT. NO. — GROUP NO. — CURRENT COVERAGE NO. — EFFECTIVE DATE

*CHAMPUS I.D. Card # 73485 01-01-80 994-02-1164
MEDICARE NO. — MEDICAID NO. — EFFECTIVE DATE — SOC. SEC. NO.

Exp. Date 1-1-9x

*This number is not required on the HCFA-1500 claim form.
REFERRED BY:

Hilda M. Mendez (friend)

DATE	PROGRESS
5-1-9x	Sunday 3 a.m. pt seen in ER hosp complaining of pain rt ear
	for 3 days. Exam revealed fluid & pus rt ear. Temp 101
	Adv mother a myringotomy was necessary. Imp: Rt otitis media
	Surg: rt myringotomy c̄ aspiration. To be seen in ofc for FU.
	Pedro Atrics, MD
5-3-9x	No pain rt ear. Pt progressing to retn in 1 wk T 98 P. Atrics
5-10-9x	T 98, no fluid or pus in rt ear. No pain. Retn prn. P. Atrics

FIGURE 13-1

STATEMENT

College Clinic
4567 Broad Avenue
Woodland Hills, XY 12345-0001
Telephone: 013-486-9002
Fax: 013-487-8976

Mr. Hernan J. Sandoval
209 West Maple Street
Woodland Hills, XY 12345-0001

DATE	PROFESSIONAL SERVICE DESCRIPTION	CHARGE	CREDITS		CURRENT BALANCE
			PAYMENTS	ADJUSTMENTS	
5-1-9x	ER, EPF hx/exam, LC decision making				
5-1-9x	Rt myringotomy with aspiration				
5-3-9x	OC				
5-10-9x	OC, EPF hx/exam, LC decision making				

Due and payable within 10 days. **Pay last amount in balance column** ⇧

Key: **PF:** Problem-focused
EPF: Expanded problem-focused
D: Detailed
C: Comprehensive
SF: Straightforward
LC: Low complexity
MC: Moderate complexity
HC: High complexity
CON: Consultation
CPX: Complete Phys Exam
E: Emergency
ER: Emergency Dept.
HCD: House Call (Day)
HCN: House Call (Night)
HV: Hospital visit
OV: Office Visit

FIGURE 13-2

HEALTH INSURANCE CLAIM FORM

PICA

MEDICAID | CHAMPUS | CHAMPVA | GROUP HEALTH PLAN | FECA BLK LUNG | OTHER

#) ☐ (Medicaid #) ☐ (Sponsor's SSN) ☐ (VA File #) ☐ (SSN or ID) ☐ (SSN) ☐ (ID)

1a. INSURED'S I.D. NUMBER (FOR PROGRAM IN ITEM 1)

NAME (Last Name, First Name, Middle Initial)

3. PATIENT'S BIRTH DATE MM DD YY SEX M ☐ F ☐

4. INSURED'S NAME (Last Name, First Name, Middle Initial)

ADDRESS (No., Street)

6. PATIENT RELATIONSHIP TO INSURED Self ☐ Spouse ☐ Child ☐ Other ☐

7. INSURED'S ADDRESS (No., Street)

STATE

8. PATIENT STATUS Single ☐ Married ☐ Other ☐

Employed ☐ Full-Time Student ☐ Part-Time Student ☐

CITY STATE

TELEPHONE (Include Area Code) ( )

ZIP CODE TELEPHONE (INCLUDE AREA CODE) ( )

URED'S NAME (Last Name, First Name, Middle Initial)

10. IS PATIENT'S CONDITION RELATED TO:

11. INSURED'S POLICY GROUP OR FECA NUMBER

URED'S POLICY OR GROUP NUMBER

a. EMPLOYMENT? (CURRENT OR PREVIOUS) ☐ YES ☐ NO

a. INSURED'S DATE OF BIRTH MM DD YY SEX M ☐ F ☐

URED'S DATE OF BIRTH YY SEX M ☐ F ☐

b. AUTO ACCIDENT? PLACE (State) ☐ YES ☐ NO

b. EMPLOYER'S NAME OR SCHOOL NAME

S NAME OR SCHOOL NAME

c. OTHER ACCIDENT? ☐ YES ☐ NO

c. INSURANCE PLAN NAME OR PROGRAM NAME

PLAN NAME OR PROGRAM NAME

10d. RESERVED FOR LOCAL USE

d. IS THERE ANOTHER HEALTH BENEFIT PLAN? ☐ YES ☐ NO ***If yes***, return to and complete item 9 a-d.

READ BACK OF FORM BEFORE COMPLETING & SIGNING THIS FORM.

OR AUTHORIZED PERSON'S SIGNATURE I authorize the release of any medical or other information necessary this claim. I also request payment of government benefits either to myself or to the party who accepts assignment

DATE

13. INSURED'S OR AUTHORIZED PERSON'S SIGNATURE I authorize payment of medical benefits to the undersigned physician or supplier for services described below.

SIGNED

PATIENT AND INSURED INFORMATION

CURRENT: YY ◀ ILLNESS (First symptom) OR INJURY (Accident) OR PREGNANCY(LMP)

15. IF PATIENT HAS HAD SAME OR SIMILAR ILLNESS. GIVE FIRST DATE MM DD YY

16. DATES PATIENT UNABLE TO WORK IN CURRENT OCCUPATION FROM MM DD YY TO MM DD YY

REFERRING PHYSICIAN OR OTHER SOURCE

17a. I.D. NUMBER OF REFERRING PHYSICIAN

18. HOSPITALIZATION DATES RELATED TO CURRENT SERVICES FROM MM DD YY TO MM DD YY

D FOR LOCAL USE

20. OUTSIDE LAB? ☐ YES ☐ NO $ CHARGES

S OR NATURE OF ILLNESS OR INJURY. (RELATE ITEMS 1,2,3 OR 4 TO ITEM 24E BY LINE)

3. ___ . ___

4. ___ . ___

22. MEDICAID RESUBMISSION CODE ORIGINAL REF. NO.

23. PRIOR AUTHORIZATION NUMBER

A				B	C	D		E	F	G	H	I	J	K
TE(S) OF SERVICE To				Place of Service	Type of Service	PROCEDURES, SERVICES, OR SUPPLIES (Explain Unusual Circumstances)		DIAGNOSIS CODE	$ CHARGES	DAYS OR UNITS	EPSDT Family Plan	EMG	COB	RESERVED FOR LOCAL USE
YY	MM	DD	YY			CPT/HCPCS	MODIFIER							

TAX I.D. NUMBER SSN EIN ☐ ☐

26. PATIENT'S ACCOUNT NO.

27. ACCEPT ASSIGNMENT? (For govt. claims, see back) ☐ YES ☐ NO

28. TOTAL CHARGE $

29. AMOUNT PAID $

30. BALANCE DUE $

E OF PHYSICIAN OR SUPPLIER G DEGREES OR CREDENTIALS t the statements on the reverse s bill and are made a part thereof.)

DATE

32. NAME AND ADDRESS OF FACILITY WHERE SERVICES WERE RENDERED (If other than home or office)

33. PHYSICIAN'S, SUPPLIER'S BILLING NAME, ADDRESS, ZIP CODE & PHONE #

PIN# GRP#

PHYSICIAN OR SUPPLIER INFORMATION

ED BY AMA COUNCIL ON MEDICAL SERVICE 8/88)

PLEASE PRINT OR TYPE

FORM HCFA-1500 (U2) (12-90)
FORM OWCP-1500 FORM RRB-1500

FIGURE 13-3

ASSIGNMENT 48

1. Complete the CHAMPUS Claim Form (Fig. 13–6) using OCR guidelines, directing it to your local CHAMPUS fiscal intermediary. See Chapter 6 of the *Handbook* for help in completing the HCFA-1500 claim form and refer to Chapter 13, Figure 13-7. Refer to Mrs. Darlene B. Drew's patient record (Fig. 13–4) and ledger card (Fig. 13–5) for information. Refer to Appendix A to fill in the fees on the ledger card. Date the claim February 3. Let us assume the patient brings in a hard copy of a signed Nonavailability Statement DD Form 1251, which shows approval of the physician to treat the patient. Dr. Ulibarri is accepting assignment. This patient met her deductible last November when seen by a previous physician.
2. Use your *CPT Code Book* or Appendix A to determine the correct five-digit code number and modifiers for each professional service rendered.
3. Record the proper information on the ledger card when you have billed CHAMPUS.

Abbreviations pertinent to this record:

adm __________	PE __________
BP __________	Pt __________
CC __________	RBC __________
cc __________	rec __________
DC __________	retn __________
Dx __________	Rx __________
Ex __________	t.i.d __________
FU __________	UA __________
hosp __________	WBC __________
I & D __________	$\bar{c}$ __________

PATIENT RECORD

LAST NAME	FIRST NAME	MIDDLE NAME	BIRTH DATE	SEX	HOME PHONE
Drew,	Darlene	B	12-22-37	F	013/466-1002

ADDRESS	CITY	STATE	ZIP CODE
720 Ganley Street,	Woodland Hills,	XY	12345

PATIENT'S OCCUPATION: seamstress — NAME OF COMPANY: J. B. Talon Company

ADDRESS OF EMPLOYER: 2111 Ventura Road, Merck, XY 12346 — PHONE: 013/733-0156

SPOUSE OR PARENT: Harry M. Drew — OCCUPATION: U.S. Navy Lieutenant Commander (L/C) Active Status

Service # 221-96-0711 Soc.Sec. # 221-96-0711 Grade 12 4-15-37 Birthdate

ADDRESS — PHONE

P.O. Box 2927, A.P.O. New York, New York 09194

SUBSCRIBER

BLUE SHIELD OR BLUE CROSS CERT. NO.	GROUP NO.	CURRENT COVERAGE NO.	EFFECTIVE DATE

MEDICAID NO.	EFFECTIVE DATE	Pt's SOC. SEC. NO.
	1-1-80	450-10-3762

CHAMPUS ID Card # 67531 Exp. 1-1-9x

REFERRED BY: Tax ID # 77 6210740

James B. Jeffers, MD, 100 S. Broadway, Woodland Hills, XY 12345

DATE	PROGRESS
1-13-9x	CC New pt comes in complaining of very large, tender mass in periurethral orifice. Incision + drainage of deep periurethral abscess + obtained 10 cc greenish pus. UA, WBC + RBC's loaded. Pt feels much better. ℞ Terramycin 20 caps 1 t.i.d. Retn 5 days Dx: suburethral cyst. Took culture + sent to lab. Gene Ulibarri, MD
1-18-9x	Cyst is filled up again. Rec hospitalization. Culture shows pseudomonas organism. Gene Ulibarri, MD
1-19-9x	Adm to College Hosp. Pt scheduled for cystoscopy prior to surgery. Surg: Marsupialization of urethral diverticulum + packing c̄ Iodoform Gene Ulibarri, MD
1-20-9x	DC from hosp. To be seen in office next wk for FU Ex. Gene Ulibarri, MD

FIGURE 13-4

STATEMENT

College Clinic
4567 Broad Avenue
Woodland Hills, XY 12345-0001
Telephone: 013-486-9002
Fax: 013-487-8976

Mr. Harry M. Drew
720 Ganley Street
Woodland Hills, XY 12345-0001

DATE	PROFESSIONAL SERVICE DESCRIPTION	CHARGE	CREDITS		CURRENT BALANCE
			PAYMENTS	ADJUSTMENTS	
1-13-9x	OC, D hx/exam, LC decision making				
1-13-9x	UA, routine				
1-13-9x	Drainage of deep periurethral abscess				
1-13-9x	Handling of culture				
1-18-9x	OC				
1-19-9x	Admit & initial hosp care, C hx/exam MC decision making				
1-19-9x	Marsupialization of urethral diverticulum				
1-20-9x	Discharge hosp				

Due and payable within 10 days. **Pay last amount in balance column** ⇧

Key:

PF: Problem-focused	**SF:** Straightforward	**CON:** Consultation	**HCD:** House Call (Day)
EPF: Expanded problem-focused	**LC:** Low complexity	**CPX:** Complete Phys Exam	**HCN:** House Call (Night)
D: Detailed	**MC:** Moderate complexity	**E:** Emergency	**HV:** Hospital visit
C: Comprehensive	**HC:** High complexity	**ER:** Emergency Dept.	**OV:** Office Visit

FIGURE 13-5

PICA

HEALTH INSURANCE CLAIM FORM

1. MEDICARE (Medicare #) MEDICAID (Medicaid #) CHAMPUS (Sponsor's SSN) CHAMPVA (VA File #) GROUP HEALTH PLAN (SSN or ID) FECA BLK LUNG (SSN) OTHER (ID)

1a. INSURED'S I.D. NUMBER (FOR PROGRAM

2. PATIENT'S NAME (Last Name, First Name, Middle Initial)

3. PATIENT'S BIRTH DATE MM DD YY SEX M F

4. INSURED'S NAME (Last Name, First Name, Middle Initial)

5. PATIENT'S ADDRESS (No., Street)

6. PATIENT RELATIONSHIP TO INSURED Self Spouse Child Other

7. INSURED'S ADDRESS (No., Street)

CITY STATE

8. PATIENT STATUS Single Married Other

CITY

ZIP CODE TELEPHONE (Include Area Code) ( )

Employed Full-Time Student Part-Time Student

ZIP CODE TELEPHONE (INCLUDE ARE ( )

9. OTHER INSURED'S NAME (Last Name, First Name, Middle Initial)

10. IS PATIENT'S CONDITION RELATED TO:

11. INSURED'S POLICY GROUP OR FECA NUMBER

a. OTHER INSURED'S POLICY OR GROUP NUMBER

a. EMPLOYMENT? (CURRENT OR PREVIOUS) YES NO

a. INSURED'S DATE OF BIRTH MM DD YY SEX M

b. OTHER INSURED'S DATE OF BIRTH MM DD YY SEX M F

b. AUTO ACCIDENT? PLACE (State) YES NO

b. EMPLOYER'S NAME OR SCHOOL NAME

c. EMPLOYER'S NAME OR SCHOOL NAME

c. OTHER ACCIDENT? YES NO

c. INSURANCE PLAN NAME OR PROGRAM NAME

d. INSURANCE PLAN NAME OR PROGRAM NAME

10d. RESERVED FOR LOCAL USE

d. IS THERE ANOTHER HEALTH BENEFIT PLAN? YES NO *If yes,* return to and complete it

READ BACK OF FORM BEFORE COMPLETING & SIGNING THIS FORM.

12. PATIENT'S OR AUTHORIZED PERSON'S SIGNATURE I authorize the release of any medical or other information necessary to process this claim. I also request payment of government benefits either to myself or to the party who accepts assignment below.

SIGNED __________ DATE __________

13. INSURED'S OR AUTHORIZED PERSON'S SIGNATURE I a payment of medical benefits to the undersigned physician or s services described below.

SIGNED __________

14. DATE OF CURRENT: MM DD YY ◀ ILLNESS (First symptom) OR INJURY (Accident) OR PREGNANCY(LMP)

15. IF PATIENT HAS HAD SAME OR SIMILAR ILLNESS. GIVE FIRST DATE MM DD YY

16. DATES PATIENT UNABLE TO WORK IN CURRENT OCCU FROM MM DD YY TO MM DD

17. NAME OF REFERRING PHYSICIAN OR OTHER SOURCE

17a. I.D. NUMBER OF REFERRING PHYSICIAN

18. HOSPITALIZATION DATES RELATED TO CURRENT SERV FROM MM DD YY TO MM DD

19. RESERVED FOR LOCAL USE

20. OUTSIDE LAB? YES NO $ CHARGES

21. DIAGNOSIS OR NATURE OF ILLNESS OR INJURY. (RELATE ITEMS 1,2,3 OR 4 TO ITEM 24E BY LINE)

1. ____ . __

3. ____ . __

2. ____ . __

4. ____ . __

22. MEDICAID RESUBMISSION CODE ORIGINAL REF. NO.

23. PRIOR AUTHORIZATION NUMBER

24. A DATE(S) OF SERVICE From MM DD YY	To MM DD YY	B Place of Service	C Type of Service	D PROCEDURES, SERVICES, OR SUPPLIES (Explain Unusual Circumstances) CPT/HCPCS MODIFIER	E DIAGNOSIS CODE	F $ CHARGES	G DAYS OR UNITS	H EPSDT Family Plan	I EMG	J COB	RESER LOC
1											
2											
3											
4											
5											
6											

25. FEDERAL TAX I.D. NUMBER SSN EIN

26. PATIENT'S ACCOUNT NO.

27. ACCEPT ASSIGNMENT? (For govt. claims, see back) YES NO

28. TOTAL CHARGE $

29. AMOUNT PAID $

30. BALA $

31. SIGNATURE OF PHYSICIAN OR SUPPLIER INCLUDING DEGREES OR CREDENTIALS (I certify that the statements on the reverse apply to this bill and are made a part thereof.)

SIGNED DATE

32. NAME AND ADDRESS OF FACILITY WHERE SERVICES WERE RENDERED (If other than home or office)

33. PHYSICIAN'S, SUPPLIER'S BILLING NAME, ADDRESS, ZIP & PHONE #

PIN# GRP#

(APPROVED BY AMA COUNCIL ON MEDICAL SERVICE 8/88)

PLEASE PRINT OR TYPE

FORM HCFA-1500 (U2) (12-90)
FORM OWCP-1500 FOR

FIGURE 13-6

ASSIGNMENT 49

1. Since this case requires three claim forms, make photocopies of the HCFA-1500 form or see Figure 13-10. Complete the CHAMPUS Claim Form (Fig. 13–9) using OCR guidelines, directing it to your local CHAMPUS fiscal intermediary. See Chapter 6 of the *Handbook* for help in completing the HCFA-1500 claim form and refer to Chapter 13, Figure 13-7. Refer to Mrs. Mae I. Abbreviate's patient record (Fig. 13–7) and ledger card (Fig. 13–8) for information. Refer to Appendix A to fill in the fees on the ledger card. Date the claim January 31. Assume that the patient brings in a hard copy of a signed Nonavailability Statement DD Form 1251, which shows approval of the physician to treat the patient. Dr. Coccidioides is not accepting assignment but is completing the claim for the patient's convenience. This patient has not previously met her deductible.
2. Use your *CPT Code Book* or Appendix A to determine the correct five-digit code number and modifiers for each professional service rendered. X-rays in this case were taken at Speedy Radiology Service at 4300 Broad Avenue, Woodland Hills, XY 12345, and laboratory work was sent to Laboratory Associates, 4100 Broad Avenue, Woodland Hills, XY 12345, provider No. 808491205. The doctor is submitting the bill for x-rays.
3. Record the proper information on the ledger card when you have billed CHAMPUS.

Abbreviations pertinent to this record:

abdom ____________________

aet ____________________

BP ____________________

Ca ____________________

CC ____________________

D & C ____________________

Dx ____________________

EENT ____________________

FH ____________________

GB ____________________

GGE ____________________

GI ____________________

Ht ____________________

I ____________________

LMP ____________________

L & W ____________________

NYD ____________________

OS ____________________

Para I ____________________

PE ____________________

PH ____________________

PND ____________________

Prog ____________________

pt ____________________

PTR ____________________

PX ____________________

RBC ____________________

Rx ____________________

surg ____________________

T & A ____________________

TPR ____________________

u ____________________

UCHD ____________________

URI ____________________

PATIENT RECORD

LAST NAME	FIRST NAME	MIDDLE NAME	BIRTH DATE	SEX	HOME PHONE
Abbreviate,	Mae	I.	01-02-42	F	013/985-7667

ADDRESS	CITY	STATE	ZIP CODE
4667 Symbol Road,	Woodland Hills,	XY	12345

PATIENT'S OCCUPATION: typist
NAME OF COMPANY: U.R. Wright Company

ADDRESS OF EMPLOYER: 6789 Abridge Road, Woodland Hills, XY 12345
PHONE: 013/988-7540

SPOUSE OR PARENT: Shorty S. Abbreviate
OCCUPATION: Army Staff Sargeant, Active Status
Birthdate: 3-25-40

ADDRESS: Service # 023-19-7866 Soc.Sec. # 012-19-7866, HHC. 2nd Batt., 27th Infantry
Grade 12, A.P.O., New York, New York 10030
PHONE:

SUBSCRIBER:

BLUE SHIELD OR BLUE CROSS CERT. NO.	GROUP NO.	CURRENT COVERAGE NO.	EFFECTIVE DATE
CHAMPUS ID Card # 97600		01-01-80	865-04-2311

	MEDICAID NO.	EFFECTIVE DATE	SOC. SEC. NO.
		Exp. Date 1-1-9x	

REFERRED BY:
Jane B. Accurate (friend)

DATE	PROGRESS
1-14-9x	Pt 45 W♀in for complete PE; CC recent URI of 2 wk duration: PND, chest pain & cough; Sweat, chills & sputum c pus X 5 days
	PH removal of T & A aet 6, UCHD; Para I, D & C aet 41; Surg on OS after accident last yr.
	FH: Father expired c Ca of kidney aet 63; Mother L & W after GB surg.
	PX: Ht 5' 7", Wt 150 #, EENT o except OS opaque; LMP 12-18-81; Chest: Dyspnea & rales, BP 120/80; TPR normal. Abdomen o. GGE; WBC 7,800,RBC 4.2 Prog: NYD. Chest x-rays reveal a cavity c a fluid level. Sputum specimen sent for culture & sensitivity tests Dx: lung abscess. Rx penicillin G 10 million u/day IV for 4 days.
	Brady Coccidioides, MD
1-15-9x	Penicillin G 10 million units IV Pt doing well. B Coccidioides
1-16-9x	Penicillin G 10 million units IV. Ordered bilateral bronchography BC
1-17-9x	Penicillin G 10 million units IV. B Coccidioides
1-18-9x	Penicillin G 10 million units IV. Pt doing well Few residual shadows on repeat of chest x-ray. PIR in 1 wk.
	Brady Coccidioides, MD

FIGURE 13-7

STATEMENT

College Clinic
4567 Broad Avenue
Woodland Hills, XY 12345-0001
Telephone: 013-486-9002
Fax: 013-487-8976

Mrs. Shorty S. Abbreviate
4667 Symbol Road
Woodland Hills, XY 12345-0001

DATE	PROFESSIONAL SERVICE DESCRIPTION	CHARGE	CREDITS		CURRENT BALANCE
			PAYMENTS	ADJUSTMENTS	
1-14-9x	OC, C hx/exam, HC decision making				
1-14-9x	AP & lat chest x-rays				
1-14-9x	Handling of sputum specimen				
1-14-9x	Penicillin inj 10 mil U.				
1-15-9x	OC, EPF hx/exam,LC decision making				
1-15-9x	Penicillin inj 10 mil U.				
1-16-9x	OC, D hx/exam, MC decision making				
1-16-9x	Penicillin inj 10 mil U.				
1-16-9x	Bilateral bronchography				
1-17-9x	OC, EPF hx/exam, LC decision making				
1-17-9x	Penicillin inj 10 mil U.				
1-18-9x	OC, D hx/exam, MC decision making				
1-18-9x	Penicillin inj 10 mil U.				
1-18-9x	AP & lat chest x-rays				

Due and payable within 10 days. **Pay last amount in balance column** ⇧

Key: PF: Problem-focused
EPF: Expanded problem-focused
D: Detailed
C: Comprehensive
SF: Straightforward
LC: Low complexity
MC: Moderate complexity
HC: High complexity
CON: Consultation
CPX: Complete Phys Exam
E: Emergency
ER: Emergency Dept.
HCD: House Call (Day)
HCN: House Call (Night)
HV: Hospital visit
OV: Office Visit

FIGURE 13-8

PICA

HEALTH INSURANCE CLAIM FORM

1. MEDICARE (Medicare #) MEDICAID (Medicaid #) CHAMPUS (Sponsor's SSN) CHAMPVA (VA File #) GROUP HEALTH PLAN (SSN or ID) FECA BLK LUNG (SSN) OTHER (ID)

1a. INSURED'S I.D. NUMBER (FOR PROGRAM

2. PATIENT'S NAME (Last Name, First Name, Middle Initial)

3. PATIENT'S BIRTH DATE MM DD YY SEX M F

4. INSURED'S NAME (Last Name, First Name, Middle Initial)

5. PATIENT'S ADDRESS (No., Street)

6. PATIENT RELATIONSHIP TO INSURED Self Spouse Child Other

7. INSURED'S ADDRESS (No., Street)

CITY STATE

8. PATIENT STATUS Single Married Other

CITY

ZIP CODE TELEPHONE (Include Area Code) ( )

Employed Full-Time Student Part-Time Student

ZIP CODE TELEPHONE (INCLUDE ARE ( )

9. OTHER INSURED'S NAME (Last Name, First Name, Middle Initial)

10. IS PATIENT'S CONDITION RELATED TO:

11. INSURED'S POLICY GROUP OR FECA NUMBER

a. OTHER INSURED'S POLICY OR GROUP NUMBER

a. EMPLOYMENT? (CURRENT OR PREVIOUS) YES NO

a. INSURED'S DATE OF BIRTH MM DD YY SEX M

b. OTHER INSURED'S DATE OF BIRTH MM DD YY SEX M F

b. AUTO ACCIDENT? PLACE (State) YES NO

b. EMPLOYER'S NAME OR SCHOOL NAME

c. EMPLOYER'S NAME OR SCHOOL NAME

c. OTHER ACCIDENT? YES NO

c. INSURANCE PLAN NAME OR PROGRAM NAME

d. INSURANCE PLAN NAME OR PROGRAM NAME

10d. RESERVED FOR LOCAL USE

d. IS THERE ANOTHER HEALTH BENEFIT PLAN? YES NO *If yes,* return to and complete it

READ BACK OF FORM BEFORE COMPLETING & SIGNING THIS FORM.

12. PATIENT'S OR AUTHORIZED PERSON'S SIGNATURE I authorize the release of any medical or other information necessary to process this claim. I also request payment of government benefits either to myself or to the party who accepts assignment below.

SIGNED DATE

13. INSURED'S OR AUTHORIZED PERSON'S SIGNATURE I a payment of medical benefits to the undersigned physician or services described below.

SIGNED

14. DATE OF CURRENT: MM DD YY ◀ ILLNESS (First symptom) OR INJURY (Accident) OR PREGNANCY(LMP)

15. IF PATIENT HAS HAD SAME OR SIMILAR ILLNESS. GIVE FIRST DATE MM DD YY

16. DATES PATIENT UNABLE TO WORK IN CURRENT OCCU FROM MM DD YY TO MM DD

17. NAME OF REFERRING PHYSICIAN OR OTHER SOURCE

17a. I.D. NUMBER OF REFERRING PHYSICIAN

18. HOSPITALIZATION DATES RELATED TO CURRENT SERV FROM MM DD YY TO MM DD

19. RESERVED FOR LOCAL USE

20. OUTSIDE LAB? YES NO $ CHARGES

21. DIAGNOSIS OR NATURE OF ILLNESS OR INJURY. (RELATE ITEMS 1,2,3 OR 4 TO ITEM 24E BY LINE)

1. ___ . __

2. ___ . __

3. ___ . __

4. ___ . __

22. MEDICAID RESUBMISSION CODE ORIGINAL REF. NO.

23. PRIOR AUTHORIZATION NUMBER

24. A DATE(S) OF SERVICE From MM DD YY To MM DD YY	B Place of Service	C Type of Service	D PROCEDURES, SERVICES, OR SUPPLIES (Explain Unusual Circumstances) CPT/HCPCS MODIFIER	E DIAGNOSIS CODE	F $ CHARGES	G DAYS OR UNITS	H EPSDT Family Plan	I EMG	J COB	RESER LOC
1										
2										
3										
4										
5										
6										

25. FEDERAL TAX I.D. NUMBER SSN EIN

26. PATIENT'S ACCOUNT NO.

27. ACCEPT ASSIGNMENT? (For govt. claims, see back) YES NO

28. TOTAL CHARGE $

29. AMOUNT PAID $

30. BALA $

31. SIGNATURE OF PHYSICIAN OR SUPPLIER INCLUDING DEGREES OR CREDENTIALS (I certify that the statements on the reverse apply to this bill and are made a part thereof.)

SIGNED DATE

32. NAME AND ADDRESS OF FACILITY WHERE SERVICES WERE RENDERED (If other than home or office)

33. PHYSICIAN'S, SUPPLIER'S BILLING NAME, ADDRESS, ZIP & PHONE #

PIN# GRP#

(APPROVED BY AMA COUNCIL ON MEDICAL SERVICE 8/88)

PLEASE PRINT OR TYPE

FORM HCFA-1500 (U2) (12-90)
FORM OWCP-1500 FOR

FIGURE 13-9

W ____________________

WBC ____________________

wk ____________________

wt ____________________

X ____________________

yr ____________________

c̄ ____________________

♀ ____________________

ō ____________________

Since only six of the professional services rendered to Mrs. Abbreviate will fit on a HCFA-1500 claim form, complete the bottom halves of these two forms (Fig. 13–10) for the remainder of her services, or make photocopies of blank HCFA-1500 claim forms to complete the assignment.

COMPUTER EXERCISE

CASE 4 CHAMPUS

Before proceeding, you may want to do an exercise based on the concepts you have learned. Additional practice material is on your computer diskette.

Directions: Insert the diskette into the computer and follow the instructions on the screen for Computer Exercise Case 4.

14. DATE OF CURRENT: MM DD YY ◀ ILLNESS (First symptom) OR INJURY (Accident) OR PREGNANCY(LMP)	15. IF PATIENT HAS HAD SAME OR SIMILAR ILLNESS. GIVE FIRST DATE MM DD YY	16. DATES PATIENT UNABLE TO WORK IN CURRENT OCCU MM DD YY FROM TO MM DD
17. NAME OF REFERRING PHYSICIAN OR OTHER SOURCE	17a. I.D. NUMBER OF REFERRING PHYSICIAN	18. HOSPITALIZATION DATES RELATED TO CURRENT SER MM DD YY FROM TO MM DD
19. RESERVED FOR LOCAL USE		20. OUTSIDE LAB? $ CHARGES ☐ YES ☐ NO
21. DIAGNOSIS OR NATURE OF ILLNESS OR INJURY. (RELATE ITEMS 1,2,3 OR 4 TO ITEM 24E BY LINE) 1. ___ . ___ 3. ___ . ___ 2. ___ . ___ 4. ___ . ___		22. MEDICAID RESUBMISSION CODE ORIGINAL REF. NO. 23. PRIOR AUTHORIZATION NUMBER

24. A DATE(S) OF SERVICE From MM DD YY	To MM DD YY	B Place of Service	C Type of Service	D PROCEDURES, SERVICES, OR SUPPLIES (Explain Unusual Circumstances) CPT/HCPCS | MODIFIER	E DIAGNOSIS CODE	F $ CHARGES	G DAYS OR UNITS	H EPSDT Family Plan	I EMG	J COB	RESE LOC
1											
2											
3											
4											
5											
6											

25. FEDERAL TAX I.D. NUMBER SSN EIN ☐ ☐	26. PATIENT'S ACCOUNT NO.	27. ACCEPT ASSIGNMENT? (For govt. claims, see back) ☐ YES ☐ NO	28. TOTAL CHARGE $	29. AMOUNT PAID $	30. BAL $
31. SIGNATURE OF PHYSICIAN OR SUPPLIER INCLUDING DEGREES OR CREDENTIALS (I certify that the statements on the reverse apply to this bill and are made a part thereof.) SIGNED DATE	32. NAME AND ADDRESS OF FACILITY WHERE SERVICES WERE RENDERED (If other than home or office)		33. PHYSICIAN'S, SUPPLIER'S BILLING NAME, ADDRESS, ZI & PHONE # PIN# GRP#		

(APPROVED BY AMA COUNCIL ON MEDICAL SERVICE 8/88) ***PLEASE PRINT OR TYPE*** FORM HCFA-1500 (U2) (12-9 FORM OWCP-1500 FO

FIGURE 13-10

CHAPTER 14

Workers' Compensation

Key Terms

Your instructor may wish to select some specific words pertinent to this chapter for a test. For definitions of the terms, further study, and/or reference, the words, phrases, and abbreviations may be found in the Glossary at the end of the textbook. *Key terms for this chapter follow:*

accident
adjudication
by report (BR)
compromise and release (C and R)
course of employment (COE)
deposition
employer's liability insurance
extraterritorial
Federal Employees' Compensation Act (FECA)
fee schedule
independent medical examiner (IME)
injury
lien
limited duty
medical service order
nondisability (ND) claim
occupational illness (or disease)
Occupational Safety and Health Administration (OSHA)
Office of Federal Employees' Compensation (OFEC)
Office of Workers' Compensation Programs (OWCP)
permanent and stationary (P and S)
permanent disability (PD)
petition
second-injury fund
sub rosa films
subsequent injury fund (SIF)
temporary disability (TD)
third-party liability
third-party subrogation
waiting period (WP)
Workers' Compensation Appeals Board (WCAB)
workers' compensation (WC) insurance
work hardening

Performance Objectives

The student will be able to

- Define and spell the key terms for this chapter, given the information from the textbook Glossary, within a reasonable period of time and with enough acccuracy to obtain a satisfactory evaluation.
- Answer the review questions after reading the chapter, with enough accuracy to obtain a satisfactory evaluation.
- Fill in the correct meaning of each abbreviation, given a list of common medical abbreviations and symbols that appear in chart notes, within a reasonable period of time and with enough accuracy to obtain a satisfactory evaluation.
- Complete each workers' compensation form for billing, given the patients' medical chart notes, ledger cards, and blank insurance forms, within a reasonable period of time and with enough accuracy to obtain a satisfactory evaluation.
- Correctly post payments, adjustments, and balances on the patients' ledger cards, using the Mock Fee Schedule in Appendix A, within a reasonable period of time and with enough accuracy to obtain a satisfactory evaluation.

Study Outline

WORKERS' COMPENSATION
- History
- Benefits
- Purposes of workers' compensation laws
- Workers' compensation reform
- Self-insurance
- Managed care

COVERAGE OF FEDERAL LAWS

COVERAGE OF STATE LAWS
- Funding
- Minimum number of employees
- Waiting periods
- Types of state compensation benefits

TYPES OF STATE CLAIMS
- Nondisability claim
  - Medical service order
  - First treatment medical report
- Temporary disability claim
  - Vocational rehabilitation
- Permanent disability claim
- Rating
  - Surveillance

FRAUD AND ABUSE
- Employee
- Employer
- Insurer
- Medical provider
- Lawyer

OCCUPATIONAL SAFETY AND HEALTH ADMINISTRATION (OSHA) ACT OF 1970
- Background
- Coverage
- Regulations
- Filing a complaint
- Inspection
- Recordkeeping, posting and reporting

SPECIAL CIRCUMSTANCES
- Third-party subrogation
- Medical testimony
- Depositions
- Liens
- Second-injury fund (Subsequent Injury fund)
- Unemployment compensation disability and workers' compensation

MEDICAL REPORTS
- Confidentiality
- Documentation
- Recordkeeping
- Terminology
- Information to be included in detailed progress or re-examination reports

BILLING CLAIMS
- Financial responsibility
- Fee schedules
- Helpful billing tips
- Electronic claims submission
- Out-of-state claims

INSTRUCTIONS FOR COMPLETING THE DOCTOR'S FIRST REPORT OF OCCUPATIONAL INJURY OR ILLNESS

DELINQUENT CLAIMS

Review Questions

Review the objectives, key terms, glossary definitions to key terms, chapter information, and figures before completing the following review questions.

1. An unforeseen, unexpected, unintended event that occurs at a particular time and place, causing injury to an individual not of his or her own making, is called a/an

   ____ .

2. Maria Cardoza works in a plastics manufacturing company and inhales some fumes that cause bronchitis. Since this condition is associated with her employment, it is called

   a/an ____ .

3. Name two kinds of statutes under workers' compensation.

   a. ____

   b. ____

4. Name the classifications of employees that fall under federal workers' compensation statutes and the four acts that cover them.

   a. ____________________ ______________________________ Act

   b. ____________________ ______________________________ Act

   c. ____________________ ______________________________ Act

   d. ____________________ ______________________________ Act

5. Fifty states have ____________________ workers' compensation and employer's liability insurance.

6. Three states have ____________________ workers' compensation and employers' liability insurance coverage.

7. State five methods used for funding workers' compensation.

   a. ____

   b. ____

   c. ____

   d. ____

   e. ____

8. Who pays the workers' compensation insurance premiums? ____________________

9. Name jobs that may not be covered by workers' compensation insurance.

   a. ____________________ d. ____________________

   b. ____________________ e. ____________________

   c. ____________________ f. ____________________

10. What is the time limit in your state for submitting the employers' and/or physicians' report of an industrial accident? ____________________

11. What is the minimum number of employees per business needed in your state before workers' compensation statutes become effective? ____________________

12. What waiting period must elapse in your state before workers' compensation payments begin? ____________________

13. List five types of workers' compensation benefits.
   a. ____________________
   b. ____________________
   c. ____________________
   d. ____________________
   e. ____________________

14. Who can treat an industrial injury? ____________________
   ____

15. Three types of workers' compensation claims are
   a. ____________________
   b. ____________________
   c. ____________________

16. What is the first thing an employee should do after he or she is injured? ____________________
   ____

17. When an individual suffers a work-related injury or illness, the employer must complete and send a form to the insurance company and workers' compensation state offices called a/an , ____________________ and if the employee is sent to a physician's office for medical care, the employer must complete a form that authorizes the physician to treat the employee, called a/an ____________________ .

18. Who selects the attending physician for an industrial accident or illness?
   ____
   ____

19. When a physician treats an industrial injury, he or she must complete a/an

_____________________________ and send it to the following:

a. ____

b. ____

c. ____

Is a stamped physician's signature acceptable on the form? ______________ Explain.

____

20. After suffering an industrial injury, Mr. Fields is in a treatment program in which he is given real work tasks for building strength and endurance. This form of therapy is called

____ .

21. Explain the differences between these three types of claims.

a. Nondisability claim: ____

____

b. Temporary disability claim: ____

____

c. Permanent disability claim: ____

____

22. Define these abbreviations.

a. TD ______________________ c. P & S ______________________

b. PD ______________________ d. C & R ______________________

23. Weekly temporary disability payments are based on ______________________

____ .

24. When an industrial case reaches the time for rating the disability, this is accomplished

by ____ .

25. May an injured person appeal his or her case if not satisfied with the rating? ________

If so, to whom does he or she appeal? ______________________________

or ____

26. When a case of fraud or abuse is suspected in a workers' compensation case, the

physician should report the situation to ______________________________ .

27. Employers are required to meet health and safety standards for their employees under

federal and state statutes known as the ______________________________ .

28. A man takes his girlfriend to a roofing job and she is injured. Is she covered under workers' compensation insurance? ______________________________
29. If the physician feels the injured employee is capable of returning to work after having been on temporary disability, what does the physician do? ______________________________

____
30. May a person receiving permanent disability benefits still work in another occupation?

____
31. Explain third-party subrogation. ______________________________
32. The process of carrying on a lawsuit is called ______________________________.
33. A proceeding during which an attorney questions a witness who answers under oath but not in open court is called a/an ______________________________.
34. The legal promise of a patient to satisfy a debt to the physician from proceeds received from a litigated case is termed a/an ______________________________.
35. When an employee with a pre-existing condition is injured at work and the injury produces a disability greater than that caused by the second injury alone, the benefits are derived from a/an ______________________________.
36. In a workers' compensation case, bills should be submitted ______________________________ or

______________________________,

and a claim becomes delinquent after a time frame of ______________________________.
37. If an individual seeks medical care for a workers' compensation injury from another state, which state's regulations are followed? ______________________________

ASSIGNMENT 50

Complete the *Doctor's First Report of Occupational Injury or Illness* (Fig. 14–3) for this nondisability type of claim. The ledger card could be photocopied after inserting procedure code numbers and fees (refer to Appendix A) and sent along with the report as a billing statement to the insurance carrier. X-rays would be billed by the hospital as inpatient diagnostic work-up. Refer to Glen Hiranuma's patient record (Fig. 14–1) and ledger card (Fig. 14–2) for information.

Abbreviations pertinent to this record:

AP ______________________

apt ______________________

DC ______________________

Dr ______________________

Ex ______________________

hosp ______________________

lat ______________________

lt ______________________

neg ______________________

PD ______________________

Pt ______________________

reg ______________________

R/O ______________________

Tr ______________________

Tx ______________________

____

PATIENT RECORD

Hiranuma,	Glen	M.	12-24-45	M	013/467-3383
LAST NAME	FIRST NAME	MIDDLE NAME	BIRTH DATE	SEX	HOME PHONE

4372 Hanley Avenue	Woodland Hills,	XY	12345
ADDRESS	CITY	STATE	ZIP CODE

house painter	Pittsburgh Paint Co. (Commercial painting Co.)
PATIENT'S OCCUPATION	NAME OF COMPANY

3725 Bonfeld Avenue Woodland Hills, XY 12345	013/486-9070
ADDRESS OF EMPLOYER	PHONE

Esme M. Hiranuma	homemaker
SPOUSE OR PARENT	OCCUPATION

EMPLOYER	ADDRESS	PHONE

State Compensation Ins. Fund	14156 Magnolia Blvd., Torres, XY 12349
NAME OF INSURANCE GROUP	SUBSCRIBER

Policy # 016-2432-211			
BLUE SHIELD OR BLUE CROSS CERT. NO.	GROUP NO.	CURRENT COVERAGE NO.	EFFECTIVE DATE

			558-40-9960
MEDICARE NO.	MEDICAID NO.	EFFECTIVE DATE	SOC. SEC. NO.

REFERRED BY:
Pittsburgh Paint Company

DATE	PROGRESS
5-22-9x	At 9:30 a.m. this ♂ pt was painting an apt ceiling. Pt slipped
	& fell from ladder & hit lt side of body. Apt located at
	3540 W. 87 St., Woodland Hills, XY 12345. Pt notified employer
	immediately. Adm. to College Hosp where x-rays of lt hip, lt femur,
	& cervical spine were taken (2 views AP & Lat)--all neg. CT of
	brain. (Dr. was called to hosp at request of employer & saw pt at
	5 p.m.) Ex & Tr for abrasions, multiple contusions & sprain of lt
	shoulder. Pt to be kept overnight in hosp to R/O head trauma &
	will be DC 5-23-9x. No PD expected. No further Tx after DC from
	hosp. Pt will resume reg work 6-1-9x. Gerald Practon, MD

FIGURE 14-1

STATEMENT

College Clinic
4567 Broad Avenue
Woodland Hills, XY 12345-0001
Telephone: 013-486-9002
Fax: 013-487-8976

TO: State Compensation Insurance Fund
14156 Magnolia Boulevard
Torres, XY 12349-0218

RE: Inj: Glen M. Hiranuma
Date of Inj: 5-22-9x
Emp: Pittsburgh Paint Company
Policy No.: 016-2432-211

DATE	PROFESSIONAL SERVICE DESCRIPTION	CPT/RVS CODES	CHARGE	CREDITS		CURRENT BALANCE
				PAYMENTS	ADJUSTMENTS	
5-22-9x	Hosp exam & initial treatment, C hx/exam, MC decision making					
5-22-9x	Medical report					
5-23-9x	Discharge hospital					

Due and payable within 10 days. **Pay last amount in balance column** ⇧

Key: PF: Problem-focused **SF:** Straightforward **CON:** Consultation **HCD:** House Call (Day)
EPF: Expanded problem-focused **LC:** Low complexity **CPX:** Complete Phys Exam **HCN:** House Call (Night)
D: Detailed **MC:** Moderate complexity **E:** Emergency **HV:** Hospital visit
C: Comprehensive **HC:** High complexity **ER:** Emergency Dept. **OV:** Office Visit

FIGURE 14-2

DOCTOR'S FIRST REPORT OF OCCUPATIONAL INJURY OR ILLNESS

Vithin 5 days of your initial examination, for every occupational injury or illness, send two copies of this report to the **employer's workers' compensation insurance carrier** **elf-insured employer.** Failure to file a timely doctor's report may result in assessment of a civil penalty. **In the case of diagnosed or suspected pesticide poisoning,** send a c his report to Division of Labor Statistics and Research, P.O. Box 420603, San Francisco, CA 94142-0603, and notify your local health officer by telephone within 24 hours.

1. **INSURER NAME AND ADDRESS**

2. **EMPLOYER NAME**

3. Address — No. and Street — City — Zip

4. Nature of business (e.g., food manufacturing, building construction, retailer of women's clothes)

5. **PATIENT NAME** (first name, middle initial, last name) — 6. Sex ☐ Male ☐ Female — 7. Date of Birth Mo. Day Yr.

8. Address: No. and Street — City — Zip — 9. Telephone number ( )

10. Occupation (Specific job title) — 11. Social Security Number

12. Injured at: No. and Street — City — County

13. Date and hour of injury or onset of illness Mo. Day Yr. Hour ________ a.m. ________ p.m — 14. Date last worked Mo. Day Yr.

15. Date and hour of first examination or treatment Mo. Day Yr. Hour ________ a.m ________ p.m. — 16. Have you (or your office) previously treated patient? ☐ Yes ☐ No

PLEASE DO USE THIS COLUMN: Case No — Industry — County — Age — Hazard — Disease — Hospitalizat — Occupatic — Return Date/

Patient please complete this portion, if able to do so. Otherwise, doctor please complete immediately. Inability or failure patient to complete this portion shall not affect his/her rights to workers' compensation under the California Labor Code.

17. **DESCRIBE HOW THE ACCIDENT OR EXPOSURE HAPPENED** (Give specific object, machinery or chemical. Use reverse side if more space is requi

18. **SUBJECTIVE COMPLAINTS** (Describe fully. Use reverse side if more space is required.)

19. **OBJECTIVE FINDINGS** (Use reverse side if more space is required.)
    A. Physical examination

    B. X-ray and laboratory results (State if none or pending.)

20. **DIAGNOSIS** (if occupational illness specify etiologic agent and duration of exposure.) Chemical or toxic compounds involved? ☐ Yes ☐ No

    ICD-9 Code __ __ __ . __

21. Are your findings and diagnosis consistent with patient's account of injury or onset of illness? ☐ Yes ☐ No If "no", please explain.

22. Is there any other current condition that will impede or delay patient's recovery? ☐ Yes ☐ No If "yes", please explain.

23. **TREATMENT RENDERED** (Use reverse side if more space is required.)

24. If further treatment required, specify treatment plan/estimated duration.

25. If hospitalized as inpatient, give hospital name and location — Date admitted Mo. Day Yr. — Estimated stay

26. **WORK STATUS**—Is patient able to perform usual work? ☐ Yes ☐ No
    If "no", date when patient can return to: Regular work ____/____/____
    Modified work ____/____/____ Specify restrictions ________

Doctor's Signature ________ CA License Number ________

Doctor Name and Degree (please type) ________ IRS Number ________

Address ________ Telephone Number (   )

FORM 5021 (REV. 4)
992

Any person who makes or causes to be made any knowingly false or fraudulent material statement or material representation for the purpose of obtaining or denying workers' compensation benefits or payments is guilty of a felony.

FIGURE 14-3

ASSIGNMENT 51

1. Complete the *First Treatment Medical Report* (Fig. 14–6) for this temporary disability type of claim. Date the form November 12. Remember to complete the report using only the pertinent information up to and including November 12, i.e., refer to only the first two entries on the patient record (Fig. 14–4). See Figure 14–5 for the patient's ledger card information. Use Dr. Parkinson's state license number as the I.D. number on the form.
2. Send in a *Doctor's Final Report and Bill* (Fig. 14–7) on December 29, and submit a complete billing in triplicate to the insurance company. Use the patient's Social Security number as the case number. Be sure to include procedure code numbers for each professional service rendered. Dr. Parkinson is a graduate of Columbia University Medical School, June, 1960. Refer to Appendix A for information on fees.

Abbreviations pertinent to this record:

Cons ______________________ PT ______________________

DC ______________________ qd ______________________

Dg ______________________ R ______________________

HV ______________________ Reg ______________________

OC ______________________ TD ______________________

p.m. ______________________ trt ______________________

P & S ______________________ W ______________________

PATIENT RECORD

LAST NAME	FIRST NAME	MIDDLE NAME	BIRTH DATE	SEX	HOME PHONE
Giovanni,	Carlos	A.	10-24-45	M	013/677-3485

ADDRESS	CITY	STATE	ZIP CODE
89 Beaumont Court,	Woodland Hills,	XY	12345

PATIENT'S OCCUPATION	NAME OF COMPANY
TV repairman	Giant Television Co. (tv repair co.)

ADDRESS OF EMPLOYER	PHONE
8764 Ocean Avenue, Woodland Hills, XY 12345	013/647-8851

SPOUSE OR PARENT	OCCUPATION
Maria B. Giovanni	homemaker

EMPLOYER	ADDRESS	PHONE

NAME OF INSURANCE GROUP	SUBSCRIBER
State Compensation Ins. Fund 600 S. Lafayette Park Pl., Ehrlich, XY 12350	

BLUE SHIELD OR BLUE CROSS CERT. NO.	GROUP NO.	CURRENT COVERAGE NO.	EFFECTIVE DATE
Policy # 57780			

MEDICARE NO.	MEDICAID NO.	EFFECTIVE DATE	SOC. SEC. NO.
			556-48-9699

REFERRED BY:
Giant Television Co.

DATE	PROGRESS
11-11-9x	Today at 2pm Pt was thrown from roof of private home (2231 Duarte St. Woodland Hills, XY 12345 in Woodland Hills County) states "When I was attaching the base of an antenna the weight of the antenna shifted + threw me off the roof." Adm. pt to College Hosp at 5pm. Pt was referred by employer. Dg: X-rays: fractured skull Pt also suffered cerebral concussion + R subdural hematoma. Brief loss of consciousness. No open wound. A.P. MD
11-12-9x	Performed R infratentorial craniotomy + removed subdural hematoma. Pt will be seen qd. TD: Pt will be disabled until 1-1-9x. Possible cranial defect + head disfigurement resulting. Pt to be hospitalized for approx 2wks for further tr. A. Parkinson, MD
11-14-9x	Pt seen in cons by Dr. Cosmo Graff who stated unable to correct cranial defect. Astro Parkinson, MD
11-30-9x	DC from hosp. Permanent cranial defect resulting from surgery.
12-29-9x	No further trt necessary. PT able to resume reg W on 1-15-9x.
	Astro Parkinson, MD

FIGURE 14-4

STATEMENT

College Clinic
4567 Broad Avenue
Woodland Hills, XY 12345-0001
Telephone: 013-486-9002
Fax: 013-487-8976

To: State Compensation Insurance Fund
600 S. Lafayette Park Place
Ehrlich, XY 1250-8900

RE: Inj: Carlos A. Giovanni
Date of Inj: 11-11-9x
Emp: Giant Television Company
Policy No.: 57780

DATE	PROFESSIONAL SERVICE DESCRIPTION	CPT/RVS CODES	CHARGE		CREDITS				CURRENT BALANCE	
					PAYMENTS		ADJUSTMENTS			
11-11-9x	HV, C hx/exam, HC decision making									
11-12-9x	Craniotomy remove subdural hematoma									
11-13 to 11-29-9x	HV, PF hx/exam, LC decision making									
11-30-9x	Hosp discharge									
12-29-9x	OC,EPF hx/exam, LC decision making, workers' compensation report									

Due and payable within 10 days. **Pay last amount in balance column** ⇧

Key: PF: Problem-focused **SF:** Straightforward **CON:** Consultation **HCD:** House Call (Day)
EPF: Expanded problem-focused **LC:** Low complexity **CPX:** Complete Phys Exam **HCN:** House Call (Night)
D: Detailed **MC:** Moderate complexity **E:** Emergency **HV:** Hospital visit
C: Comprehensive **HC:** High complexity **ER:** Emergency Dept. **OV:** Office Visit

FIGURE 14-5

printed on recycled paper

NEBRASKA WORKERS' COMPENSATION COURT

First Treatment Medical Report

(Must be filed with Compensation Court & Employer within 14 days of first treatment)

(Shaded sections are not required)

YPE OR PRINT

PATIENT & INSURED (SUBSCRIBER) INFORMATION

1. PATIENT'S NAME (First name, middle initial, last name)
2. PATIENT'S DATE OF BIRTH
3. INSURED'S NAME (Employer)
4. PATIENT'S ADDRESS (Street, City, State, ZIP Code)
5. PATIENT'S SEX — MALE — FEMALE
6. INSURED'S I.D. NO. (Include any letters)
7. PATIENT'S RELATIONSHIP TO INSURED — SELF — SPOUSE — CHILD — OTHER
8. INSURED'S GROUP NO. (Or Group Name)
9. OTHER HEALTH INSURANCE COVERAGE – Enter Name of Policyholder and Plan Name and Address and Policy or Medical Assistance Number
10. WAS CONDITION RELATED TO
   A. PATIENT'S EMPLOYMENT — YES — NO
   B. AN AUTO ACCIDENT — YES — NO
11. INSURED'S ADDRESS (Street, City, State, ZIP Code)
12. PATIENT'S OR AUTHORIZED PERSON'S SIGNATURE
   I Authorize the Release of any Medical Information Necessary to Process this Claim
   SIGNED
12A. PATIENT'S SOCIAL SECURITY NO.
   DATE
13. I AUTHORIZE PAYMENT OF MEDICAL BENEFITS TO UNDERSIGNED PHYSI OR SUPPLIER FOR SERVICE DESCRIBED BELOW
   SIGNED (Insured or Authorized Person)

PHYSICIAN OR SUPPLIER INFORMATION

14. DATE OF: ILLNESS (FIRST SYMPTOM OR INJURY (ACCIDENT)
15. DATE FIRST CONSULTED YOU FOR THIS CONDITION
16. HAS PATIENT EVER HAD SAME OR SIMILAR SYMPTOMS? — YES — NO
17. DATE PATIENT ABLE TO RETURN TO WORK
18. DATES OF TOTAL DISABILITY — FROM — THROUGH
   DATES OF PARTIAL DISABILITY — FROM — THROUGH
19. NAME OF REFERRING PHYSICIAN
20. FOR SERVICES RELATED TO HOSPITALIZATION GIVE HOSPITALIZATION D
   ADMITTED — DISCHARGED
21. NAME & ADDRESS OF FACILITY WHERE SERVICES RENDERED (If other than home or office)
22. WAS LABORATORY WORK PERFORMED OUTSIDE YOUR OFFICE? — YES — NO — CHARGES:
23. DIAGNOSIS OR NATURE OF ILLNESS OR INJURY. RELATE DIAGNOSIS TO PROCEDURE IN COLUMN D BY REFERENCE TO NUMBERS 1, 2, 3, ETC. OR DX CODE

1.
2.
3.
4.

24 A DATE OF SERVICE	B* PLACE OF SERVICE	C. FULLY DESCRIBE PROCEDURES, MEDICAL SERVICE OR SUPPLIES FURNISHED FOR EACH DATE GIVEN — PROCEDURE CODE (IDENTIFY:)	(EXPLAIN UNUSUAL SERVICES OR CIRCUMSTANCES)	D DIAGNOSIS CODE	E CHARGES	F

24A. HISTORY: GIVE BRIEF DESCRIPTION OF WHAT OCCURRED. PATIENT'S ACCOUNT OF ACCIDENT.

25. SIGNATURE OF PHYSICIAN OR SUPPLIER
   SIGNED — DATE
26. ACCEPT ASSIGNMENT GOVERNMENT CLAIMS ONLY) — YES — NO
27. TOTAL CHARGE
28. AMOUNT PAID
29. BALANCE DUE
   PHYSICIAN'S SOCIAL SECURITY NO.
31. PHYSICIAN'S OR SUPPLIER'S NAME, ADDRESS, ZIP CODE & TELEPHONE
   I.D. NO.
32. YOUR PATIENT'S ACCOUNT NO.
33. YOUR EMPLOYER I.D. NO.

PLACE OF SERVICE CODES

–(IH) INPATIENT HOSPITAL	4—(H) – PATIENT'S HOME	7—(NH) – NURSING HOME	O—(OL) OTHER LOCATIONS
–(OH) – OUTPATIENT HOSPITAL	5— – DAY CARE FACILITY (PSY)	8—(SNF) – SKILLED NURSING FACILITY	A—(IL) – INDEPENDENT LABORATORY
–(O) – DOCTOR'S OFFICE	6— – NIGHT CARE FACILITY (PSY)	9— – AMBULANCE	B— – OTHER MEDICAL/SURGICAL FACIL

WCC FORM 45 (Rev. 86)

FIGURE 14-6

STATE COMPENSATION INSURANCE FUND

DOCTOR'S FINAL (OR MONTHLY) REPORT AND BILL

Monthly itemized bills required on all cases under continuing treatment.
Services beginning late in month and extending into succeeding month may be itemized on one statement.

CASE No. ____________

EMPLOYEE ____________
DATE OF INJURY ____________
EMPLOYER ____________

SERVICES FOR MONTH OF ____________ 19 ____

Patient refused treatment ____________ 19 ____
Patient stopped treatment without orders ____________ 19 ____
Patient entered hospital ____________ 19 ____
Further treatment anticipated? ______ (Yes) ______ (No)

Patient able to return to work ____________ 19 ____
Patient discharged as cured ____________ 19 ____
Condition at time of last visit ____________

Any other charges authorized such as Drugs? ______ (Check) Hospital? ______ (Check)

Code: O—Office; V—Home Visit; H—Hospital Visit; N—Night Visit; S—Operation; X—X-ray.

Month	1	2	3	4	5	6	7	8	9	10	11	12	13	14	15	16	17	18	19	20	21	22	23	24	25	26	27	28	29	30	31

	RVS CODE	TOTALS
First aid treatment *(describe)* ____________	# ______	$ ______
Office Visits ____________	# ______	$ ______
Home Visits ____________	# ______	$ ______
Hospital Visits ____________	# ______	$ ______
Operations ____________	# ______	$ ______
MATERIAL *(Itemize at cost)* ____________	# ______	$ ______

Any charges shown above which are in excess of the scheduled fee must be explained regarding nature of such services, indicating the date rendered. TOTAL $ ____________

Make check payable to:

Doctor ____________

Address ____________ (Street)

____________ (City) (Zip)

Signature ____________

Date ____________

LEAVE BLANK

APPROVED

(Dollars) (Cents)

BY ____________

DATE ____________

Internal Revenue Code Section 6109 requires you to furnish your Internal Revenue Service Employer Identification Number or Social Security Number. Please enter the Identification Number here ____________ .

IMPORTANT.—
Bills Must Be Submitted in Duplicate

SCIF FORM 60 (REV. 5-78)
66744-218 30 M - OSP

FIGURE 14-7

ASSIGNMENT 52

1. Complete the *Attending Physician's Report* (Fig. 14–10). Date it October 17. The claim number will be the patient's Social Security number. Remember to complete the report using only the pertinent information up to and including October 16, i.e., refer to the first three entries on the patient record (Fig. 14–8). Be sure to include procedure code numbers for each professional service rendered. Mr. Weston was seen previously by another physician, and Dr. Gaston Input is taking over this case on October 1. Appendix A may be used for reference for fees and procedure codes.
2. Mr. Weston returns to see Dr. Input on November 12. Complete a *Doctor's Supplemental Report* (Fig. 14–11), and date it November 12, 199X. The November 12 office visit was limited. Refer to Appendix A for the fee. Record the proper information on the ledger card (Fig. 14–9) for all these transactions.
   Note: Some states have workers' compensation laws specific to maximum fees for industrial reports as well as insurance carriers' payments.

Abbreviations pertinent to this record:

adv ______________________ PD ______________________

CO ______________________ Pt ______________________

DC ______________________ retn ______________________

exam ______________________ rev ______________________

HX ______________________ rt ______________________

imp ______________________ slt ______________________

inj ______________________ trt ______________________

med ______________________ wks ______________________

orig ______________________

COMPUTER EXERCISE

CASE 5 PRIVATE ACCIDENT

Before proceeding, you may want to do an exercise based on the concepts you have learned throughout the textbook. Additional practice material is on your computer diskette. Although Case 5 is not a workers' compensation scenario, it is more difficult than Cases 1 through 4 and will give you experience in handling a claim for a private insurance accident case.

Directions: Insert the diskette into the computer and follow the instructions on the screen for Computer Exercise Case 5.

PATIENT RECORD

Weston,	Keith	P.	01-03-48	M	013/567-8898
LAST NAME	FIRST NAME	MIDDLE NAME	BIRTH DATE	SEX	HOME PHONE

4201 Huntington Drive,	Woodland Hills,	XY	12345
ADDRESS	CITY	STATE	ZIP CODE

delivery man	Hathaway Service Co. (parcel delivery co)
PATIENT'S OCCUPATION	NAME OF COMPANY

200 Holloway Drive, Woodland Hills, XY 12345	013/466-7887
ADDRESS OF EMPLOYER	PHONE

Jane F. Weston	homemaker
SPOUSE OR PARENT	OCCUPATION

EMPLOYER	ADDRESS	PHONE

State Compensation Ins. Fund 14156 Magnolia Blvd., Torres, XY 12349	
NAME OF INSURANCE GROUP	SUBSCRIBER

Policy # 578099			
BLUE SHIELD OR BLUE CROSS CERT. NO.	GROUP NO.	CURRENT COVERAGE NO.	EFFECTIVE DATE

			174-98-0080
MEDICARE NO.	MEDICAID NO.	EFFECTIVE DATE	SOC. SEC. NO.

REFERRED BY:
Hathaway Service Company

DATE	PROGRESS
10-1-9x	CO recurrent pain lower rt abdomen. Records forwarded from prior exams for evaluation. Orig inj 8-18-9x at 2 p.m. Hx & exam showed right inguinal hernia. Reviewed prior med records & assessed data & evaluations. Imp: rt recurrent inguinal hernia Recommended trt: herniorrhaphy on outpt basis. Gaston Input, MD
10-11-9x	Outpt Surg: R recurrent inguinal herniorrhaphy at College Hospital. See short-stay op report. Gaston Input, MD
10-16-9x	Improved as expected. Adv to rest a home for 3 wks. Pt able to retn to work 11-15-9x. No PD anticipated. Gaston Input, MD
11-12-9x	Pt continues to have slt pain. Unable to retn to work on 11-15-9x. Some pain on forward bending + lt lateral bending. To retn in 1 wk for re-exam. Pt should be able to resume work on 11-25-9x. Full recovery expected by 12-30-9x. Gaston Input, MD

FIGURE 14-8

STATEMENT

College Clinic
4567 Broad Avenue
Woodland Hills, XY 12345-0001
Telephone: 013-486-9002
Fax: 013-487-8976

TO: State Compensation Insurance Fund
14156 Magnolia Boulevard
Torres, XY 12349-9860

RE: Case No.: 174-98-0080
Injured: Keith P. Weston
Date of Inj: 8-18-9x
Employer: Hathaway Service Company

DATE	PROFESSIONAL SERVICE DESCRIPTION	CPT/RVS	CHARGE	CREDITS		CURRENT BALANCE
				PAYMENTS	ADJUSTMENTS	
10-1-9x	Extensive rev of prior med records & assessment of data, evaluation & written report					
10-11-9x	Rt recurrent inguinal herniorrhaphy					
11-12-9x	OC					

Due and payable within 10 days. **Pay last amount in balance column**

Key: PF: Problem-focused	**SF:** Straightforward	**CON:** Consultation	**HCD:** House Call (Day)
EPF: Expanded problem-focused	**LC:** Low complexity	**CPX:** Complete Phys Exam	**HCN:** House Call (Night)
D: Detailed	**MC:** Moderate complexity	**E:** Emergency	**HV:** Hospital visit
C: Comprehensive	**HC:** High complexity	**ER:** Emergency Dept.	**OV:** Office Visit

FIGURE 14-9

ATTENDING PHYSICIAN'S REPORT

nployee: ______________________ Claim Number: ______________________

nployer: ______________________ Date of Injury(ies): ________ Date of Next Exam: ________

ate of This Exam: ______________________ Patient Social Security No.: ______________________

urrent Diagnosis: ______________________
clude ICD•9 Code)
____

PATIENT STATUS

nce the last exam, this patient's condition has:

☐ improved as expected. ☐ improved, but slower than expected. ☐ not improved significantly.

☐ worsened. ☐ plateaued, no further improvement is expected. ☐ has been determined to be non-work related.

riefly describe any change in objective or subjective complaint: ______________________
____

TREATMENT

reatment plan: (only list changes from prior status) ☐ No change ☐ Patient is/was discharged from care on ________

st. Discharge Date: ______________ Medications: ______________

herapy: Type ______________ Times per week ________ Estimated Date of Completion ________

iagnostic Studies: ______________________

ospitalization/Surgery: ______________________

onsult/Other Service: ______________________

WORK STATUS

he patient has been instructed to:

☐ return to full duty with no limitations or restrictions.

☐ remain off the rest of the day and return to work tomorrow:
_____ with no limits or restrictions. _____ with limits listed below.

☐ return to work on ______________________
work limitations: ______________________

☐ remain off work until ______________________

stimated date patient can return full duty: ______________________

DISABILITY STATUS

☐ Patient discharged as cured.

lease supply a brief narrative report if any of the below apply:

☐ Patient will be permanently precluded from engaging in his/her usual and customary occupation.

☐ Patient's condition is permanent and stationary.

☐ Patient will have permanent residuals. ☐ Patient will require future medical care.

hysician Name: ______________________ Address: ______________________

)ate: ______________________ Telephone: (______) ______________________

ignature: ______________________

FIGURE 14-10

STATE
FUND

Case No.:
Injured:
Injury date:

DOCTOR'S SUPPLEMENTAL REPORT

The information requested in this report is necessary to establish eligibility for further benefits.
You may make your notations on this form (including reverse side if more space required) or, if more convenient, forward a brief report containing the necessary information.

1. Have you discharged patient?__________If so, when?______________________________
(if answer to above is yes and you expect no permanent residuals, you may disregard remainder of form, sign and return)

2. Date of last examination______________________________________

3. Present condition and prognosis (indicate if diagnosis changed since last report)________________

4. Treatment required by injury in question (type, length and frequency)________________

5. Date injured was or will be able to return to work________________________
6. When do you expect full recovery from injury in question?____________________

______________________________ _______________
(Doctor's Signature) (Date)

If you wish to discuss this case in greater detail, please contact our Claims Department at the above address.

SCIF 3036 (REV. 5-74) OLD

FIGURE 14-11

CHAPTER 15

Disability Income Insurance and Disability Benefit Programs

Key Terms

Your instructor may wish to select some specific words pertinent to this chapter for a test. For definitions of the terms, further study, and/or reference, the words, phrases, and abbreviations may be found in the Glossary at the end of the textbook. Key terms for this chapter follow:

accidental death and dismemberment
armed services disability
Civil Service Retirement System (CSRS)
consultative examiner (CE)
cost-of-living adjustment
Disability Determination Services (DDS)
disability income insurance
double indemnity
elimination period
Federal Employees Retirement System (FERS)
future purchase option
hearing
long-term disability insurance
nonoccupational policy
partial disability
reconsideration
regional office (RO)
short-term disability income insurance
Social Security Administration (SSA)
Social Security Disability Insurance (SSDI) program
State Disability Insurance (SDI)
supplemental benefits
Temporary Disability Insurance (TDI)
total disability
Unemployment Compensation Disability (UCD)
Veterans Administration Disability program
Veterans Administration (VA) Outpatient Clinics
voluntary disability insurance
waiver of premium

Performance Objectives

The student will be able to

- Define and spell the key terms for this chapter, given the information from the textbook Glossary, within a reasonable period of time and with enough accuracy to obtain a satisfactory evaluation.
- Answer the review questions after reading the chapter, with enough accuracy to obtain a satisfactory evaluation.
- Fill in the correct meaning of each abbreviation, given a list of common medical abbreviations and symbols that appear in chart notes, within a reasonable period of time and with enough accuracy to obtain a satisfactory evaluation.
- Complete each state disability form, given the patients' medical chart notes and blank state disability forms, within a reasonable period of time and with enough accuracy to obtain a satisfactory evaluation.

Study Outline

INTRODUCTION
HISTORY
DISABILITY INCOME INSURANCE
- Individual
  - Waiting period
  - Benefit period
  - Clauses
  - Benefits
  - Exclusions
  - AIDS and HIV
- Group

FEDERAL DISABILITY PROGRAMS
- Workers' Compensation
- Disability benefit programs
- Social Security disability insurance program
  - Background
  - Disability
  - Eligibility
- Supplemental Security Income
  - Eligibility
- Civil Service and federal employees disability benefits
- Armed services disability benefits
- Veterans Administration disability benefits
  - Benefits
  - Emergency outpatient treatment

STATE DISABILITY INSURANCE
- Background
- Funding
- Eligibility
- Benefits
  - Limited benefits
  - Reduced benefits
- Time limits
- Medical examinations
- Limitations
- Voluntary disability insurance plan

INSTRUCTIONS AND PROCEDURES FOR CLAIMS SUBMISSION
- Disability income claims
- Federal disability claims
- Veterans Administration disability outpatient clinic claims
- State disability claims

Review Questions

Review the objectives, key terms, glossary definitions to key terms, chapter information, tables, and figures before completing the following review questions.

1. Health insurance that provides monthly or weekly income when an individual is unable to work because of a nonindustrial illness or injury is called ________________ .

2. Another insurance term for *benefits* is ____ .

3. When an individual who is insured under a disability income insurance policy cannot perform *one or more* of his or her regular job duties, this is known as __________ or ______________________________ disability.

4. When a person insured under a disability income insurance policy cannot perform *all functions* of his or her regular job duties for a limited period of time, this is known as ________________________ disability.
5. When investigating the purchase of insurance, the word(s) to look for in the insurance contract that mean the premium cannot be increased at renewal time is/are ____ .
6. When an individual becomes permanently disabled and cannot pay the insurance premium, a desirable provision in an insurance contract is __________________ .
7. Some insurance contracts that pay twice the face amount of the policy if accidental death occurs may have a provision entitled ___________________________________ .
8. Provisions that limit the scope of insurance coverage are known as __________ .
9. Ezra Jackson has disability income insurance under a group policy paid for by his employer. One evening he goes roller blading and suffers a complex fracture of the patella requiring several months off work. Are his monthly disability benefits taxable? ____________________ Why? _______________________________________

____
10. Two federal programs for individuals under 65 years of age who suffer from a severe disability are:

    a. ____

    b. ____
11. To be eligible to apply for disability benefits under Social Security, an individual must be unable to do any type of work for a period of ________________________ .
12. Social Security may hire a physician to evaluate an applicant's disability. A physician's role may be any one of the following:

    a. ____

    b. ____

    c. ____
13. A Social Security division that determines an individual's eligibility to be placed under the federal disability program is called _______________________________ .
14. Jamie Woods, a Navy petty officer, suffers an accident aboard the USS Denebola just before his honorable discharge. To receive veteran's benefits for this injury, the time limit in which a claim must be filed is _________________________________ .

15. Name the states that have nonindustrial state disability programs.

a. ____________________

b. ____________________

c. ____________________

d. ____________________

e. ____________________

f. ____________________

16. List two states where hospital benefits may be paid for nonoccupational illness or injury under a state's temporary disability benefit program.

a. ____________________

b. ____________________

17. Temporary disability insurance claims must be filed within how many days in your state? ____________________

18. How long can a person continue to draw temporary disability insurance benefits?

____

19. After a claim begins, when do basic state disability benefits become payable if the patient is confined at home? ____________________

If the patient is hospitalized? ____________________

20. Nick Tyson has recovered from a previous temporary disability and becomes ill again with the same ailment. Is he entitled to state disability benefits? __________

21. Peggy Jonson has an ectopic pregnancy and is unable to work because of this complication of her pregnancy. Can she receive state temporary disability benefits? ______

22. If a woman has an abnormal condition that arises out of her pregnancy (such as diabetes or varicose veins) and is unable to work because of the condition, can she receive state disability benefits? ______________ Four states that allow for maternity benefits in normal pregnancy are

a. ____________________

b. ____________________

c. ____________________

d. ____________________

23. John S. Thatcher stubbed his toe as he was leaving work. Since the injury was only slightly uncomfortable, he thought no more about it. The next morning he found that his foot was too swollen to fit in his shoe, so he stayed home. When the swelling did not subside after 3 days, John went to the doctor. X-rays showed a broken toe, which kept John home for 2 weeks. After 1 week he applied for temporary state disability benefits.

Will he be paid? ________________ Why? ______________________________

____

24. Betty T. Kraft had to stay home from her job because her 10-year-old daughter had measles. She applied for temporary state disability benefits. Will she be paid?

________________ Why? ______________________________________

____

25. Vincent P. Michael was ill with a bad cold for 1 week. Will he receive temporary state disability benefits? ________________ Why? ____________________

26. Betsy C. Palm had an emergency appendectomy and was hospitalized for 3 days. Will she receive state disability benefits? ______________ Why? ______________

____

27. Frank E. Thompson is a box boy at a supermarket on Saturdays and Sundays while a full-time student at college. He broke his leg while skiing so he cannot work at the market, but he is able to attend classes with his leg in a cast. Can he collect state disability benefits for his part-time job? ________________ Why? ________________

____

28. Jerry L. Slate is out of a job and is receiving unemployment insurance benefits. He is now suffering from a severe case of intestinal flu. The employment office calls him to interview for a job, but he is too ill to go. Can he collect temporary state disability benefits for this illness when he might have been given a job? ________________ Why? _______

____

____

29. Joan T. Corman has diabetes, which sometimes makes her weak so that she has to leave work early in the afternoon. She loses pay for each hour she cannot work. Can she collect temporary state disability benefits? ________________ Why? ____________

____

30. While walking the picket line with other employees on strike, Gene J. Berry came down with pneumonia and was ill for 2 weeks. Can he collect temporary state disability benefits? ________________ Why?________________________________

____

Gene went back to work for 3 weeks and then developed a slight cold and cough, which again was diagnosed as pneumonia. The doctor told him to stay home from work. Would he be able to collect temporary disability benefits again?
________________ Why?

____

31. A month after he retired, Roger Reagan had a gallbladder operation. Can he receive temporary state disability benefits? ________________ Why? ____________

____

32. Jane M. Lambert fell in the backyard of her home and fractured her left ankle. She had a nonunion fracture and was out of work for 28 weeks. For how long will she collect temporary state disability benefits? ________________

33. Dr. Kay examines Ben Yates and completes a claim form for state disability income due to a prolonged illness. On receiving the information, the insurance adjuster notices some conflicting data. Name other documents that may be requested to justify payment of benefits.

a. ____

b. ____

c. ____

34. Trent Walters, a permanently disabled individual, applies for federal disability benefits.

To establish eligibility for benefits under this program, data allowed must be _____ year(s) old.

35. A Veterans Affairs patient is seen as an emergency by Dr. Onion. Name the two methods or options for billing this case.

a. ____

b. ____

36. When submitting a claim form for a patient applying for state disability benefits, the most important item required on the form is ________________________________.

ASSIGNMENT 53

To familiarize you with what information the employee must furnish, this assignment will encompass completing both the *Claim Statement of Employee* (Fig. 15–2) and the *Doctor's Certificate* (Fig. 15–3). Mr. Broussard (Fig. 15–1) is applying for state disability benefits, and he does not receive sick leave pay from his employer. Date the Claim Statement of Employee November 5, and date the Doctor's Certificate November 10. Remember that this is not a claim for payment to the physician, so no ledger card has been furnished for this patient.

Abbreviations pertinent to this record:

exam ______________________ retn ______________________

hosp ______________________ rt ______________________

imp ______________________ SLR ______________________

lt ______________________ wk ______________________

pt ______________________ WNL ______________________

PATIENT RECORD

Broussard,	Jeff	L.	03-09-52	M	013/466-2490
LAST NAME	FIRST NAME	MIDDLE NAME	BIRTH DATE	SEX	HOME PHONE

3577 Plain Street,	Woodland Hills,	XY	12345
ADDRESS	CITY	STATE	ZIP CODE

carpenter   Payroll # 2156 — Ace Construction Company
PATIENT'S OCCUPATION — NAME OF COMPANY

4556 West Eighth Street, Dorland, XY 12347 — 013/477-8900
ADDRESS OF EMPLOYER — PHONE

Harriet M. Broussard — secretary
SPOUSE OR PARENT — OCCUPATION

Merit Accounting Co. — 6743 Main St., Woodland Hills, XY 12345 — 013/478-0980
EMPLOYER — ADDRESS — PHONE

Blue Cross — Jeff L. Broussard
NAME OF INSURANCE GROUP — SUBSCRIBER

466-23-9979		6131	1-1-80
BLUE SHIELD OR BLUE CROSS CERT. NO.	GROUP NO.	CURRENT COVERAGE NO.	EFFECTIVE DATE
			566-12-0090
MEDICARE NO.	MEDICAID NO.	EFFECTIVE DATE	SOC. SEC. NO.

REFERRED BY:
Harold B. Hartburn (friend)

DATE	PROGRESS
10-21-9x	On 8-15-9x after swinging a golf club, pt had sudden onset of severe pain in low back with radiation to lt side. Pt unable to work on 8-16 but resumed wk on 8-17 and has been working full time but doing no lifting while working. Exam showed SLR strongly positive on lt, on rt causes pain into lt side. Neurological exam WNL. Raymond Skelton, MD
10-29-9x	At 10 a.m. pt admitted to College Hosp. Myelogram ordered. R.S. MD
10-30-9x	Myelogram showed huge defect L4-5 on lt. Imp: acute herniated disc L4-5 on lt. Raymond Skelton, MD
11-1-9x	Operation: Lumbar laminotomy & disc excision L4-5. Pt seen daily in hosp. Raymond Skelton MD
11-10-9x	At 3 p.m. pt discharged to home. Will retn to wk 12-15-9x. Raymond Skelton, MD

FIGURE 15-1

LAIM STATEMENT OF EMPLOYEE

OMPLETE *ALL* ITEMS. IF INCOMPLETE, THIS FORM WILL BE RETURNED, CAUSING A DELAY IN BENEFIT PAYMENTS

o you need assistance in a language other than English? ☐ No ☐ Yes **If yes, write that language here** ____________

'refiere Ud. formularios escritos en español? ☐ No ☐ Sí

Print your full name: FIRST INITIAL LAST

2. **IMPORTANT: Enter your Social Security Account Number**

Other Names (including maiden, married and ethnic surnames) Used:

2A. If you have used another Social Security number, enter that number here

Your Mailing Address:
REET ADDRESS, P.O. BOX OR RFD APT. NO. CITY OR TOWN STATE AND ZIP CODE

3. What was the first day you were too sick to perform all the duties of your regular or customary work, even if it was a Saturday, Sunday, holiday, or a normal day off?

MONTH DAY YEAR

Your Home Address: (if different from mailing address)
REET ADDRESS, OR SPECIFIC DIRECTIONS TO YOUR HOME IF P.O. BOX OR RFD

ALE ☐ FEMALE ☐ Birthdate Mo. Day Yr.

4. What was the last day you worked?

MONTH DAY YEAR

5. Employer's Business Name: Telephone Number ( )

Employer's Business Address: NUMBER AND STREET CITY STATE AND ZIP CODE

6. Your occupation with this employer. Your Badge or Payroll number:

7. What is your usual occupation?

8. Are you self-employed? Yes ☐ No ☐

9. Did you lose any time from work because of this illness or injury during the two weeks before the last day you worked as shown in item (4) above? Yes ☐ No ☐

0. Did you stop work because of sickness, injury or pregnancy? If "No," please give reason: Yes ☐ No ☐

1. Have you filed for or received UNEMPLOYMENT INSURANCE benefits between the last day you worked and the first day you became disabled? Yes ☐ No ☐

2. a. Has, or will your employer continue your pay by means of sick leave, vacation, pension, gift or other means? Yes ☐ No ☐

b. Do you authorize the Employment Development Department to disclose benefit eligibility information to your employer to be used only for the purpose of integrating your employer's wage continuation/sick leave program with your benefits? (This information is limited to the claim effective date; the weekly and maximum benefit amounts; and the periods covered by benefit payments.) Yes ☐ No ☐

3. Was this disability or any other disability during this claim period caused by your work? Yes ☐ No ☐
If "Yes," please provide the name and address of any insurance carrier from whom you are claiming or receiving Workers' Compensation Benefits:

4. Have you recovered from your disability? If "Yes," enter date of recovery: Yes ☐ No ☐

5. Have you returned to work for any day, part-time or full-time after the beginning date of your disability as shown in item (3) above? If "Yes," please enter such dates: Yes ☐ No ☐

6. Were you, as a result of an arrest, confined to a jail, detention center, prison, medical center or other correctional institution or any other place at any time during your disability? If "Yes," give dates: Yes ☐ No ☐

hereby claim benefits and certify that for the period covered by this claim I was unemployed and disabled, that the foregoing statements including any accompanying atements are to the best of my knowledge and belief true, correct and complete. I hereby authorize my attending physician, practitioner, hospital and employer to furish and disclose all facts concerning my disability and wages or earnings that are within their knowledge and to allow inspection of and provide copies of any hospital ecords concerning my disability that are under their control. I understand that authorizations contained in this claim statement are granted for a period of 18 months om the date of my signature or the effective date of the claim, whichever is later. I agree that a photocopy of this release shall be as valid as the original.

laim signed on: MONTH DAY YEAR | Claimant's signature: (DO NOT PRINT) ▶ | Telephone Number ( )

Under Section 2101 of the California Unemployment Insurance Code, it is a violation to willfully make a false statement or knowingly conceal a material fact in order to obtain the payment of any benefits, such violation being punishable by imprisonment and/or by a fine not exceeding $20,000 or both.

If your signature is made by mark (X) it must be attested by two witnesses with their addresses.

SIGNATURE-WITNESS | SIGNATURE-WITNESS

ADDRESS | ADDRESS

If an authorized agent is filing for benefits for an INCAPACITATED or DECEASED claimant, or a spouse is filing for a MENTALLY INCAPACITATED individual, contact the office below for the required forms and instructions.

FIGURE 15-2

DOCTOR'S CERTIFICATE

Certification may be made by a licensed medical or osteopathic physician and surgeon, chiropractor, dentist, podiatrist, optometrist, designated psychologist or an authorized medical officer of a United States Government facility. Certification may also be made by a licensed nurse-midwife or nurse practitioner for the purposes of disability related to normal pregnancy or childbirth. All items on this sheet must be completed legibly.

Patient File No.	Name	Social Security Number

17. I attended the patient for the present medical problem from: MONTH DAY YEAR To MONTH DAY YEAR At intervals of:

18. Are you completing this form for the sole purpose of referral or recommendation to an alcoholic recovery home or drug-free residential facility? Yes ☐ No ☐ If yes, please enter facility name and address in item #28.

19. History:
Findings (state nature, severity and bodily extent of the incapacitating disease or injury):
Diagnosis:
ICD Disease Code, Primary: (REQUIRED)
ICD Disease Code, Secondary:
Type of treatment and/or medication rendered to patient:

20. Diagnosis confirmed by: **(Specify type of test or X-ray)**

21. Is this patient now pregnant or has she been pregnant since the date of treatment as reported above? Yes ☐ No ☐ If "Yes", date pregnancy terminated or future EDC.
Is the pregnancy normal? Yes ☐ No ☐ If "No," state the abnormal and involuntary complication causing maternal disability:

22. Operation: Date performed or to be performed ☐ Type of Operation: ICD Procedure Code: (REQUIRED)

23. Has the patient at any time during your attendance for this medical problem, been incapable of performing his or her regular work? Yes ☐ No ☐ If "Yes" the disability commenced on:

24. APPROXIMATE date, based on your examination of patient, disability (if any) should end or has ended sufficiently to permit the patient to resume regular or customary work. Even if considerable question exists, make SOME "estimate." This is a requirement of the Code, and the claim will be delayed if such date is not entered. Such answers as "Indefinite" or "don't know" will not suffice. (ENTER DATE)

25. Based on your examination of patient, is this disability the result of "occupation" either as an "industrial accident" or as an "occupational disease"?
Yes ☐ No ☐ (This should include aggravation of pre-existing conditions by occupation.)

26. Have you reported this OR A CONCURRENT DISABILITY to any insurance carrier as a Workers' Compensation Claim?
Yes ☐ No ☐ If "Yes," to whom? (Name of carrier or firm)

27. Was patient in a hospital surgical unit, surgical unit, ambulatory surgical center certified to participate in the federal Medicare program or a postsurgical recovery care unit as designated by section 1250.9 of the Health and Safety Code? Yes ☐ No ☐
If "Yes," please provide name and address:

28. Was or is patient a resident in an alcoholic recovery home or drug-free residential facility? Yes ☐ No ☐
If "Yes," please provide name and address:

29. Was or is patient confined as a registered bed patient in a hospital? Yes ☐ No ☐
If "Yes," please provide name and address:

Date and hour entered as a registered bed patient and discharged pursuant to your orders:

ENTERED	**STILL CONFINED**	**DISCHARGED**
on , 19 , at A.M. P.M.	on , 19	on , 19 , at A.M. P.M.

30. Would the disclosure of this information to your patient be medically or psychologically detrimental to the patient?
Yes ☐ No ☐

I hereby certify that, based on my examination, the above statements truly describe the patient's disability (if any) and the estimated duration thereof, and that I am a ______________________ licensed to practice by the State of ______________________
(TYPE OF DOCTOR)

▶ PRINT OR TYPE DOCTOR'S NAME AS SHOWN ON LICENSE

▶ SIGNATURE OF ATTENDING DOCTOR

▶ NO. AND STREET CITY ZIP CODE

▶ STATE LICENSE NUMBER ( ) TELEPHONE NO. DATE OF SIGNING THIS FORM

"Under Section 2116 of the California Unemployment Insurance Code, it is a violation for any individual who, with the intent to defraud, falsely certifies the medical condition of any person in order to obtain disability insurance benefits, whether for the maker or for any other person, and is punishable by imprisonment and/or a fine not exceeding twenty thousand dollars.

FIGURE 15-3

ASSIGNMENT 54

1. Let us assume that the Claim Statement of Employee has been completed satisfactorily by Mr. Fred E. Thorndike (Fig. 15–4). Complete the *Doctor's Certificate* portion of the First Claim Form (Fig. 15–5), and date it December 2. In completing this portion of the assignment, look at the first entry made by Dr. Practon on November 25 only.

2. Mr. Thorndike returns to see Dr. Practon on December 7, at which time his disability leave needs to be extended. Complete the *Physician's Supplementary Certificate* (Fig. 15–6) by referring to the entry made during the second visit, and date the Certificate December 7. Remember that this is not a claim for payment to the physician, so no ledger card has been furnished for this patient.

Abbreviations pertinent to this record:

Dx ______________________ SD ______________________

PE ______________________ slt ______________________

Pt ______________________ wk ______________________

Reg ______________________ wks ______________________

PATIENT RECORD

Thorndike,	Fred	E.	02-17-44	M	013/465-7820
LAST NAME	FIRST NAME	MIDDLE NAME	BIRTH DATE	SEX	HOME PHONE

5784 Helen Street,	Woodland Hills,	XY	12345
ADDRESS	CITY	STATE	ZIP CODE

salesman   Payroll No. 6852   Easy On Paint Company
PATIENT'S OCCUPATION   NAME OF COMPANY

4586 West 20th Street, Woodland Hills, XY 12345   013/467-8898
ADDRESS OF EMPLOYER   PHONE

Jennifer B. Thorndike   homemaker
SPOUSE OR PARENT   OCCUPATION

EMPLOYER   ADDRESS   PHONE

Pacific Mutual Insurance Co.   Fred E. Thorndike
NAME OF INSURANCE GROUP   SUBSCRIBER

120 So. Main Street, Merck, XY	12346	Group #6709	1-9-80
BLUE SHIELD OR BLUE CROSS CERT. NO.	GROUP NO.	CURRENT COVERAGE NO.	EFFECTIVE DATE

			549-23-8721
MEDICARE NO.	MEDICAID NO.	EFFECTIVE DATE	SOC. SEC. NO.

REFERRED BY:
John Diehl (friend)

DATE	PROGRESS
11-25-9x	On or about 11-3-9x pt began to have chest pain & much coughing. On 11-24-9x pt too ill to work & decided to file for SDI benefits. Pt states illness is not work connected & he does not receive sick leave pay.
	PE: Pt examined & complained of productive cough of 3wks duration & chest pain. Chest x-rays confirmed dx - bronchitis. Cont home rest & prescribed antibiotic medication. Pt will be capable of returning to wk 12/8/9x. Gerald Practon, MD
12-7-9x	Pt has bronchitis with recurring chest pain & slt cough. Will extend disability to 12/15/9x at which time pt can resume reg work. No complications anticipated. Gerald Practon, MD

FIGURE 15-4

CTOR'S CERTIFICATE

fication may be made by a licensed medical or osteopathic physician and surgeon, chiropractor, dentist, podiatrist, optometrist, designated nologist or an authorized medical officer of a United States Government facility. Certification may also be made by a licensed nurse-midwife urse practitioner for the purposes of disability related to normal pregnancy or childbirth. All items on this sheet must be completed legibly.

nt File No.	Name	Social Security Number

I attended the patient for the present medical problem from: MONTH DAY YEAR To MONTH DAY YEAR At intervals of:

Are you completing this form for the sole purpose of referral or recommendation to an alcoholic recovery home or drug-free residential facility?
Yes ☐ No ☐ If yes, please enter facility name and address in item #28.

History:

Diagnosis:

Findings (state nature, severity and bodily extent of the incapacitating disease or injury):

ICD Disease Code, Primary: (REQUIRED)

ICD Disease Code, Secondary:

Type of treatment and/or medication rendered to patient:

Diagnosis confirmed by: **(Specify type of test or X-ray)**

Is this patient now pregnant or has she been pregnant since the date of treatment as reported above? Yes ☐ No ☐ If "Yes", date pregnancy terminated or future EDC.

Is the pregnancy normal? Yes ☐ No ☐ If "No," state the abnormal and involuntary complication causing maternal disability:

Operation: Date performed or to be performed ☐ Type of Operation: ICD Procedure Code: (REQUIRED)

Has the patient at any time during your attendance for this medical problem, been incapable of performing his or her regular work? Yes ☐ No ☐ If "Yes" the disability commenced on:

APPROXIMATE date, based on your examination of patient, disability (if any) should end or has ended sufficiently to permit the patient to resume regular or customary work. Even if considerable question exists, make SOME "estimate." This is a requirement of the Code, and the claim will be delayed if such date is not entered. Such answers as "Indefinite" or "don't know" will not suffice. (ENTER DATE) ☐

Based on your examination of patient, is this disability the result of "occupation" either as an "industrial accident" or as an "occupational disease"?

Yes ☐ No ☐ (This should include aggravation of pre-existing conditions by occupation.)

Have you reported this OR A CONCURRENT DISABILITY to any insurance carrier as a Workers' Compensation Claim?

Yes ☐ No ☐ If "Yes," to whom? (Name of carrier or firm)

Was patient in a hospital surgical unit, surgical unit, ambulatory surgical center certified to participate in the federal Medicare program or a postsurgical recovery care unit as designated by section 1250.9 of the Health and Safety Code? Yes ☐ No ☐
If "Yes," please provide name and address:

Was or is patient a resident in an alcoholic recovery home or drug-free residential facility? Yes ☐ No ☐
If "Yes," please provide name and address:

Was or is patient confined as a registered bed patient in a hospital? Yes ☐ No ☐
If "Yes," please provide name and address:

Date and hour entered as a registered bed patient and discharged pursuant to your orders:

ENTERED	STILL CONFINED	DISCHARGED
on , 19 , at A.M. P.M.	on , 19	on , 19 , at A.M. P.M.

Would the disclosure of this information to your patient be medically or psychologically detrimental to the patient?

Yes ☐ No ☐

eby certify that, based on my examination, the above statements truly describe the patient's disability (if any) and the estimated duration thereof, and that a ______________ licensed to practice by the State of ______________
(TYPE OF DOCTOR)

PRINT OR TYPE DOCTOR'S NAME AS SHOWN ON LICENSE ▶ SIGNATURE OF ATTENDING DOCTOR

. AND STREET CITY ZIP CODE ▶ STATE LICENSE NUMBER ( ) TELEPHONE NO. DATE OF SIGNING THIS FORM

der Section 2116 of the California Unemployment Insurance Code, it is a violation for any individual who, with the intent to defraud, falsely fies the medical condition of any person in order to obtain disability insurance benefits, whether for the maker or for any other person, and is ishable by imprisonment and/or a fine not exceeding twenty thousand dollars.

FIGURE 15-5

NOTICE OF FINAL PAYMENT

The information contained in your claim for Disability Insurance indicates that you are now able to work, therefore, this is the check that you will receive on this claim.

IF YOU ARE ***STILL*** DISABLED: You should complete the Claimant's Certification portion of this form and contact your doct mediately to have him/her complete the Physician's Supplementary Certificate below.

IF YOU BECOME DISABLED ***AGAIN:*** File a new Disability Insurance claim form.

IF YOU ARE UNEMPLOYED AND AVAILABLE FOR WORK: Report to the nearest Unemployment Insurance office of the Depart for assistance in finding work and to determine your entitlement to Unemployment Insurance Benefits.

This determination is final unless you file an appeal within twenty (20) days from the date of mailing of this notification. You appeal by giving a detailed statement as to why you believe the determination is in error. All communications regarding this Disa Insurance claim should include your Social Security Account Number and be addressed to the office shown.

CLAIMANT'S CERTIFICATION

I certify that I continue to be disabled and incapable of doing my regular work, and that I have reported all wa Workers' Compensation benefits and other monies received during the claim period to the Employment Developr Department.

ENTER YOUR SOCIAL SECURITY NUMBER 549 23 8721

Sign Your Name Fred E. Thorndike **Date Signed** December 6, 199x

PHYSICIAN'S SUPPLEMENTARY CERTIFICATE

Department Use On	

1. Are you still treating patient?________ Date of last treatment ________________, 19 ____.
2. What present condition continues to make the patient disabled?

____

____

____

3. Date patient recovered, or will recover sufficiently (even if under treatment) to be able to perform his/her regular and customary ________________, 19 ____. Please enter a specific or estimated recovery date.
4. Would the disclosure of this information to your patient be medically or psychologically detrimental to the patient?

   Yes ☐ No ☐

I hereby certify that the above statements in my opinion truly describe the claimant's condition and the estimated duration thereof.

________________, 19 ____. Doctor's Signature ________________
Date

Phone Number ________________

DE 2525XX Rev. 13 (3-86) — Versión en español en el dorso —

FIGURE 15-6

ASSIGNMENT 55

Assume that the Claim Statement of Employee has been completed satisfactorily by Mr. James T. Fujita (Fig. 15–7). Complete the *Doctor's Certificate* portion of the First Claim Form (Fig. 15–8), and date it December 15. Remember that this is not a claim for payment to the physician, so no ledger card has been furnished for this patient.

Abbreviations pertinent to this record:

exam ______________________

imp ______________________

neg ______________________

pt ______________________

SD ______________________

WBC ______________________

wk ______________________

PATIENT RECORD

LAST NAME	FIRST NAME	MIDDLE NAME	BIRTH DATE	SEX	HOME PHONE
Fujita,	James	T.	03-27-34	M	013/677-2881

ADDRESS	CITY	STATE	ZIP CODE
3538 South A Street,	Woodland Hills,	XY	12345

PATIENT'S OCCUPATION	NAME OF COMPANY
electrician Payroll No. 8834	Macy Electric Company

ADDRESS OF EMPLOYER	PHONE
2671 North C Street, Woodland Hills, XY 12345	013/677-2346

SPOUSE OR PARENT	OCCUPATION
Mary J. Fujita	homemaker

EMPLOYER	ADDRESS	PHONE

NAME OF INSURANCE GROUP	SUBSCRIBER
Atlantic Mutual Ins. Co. 111 S. Main St.,	James T. Fujita

BLUE SHIELD OR BLUE CROSS CERT. NO.	GROUP NO.	CURRENT COVERAGE NO.	EFFECTIVE DATE
Woodland Hills, XY 12345	Policy # F20015		1-3-80

MEDICARE NO.	MEDICAID NO.	EFFECTIVE DATE	SOC. SEC. NO.
			567-43-8898

REFERRED BY:
Cherry Hotta (aunt)

DATE	PROGRESS
12-7-9x	Today pt could not go to work & came for exam complaining of pain in abdomen, nausea, no vomiting. Will file for SDI benefits. Pt states illness is not work connected & he receives sick leave pay of $50/wk. Exam neg except abdomen showed tenderness all over with voluntary guarding. WBC 10,000. Imp: mesenteric adenitis. Advised strict bed rest at home & bland diet. To return in 1 wk. *Gaston Input MD*
12-15-9x	Exam showed normal abdomen. WBC 7,500. Pt will be capable of returning to work 12-22-9x *Gaston Input MD*

FIGURE 15-7

OCTOR'S CERTIFICATE

ertification may be made by a licensed medical or osteopathic physician and surgeon, chiropractor, dentist, podiatrist, optometrist, designated ychologist or an authorized medical officer of a United States Government facility. Certification may also be made by a licensed nurse-midwife nurse practitioner for the purposes of disability related to normal pregnancy or childbirth. All items on this sheet must be completed legibly.

tient File No.	Name	Social Security Number

'. I attended the patient for the present medical problem from: MONTH DAY YEAR To MONTH DAY YEAR At intervals of:

3. Are you completing this form for the sole purpose of referral or recommendation to an alcoholic recovery home or drug-free residential facility?
Yes ☐ No ☐ If yes, please enter facility name and address in item #28.

9. History:

Findings (state nature, severity and bodily extent of the incapacitating disease or injury):

Diagnosis:

ICD Disease Code, Primary: (REQUIRED)

ICD Disease Code, Secondary:

Type of treatment and/or medication rendered to patient:

). Diagnosis confirmed by: **(Specify type of test or X-ray)**

1. Is this patient now pregnant or has she been pregnant since the date of treatment as reported above? Yes ☐ No ☐
If "Yes", date pregnancy terminated or future EDC.
Is the pregnancy normal? Yes ☐ No ☐
If "No," state the abnormal and involuntary complication causing maternal disability:

2. Operation: Date performed or to be performed

Type of Operation:

ICD Procedure Code: (REQUIRED)

3. Has the patient at any time during your attendance for this medical problem, been incapable of performing his or her regular work? Yes ☐ No ☐
If "Yes" the disability commenced on:

4. APPROXIMATE date, based on your examination of patient, disability (if any) should end or has ended sufficiently to permit the patient to resume regular or customary work. Even if considerable question exists, make SOME "estimate." This is a requirement of the Code, and the claim will be delayed if such date is not entered. Such answers as "Indefinite" or "don't know" will not suffice.
(ENTER DATE)

5. Based on your examination of patient, is this disability the result of "occupation" either as an "industrial accident" or as an "occupational disease"?
Yes ☐ No ☐ (This should include aggravation of pre-existing conditions by occupation.)

6. Have you reported this OR A CONCURRENT DISABILITY to any insurance carrier as a Workers' Compensation Claim?
Yes ☐ No ☐ If "Yes," to whom? (Name of carrier or firm)

7. Was patient in a hospital surgical unit, surgical unit, ambulatory surgical center certified to participate in the federal Medicare program or a postsurgical recovery care unit as designated by section 1250.9 of the Health and Safety Code? Yes ☐ No ☐
If "Yes," please provide name and address:

3. Was or is patient a resident in an alcoholic recovery home or drug-free residential facility? Yes ☐ No ☐
If "Yes," please provide name and address:

9. Was or is patient confined as a registered bed patient in a hospital? Yes ☐ No ☐
If "Yes," please provide name and address:

Date and hour entered as a registered bed patient and discharged pursuant to your orders:

ENTERED	STILL CONFINED	DISCHARGED
on , 19 , at A.M. P.M.	on , 19	on , 19 , at A.M. P.M.

). Would the disclosure of this information to your patient be medically or psychologically detrimental to the patient?
Yes ☐ No ☐

hereby certify that, based on my examination, the above statements truly describe the patient's disability (if any) and the estimated duration thereof, and that am a ______________ licensed to practice by the State of ______________
(TYPE OF DOCTOR)

PRINT OR TYPE DOCTOR'S NAME AS SHOWN ON LICENSE ▶ SIGNATURE OF ATTENDING DOCTOR

NO. AND STREET CITY ZIP CODE ▶ STATE LICENSE NUMBER ( ) TELEPHONE NO. DATE OF SIGNING THIS FORM

Under Section 2116 of the California Unemployment Insurance Code, it is a violation for any individual who, with the intent to defraud, falsely certifies the medical condition of any person in order to obtain disability insurance benefits, whether for the maker or for any other person, and is punishable by imprisonment and/or a fine not exceeding twenty thousand dollars.

FIGURE 15-8

ASSIGNMENT 56

1. Mr. Jake J. Burrows (Fig. 15–9) has previously applied for state disability benefits. After 2 months he is referred to another doctor for further care. Complete the form (Fig. 15–10) and date it June 25. You will notice that this form is almost identical to the Doctor's Certificate and is mailed to the claimant to secure the certification of a new physician or to clarify a specific claimed period of disability. In completing this part of the assignment, look at the first three entries on the patient record only.

2. Complete the *Request for Additional Medical Information Form* (Fig. 15–11) by looking at the last entry made on Mr. Burrows' record, and date the report July 15. Remember that this is not a claim for payment to the physician, so no ledger card has been furnished for this patient.

Abbreviations pertinent to this record:

approx ______________________________ imp ______________________________

C 5/6 ______________________________ Pt ______________________________

exam ______________________________ retn ______________________________

hosp ______________________________ c̄ ______________________________

PATIENT RECORD

Burrows,	Jake	J.	04-26-50	M	013/478-9009
LAST NAME	FIRST NAME	MIDDLE NAME	BIRTH DATE	SEX	HOME PHONE

319 Barry Street,	Woodland Hills,	XY	12345
ADDRESS	CITY	STATE	ZIP CODE

assembler	Convac Electronics Company
PATIENT'S OCCUPATION	NAME OF COMPANY

3440 West 7th Street, Woodland Hills, XY 12345	013/467-9008
ADDRESS OF EMPLOYER	PHONE

Jane B. Burrows	homemaker
SPOUSE OR PARENT	OCCUPATION

EMPLOYER	ADDRESS	PHONE

Blue Shield	Jake J. Burrows
NAME OF INSURANCE GROUP	SUBSCRIBER

T8471811A	535537AT		1-1-80
BLUE SHIELD OR BLUE CROSS CERT. NO.	GROUP NO.	CURRENT COVERAGE NO.	EFFECTIVE DATE

			457-99-0801
MEDICARE NO.	MEDICAID NO.	EFFECTIVE DATE	SOC. SEC. NO.

REFERRED BY:

Clarence Butler, MD 300 Sixth Street, Woodland Hills, XY 12345

DATE	PROGRESS
6-2-9x	Pt referred by Dr. Butler. Pt states on 4-19-9x was wrestling c̄ son and jerked his neck the wrong way. 2 days later had much pain & muscle spasm cervical region. X-rays show degenerated disc C5/6. Exam - limited range of neck motion & limited abduction both shoulders. Imp: Degenerated cervical disc C5/6. Pt unable to work as of this date. Myelogram ordered. RS, MD
6-24-9x	Myelogram positive at C5/6. Scheduled for surgery the following day. Raymond Skelton, MD
6-25-9x	Pt adm to College Hospital for surgery. Disc excision & anterior cervical fusion at C5/6. Pt will be discharged from hosp on 6-29-9x. Approx date of retn to work 10-1-9x. Raymond Skelton, MD
6-26- to	29. Pt seen daily in hosp. Discharged 6-29. RTO 2 wks. RS, MD
7-15-9x	Has some restriction of cervical motion. No muscle spasm. Very little cervical pain. Pt to be seen monthly. To retn to work 10-1-9x. Raymond Skelton, MD

FIGURE 15-9

In order that any disability insurance to which you may be entitled may be paid without und please have the physician who treats or treated you during the period indicated below complete and return it to us at his earliest convenience.

Para que cualquier beneficio del Seguro de Incapacidad a que Ud. pueda tener derecho a recibir se sin demoras excesivas, haga el favor de hacer que el médico que le atiende o atendió, durante e indicado abajo, complete este formulario y que lo regrese a nuestra oficina cuanto antes.

Henry B. Garcia
Disability Insurance Program Representative

6-2 thru 7-25-9x
Period Dates – Fechas del Periodo

457-99-0801
S.S.A. – No. del S.S.

1. I attended the patient for the present medical problem from: Month Day Year To Month Day Year At intervals of:

2. History:

State the nature, severity and the bodily extent of the incapacitating disease or injury.
Findings:
Diagnosis:
Type of treatment and/or medication rendered to patient:

3. Diagnosis confirmed by: *(Specify type of test or X-ray)*

4. Is this patient now pregnant or has she been pregnant since the date of treatment as reported above? Yes ☐ No ☐ If "Yes", date pregnancy terminated or future EDC:
Is the pregnancy normal? Yes ☐ No ☐ If "No", state the abnormal and involuntary complication causing maternal disability:

5. Operation: Date performed: ☐ Date to be performed: ☐ Type of Operation:

6. Has the patient at any time during your attendance for this medical problem, been incapable of performing his/her regular work? Yes ☐ No ☐ If "Yes", the disability commenced on:

7. APPROXIMATE date, based on your examination of patient, disability (if any) should end or has ended sufficiently to permit the patient to resume regular or customary work. Even if considerable question exists, make *SOME* "estimate". This is a requirement of the Code, and the claim will be delayed if such date is not entered. Such answers as "Indefinite" or "don't know" will not suffice. (ENTER DATE) ☐

8. Based on your examination of patient, is this disability the result of "occupation" either as an "industrial accident" or as an "occupational disease"?
(This should include aggravation of pre-existing conditions by occupation.) Yes ☐ No ☐

9. Have you reported this *OR A CONCURRENT DISABILITY* to any insurance carrier as a Workers' Compensation Claim?
Yes ☐ No ☐ If "Yes," to whom?

10. Was or is patient confined as a registered bed patient in a hospital? Yes ☐ No ☐
Was patient treated in the surgical unit of a hospital or surgical clinic? Yes ☐ No ☐
If "Yes", please provide name and address:

11. Date and hour entered as a registered bed patient and discharged from such Hospital pursuant to your orders:

ENTERED	STILL CONFINED	DISCHARGED
on , 19 , at A.M. P.M.	on , 19	on , 19 , at A. P.

12. Would the disclosure of this information to your patient be medically or psychologically detrimental to the patient?
Yes ☐ No ☐

I hereby certify that the above statements in my opinion truly describe the patient's disability (if any) and the estimate duration thereof, and that I am a ____________ *licensed to practice by the State of* ____________
(TYPE OF DOCTOR)

PRINT OR TYPE DOCTOR'S NAME AS SHOWN ON LICENSE — SIGNATURE OF ATTENDING DOCTOR

NO. AND STREET — CITY — ZIP CODE — STATE LICENSE NO. — TELEPHONE NO. — DATE OF SIGNING THIS

Certification may be made by a licensed physician and surgeon, osteopath, chiropractor, dentist, podiatrist, optometrist, designated psychologist, or an authorized medical officer of a United States Government facility. All items on this sheet must be completed.

M

8

FIGURE 15-10

STATE OF CALIFORNIA
EMPLOYMENT DEVELOPMENT DEPARTMENT

REFER TO
↓

457-99-0801 — Our File No.
Jack J. Burrows — Your Patient
— Regular or Customary Work

REQUEST FOR ADDITIONAL MEDICAL INFORMATION

Raymond Skelton, M. D.
4567 Broad Avenue
Woodland Hills, XY 12345

The original basic information and estimate of duration of your patient's disability have been carefully evaluated. At the present time, the following additional information based upon the progress and present condition of this patient is requested. This will assist the Department in determining eligibility for further disability insurance benefits. Return of the completed form as soon as possible will be appreciated.

WM. C. SCHMIDT, M.D., MEDICAL DIRECTOR

CLAIMS EXAMINER

DOCTOR: Please complete either Part A or B, date and sign.

RT A IF YOUR PATIENT HAS RECOVERED SUFFICIENTLY TO BE ABLE TO RETURN TO HIS/HER REGULAR OR CUSTOMARY WORK LISTED ABOVE, PLEASE GIVE THE DATE, ____________ 19 ___

RT B THIS PART REFERS TO PATIENT WHO IS STILL DISABLED.

Are you still treating the patient? YES ☐ NO ☐ ____________ 19 ___.
DATE OF LAST TREATMENT

What are the medical circumstances which continue to make your patient disabled?

____

____

____

____

What is your present estimate of the date your patient will be able to perform his/her regular or customary work listed above? Date ____________ 19 ___.

Further Comments: ____

____

____

Would the disclosure of this information to your patient be medically or psychologically detrimental to the patient? YES ☐ NO ☐

Date ____________ 19 ___ ____________________
DOCTOR'S SIGNATURE

SE
ENCLOSED IS A STAMPED PREADDRESSED ENVELOPE FOR YOUR CONVENIENCE.

DE 2547 Rev. 17 (4-84)

FIGURE 15-11

ASSIGNMENT 57

Mr. Vincent P. Michael (Fig. 15–12) is applying for state disability benefits. Complete the *Doctor's Certificate* portion of the form (Fig. 15–13), and date it September 21. Assume that the Claim Statement of Employee has been completed satisfactorily by Mr. Michael. Remember that this is not a claim for payment to the physician, so no ledger card has been furnished for this patient.

Abbreviations pertinent to this record:

approx ____________________ imp ____________________

CVA ____________________ mm ____________________

ESR ____________________ pt ____________________

L ____________________ retn ____________________

hr ____________________ wk ____________________

PATIENT RECORD

LAST NAME	FIRST NAME	MIDDLE NAME	BIRTH DATE	SEX	HOME PHONE
Michael,	Vincent	P.	05-17-45	M	013/567-9001

ADDRESS	CITY	STATE	ZIP CODE
15291/2 Thompson Boulevard,	Woodland Hills,	XY	12345

PATIENT'S OCCUPATION	NAME OF COMPANY
assembler "A"	Burroughs Corporation

ADDRESS OF EMPLOYER	PHONE
5411 North Lindero Canyon Road, Woodland Hills, XY 12345	013/560-9008

SPOUSE OR PARENT	OCCUPATION
Helen J. Michael	homemaker

EMPLOYER	ADDRESS	PHONE

NAME OF INSURANCE GROUP	SUBSCRIBER
Blue Shield	Vincent P. Michael

BLUE SHIELD OR BLUE CROSS CERT. NO.	GROUP NO.	CURRENT COVERAGE NO.	EFFECTIVE DATE
T8411981A	677899 AT		1-1-80

MEDICARE NO.	MEDICAID NO.	EFFECTIVE DATE	SOC. SEC. NO.
			562-90-8888

REFERRED BY: Robert T. Smith (friend)

DATE	PROGRESS
9-20-9x	Pt complains of having had the flu, headache and of being tired.
	Pt unable to go to work today. Exam shows weakness of L hand.
	Hyperreflexia on L. Chest x-ray shows cardiomegaly and slight
	pulmonary congestion. ESR 46 mm/hr. Imp: Post flu syndrome,
	transient ischemia attack; possible CVA. Prescribed medication
	for congestion & adv pt to take aspirin 1/day. Pt to retn in 1 wk.
	Approx. date to retn to work 10-16-9x. Brady Coccidioides, MD

FIGURE 15-12

DOCTOR'S CERTIFICATE

Certification may be made by a licensed medical or osteopathic physician and surgeon, chiropractor, dentist, podiatrist, optometrist, designated psychologist or an authorized medical officer of a United States Government facility. Certification may also be made by a licensed nurse-midwife or nurse practitioner for the purposes of disability related to normal pregnancy or childbirth. All items on this sheet must be completed legibly.

Patient File No.	Name	Social Security Number

17. I attended the patient for the present medical problem from: MONTH DAY YEAR To MONTH DAY YEAR At intervals of:

18. Are you completing this form for the sole purpose of referral or recommendation to an alcoholic recovery home or drug-free residential facility?
Yes ☐ No ☐ If yes, please enter facility name and address in item #28.

19. History: | Objective Findings/Detailed Statement of Symptoms

Diagnosis:

ICD Disease Code, Primary: (REQUIRED) | ICD Disease Code, Secondary:

Type of treatment and/or medication rendered to patient:

20. Diagnosis confirmed by: **(Specify type of test or X-ray)**

21. Is this patient now pregnant or has she been pregnant since the date of treatment as reported above? Yes ☐ No ☐ If "Yes", date pregnancy terminated or future EDC.
Is the pregnancy normal? Yes ☐ No ☐ If "No," state the abnormal and involuntary complication causing maternal disability:

22. Operation: Date performed or to be performed ☐ Type of Operation: ICD Procedure Code: (REQUIRED)

23. Was or is patient confined as a registered bed patient in a hospital? Yes ☐ No ☐
If "Yes," please provide dates:

Entered hospital on ______________________, 19 ___

Discharged from hospital on ______________________, 19 ___.

24. Has the patient at any time during your attendance for this medical problem, been incapable of performing his or her regular work? Yes ☐ No ☐ If "Yes" the disability commenced on:

25. APPROXIMATE date, based on your examination of patient, disability (if any) should end or has ended sufficiently to permit the patient to resume regular or customary work. Even if considerable question exists, make SOME "estimate." This is a requirement of the Code, and the claim will be delayed if such date is not entered. Such answers as "Indefinite" or "don't know" will not suffice. (ENTER DATE) ☐

26. Based on your examination of patient, is this disability the result of "occupation" either as an "industrial accident" or as an "occupational disease"?
Yes ☐ No ☐ (This should include aggravation of pre-existing conditions by occupation.)

27. Have you reported this OR A CONCURRENT DISABILITY to any insurance carrier as a Workers' Compensation Claim?
Yes ☐ No ☐ If "Yes," to whom? (Name of carrier or firm)

28. Was or is patient a resident in an alcoholic recovery home or drug-free residential facility? Yes ☐ No ☐
If "Yes," please provide name and address:

29. Would the disclosure of this information to your patient be medically or psychologically detrimental to the patient?
Yes ☐ No ☐

I hereby certify that, based on my examination, the above statements truly describe the patient's disability (if any) and the estimated duration thereof, and that I am a ______________________ (TYPE OF DOCTOR) licensed to practice by the State of ______________________

▶ ______________________ PRINT OR TYPE DOCTOR'S NAME AS SHOWN ON LICENSE

▶ ______________________ ORIGINAL SIGNATURE OF ATTENDING DOCTOR - RUBBER STAMP IS NOT ACCEPTABLE -

▶ NO. AND STREET | CITY | ZIP CODE

▶ STATE LICENSE NUMBER | ( ) TELEPHONE NO. | DATE OF SIGNING THIS FORM

"Under Section 2116 of the California Unemployment Insurance Code, it is a violation for any individual who, with the intent to defraud, falsely certifies the medical condition of any person in order to obtain disability insurance benefits, whether for the maker or for any other person, and is punishable by imprisonment and/or a fine not exceeding twenty thousand dollars.

FIGURE 15-13

CHAPTER 16

Hospital Billing

Key Terms

Your instructor may wish to select some specific words pertinent to this chapter for a test. For definitions of the terms, further study, and/or reference, the words, phrases, and abbreviations may be found in the Glossary at the end of the textbook. *Key terms for this chapter are:*

admission review
ambulatory patient groups (APGs)
ambulatory visit groups (AVGs)
appropriateness evaluation protocol (AEP)
capitation
case rate
charges
clinical outlier
coding
comorbidity
complication
cost outlier
cost outlier review
day outlier review
diagnosis-related groups (DRGs)
discharge face sheet
discharge status
DRG creep
DRG rate
elective surgery
grouper
inpatient
International Classification of Diseases, 9th Revision, Clinical Modification (ICD-9-CM)
looping
low-volume DRGs
major diagnostic categories (MDCs)
outpatient
outliers (atypical cases)
percentage of revenue
per diem
preadmission testing (PAT)
principal diagnosis
principal procedure
procedure review
professional review organizations (PROs)
readmission review
stop loss
transfer
transfer review
Uniform Bill (UB-92) claim form
utilization review (UR)

Performance Objectives

The student will be able to

- Define and spell the key terms for this chapter, given the information from the textbook Glossary, within a reasonable period of time and with enough accuracy to obtain a satisfactory evaluation.
- Answer the review questions after reading the chapter, with enough accuracy to obtain a satisfactory evaluation.
- State the reasons why claims may be either rejected, delayed, or incorrect payment received, given computer-generated UB-92 claim forms, within a reasonable period of time and with enough accuracy to obtain a satisfactory evaluation.
- Analyze, edit, and insert entries on computer-generated UB-92 claim forms so payment will be accurate, within a reasonable period of time and with enough accuracy to obtain a satisfactory evaluation.

Study Outline

INTRODUCTION
REIMBURSEMENT METHODS
MEDICOLEGAL
  Confidentiality
BILLING ERRORS
HOSPITAL BILLING PROCESS
ELECTRONIC DATA INTERCHANGE
PAYMENTS
OUTPATIENT INSURANCE CLAIMS
INPATIENT INSURANCE CLAIMS
  Private Insurance (Group or Individual)
  Blue Plans
  Workers' Compensation
  Managed Care
  Medicare
  Medicaid
  CHAMPUS, CHAMPVA, and TRICARE
DIAGNOSTIC CODING
  ICD-9-CM Volume 3 Procedures—Tabular List and Alphabetic Index
  Tabular List
  Alphabetic Index
  Special Points to Remember in Volume 3
  Diagnostic Coding Handy Hints
PROCEDURAL CODING
  Current Procedural Terminology
  Procedural Coding Hospital Billing Handy Hints
  Health Care Finance Administration Common Procedure Coding System
HOSPITAL BILLING CLAIM FORM
  Uniform Bill Inpatient and Outpatient Claim Form
  Instructions for Completing the UB-92 Claim Form
DIAGNOSIS RELATED GROUPS
  History
  The DRG System
  DRGs and the Medical Assistant/Insurance Billing Specialist
  Handy Hints for the Physician's Practice
Diagnostic Related Groups and Medical Records
  Outpatient Classifications
    Ambulatory Patient Groups
    Ambulatory Care Groups
UTILIZATION REVIEW
PEER REVIEW ORGANIZATION
APPROPRIATENESS EVALUATION PROTOCOLS
  Appropriateness Evaluatuion Protocol Criteria for Admission Certification

Review Questions

Review the objectives, key terms, glossary definitions to key terms, chapter information, and figures before completing the following review questions.

1. Match the words or phrases used for managed care reimbursement methods in the first column with the definitions in the second column. Write the correct letters in the blanks.

sliding scales for discounts and per diem ____

discounts in the form of sliding scale ____

stop loss ____

withholds ____

charges ____

ambulatory patient groups ____

case rate ____

diagnostic related groups ____

differential by service type ____

periodic interim payments ____

bed leasing ____

differential by day in hospital ____

capitation ____

per diem ____

percentage of revenue ____

a. Most hospitalizations are more expensive on the first day.

b. Reimbursement to the hospital on a per member per month basis.

c. Plan advances cash to cover expected claims to the hospital.

d. Fixed percentage of collected premium rate paid to the hospital.

e. Single charge for a day in the hospital regardless of actual cost.

f. Interim per diem paid for each day in the hospital, based on total volume.

g. Classification system categorizing patients who are medically related with respect to diagnosis and treatment and statistically similar in lengths of hospital stay.

h. Hospital receives a flat per-admission payment for the particular service type the patient is admitted to.

i. An averaging after a flat rate is given to certain categories of procedures.

j. Outpatient classification based on procedures rather than on diagnoses.

k. Form of reinsurance which limits losses on certain expensive hospital claims.

l. Part of plan's payment to the hospital may be withheld and paid at the end of the year.

m. When a managed care plan leases beds from a hospital and pays per bed whether used or not.

n. A percentage reduction in charges for total bed days per year with incremental increases in the discount up to a maximum percentage.

o. Dollar amount a hospital bills a case for services rendered.

2. You are reviewing a computer-generated insurance claim before it is sent to the insurance carrier and notice the patient's name as being an old friend. You quickly read the code for the diagnosis. Is this a breach of confidentiality? ____________

3. You are coding in a medical records department when an agent from the Federal Bureau of Investigation walks in and asks for a patient's address. You ask, "Why do you need Mrs. Doe's address. Do you have a signed authorization from Mrs. Doe for release of information from our facility?" The FBI agent responds, "I'm trying to locate this person because of counterfitting charges. No, I don't have a signed authorization form." Would there be any breach of confidentiality if you release the patient's address? Explain. ______________________________

4. The inpatient and outpatient hospital billing department uses a summary form for submitting an insurance claim to an insurance plan called ______________________________

5. Define the term *outpatient*. ______________________________

6. Define the term *elective surgery*. ______________________________

7. Baby Stephens falls from a high stool cutting his head. His mother rushes him to St. Joseph's Medical Center for emergency care. The physician examines the baby, takes two stiches closing the laceration, sends the child for skull x-rays, and then discharges him to home. Will the emergency room care be billed as an inpatient or outpatient? ______________________________

8. In what type of situation would a patient not have an insurance identification card?
____

9. If a patient under a managed care plan goes to a hospital that is under contract with the plan for admission, what is necessary for inpatient admission? ______________________________

10. The primary diagnosis listed for admission to the hospital for an illness or injury is called a/an __________________ diagnosis.

11. From the list of ICD-9-CM descriptions shown, place in correct sequential order (1, 2, 3) for billing purposes. In this case, the medical procedure is a repair of other hernia of anterior abdominal wall, incisional hernia repair with prosthesis, ICD-9-CM code 53.61.

	Diagnosis	ICD-9-CM Code
____	Chronic liver disease, liver damage unspecified	571.3
____	Alcohol dependence syndrome (other and unspecified)	303.9
____	Other hernia of abdominal cavity without mention of obstruction or gangrene (incisional hernia)	553.21

12. You can determine if a UB-92 claim form is for an inpatient or an outpatient by the following observations:

    a. When the inpatient block number 4 shows three-digit billing code(s) __________

    b. When the outpatient block number 4 shows three-digit billing code(s) __________

    c. When revenue codes and block number(s) ______________________________ indicate type of service rendered

13. Name five different payment types under managed care contracts.

    a. ______________________________

    b. ______________________________

    c. ______________________________

    d. ______________________________

    e. ______________________________

14. List three instances of breaching confidentiality in a hospital setting.

    a. ______________________________

    b. ______________________________

    c. ______________________________

15. Describe the significance of Blocks 42, 43, 44, 46, and 47 of the UB-92 claim form.

    a. Block 42 ______________________________

    b. Block 43 ______________________________

    c. Block 44 ______________________________

    d. Block 46 ______________________________

    e. Block 47 ______________________________

16. Why did Medicare implement the DRG-based system of reimbursement?

    ____

17. Name the six variables that affect Medicare reimbursement under the DRG system.

    a. ______________________________

    b. ______________________________

    c. ______________________________

    d. ______________________________

    e. ______________________________

    f. ______________________________

18. Define the following abbreviations.

AEP ____________________

PAT ____________________

MDC ____________________

PPS ____________________

TEFRA ____________________

UR ____________________

IS ____________________

SI ____________________

19. Name the most important factor in reimbursement. ____________________

20. Define comorbidity. ____________________

21. Define cost outliners. ____________________

22. Mrs. Benson, a Medicare patient, is admitted by Dr. Dalton to the hospital on January 4 and is seen in consultation by Dr. Frank on January 5. On January 6, Mrs. Benson is discharged with a diagnosis of coronary atherosclerosis. State some of the problems regarding payment and Medicare policies that would affect this case.

____

23. What hospital document begins the reimbursement process and what important items must it contain? ____________________

24. What is the purpose of appropriateness evaluation protocols (AEP)? ____________________

ASSIGNMENT 58

Read the computer-generated UB-92 claim form (Fig. 16-1) and circle in red any errors you discover. In addition, you notice that the second line entry for pharmacy shows a total of $6806. However, you know from reviewing the case that one injection of a drug known as TPA (Revenue code 259 and fee $5775), which dissolves clots and opens vessels when a patient has a cardiac infarct, was not broken out of the fee. Handwrite this final entry. On line two cross out the total charge $6806 and insert the correct pharmacy reduced amount. Then write a list of the reasons why the claim may be either rejected, delayed, or incorrect payment generated because of errors discovered.

APPROVED OMB NO.

013-487-6789
COLLEGE HOSPITAL
4500 BROAD AVENUE
WOODLAND HILLS XY 12345-0001

2

3 PATIENT CONTROL NO.: 10687127

5 FED. TAX NO.	6 STATEMENT COVERS PERIOD FROM	THROUGH	7 COV D.	8 N-C D.	9 C-I D.	10 L-R D.	11
95-0731067	07119X	07149X	003				

12 PATIENT NAME: TORRE, MARY J.

13 PATIENT ADDRESS: 452 JEME STREET WOODLAND HILLS, XY 12345-0001

14 BIRTHDATE	15 SEX	16 MS	17 ADMISSION DATE	18 HR	19 TYPE	20 SRC	21 D HR	22 STAT	23 MEDICAL RECORD NO.	24 CONDITION CODES	25	26	27	28	29	30	31
12031918	F	M	07119X	21	2	7	17	01	2018856	C5	04						

	32 OCCURRENCE CODE	DATE	33 OCCURRENCE CODE	DATE	34 OCCURRENCE CODE	DATE	35 OCCURRENCE CODE	DATE	36 OCCURRENCE SPAN CODE	FROM	THROUGH	37
a	11	071197										A
b												B
												C

38
TORRE, MARY J
452 JEME STREET
WOODLAND HILLS XY 12345-0001

	39 VALUE CODES CODE	AMOUNT	40 VALUE CODES CODE	AMOUNT	41 VALUE CODES CODE	AMOUNT
a	01	650 00				
b						
c						
d						

	42 REV. CD.	43 DESCRIPTION	44 HCPCS / RATES	45 SERV. DATE	46 SERV. UNITS	47 TOTAL CHARGES	48 NON-COVERED CHARGES	49
1	210	ROOM & CARE CCU	1600.00		3	4800 00		
2	250	PHARMACY			121	6806 00		
3	270	MED-SUR SUPPLIES			31	700 50		
4	300	LABORATORY			45	1710 50		
5	310	PATHOLOGY LABORATORY			1	99 50		
6	320	RADIOLOGY			3	159 00		
7	450	EMERGENCY ROOM SERVICE			5	196 00		
8	730	ELECTROCARDIOLOGY			7	700 00		
9								
10								
11								
12								
13								
14								
15								
16								
17								
18								
19								
20								
21								
22								
23								

	50 PAYER	51 PROVIDER NO.	52 REL INFO	53 ASG BEN	54 PRIOR PAYMENTS	55 EST. AMOUNT DUE	56
A	MEDIPRIME - HPR		Y	Y		15171 50	
B							
C							

57 DUE FROM PATIENT ▶

	58 INSURED'S NAME	59 P.REL	60 CERT. - SSN - HIC. - ID NO.	61 GROUP NAME	62 INSURANCE GROUP NO.
A	TORRE, MARY J	01	54626897101		6500-0000
B					
C					

	63 TREATMENT AUTHORIZATION CODES	64 ESC	65 EMPLOYER NAME	66 EMPLOYER LOCATION
A		9	RETIRED 080184	
B				
C				

67 PRIN. DIAG. CD.	68 CODE	69 CODE	70 CODE	71 CODE	72 CODE	73 CODE	74 CODE	75 CODE	76 ADM. DIAG. CD.	77 E-CODE
41011	4589	5780	E9444	E9424	E8490	E9344	E8497		41011	

(68–75: OTHER DIAG. CODES)

79 P.C.: 9

80 PRINCIPAL PROCEDURE CODE / DATE

81 OTHER PROCEDURE CODE / DATE (A, B, C, D, E)

82 ATTENDING PHYS. ID: 642110670 CARDI PERRY

83 OTHER PHYS. ID

OTHER PHYS. ID

84 REMARKS
a
b
c
d

85 PROVIDER REPRESENTATIVE: X Perry Cardi, MD

86 DATE: 07169X

I CERTIFY THE CERTIFICATIONS ON THE REVERSE APPLY TO THIS BILL AND ARE MADE A PART HEREOF

UB-92 HCFA-1450

OCR/ **ORIGINAL**

FIGURE 16-1

ASSIGNMENT 59

Read the computer-generated UB-92 claim form (Fig. 16-2) and circle in red any errors you discover. Write a list of reasons why the claim may be either rejected, delayed, or incorrect payment generated because of errors discovered.

APPROVED OMB NO. 09

COLLEGE HOSPITAL 4500 BROAD AVENUE WOODLAND HILLS XY 12345-0001 013-487-6789	2	3 PATIENT CONTROL NO. 10453462

5 FED. TAX NO.	6 STATEMENT COVERS PERIOD FROM	THROUGH	7 COV D.	8 N-C D.	9 C-I D.	10 L-R D.	11
95-0731067	03159X	03159X					

12 PATIENT NAME	13 PATIENT ADDRESS
COSBY HENRY M	1501 PACIFIC WAY WOODLAND HILLS XY 12345-0001

14 BIRTHDATE	15 SEX	16 MS	ADMISSION 17 DATE	18 HR	19 TYPE	20 SRC	21 D HR	22 STAT	23 MEDICAL RECORD NO.	CONDITION CODES 24	25	26	27	28	29	30	31
03101956	M	M	03159X	13	3	2	99	01	2084100	C5							

	32 OCCURRENCE CODE	DATE	33 OCCURRENCE CODE	DATE	34 OCCURRENCE CODE	DATE	35 OCCURRENCE CODE	DATE	36 OCCURRENCE SPAN CODE	FROM	THROUGH	37
a	05	072194										A
b												B
												C

38
COSBY, HENRY M
1501 PACIFIC WAY
WOODLAND HILLS XY 12345

	39 VALUE CODES CODE	AMOUNT	40 VALUE CODES CODE	AMOUNT	41 VALUE CODES CODE	AMOUNT
a						
b						
c						
d						

	42 REV. CD.	43 DESCRIPTION	44 HCPCS / RATES	45 SERV. DATE	46 SERV. UNITS	47 TOTAL CHARGES		48 NON-COVERED CHARGES	49
1	110	ROOM - BOARD/SEMI/PVT	650.00		1	650	00		
2	250	PHARMACY			11	207	20		
3	270	MED-SUR SUPPLIES			4	1041	28		
4	360	OPERATING ROOM				865	00		
5	370	ANESTHESIA				64	50		
6	730	ELECTROCARDIOGRAM, COMPL	93000	03139X	03139X	100	00		
7									
8									
9									
10									
11									
12									
13									
14									
15									
16									
17									
18									
19									
20									
21									
22									
23									

	50 PAYER	51 PROVIDER NO.	52 REL INFO	53 ASG BEN	54 PRIOR PAYMENTS	55 EST. AMOUNT DUE		56
A	BLUE SHIELD OF CA	Z22C49122	Y	Y		2277	98	
B								
C								

57 **DUE FROM PATIENT ▶**

	58 INSURED'S NAME	59 P.REL	60 CERT. - SSN - HIC. - ID NO.	61 GROUP NAME	62 INSURANCE GROUP NO.
A	COSBY, HENRY M	01	564729922		PA 0132
B					
C					

	63 TREATMENT AUTHORIZATION CODES	64 ESC	65 EMPLOYER NAME	66 EMPLOYER LOCATION
A		4	DBA: COSBY AUTO BODY	
B				
C				

67 PRIN. DIAG. CD.	OTHER DIAG. CODES 68 CODE	69 CODE	70 CODE	71 CODE	72 CODE	73 CODE	74 CODE	75 CODE	76 ADM. DIAG. CD.	77 E-CODE	78
8408											

79 P.C.	80 PRINCIPAL PROCEDURE CODE	DATE	81 OTHER PROCEDURE CODE	DATE	OTHER PROCEDURE CODE	DATE
9	8301	031597				
	OTHER PROCEDURE CODE	DATE	OTHER PROCEDURE CODE	DATE	OTHER PROCEDURE CODE	DATE

82 ATTENDING PHYS. ID
126785470 SKELTON RAYMOND

83 OTHER PHYS. ID

OTHER PHYS. ID

84 REMARKS
a
b FELL WATERSKIING 7/21/94
c
d

85 PROVIDER REPRESENTATIVE
X SIGNATURE ON FILE

86 DATE
03169X

I CERTIFY THE CERTIFICATIONS ON THE REVERSE APPLY TO THIS BILL AND ARE MADE A PART HEREOF.

UB-92 HCFA-1450 OCR/ **ORIGINAL**

FIGURE 16-2

ASSIGNMENT 60

Read the computer-generated UB-92 claim form (Fig. 16-3) and circle in red any errors you discover. You notice that the seventh CPT/HCPCS code 43450 for operating room is missing. On hospital claims the entry for operating room is usually blank and must be handwritten in as this is the code for the surgical procedure. Then write a list of reasons why the claim may be either rejected, delayed, or incorrect payment generated because of errors discovered.

APPROVED OMB NO. 09

1	2	3 PATIENT CONTROL NO.
COLLEGE HOSPITAL 4500 BROAD AVENUE WOODLAND HILLS XY 12345-0001 013-487-6789		10670685

5 FED. TAX NO.	6 STATEMENT COVERS PERIOD FROM	THROUGH	7 COV D.	8 N-C D.	9 C-I D.	10 L-R D.	11
95-0731067	07059X	07059X					

12 PATIENT NAME	13 PATIENT ADDRESS
MCDONALD HAROLD M	22 BEACON ROAD WOODLAND HILLS XY 12345-0001

14 BIRTHDATE	15 SEX	16 MS	ADMISSION 17 DATE	18 HR	19 TYPE	20 SRC	21 D HR	22 STAT	23 MEDICAL RECORD NO.	CONDITION CODES 24	25	26	27	28	29	30	31
04261929	M	M	07059X	12	3	1	99	01	2071307	C5							

32 OCCURRENCE CODE DATE · 33 OCCURRENCE CODE DATE · 34 OCCURRENCE CODE DATE · 35 OCCURRENCE CODE DATE · 36 OCCURRENCE SPAN CODE FROM THROUGH · 37 A B C

a

b

38

MCDONALD HAROLD M
22 BEACON ROAD
WOODLAND HILLS XY 12345-0001

39 VALUE CODES CODE AMOUNT · 40 VALUE CODES CODE AMOUNT · 41 VALUE CODES CODE AMOUNT

a b c d

	42 REV. CD.	43 DESCRIPTION	44 HCPCS / RATES	45 SERV. DATE	46 SERV. UNITS	47 TOTAL CHARGES		48 NON-COVERED CHARGES	49
1	250	PHARMACY			5	90	90		
2	270	MED - SUR SUPPLIES			16	2519	50		
3	300	DRAWING BLOOD	36415	07059X	1	8	50		
4	300	13-16 BLOOD/URINE TESTS	80016	07059X	1	28	00		
5	300	CREATININE CLEARANCE TEST	82575	07059X	1	20	00		
6	300	CBC	85025 24	07059X	1	16	50		
7	320	CONTRAST XRAY EXAM, ESOPH	74220	07059X	1	114	00		
8	320	X-RAY GUIDE,GI DILATION	74360	07059X	1	750	00		
9	360	OPERATING ROOM				500	00		
10	410	CONT OXIMETER HOURS	82805 22	07059X	1	8	00		
11									
12									
13									
14									
15									
16									
17									
18									
19									
20									
21									
22									
23									

	50 PAYER	51 PROVIDER NO.	52 REL INFO	53 ASG BEN	54 PRIOR PAYMENTS	55 EST. AMOUNT DUE	56
A	HEALTH PLAN REDWOO	278654901	Y	Y		4055 40	
B							
C							

57 **DUE FROM PATIENT ▶**

	58 INSURED'S NAME	59 P.REL	60 CERT. - SSN - HIC. - ID NO.	61 GROUP NAME	62 INSURANCE GROUP NO.
A	MCDONALD HAROLD M	01	31424435401		1320-0000 PLAN GO
B					
C					

	63 TREATMENT AUTHORIZATION CODES	64 ESC	65 EMPLOYER NAME	66 EMPLOYER LOCATION
A		9	WC PEDERSON FORD	
B				
C				

67 PRIN. DIAG. CD.	OTHER DIAG. CODES 68 CODE	69 CODE	70 CODE	71 CODE	72 CODE	73 CODE	74 CODE	75 CODE	76 ADM. DIAG. CD.	77 E-CODE	78
1509	V725										

79 P.C.	80 PRINCIPAL PROCEDURE CODE DATE	81 OTHER PROCEDURE CODE DATE	OTHER PROCEDURE CODE DATE	82 ATTENDING PHYS. ID
9				124589770 ANTRUM CONCHA

OTHER PROCEDURE CODE DATE · OTHER PROCEDURE CODE DATE · OTHER PROCEDURE CODE DATE

83 OTHER PHYS. ID

OTHER PHYS. ID

84 REMARKS

a
b HPR
c
d

85 PROVIDER REPRESENTATIVE: X Concha Antrum, MD

86 DATE: 07069X

UB-92 HCFA-1450

OCR/ ORIGINAL

I CERTIFY THE CERTIFICATIONS ON THE REVERSE APPLY TO THIS BILL AND ARE MADE A PART HEREOF.

FIGURE 16-3

ASSIGNMENT 61

Read the computer-generated UB-92 claim form (Fig. 16-4) and circle in red any errors you discover. Then write a list of the reasons why the claim may be either rejected, delayed, or incorrect payment generated because of errors discovered.

ASSIGNMENT 62

These cases point out the value of proper versus improper coding regarding correct sequence, indicating the variance of payment. Fill in the correct *ICD-9-CM* code numbers. Note how the same case was coded listing different principal and secondary hospital diagnoses and that the DRG payment for each is substantially different. Also note the difference in the major diagnostic category (MDC).

Case 1
Age: 62 Sex: Female

MDC: Six diseases and disorders of the digestive system
DRG: Code 188: Other digestive system diagnoses, age >69 and/or CC

Principal Diagnosis

Descending colon inj—closed __________

Secondary Diagnoses

Liver injury NOS—closed __________

Open wnd knee/leg—compl __________

Firearm accident NOS __________

No procedures performed

DRG Payment: $4710

MDC: Seven diseases and disorders of the hepatobiliary system and pancreas
DRG: Code 205: Disorders of the liver exc malig, cirr, alc hepa, age >69 and/or CC

Principal Diagnosis

Liver injury NOS—closed __________

Secondary Diagnoses

Atrial fibrillation __________

Urin tract infection NOS __________

Descending colon inj—closed __________

Open wnd knee/leg—compl __________

Firearm accident NOS __________

E. coli infect NOS __________

DRG Payment: $6847

Case 2
Age: 65 Sex: Male

MDC: Five diseases and disorders of the circulatory system
DRG: Code 468: Unrelated OR proc

Principal Diagnosis

Hypertensive heart disease NOS __________

MDC: Twelve diseases and disorders of the male reproductive system
DRG: Code 336: Transurethral prostatectomy, age >69 and/or CC

Principal Diagnosis

Malig neopl prostate __________

APPROVED OMB NO. 0

COLLEGE HOSPITAL
4500 BROAD AVENUE
WOODLAND HILLS XY 12345-0001
013-487-6789

2

3 PATIENT CONTROL NO. 10630911

5 FED. TAX NO.	6 STATEMENT COVERS PERIOD FROM	THROUGH	7 COV D.	8 N-C D.	9 C-I D.	10 L-R D.	11
95-0731067	06119X	06219X	010				

12 PATIENT NAME: MARTINEZ PEDRO

13 PATIENT ADDRESS: 7821 SENSOR AVE WOODLAND HILLS XY 12345-0001

14 BIRTHDATE	15 SEX	16 MS	ADMISSION 17 DATE	18 HR	19 TYPE	20 SRC	21 D HR	22 STAT	23 MEDICAL RECORD NO.	CONDITION CODES 24	25	26	27	28	29	30	31
092218	M	W	06109X	20	1	7	19	03	3567811	C5	04						

	32 OCCURRENCE CODE	DATE	33 OCCURRENCE CODE	DATE	34 OCCURRENCE CODE	DATE	35 OCCURRENCE CODE	DATE	36 OCCURRENCE SPAN CODE	FROM	THROUGH	37
a												A
b												B
												C

38
MARTINEZ PEDRO
7821 SENSOR AVENUE
WOODLAND HILLS XY 12345-0001

	39 VALUE CODES CODE	AMOUNT	40 VALUE CODES CODE	AMOUNT	41 VALUE CODES CODE	AMOUNT
a	01	650 00				
b						
c						
d						

	42 REV. CD.	43 DESCRIPTION	44 HCPCS / RATES	45 SERV. DATE	46 SERV. UNITS	47 TOTAL CHARGES	48 NON-COVERED CHARGES	49
1	110	ROOM - BOARD/SEMI/PVT	650.00		1	650 00		
2	120	ROOM & CARE SEMI	650.00		1	650 00		
3	210	ROOM & CARE CCU	1600.00		8	12800 00		
4	250	PHARMACY			500	7133 90		
5	270	MED - SUR SUPPLIES			149	3689 50		
6	300	LABORATORY			97	5399 33		
7	320	RADIOLOGY			27	1544 00		
8	350	CT SCAN			1	622 00		
9	410	RESPIRATORY THERAPY			240	6698 50		
10	420	PHYSICAL THERAPY			9	470 00		
11	450	EMERGENCY ROOM SERV			6	197 00		
12	460	PULMONARY FUNCTION				29 00		
13	730	ELECTROCARDIOLOGY			1	100 00		
14	942	EDUCATION			6	82 50		
15								
16								
17								
18								
19								
20								
21								
22								
23								

	50 PAYER	51 PROVIDER NO.	52 REL INFO	53 ASG BEN	54 PRIOR PAYMENTS	55 EST. AMOUNT DUE	56
A	MEDIPRIME - HPR		Y	Y			
B							
C							

57 DUE FROM PATIENT ▶

	58 INSURED'S NAME	59 P.REL	60 CERT. - SSN - HIC. - ID NO.	61 GROUP NAME	62 INSURANCE GROUP NO.
A	MARTINEZ PEDRO	01	55025897001		6500-0000
B					
C					

	63 TREATMENT AUTHORIZATION CODES	64 ESC	65 EMPLOYER NAME	66 EMPLOYER LOCATION
A		5	RETIRED 1975	
B				
C				

67 PRIN. DIAG. CD.	68 CODE	69 CODE	70 CODE	71 CODE	72 CODE	73 CODE	74 CODE	75 CODE	76 ADM. DIAG. CD.	77 E-CODE	78
4169	51881	49121							51881		

(68–75: OTHER DIAG. CODES)

79 P.C.: 9

80 PRINCIPAL PROCEDURE CODE / DATE; 81 OTHER PROCEDURE CODE / DATE; OTHER PROCEDURE CODE / DATE; OTHER PROCEDURE CODE / DATE; OTHER PROCEDURE CODE / DATE; OTHER PROCEDURE CODE / DATE

82 ATTENDING PHYS. ID: 642110670 COCCIDIOIDES BRADY

83 OTHER PHYS. ID

OTHER PHYS. ID

84 REMARKS
a
b
c
d

85 PROVIDER REPRESENTATIVE: X

86 DATE

UB-92 HCFA-1450

OCR/ ORIGINAL

I CERTIFY THE CERTIFICATIONS ON THE REVERSE APPLY TO THIS BILL AND ARE MADE A PART HEREOF.

FIGURE 16-4

Secondary Diagnoses

Hematuria ______________________

Hyperplasia of prostate ______________

Hemiplegia NOS ____________________

Late eff cerebrovasc dis ______________

Malign neopl prostate _______________

Secondary Diagnoses

Hematuria ______________________

Hypertensive heart disease NOS ________

Hemiplegia NOS ____________________

Late eff cerebrovasc dis ______________

Hyperplasia of prostate ______________

Procedures

Transurethral prostatect ____________

Urethral dilation _________________

Cystoscopy NEC __________________

Intravenous pyelogram ____________

Nephrotomogram NEC _____________

DRG Payment: $13,311

DRG Payment: $6,377

Note: Since this is a hospital case, *ICD-9-CM* Volume 3 should be used to code the procedures. However, Volume 3 is not used in the medical office.

Case 3

Age: 42 Sex: Male

MDC: Nineteen mental diseases and disorders
DRG: Code 426: Depressive neuroses

Principal Diagnosis

Neurotic depression_______________

Secondary Diagnoses

Acute myocardial infarction anterior wall

NEC ___________________________

Chest pain NOS___________________

Heart disease NOS ________________

Paranoid personality ______________

MDC: Five diseases and disorders of the circulatory system
DRG: Code 122: Circulatory disorders with ami w/o cv comp disch alive

Principal Diagnosis

Acute myocardial infarction anterior wall

NEC ___________________________

Secondary Diagnoses

Neurotic depression_______________

Chest pain NOS___________________

Heart disease NOS ________________

Paranoid personality ______________

Procedures

Dx ultrasound—heart ________________

Other resp procedures ________________

DRG Payment: $6007

DRG Payment: $8637

Note: Since this is a hospital case, *ICD-9-CM* Volume 3 should be used to code the procedures. However, Volume 3 is not used in the medical office.

Case 4

Age: 77 Sex: Male

MDC: Five diseases and disorders of the circulatory system
DRG: Code 138: Cardiac arrhythmia and conduction disorders, age >69 and/or CC

Principal Diagnosis

Atrial fibrillation ____________________

Secondary Diagnoses

Fracture six ribs—closed ______________

Trans cereb ischemia NOS ___________

Syncope and collapse ________________

Fx scapula NOS—closed ____________

Fall NEC & NOS ____________________

MDC: Four diseases and disorders of the respiratory system
DRG: Code 83: Major chest trauma, age >69 and/or CC

Principal Diagnosis

Fracture six ribs—closed ______________

Secondary Diagnoses

Atrial fibrillation ____________________

Trans cereb ischemia NOS ___________

Syncope and collapse ________________

Fx scapula NOS—closed ____________

Fall NEC & NOS ____________________

Procedures

Contrast cerebr arteriogram ___________

CAT scan of head ____________________

Dx ultrasound—heart ________________

Physical therapy NEC ________________

DRG Payment: $5882

DRG Payment: $6206

Note: Since this is a hospital case, *ICD-9-CM* Volume 3 should be used to code the procedures. However, Volume 3 is not used in the medical office.

Case 5

Age: 12 Sex: Male

MDC: Four diseases and disorders of the respiratory system
DRG: Code 98: Bronchitis and asthma age 0–17

Principal Diagnosis

Asthma w/o status asthmaticus ________

MDC: Four diseases and disorders of the respiratory system
DRG: Code 91: Simple pneumonia and pleurisy age 0–17

Principal Diagnosis

Pneumonia, organism NOS ___________

Secondary Diagnoses

Pneumonia, organism NOS ____________

Otitis media NOS ____________________

DRG Payment: $2705

Secondary Diagnoses

Asthma w/o status asthmaticus ________

Otitis media NOS ____________________

DRG Payment: $3246

CHAPTER 17

Seeking a Position as an Insurance Billing Specialist

Key Terms

Your instructor may wish to select some specific words pertinent to this chapter for a test. For definitions of the terms, further study, and/or reference, the words, phrases, and abbreviations may be found in the Glossary at the end of the textbook. Key terms for this chapter follow.

alien
application form
Certified Claims Assistance Professional (CCAP)
Certified Coding Specialist (CCS)
Certified Electronic Claims Professional (CECP)
Certified Procedural Coder (CPC)
chronologic resume
Claims Assistance Professional (CAP)
coding specialist
combination resume
cover letter
electronic claims processor (ECP)
employment agency
free-lancer
functional resume
insurance billing specialist
interview
portfolio
resume
self-employment

Performance Objectives

The student will be able to

- Define and spell the key terms for this chapter, given the information from the textbook Glossary, within a reasonable period of time and with enough accuracy to obtain a satisfactory evaluation.
- Answer the review questions after reading the chapter with enough accuracy to obtain a satisfactory evaluation.
- Research information in preparation for typing a resume, given a worksheet to complete within a reasonable period of time and with enough accuracy to obtain a satisfactory evaluation.
- Type an accurate resume in attractive format, using plain typing paper, within a reasonable period of time to obtain a satisfactory evaluation.
- Compose and type a letter of introduction to go with the resume and place in a typed envelope, using one sheet of plain typing paper and a number 10 envelope, within a reasonable period of time to obtain a satisfactory evaluation.
- Complete an application form for a job, given an application for position form, within a reasonable period of time and with enough accuracy to obtain a satisfactory evaluation.
- Compose and type a follow-up thank you letter and place in a typed envelope, using one sheet of plain typing paper and a number 10 envelope, within a reasonable period of time to obtain a satisfactory evaluation.

Study Outline

EMPLOYMENT OPPORTUNITIES
JOB SEARCH
  Insurance billing specialist
  On-line job search
  Electronic resume
  Claims assistance professional
  Electronic claims professional
  Application
  Letter of introduction
  Resume
  Interview
    Portfolio
    After the interview
SELF-EMPLOYMENT OR FREELANCING
  Setting up an office
  Finances
  Equipment
  Insurance
  Marketing, advertising, promotion and public relations
  Contracts or agreements
  Documentation
  Statements and pricing
  Networking

Review Questions

Review the objectives, key terms, glossary definitions to key terms, chapter information, and figures before completing the following review questions.

1. Read each statement and indicate whether True (T) or False (F).

____ a. An insurance billing specialist is NOT required to report insurance fraud or abuse.

____ b. Enhancing knowledge and keeping up-to-date are responsibilities of an insurance billing specialist.

____ c. A claims assistance professional assists clients in challenging an insurance company's denial of payment.

____ d. Professional status of an electronic claims processor may be obtained when passing a national examination for a CECP.

____ e. Professional status of a claims assistance professional may be obtained when passing a national examination as a CCS.

2. Read the job descriptions in Chapter 17. An ability to read handwritten and transcribed documents in the medical record, interpret information, and input accurate code data to the computer system are technical skills required in the job of a/an ____________________

3. You have just completed a one-year medical insurance billing course at a college. Name some preliminary job search contacts to make on campus.

a. ____________________

b. ____________________

c. ____________________

d. ____________________

4. Name skills that may be listed on an application form or in a resume when seeking a position as an insurance billing specialist.

a. ____________________

b. ____________________

c. ____________________

d. ____________________

e. ____________________

5. A question appears on a job application form about salary. Two ways in which to handle this question are

a. ____________________

b. ____________________

6. State the chief purpose of a cover letter when sending a resume to a prospective employer. ____________________

____

7. A resume style that emphasizes work experience dates is known as a/an ____________ format; the ____________ format stresses job skills.

8. When job applicants have similar skills and education, surveys have shown that hiring by employers has been based on ____________________

____

9. List the items to be compiled in a portfolio.

a. ______________________________

b. ______________________________

c. ______________________________

d. ______________________________

e. ______________________________

f. ______________________________

g. ______________________________

h. ______________________________

i. ______________________________

10. You are being interviewed for a job and the interviewer asks this question, "What is your religious preference?" What would you respond? ______________________________

____

11. If a short period of time elapses after an interview and the applicant has received no word from the prospective employer, what follow-up steps may be taken?

a. ______________________________

b. ______________________________

12. When planning to start an insurance reimbursement business, enough funds to operate the business for a period of time from ______________________________ are vital.

13. Once an individual has begun his or her own business, the most common reason that a business might fail is ______________________________

14. In regard to the Internal Revenue Service, estimated tax payments must be made ____________ when the net income is ____________ or more.

15. Hugh Beason was the owner of XYZ Medical Reimbursement Service. A fire occurred, damaging some of the equipment and part of the office premises, requiring him to stop his work for a month so that repairs could be made. What type(s) of insurance would be helpful for this type of problem? ______________________________

16. Name three situations in which an established insurance reimbursement service may require additional help.

a. ______________________________

b. ______________________________

c. ______________________________

17. Jerry Hahn is pursuing a career as a claims assistance professional. When marketing his business, the target audience should be ______________ and ______________.

18. When composing an insurance reimbursement service contract or agreement with a client, important basic terms may include

a. ______________________________

b. ______________________________

c. ______________________________

d. ______________________________

e. ______________________________

19. Jennifer Inouye has been hired as a coding specialist by a hospital and needs to keep documentation when working. This may consist of

a. ______________________________

b. ______________________________

c. ______________________________

20. List various methods used for pricing services as a self-employed insurance billing specialist.

a. ______________________________

b. ______________________________

ASSIGNMENT 63

COMPLETE A RESUME WORKSHEET

Complete a worksheet in preparation for typing your resume. Some of the information requested on the worksheet should not appear on the resume but should be available if you are asked to provide it.

ASSIGNMENT 64

TYPE A RESUME

An advertisement appeared in your local newspaper (Fig. 17–1). You decide to apply for the position. Abstract data you think are relevant from your information worksheet and type a resume in rough draft. Ask the instructor for suggestions to improve the rough draft. Refer to Chapter 17, Figure 17–7, to help organize your resume into an attractive format before typing the final copy.

Medical Insurance Coding/Reimbursement Specialist

Mid-Atlantic Clinic, a 20 physician, multi-specialty group practice in Chicago, Illinois has a need for a coding and reimbursement specialist. Knowledge of medical terminology, CPT and ICD-9-CM coding systems, Medicare regulations, third-party insurance reimbursement and physician billing procedures required. Proficiency in the interpretation and coding of procedural and diagnostic codes is strongly preferred. Successful candidates must have excellent communication and problem-solving skills. This position offers a competitive salary and superior benefits. Please send resume to:

George B. Pason, Personnel Director
Mid-Atlantic Clinic
1230 South Main Street
Chicago, IL 60611

FIGURE 17-1

ASSIGNMENT 65

COMPOSE A COVER LETTER

Compose a cover letter introducing yourself and type a rough draft. Consult the instructor for suggestions. Type the cover letter on plain bond paper in mailable form. Refer to the sample letter in Chapter 17, Figure 17–6, as a guide to help organize thoughts. Type a number 10 envelope and insert the letter with the resume from Assignment 64.

ASSIGNMENT 66

COMPLETE AN APPLICATION FORM

Assume the employer asked you to come to his or her place of business to complete an application form and make an appointment for an interview. Using your data and resume, complete an application form (Fig. 17–2A and B).

APPLICATION FOR POSITION / Medical or Dental Office

AN EQUAL OPPORTUNITY EMPLOYER

(In answering questions, use extra blank sheet if necessary)

...nployee, applicant, or candidate for promotion, training or other advantage shall be discriminated against (or given preference) ...use of race, color, religion, sex, age, physical handicap, veteran status, or national origin.

Date of Application

...SE READ CAREFULLY AND WRITE OR PRINT ANSWERS TO ALL QUESTIONS. DO NOT TYPE.

...PERSONAL INFORMATION

...- Last	First	Middle	Social Security No.	Area Code/Phone No. ( )

...nt Address: - Street	(Apt #)	City	State	Zip	How Long At This Address?:

...us Address: - Street	City	State	Zip	Person to notify in case of Emergency or Accident - Name:
	To:			Address: Telephone:

...EMPLOYMENT INFORMATION

...hat Position Are You Applying?:	☐ Full-Time ☐ Part-Time ☐ Either	Date Available For Employment?:	Wage/Salary Expectations:
...s./Days You Prefer To Work:	List Any Hrs./Days You Are Not Available: (Except for times required for religious practices or observances)		Can You Work Overtime, If Necessary? ☐ Yes ☐ No
...u Employed Now?: ...☐ No	If So, May We Inquire Of Your Present Employer?: ☐ No ☐ Yes, If Yes: Name Of Employer:	Phone Number: ( )	
...ou Ever Been Bonded? ...☐ No	If Required For Position, Are You Bondable? ☐ Yes ☐ No ☐ Uncertain	Have You Applied For A Position With This Office Before?: ☐ No ☐ Yes, If Yes, When?:	

...ed By / Or Where Did You Learn Of This Job?:

...ou, Upon Employment, Submit Verification Of Your Legal Right ...k In The United States?: ☐ Yes ☐ No ...it Proof That You Meet Legal Age Requirement For Employment? ☐ Yes ☐ No	Language(s) Applicant Speaks or Writes (If Use Of A Language Other Than English Is Relevant To The Job For Which The Applicant Is Applying:

...EDUCATIONAL HISTORY

Name & Address Of Schools Attended (Include Current)	Dates From	Dates Thru	Highest Grade/Level Completed	Diploma/Degree(s) Obtained/Areas of Study
...School				
...e				Degree/Major
...raduate				Degree/Major
				Course/Diploma/License/ Certificate

...c Training, Education, Or Experiences Which Will Assist You In The Job For Which You Have Applied.

...Educational Plans

...SPECIAL SKILLS

...ECK BELOW THE KINDS OF WORK YOU HAVE DONE:		☐ MEDICAL INSURANCE FORMS	☐ RECEPTIONIST
☐ BLOOD COUNTS	☐ DENTAL ASSISTANT	☐ MEDICAL TERMINOLOGY	☐ TELEPHONES
☐ BOOKKEEPING	☐ DENTAL HYGIENIST	☐ MEDICAL TRANSCRIPTION	☐ TYPING
☐ COLLECTIONS	☐ FILING	☐ NURSING	☐ STENOGRAPHY
☐ COMPOSING LETTERS	☐ INJECTIONS	☐ PHLEBOTOMY (Draw Blood)	☐ URINALYSIS
☐ COMPUTER INPUT	☐ INSTRUMENT STERILIZATION	☐ POSTING	☐ X-RAY
...FICE ...UIPMENT USED: ☐ COMPUTER	☐ DICTATING EQUIPMENT	☐ WORD PROCESSOR	☐ OTHER:
...er Kinds Of Tasks Performed Or Skills That May Be Applicable To Position:		Typing Speed	Shorthand Speed

...O 72-110 © 1976 BIBBERO SYSTEMS, INC. • PETALUMA, CA (MB-CO) # 2-5 (REV. 10/92)
...RDER CALL 800-BIBBERO (800) 242-2376

(PLEASE COMPLETE OTHER SIDE)

FIGURE 17-2A

E. EMPLOYMENT RECORD

LIST MOST RECENT EMPLOYMENT FIRST **May We Contact Your Previous Employer(s) For A Reference?** ☐ Yes ☐

1) Employer

Address Street City State Zip Code

Phone Number ( )

Type of Business | Dates Mo. Yr. Mo. Yr. From To

Your Position | Hourly Rate/Salary Starting Final

Supervisor's Name

Reason For Leaving

Work Performed. Be Specific:

2) Employer

Address Street City State Zip Code

Phone Number ( )

Type of Business | Dates Mo. Yr. Mo. Yr. From To

Your Position | Hourly Rate/Salary Starting Final

Supervisor's Name

Reason For Leaving

Work Performed. Be Specific:

3) Employer

Address Street City State Zip Code

Phone Number ( )

Type of Business | Dates Mo. Yr. Mo. Yr. From To

Your Position | Hourly Rate/Salary Starting Final

Supervisor's Name

Reason For Leaving

Work Performed. Be Specific:

F. REFERENCES — FRIENDS / ACQUAINTANCES NON-RELATED

(1) Name Address Telephone Number (☐ Work ☐ Home) Occupation Years Acquain

(1) Name Address Telephone Number (☐ Work ☐ Home) Occupation Years Acquain

Please Feel Free To Add Any Information Which You Feel Will Help Us Consider You For Employment.

READ THE FOLLOWING CAREFULLY, THEN SIGN AND DATE THE APPLICATION

"I certify that all answers given by me on this application are true, correct and complete to the best of my knowledge. I acknowledge notice that the informati contained in this application is subject to check. I agree that, if hired, my continued employment may be contingent upon the accuracy of that information. If employed, I further agree to comply with Company / Office rules and regulations."

Signature: ______________________ Date: ____________

FORM NO. 72-110 © 1976 BIBBERO SYSTEMS, INC. • PETALUMA, CA (MB-CO) # 6-7 (REV. 4/92) TO REORDER CALL: 800-BIBBERO (800) 242-2

B

FIGURE 17-2B

ASSIGNMENT 67

PREPARE A FOLLOW-UP THANK YOU LETTER

After the interview, you decide to send a follow-up thank you letter to the person who interviewed you. Type a letter and address a number 10 envelope. Refer to Chapter 17, Figure 17–9, to help organize your thoughts.

Tests

Test 1: Evaluation and Management and Medicine Procedure Code Test

---

Directions: Using a *Current Procedural Terminology* (CPT) code book or Appendix A, insert the correct code numbers and modifiers for each service rendered. Give a brief description for each professional service rendered, although this is not needed when completing the HCFA–1500 claim form.

1. Dr. Input sees a new patient, Mrs. Post, in the office for acute abdominal distress. The physician spends approximately 1 hour doing a comprehensive history and physical examination with high-complexity decision making. Several diagnostic studies are ordered, and she is given an appointment to return in 1 week.
   Professional Service Rendered — Code

   ____________________ ________

2. Mr. Nakahara, an established patient, sees Dr. Practon in the office on January 11 for a re-evaluation of his diabetic condition. Dr. Practon takes a detailed history and performs a detailed examination. Decision making is moderately complex.
   Professional Service Rendered — Code

   ____________________ ________

3. Dr. Cardi sees Mrs. Franklin for a follow-up office visit for her hypertension (problem-focused history). A problem-focused examination of her cardiovascular system was done, revealing BP 140/100. Straightforward decision making with medication being prescribed. Pt. advised to return in 2 weeks to have her blood pressure checked by the nurse. Mrs. Franklin returns 2 weeks later, and the nurse checks her blood pressure.
   Professional Service Rendered — Code

   ____________________ ________

   ____________________ ________

4. Dr. Skelton receives a call at 7 p.m. from Mrs. Snyder. Her husband, a patient of Dr. Skelton's, has been very ill for 2 hours. Dr. Skelton goes to their home to see Mr. Snyder and spends considerable time doing a detailed history and examination. The medical decision making was of a highly complex nature. Physician administered an injection of Compazine.
   Professional Service Rendered — Code

   ____________________ ________

   ____________________ ________

5. Dr. Cutis sees an established patient, a registered nurse, for determination of pregnancy. Detailed hx/exam are done. A Papanicolaou smear is taken, a blood sample is drawn, and the specimens are sent to an independent laboratory for a qualitative hCG (human chorionic gonadotropin) test. This laboratory requires CPT coding on the lab requisition. List how these lab procedures would appear on the requisition sheet. The Pap smear is processed using the Bethesda System and done under physician supervision. The patient also complains of something she has discovered under her armpit. On examination, there is a furuncle of the left axilla, which is incised and drained during this visit. A sterile tray is required. Decision making is of moderate complexity.

Professional Service Rendered by Dr. Cutis	Code
______________________________	________
______________________________	________
______________________________	________
______________________________	________

Laboratory Service on Requisition Sheet	Code
______________________________	________
______________________________	________

6. Dr. Antrum makes a house call on Betty Mason, an established patient, for a problem-focused history of acute otitis media. A problem-focused examination is performed, with decision making of moderate complexity. While there, she also sees Betty's younger sister, Sandra, whom she has seen previously in the office for tonsillitis. A problem-focused hx/exam is performed with low-complexity decision making. In addition to the examinations, she gives both children injections of penicillin.

Professional Service Rendered to Betty	Code
______________________________	________
______________________________	________

Professional Service Rendered to Sandra	Code
______________________________	________
______________________________	________

7. Two weeks later Dr. Antrum is called to the emergency department at College Hospital at 2 a.m. on Sunday to see Betty Mason for recurrent otitis media. A problem-focused hx/exam is performed with low-complexity decision making.

Professional Service Rendered	Code
______________________________	________

8. While at the hospital, Dr. Antrum is asked to see another patient in the Emergency Department, who is new to her. A problem-focused history is taken. She does a problem-focused examination and low-complexity decision making for an intermediate 3.5–cm laceration of the scalp. It is sutured and pt is advised to come to the office in 4 days for a dressing change. Four days later the patient comes into the office for a dressing change by the nurse.

Professional Service Rendered Code

_______________________________________ _________

_______________________________________ _________

_______________________________________ _________

9. Dr. Menter, a psychiatrist, sees the following patients in the hospital. Code the procedures.
Professional Service Rendered Code
Ms. Blake: Consultation, expanded problem-focused hx/exam and straightforward decision making.

Referred by Dr. Practon. _________

Mrs. Clark: Group therapy (50 min) _________

Mrs. Samson: Group therapy (50 min) _________

Mr. Shoemaker: Group therapy (50 min) _________

Miss James: Psychotherapy (25 min) _________

10. Dr. Input, a gastroenterologist, sees Mrs. Chan in the hospital at the request of Dr. Practon. In addition to the detailed history/examination and low-complexity decision making, he does a gastric intubation and washings and prepares slides for cytology. Two days later he sees Mrs. Chan in follow-up inpt consultation and does a problem-focused interval hx/exam and low-complexity decision making. He performs an esophageal intubation and collects washings for cytology.
Professional Service Rendered Code

_______________________________________ _________

_______________________________________ _________

_______________________________________ _________

_______________________________________ _________

11. Mrs. Galati, a new patient, goes to Dr. Cardi because of chest pain (moderate to severe), weakness, fatigue, and dizziness. Dr. Cardi takes a comprehensive history and does a comprehensive examination, including ECG with interpretation and report, a vital capacity test, treadmill ECG, and urinalysis, and draws blood for a SMA-C (16 panel tests including CBC) and T–3 that are sent to and billed by a laboratory. Medical decision making was of high complexity.
Professional Service Rendered Code

_______________________________________ _________

_______________________________________ _________

_______________________________________ _________

_______________________________________ _________

_______________________________________ _________

12. Jake Wonderhill has not had his eyes examined by Dr. Lenser for about 5 years. He is seen by Dr. Lenser, who performs the following ophthalmologic procedures in addition to a comprehensive eye examination: fluorescein angioscopy and electroretinography.

Professional Service Rendered	Code
______________________	________
______________________	________
______________________	________

13. Dr. Practon is making rounds at the College Hospital and answers an urgent call on 3rd Floor East. He performs resuscitation on Mr. Sanchez and orders the patient taken to the critical care unit. Chest x-rays, lab work, blood gases, and ECG are performed. The physician is detained 2 hours in constant attendance on the patient.

Professional Service Rendered	Code
______________________	________
______________________	________

14. Mrs. Powers, new patient, sees Dr. Skelton, who takes a detailed history and does a detailed examination of her lower back and extremities. Medical decision making is of low complexity. Diathermy (30 min) is given. The next day she comes in for therapeutic exercises in the Hubbard tank (30 min).

Professional Service Rendered	Code
______________________	________
______________________	________
______________________	________

15. Mrs. Garcia, a new patient, is seen by Dr. Caesar for irregular vaginal bleeding (detailed hx/exam and low-complexity decision making). The doctor asks her to return in 3 days for cauterization of the cervix by cryocautery. The doctor takes a Pap smear and wet mount for bacterial fungi, which is sent to and billed by a laboratory. During the initial examination, Mrs. Garcia asks for an evaluation for possible infertility. Three weeks later, an endometrial biopsy and injection procedure for hysterosalpingography are performed.

Professional Service Rendered	Code
______________________	________
______________________	________
______________________	________
______________________	________
______________________	________

Multiple Choice. After reading the codes with descriptions, select the answer(s) that is/are best in each case.

59120	Surgical treatment of ectopic pregnancy; tubal or ovarian, requiring salpingectomy and/or oophorectomy, abdominal or vaginal approach.
59121	tubal or ovarian, without salpingectomy and/or oophorectomy
59130	abdominal pregnancy
59135	interstitial, uterine pregnancy requiring total hysterectomy
59136	interstitial, uterine pregnancy with partial resection of uterus
59140	cervical, with evacuation

16. In regard to this section of CPT codes, which of the following statements is true about codes 59120 through 59140 (mark all that apply):
   a. they refer to abdominal hysterotomy
   b. they involve laparoscopic treatment of ectopic pregnancy
   c. they refer to treatment of ectopic pregnancy by surgery
   d. they involve tubal ligation
17. In regard to this section of CPT codes, for treatment of an ectopic pregnancy, tubal, requiring oophorectomy, the code to select is:
   a. 59121
   b. 59120
   c. 59135
   d. 59136
   e. 59130
18. In regard to this section of CPT codes, for treatment of an ectopic pregnancy (interstitial, uterine) requiring a total hysterectomy, the code(s) to select is/are:
   a. 59135
   b. 59135 and 59120
   c. 59120
   d. 59130 and 59120
   e. 59121

Test 2: Procedure Code and Modifiers Test

Match the description given in the right column with the procedure code/modifier combination in the left column. Write the letter in the blank.

1. 99214–52 _____ A. Initial hospital admission with 40 minutes spent in counseling of patient.

2. 99244–24 _____ B. Established patient in a nursing facility with service of detailed hx/exam and highly complex decision making (unrelated service during postoperative period).

3. 99222–52 _____ C. Office consultation with comprehensive hx/exam unrelated to surgery during postoperative period. Moderately complex decision making.

4. 99291–25 _____ D. Hospital consultation with comprehensive hx/exam and moderately complex decision making (prolonged E/M service).

5. 99313–24 _____ E. Established patient office visit with detailed hx/exam and moderately complex decision making (reduced service).

6. 99233–21 _____ F. Patient discharged from hospital (separate E/M service rendered on same day).

7. 99238–25 _____ G. After diagnostic tests on Monday, patient seen for hospital visit with detailed hx/exam and highly complex decision making (prolonged E/M service).

8. 99254–21 _____ H. Inpatient critical care service (not related to surgery on the same day).

Directions: Using a *Current Procedural Terminology* (CPT) code book or Appendix A, insert the correct code numbers and modifiers for each service rendered. Give a brief description for each professional service rendered although this is not needed when completing the HCFA–1500 claim form.

9. Dr. Input performs a gastrojejunostomy and calls in Dr. Scott to do the anesthesia and Dr. Cutler to assist. Surgery takes 2 hours, 30 minutes. The patient is normal and healthy. List the procedure code numbers for each physician.

Professional Service Rendered by Dr. Input	Code
______________________________	________

Professional Service Rendered by Dr. Scott	Code
______________________________	________

Professional Service Rendered by Dr. Cutler	Code
______________________________	________

10. Dr. Rumsey assists Dr. Cutler with a total colectomy (intraperitoneal procedure). Dr. Scott is the anesthesiologist. Surgery takes 2 hours, 55 minutes. The patient is normal and healthy. List the procedure code numbers for each physician.

Professional Service Rendered by Dr. Rumsey	Code
______________________________	________

Professional Service Rendered by Dr. Scott	Code
______________________________	________

Professional Service Rendered by Dr. Cutler	Code
______________________________	________

11. Dr. Cutis removes a malignant lesion from the back (1.5 cm) and does the regional anesthesia herself.

Professional Service Rendered	Code
______________________________	________
______________________________	________

12. Dr. Skelton sees Mr. Richmond, a new patient, worked into the office schedule as an emergency following an automobile accident. He has multiple lacerations and fractures. The physician takes a comprehensive history and does a comprehensive examination. Decision making moderately complex. He orders bilateral x-rays of the tibia and fibula, two views of the chest, and left wrist to be taken in his office. Then he closes the following lacerations: 2.6 cm, simple, face; 2.0 cm, intermediate, face; 7.5 cm, intermediate, right arm; 4.5 cm, intermediate, chest. All x-rays are negative except the left tibia. Dr. Skelton performs a manipulative reduction of the left tibia and applies a cast.

Professional Service Rendered | Code

Six weeks later Dr. Skelton sees the same patient for an office visit and takes x-rays (2 views) of the left tibia and fibula. Treatment involves application of a cast below the left knee to the toes, including a walking heel.

Professional Service Rendered | Code

13. Dr. Cutler performs an incisional biopsy of the breast requiring 40 minutes of anesthesia. Dr. Scott is the anesthesiologist. The patient is normal and healthy. List the procedure code numbers for each physician.

Professional Service Rendered Dr. Cutler | Code

Professional Service Rendered Dr. Scott | Code

14. Mrs. DeBeau is aware that Dr. Input will be out of town for 6 weeks; however, she decides to have him perform the recommended combined anterior-posterior colporrhaphy with enterocele repair. Dr. Practon agrees to do the follow-up care and assist. Dr. Scott is the anesthesiologist. The anesthesia time is 2 hours, 15 minutes. The patient is normal and healthy. List the procedure code numbers for each physician.

Professional Service Rendered by Dr. Input | Code

Professional Service Rendered by Dr. Practon | Code

Professional Service Rendered by Dr. Scott | Code

15. Mr. Wong, a new patient, is seen in the College Hospital and undergoes a comprehensive H & P with moderately complex decision making. Dr. Coccidioides performs a bronchoscopy with biopsy. Results of the biopsy confirm the diagnosis. The following day he performs a total pneumonectomy. Dr. Cutler assists on the total pneumonectomy (pulmonary resection), and Dr. Scott is the anesthesiologist. Surgery takes 3 hours, 45 minutes. Patient has mild systemic disease. List the procedure code numbers for each physician.

Professional Service Rendered by Dr. Coccidioides — Code

__________ __________

__________ __________

__________ __________

Professional Service Rendered by Dr. Cutler — Code

__________ __________

Professional Service Rendered by Dr. Scott — Code

__________ __________

When completing the HCFA–1500 claim form for Dr. Scott, in which block would you list anesthesia minutes? __________

Test 3: Radiology and Pathology Procedure Code Test

Directions: Using a *Current Procedural Terminology* (CPT) code book or Appendix A, insert the correct code numbers and modifiers for each service rendered. Give a brief description for each professional service rendered, although this is not needed when completing the HCFA–1500 claim form.

1. Mrs. Cahn sees Dr. Skelton because of severe pain in her right shoulder. She is a new patient. Dr. Skelton takes a detailed history and performs a detailed examination. A complete x-ray study of the right shoulder is done. Decision making is of low complexity. Diagnosis of bursitis is made, and an injection of the bursa is carried out requiring the use of a sterile tray.

   Professional Service Rendered — Code

   __________ __________

   __________ __________

   __________ __________

   __________ __________

2. Broxton Radiologic Group, Inc., performs the following procedures on Mrs. Stephens at the request of Dr. Input. List the procedure code numbers after each radiologic procedure.

   Professional Service Rendered — Code

   Barium enema __________

   Upper GI tract with small bowel __________

   Complete chest x-ray __________

3. Two weeks later Mrs. Stephens is referred again for further radiologic studies. List the procedure code numbers after each radiologic procedure.

Professional Service Rendered	Code
IVP with drip infusion	________
Oral cholecystography	________

4. Jean Murphy comes into the Broxton Radiologic Group, Inc., for an extended radiation therapy consultation. The radiologist takes a detailed history and does a detailed examination. Decision making is of low complexity, and he orders simple tumor localization. One week later Mrs. Murphy returns to begin daily radiation therapy, complex megaelectron volt treatments (3 MeV) for 2 weeks. At the end of 2 weeks' treatment, dosimetry is performed. The next week radiation treatment is given to a single treatment area, simple block, up to 5 MeV.

Professional Service Rendered	Code
______________________________	________
______________________________	________
______________________________	________
______________________________	________
______________________________	________

5. Dr. Input refers Mrs. Horner to the Broxton Radiologic Group, Inc., for a bone marrow imaging of the whole body and imaging of the liver and spleen. List the procedure code numbers after each radiologic procedure to show how the radiology group would bill.

Professional Service Rendered	Code
Bone marrow, imaging	________
Isotope (supplies and materials)	________
Liver and spleen imaging	________
Isotope	________

6. Dr. Input also refers Mrs. Horncr to XYZ Laboratory for the following tests. List the procedure code numbers to indicate how the laboratory would bill.

Professional Service Rendered	Code
CBC (manual)	________
Bone marrow aspiration	________
Urinalysis, microscopic only	________

7. The general laboratory at College Hospital receives a surgical tissue specimen (ovary, biopsy) for gross and microscopic examination. List the procedure code number to indicate what the hospital pathology department would bill.

Professional Service Rendered	Code
______________________________	________

8. Dr. Langerhans refers Jerry Cramer to XYZ Laboratory for the following automated laboratory tests: cholesterol, glucose, sodium, and uric acid. List the procedure code number(s) to indicate how the laboratory would bill.

Professional Service Rendered	Code
______________________________	________

9. Dr. Caesar is an Ob-Gyn specialist who has her own ultrasound machine. During prenatal care, an amniocentesis is done on Carmen Cardoza, an established patient age 45, using ultrasonic guidance. The doctor performs a detailed history and physical and decision making of moderate complexity.

Professional Service Rendered	Code
______________________________	________
______________________________	________
______________________________	________

10. Mr. Marcos' medical record indicates that a retrograde pyelogram followed by a percutaneous nephrostolithotomy, with basket extraction of a stone 1 cm in size, was performed by Dr. Ulibarri.

Professional Service Rendered	Code
______________________________	________
______________________________	________

Test 4

Complete the Health Insurance Claim Form HCFA–1500 (Fig. 1) using OCR guidelines, on Miss Jennifer Lacey by referring to her patient record and ledger card (Figs. 2 and 3) and direct it to American Commercial Insurance Company. Date the claim October 15.

Use your *CPT Code Book* or Appendix A to determine the correct five-digit code number and fees for each professional service rendered. Remember to include modifiers if necessary.

Record on the ledger card when you have billed the insurance company.

HEALTH INSURANCE CLAIM FORM

PICA

E MEDICAID CHAMPUS CHAMPVA GROUP HEALTH PLAN FECA BLK LUNG OTHER

#) (Medicaid #) (Sponsor's SSN) (VA File #) (SSN or ID) (SSN) (ID)

1a. INSURED'S I.D. NUMBER (FOR PROGRAM IN ITEM 1)

NAME (Last Name, First Name, Middle Initial)

3. PATIENT'S BIRTH DATE MM DD YY SEX M F

4. INSURED'S NAME (Last Name, First Name, Middle Initial)

ADDRESS (No., Street)

6. PATIENT RELATIONSHIP TO INSURED Self Spouse Child Other

7. INSURED'S ADDRESS (No., Street)

STATE

8. PATIENT STATUS Single Married Other

Employed Full-Time Student Part-Time Student

CITY STATE

TELEPHONE (Include Area Code) ( )

ZIP CODE TELEPHONE (INCLUDE AREA CODE) ( )

URED'S NAME (Last Name, First Name, Middle Initial)

10. IS PATIENT'S CONDITION RELATED TO:

11. INSURED'S POLICY GROUP OR FECA NUMBER

URED'S POLICY OR GROUP NUMBER

a. EMPLOYMENT? (CURRENT OR PREVIOUS) YES NO

a. INSURED'S DATE OF BIRTH MM DD YY SEX M F

URED'S DATE OF BIRTH YY SEX M F

b. AUTO ACCIDENT? PLACE (State) YES NO

b. EMPLOYER'S NAME OR SCHOOL NAME

'S NAME OR SCHOOL NAME

c. OTHER ACCIDENT? YES NO

c. INSURANCE PLAN NAME OR PROGRAM NAME

E PLAN NAME OR PROGRAM NAME

10d. RESERVED FOR LOCAL USE

d. IS THERE ANOTHER HEALTH BENEFIT PLAN? YES NO ***If yes***, return to and complete item 9 a-d.

READ BACK OF FORM BEFORE COMPLETING & SIGNING THIS FORM.

S OR AUTHORIZED PERSON'S SIGNATURE I authorize the release of any medical or other information necessary this claim. I also request payment of government benefits either to myself or to the party who accepts assignment

DATE

13. INSURED'S OR AUTHORIZED PERSON'S SIGNATURE I authorize payment of medical benefits to the undersigned physician or supplier for services described below.

SIGNED

PATIENT AND INSURED INFORMATION

CURRENT: YY ILLNESS (First symptom) OR INJURY (Accident) OR PREGNANCY(LMP)

15. IF PATIENT HAS HAD SAME OR SIMILAR ILLNESS. GIVE FIRST DATE MM DD YY

16. DATES PATIENT UNABLE TO WORK IN CURRENT OCCUPATION FROM MM DD YY TO MM DD YY

REFERRING PHYSICIAN OR OTHER SOURCE

17a. I.D. NUMBER OF REFERRING PHYSICIAN

18. HOSPITALIZATION DATES RELATED TO CURRENT SERVICES FROM MM DD YY TO MM DD YY

D FOR LOCAL USE

20. OUTSIDE LAB? YES NO $ CHARGES

S OR NATURE OF ILLNESS OR INJURY. (RELATE ITEMS 1,2,3 OR 4 TO ITEM 24E BY LINE)

3. ___ . ___

4. ___ . ___

22. MEDICAID RESUBMISSION CODE ORIGINAL REF. NO.

23. PRIOR AUTHORIZATION NUMBER

TE(S) OF SERVICE To YY MM DD YY	B Place of Service	C Type of Service	D PROCEDURES, SERVICES, OR SUPPLIES (Explain Unusual Circumstances) CPT/HCPCS MODIFIER	E DIAGNOSIS CODE	F $ CHARGES	G DAYS OR UNITS	H EPSDT Family Plan	I EMG	J COB	K RESERVED FOR LOCAL USE

TAX I.D. NUMBER SSN EIN

26. PATIENT'S ACCOUNT NO.

27. ACCEPT ASSIGNMENT? (For govt. claims, see back) YES NO

28. TOTAL CHARGE $

29. AMOUNT PAID $

30. BALANCE DUE $

E OF PHYSICIAN OR SUPPLIER G DEGREES OR CREDENTIALS t the statements on the reverse s bill and are made a part thereof.)

DATE

32. NAME AND ADDRESS OF FACILITY WHERE SERVICES WERE RENDERED (If other than home or office)

33. PHYSICIAN'S, SUPPLIER'S BILLING NAME, ADDRESS, ZIP CODE & PHONE #

PIN# GRP#

PHYSICIAN OR SUPPLIER INFORMATION

ED BY AMA COUNCIL ON MEDICAL SERVICE 8/88)

PLEASE PRINT OR TYPE

FORM HCFA-1500 (U2) (12-90)
FORM OWCP-1500 FORM RRB-1500

FIGURE 1

PATIENT RECORD

LAST NAME	FIRST NAME	MIDDLE NAME	BIRTH DATE	SEX	HOME PHONE
Lacey,	Jennifer	T. (Miss)	11-12-45	F	013/549-0098

ADDRESS	CITY	STATE	ZIP CODE
451 Roberts Street,	Woodland Hills,	XY	12345

PATIENT'S OCCUPATION	NAME OF COMPANY
legal secretary	Higgins and Higgins (attorneys)

ADDRESS OF EMPLOYER	PHONE
430 Second Avenue, Woodland Hills, XY 12345	013/540-6675

SPOUSE OR PARENT	OCCUPATION

EMPLOYER	ADDRESS	PHONE

NAME OF INSURANCE GROUP	SUBSCRIBER
American Commercial Ins. Co. 5682 Bendix Blvd., Woodland Hills, XY 12345	

BLUE SHIELD OR BLUE CROSS CERT. NO.	GROUP NO.	CURRENT COVERAGE NO.	EFFECTIVE DATE
Policy No. 5789022			6-1-79

MEDICARE NO.	MEDICAID NO.	EFFECTIVE DATE	SOC. SEC. NO.
			430-98-7709

REFERRED BY:

Clarence Cutler, MD 4567 Broad Avenue, Woodland Hills, XY 12345

DATE	PROGRESS
8-1-9x	New pt came in for consultation & additional opinion referred by Dr. Cutler. CC: full feeling in stomach. BM difficulty for 5 days. Sometimes difficulty c̄ urination. PE revealed lg tumor extending out of pelvis & felt halfway to umbilicus. Ultrasonic exam showed rt ovarian mass and leiomyomata uteri. Adv expl. pelvic laparotomy with abdominal hysterectomy; possible bilateral salpingo-oophorectomy & pelvic exenteration for malignancy. Pap smear Class 1. Bertha Caesar, MD
8-3-9x	Adm to College Hosp. After IVP, barium enema & bone scan decided to schedule surg next day. B Caesar, MD
8-4-9x	Perf abdominal hysterectomy with bilateral salpingo-oophorectomy. Path report revealed leiomyometa uteri and cystoma of rt ovary. BC
8-5-9x to 8-8-9x	Pt seen daily and DC to home 8-8-9x. Bertha Caesar, MD

FIGURE 2

STATEMENT

College Clinic
4567 Broad Avenue
Woodland Hills, XY 12345-0001
Telephone: 013-486-9002
Fax: 013-487-8976

Miss Jennifer T. Lacey
451 Roberts Street
Woodland Hills, XY 12345

DATE	PROFESSIONAL SERVICE DESCRIPTION	CHARGE	CREDITS		CURRENT BALANCE
			PAYMENTS	ADJUSTMENTS	
8-1-9x	Consultation, EPF hx/exam, SF decision making				
8-3-9x	Init hosp care: comp hx/exam, hist incl prep of hosp documents & adm, HC decision making				
8-4-9x	Total abdominal hysterectomy with salpingo-oorphorectomy				
8-5-9x	HV				
8-6-9x	HV				
8-7-9x	HV				
8-8-9x	Hosp discharge				

Due and payable within 10 days. **Pay last amount in balance column**

Key: PF: Problem-focused
EPF: Expanded problem-focused
D: Detailed
C: Comprehensive
SF: Straightforward
LC: Low complexity
MC: Moderate complexity
HC: High complexity
CON: Consultation
CPX: Complete Phys Exam
E: Emergency
ER: Emergency Dept.
HCD: House Call (Day)
HCN: House Call (Night)
HV: Hospital visit
OV: Office Visit

FIGURE 3

Test 5

This case requires two HCFA-1500 claim forms, so make a photocopy of the form for the September bill.

Complete the Health Insurance Claim Form HCFA-1500 (Fig. 4) using OCR guidelines, on Mrs. Gertrude C. Hamilton by referring to her patient record and ledger card (Figs. 5 and 6) and direct it to Colonial Health Insurance. Date the claim October 15.

Use your *CPT Code Book* or Appendix A to determine the correct five-digit code number and fees for each professional service rendered. Remember to include modifiers if necessary.

Record on the ledger card when you have billed the insurance company. Mrs. Hamilton makes a payment of $200, check No. 5362, on October 16. Make the proper entry after this transaction.

HEALTH INSURANCE CLAIM FORM

PICA

E | MEDICAID | CHAMPUS | CHAMPVA | GROUP HEALTH PLAN | FECA BLK LUNG | OTHER
#) ☐ (Medicaid #) ☐ (Sponsor's SSN) ☐ (VA File #) ☐ (SSN or ID) ☐ (SSN) ☐ (ID)

1a. INSURED'S I.D. NUMBER (FOR PROGRAM IN ITEM 1)

NAME (Last Name, First Name, Middle Initial)

3. PATIENT'S BIRTH DATE MM | DD | YY SEX M ☐ F ☐

4. INSURED'S NAME (Last Name, First Name, Middle Initial)

ADDRESS (No., Street)

6. PATIENT RELATIONSHIP TO INSURED Self ☐ Spouse ☐ Child ☐ Other ☐

7. INSURED'S ADDRESS (No., Street)

STATE

8. PATIENT STATUS Single ☐ Married ☐ Other ☐ Employed ☐ Full-Time Student ☐ Part-Time Student ☐

CITY | STATE

TELEPHONE (Include Area Code) ( )

ZIP CODE | TELEPHONE (INCLUDE AREA CODE) ( )

SURED'S NAME (Last Name, First Name, Middle Initial)

10. IS PATIENT'S CONDITION RELATED TO:

11. INSURED'S POLICY GROUP OR FECA NUMBER

SURED'S POLICY OR GROUP NUMBER

a. EMPLOYMENT? (CURRENT OR PREVIOUS) ☐ YES ☐ NO

a. INSURED'S DATE OF BIRTH MM | DD | YY SEX M ☐ F ☐

SURED'S DATE OF BIRTH) | YY SEX M ☐ F ☐

b. AUTO ACCIDENT? PLACE (State) ☐ YES ☐ NO

b. EMPLOYER'S NAME OR SCHOOL NAME

R'S NAME OR SCHOOL NAME

c. OTHER ACCIDENT? ☐ YES ☐ NO

c. INSURANCE PLAN NAME OR PROGRAM NAME

E PLAN NAME OR PROGRAM NAME

10d. RESERVED FOR LOCAL USE

d. IS THERE ANOTHER HEALTH BENEFIT PLAN? ☐ YES ☐ NO *If yes*, return to and complete item 9 a-d.

READ BACK OF FORM BEFORE COMPLETING & SIGNING THIS FORM.

S OR AUTHORIZED PERSON'S SIGNATURE I authorize the release of any medical or other information necessary s this claim. I also request payment of government benefits either to myself or to the party who accepts assignment

DATE

13. INSURED'S OR AUTHORIZED PERSON'S SIGNATURE I authorize payment of medical benefits to the undersigned physician or supplier for services described below.

SIGNED

PATIENT AND INSURED INFORMATION

CURRENT:) | YY ◀ ILLNESS (First symptom) OR INJURY (Accident) OR PREGNANCY(LMP)

15. IF PATIENT HAS HAD SAME OR SIMILAR ILLNESS. GIVE FIRST DATE MM | DD | YY

16. DATES PATIENT UNABLE TO WORK IN CURRENT OCCUPATION FROM MM | DD | YY TO MM | DD | YY

REFERRING PHYSICIAN OR OTHER SOURCE

17a. I.D. NUMBER OF REFERRING PHYSICIAN

18. HOSPITALIZATION DATES RELATED TO CURRENT SERVICES FROM MM | DD | YY TO MM | DD | YY

ED FOR LOCAL USE

20. OUTSIDE LAB? ☐ YES ☐ NO $ CHARGES

SIS OR NATURE OF ILLNESS OR INJURY. (RELATE ITEMS 1,2,3 OR 4 TO ITEM 24E BY LINE)

. __ 3. ___ . __

. __ 4. ___ . __

22. MEDICAID RESUBMISSION CODE | ORIGINAL REF. NO.

23. PRIOR AUTHORIZATION NUMBER

ATE(S) OF SERVICE YY	To MM DD YY	B Place of Service	C Type of Service	D PROCEDURES, SERVICES, OR SUPPLIES (Explain Unusual Circumstances) CPT/HCPCS | MODIFIER	E DIAGNOSIS CODE	F $ CHARGES	G DAYS OR UNITS	H EPSDT Family Plan	I EMG	J COB	K RESERVED FOR LOCAL USE

TAX I.D. NUMBER SSN EIN ☐ ☐

26. PATIENT'S ACCOUNT NO.

27. ACCEPT ASSIGNMENT? (For govt. claims, see back) ☐ YES ☐ NO

28. TOTAL CHARGE $

29. AMOUNT PAID $

30. BALANCE DUE $

RE OF PHYSICIAN OR SUPPLIER NG DEGREES OR CREDENTIALS hat the statements on the reverse his bill and are made a part thereof.)

DATE

32. NAME AND ADDRESS OF FACILITY WHERE SERVICES WERE RENDERED (If other than home or office)

33. PHYSICIAN'S, SUPPLIER'S BILLING NAME, ADDRESS, ZIP CODE & PHONE #

PIN# | GRP#

PHYSICIAN OR SUPPLIER INFORMATION

VED BY AMA COUNCIL ON MEDICAL SERVICE 8/88)

PLEASE PRINT OR TYPE

FORM HCFA-1500 (U2) (12-90)
FORM OWCP-1500 FORM RRB-1500

FIGURE 4

PATIENT RECORD

LAST NAME	FIRST NAME	MIDDLE NAME	BIRTH DATE	SEX	HOME PHONE
Hamilton,	Gertrude	C.	3-6-43	F	013/798-3321

ADDRESS	CITY	STATE	ZIP CODE
5320 Phillips Street,	Woodland Hills	XY	12345

PATIENT'S OCCUPATION	NAME OF COMPANY
retired secretary	

ADDRESS OF EMPLOYER	PHONE

SPOUSE OR PARENT	OCCUPATION
deceased	

EMPLOYER	ADDRESS	PHONE

NAME OF INSURANCE GROUP	SUBSCRIBER
Colonial Health Insurance 1011 Main St., Woodland Hills, XY 12345	

BLUE SHIELD OR BLUE CROSS CERT. NO.	GROUP NO.	CURRENT COVERAGE NO.	EFFECTIVE DATE
	4566		

MEDICARE NO.	MEDICAID NO.	EFFECTIVE DATE	SOC. SEC. NO.
			540-98-7677

REFERRED BY:

Gerald Practon, M.D. 4567 Broad Avenue, Woodland Hills, XY 12345

DATE	PROGRESS
7-29-9x	This 57 yr old pt adm to College Hosp today by Dr. Practon c̄ an adm Dx of bilateral carotid stenosis. Dr. Practon asked me to see pt in consultation. Hx: suffered CVA lt hemisphere 1 yr prior to adm. Marked rt arm & leg weakness c̄ weakness of rt face & slurring of speech. PE reveals lt carotid bruit, III/IV & a rt carotid bruit, II/IV. Adv brain scan & lt carotid thromboendarterectomy. Will follow patient's progress and take over care of pt. P. Cardi, MD
7-30, 31 & 8-1-9x	Hosp visits daily. P. Cardi, MD
8-2-9x	Lt carotid thromboendarterectomy. See op report. P Cardi, MD
8-4-9x	DC hosp. To be seen in office in 1 week. P Cardi, MD
8-12-9x	PO visit. Making satisfactory PO progress. Adv rt carotid arterectomy. P Cardi, MD
9-16-9x	Adm College Hosp. Rt carotid thromboendarterectomy performed. Dx: bilateral carotid stenosis, status postoperative lt carotid thromboendarterectomy & HCVD. DC hosp. 9-18. PC MD
10-4-9x	PO visit - making satisfactory PO recovery. Retn 1 month. P Cardi, MD

FIGURE 5

STATEMENT

College Clinic
4567 Broad Avenue
Woodland Hills, XY 12345-0001
Telephone: 013-486-9002
Fax: 013-487-8976

Mrs. Gertrude C. Hamilton
5320 Phillips Street
Woodland Hills, XY 12345-0001

DATE	PROFESSIONAL SERVICE DESCRIPTION	CHARGE	CREDITS		CURRENT BALANCE
			PAYMENTS	ADJUSTMENTS	
7-29-9x	Consult, comp hx/exam, HC decision making				
7-30-9x	HV, PF hx/exam, LC decision making				
7-31-9x	HV, PF hx/exam, LC decision making				
8-1-9x	HV, PF hx, exam, LC decision making				
8-2-9x	L carotid thromboendarterectomy				
8-3-9x	HV				
8-4-9x	HV				
8-12-9x	OV				
9-16-9x	Hosp adm, D hx/exam, LC decision making				
9-17-9x	Rt carotid thromboendarterectomy				
10-4-9x	OV				

Due and payable within 10 days. **Pay last amount in balance column** ⇧

Key: **PF:** Problem-focused; **EPF:** Expanded problem-focused; **D:** Detailed; **C:** Comprehensive; **SF:** Straightforward; **LC:** Low complexity; **MC:** Moderate complexity; **HC:** High complexity; **CON:** Consultation; **CPX:** Complete Phys Exam; **E:** Emergency; **ER:** Emergency Dept.; **HCD:** House Call (Day); **HCN:** House Call (Night); **HV:** Hospital visit; **OV:** Office Visit

FIGURE 6

Appendix A

Mock Fee Schedule

Refer to the following mock fee schedule to complete the ledger cards and claim forms in this *Workbook*. The fees listed are hypothetical and are intended only for use in completing the questions. When completing the insurance claim forms, use the latest edition of *Physicians' Current Procedural Terminology (CPT)*, the professional code book published by the American Medical Association, to find the correct code numbers and modifiers for the services rendered. If you do not have access to the latest edition of *CPT*, you may use the code numbers provided in the mock fee schedule; however, do so with the understanding that the code numbers and descriptions provided in this schedule are not comprehensive. They are based on the information found in *CPT*; however, students are cautioned not to use it as a substitute for *CPT*. Because the code numbers are subject to change, every medical office must have on hand the most recent edition of *CPT*.

The mock fee schedule is arranged in the same sequence as the six *CPT Code Book* sections (i.e., Evaluation and Management; Anesthesia; Surgery; Radiology, Nuclear Medicine, and Diagnostic Ultrasound; Pathology and Laboratory; and Medicine) with a comprehensive list of modifiers placed at the beginning. An index at the end of the mock fee schedule can assist you in locating code numbers. Mock fees for the modifiers are not listed, since these can vary from one claim to another depending on the circumstances.

Remember that fees can vary with the region of the United States (West, Midwest, South, and East), the specialty of the practitioner, the type of community (urban, suburban, or rural), the type of practice (incorporated or unincorporated—solo, partners or shareholders), the overhead, and a number of other factors.

College Clinic Mock Fee Schedule

Modifier Code No.	Description	Mock Fee ($)
-20	*Microsurgery:* When the surgical service is performed using the techniques of microsurgery, including the aid of an operating microscope, modifier -20 may be added to the surgical procedure code number, or the separate five-digit modifier code number 09920 may be used. The use of this modifier is not warranted when surgery is done with the aid of a magnifying surgical loupe, whether attached to the eyeglasses or on a headband. A special report may be appropriate to document the necessity of the microsurgical approach.	Variable
-21	*Prolonged Evaluation and Management Services:* When the face-to-face or floor/unit service(s) provided is prolonged or otherwise greater than that usually required for the highest level of evaluation and management service within a given category, it may be identified by adding modifier -21 to the evaluation and management	Variable

Table continued on following page

College Clinic Mock Fee Schedule *Continued*

Modifier Code No.	Description	Mock Fee ($)
	code number or by use of the separate five-digit modifier code 09921. A report may also be appropriate.	
-22	*Unusual Services:* When the service(s) provided is greater than that usually required for the listed procedure, it may be identified by adding modifier -22 to the usual procedure code number or by using the separate five-digit modifier code number 09922. A report may also be appropriate.	Variable
-23	*Unusual Anesthesia:* Occasionally, a procedure that usually requires either no anesthesia or local anesthesia must be done under general anesthesia because of unusual circumstances. These circumstances may be reported by adding the modifier -23 to the procedure code number of the basic service or by using the separate five-digit modifier code number 09923.	Variable
-24	*Unrelated Evaluation and Management Service by the Same Physician During a Postoperative Period:* The physician may need to indicate that an evaluation and management service was performed during a postoperative period for a reason(s) unrelated to the original procedure. This circumstance may be reported by adding the modifier -24 to the appropriate level of E/M service, or the separate five-digit modifier 09924 may be used.	Variable
-25	*Significant, Separately, Identifiable Evaluation and Management Service by the Same Physician on the Same Day of a Procedure or Other Service:* The physician may need to indicate that on the day a procedure or service identified by a CPT code was performed, the patient's condition required a significant, separately identifiable E/M service above and beyond the other service provided or beyond the usual preoperative and postoperative care associated with the procedure that was performed. This circumstance may be reported by adding the modifier -25 to the appropriate level of E/M service, or the separate five-digit modifier 09925 may be used. NOTE: This modifier is not used to report an E/M service that resulted in a decision to perform surgery. See modifier -57.	Variable
-26	*Professional Component:* Certain procedures are a combination of a physician component and a technical component. When the physician component is reported separately, the service may be identified by adding the modifier -26 to the usual procedure code number, or the service may be reported by using the five-digit modifier code number 09926.	Variable
-32	*Mandated Services:* Services related to mandated consultation and/or related services (e.g., PRO, 3rd party payor) may be identified by adding the modifier -32 to the basic procedure, or the service may be reported by use of the five-digit modifier 09932.	Variable
-47	*Anesthesia by Surgeon:* Regional or general anesthesia provided by the surgeon may be reported by adding the modifier -47 to the basic service or by using the separate five-digit modifier code number 09947 (this does not include local anesthesia). NOTE: Modifier -47 or code number 09947 would not be used as a modifier for the anesthesia procedures 00100 through 01999.	Variable

College Clinic Mock Fee Schedule *Continued*

Modifier Code No.	Description	Mock Fee ($)
-50	*Bilateral Procedure:* Unless otherwise identified in the listings, bilateral procedures that are performed at the same operative session should be identified by the appropriate five-digit code number describing the first procedure. The second (bilateral) procedure is identified either by adding modifier -50 to the procedure code number or by using the separate five-digit modifier code 09950.	Variable
-51	*Multiple Procedures:* When multiple procedures are performed on the same day or at the same session, the major procedure or service may be reported as listed. The secondary, additional, or lesser procedure(s) or service may be identified by adding the modifier -51 to the secondary procedure or service code(s) or by using the separate five-digit modifier code 09951. This modifier may be used to report multiple medical procedures performed at the same session, as well as a combination of medical and surgical procedures, or several surgical procedures performed at the same operative session.	Variable
-52	*Reduced Services:* Under certain circumstances a service or procedure is partially reduced or eliminated at the physician's election. Under these circumstances the service provided can be identified by its usual procedure number and the addition of the modifier -52, signifying that the service is reduced. This provides a means of reporting reduced services without disturbing the identification of the basic service. Modifier code 09952 may be used as an alternative to modifier -52.	Variable
-54	*Surgical Care Only:* When one physician performs a surgical procedure and another provides preoperative and/or postoperative management, surgical services may be identified by adding the modifier -54 to the usual procedure number or by using the separate five-digit modifier code 09954.	Variable
-55	*Postoperative Management Only:* When one physician performs the postoperative management and another physician performs the surgical procedure, the postoperative component may be identified by adding modifier -55 to the usual procedure number or by using the separate five-digit modifier code 09955.	Variable
-56	*Preoperative Management Only:* When one physician performs the preoperative care and evaluation and another physician performs the surgical procedure, the preoperative component may be identified by adding the modifier -56 to the usual procedure number or by using the separate five-digit modifier code 09956.	Variable
-57	*Decision for Surgery:* An evaluation and management service that resulted in the initial decision to perform the surgery may be identified by adding the modifier -57 to the appropriate level of E/M service, or the separate five-digit modifier 09957 may be used.	Variable
-58	*Staged or Related Procedure or Service by the Same Physician During the Postoperative Period:* The physician may need to indicate that the performance of a proce-	Variable

Table continued on following page

College Clinic Mock Fee Schedule *Continued*

Modifier Code No.	Description	Mock Fee ($)
	dure or service during the postoperative period was: (a) planned prospectively at the time of the original procedure (staged); (b) more extensive than the original procedure; or (c) for therapy following a diagnostic surgical procedure. This circumstance may be reported by adding the modifier -58 to the staged or related procedure, or the separate five-digit modifier 09958 may be used. NOTE: This modifier is not used to report the treatment of a problem that requires a return to the operating room. See modifier -78.	
-62	*Two Surgeons:* Under certain circumstances the skills of two surgeons (usually with different skills) may be required in the management of a specific surgical procedure. Under such circumstances the separate services may be identified by adding the modifier -62 to the procedure number used by each surgeon for reporting his or her services. Modifier code 09962 may be used as an alternative to modifier -62.	Variable
-66	*Surgical Team:* Under some circumstances, highly complex procedures (requiring the concomitant services of several physicians, often of different specialties, plus other highly skilled, specially trained personnel and various types of complex equipment) are carried out under the "surgical team" concept. Such circumstances may be identified by each participating physician with the addition of the modifier -66 to the basic procedure code number used for reporting services. Modifier code 09966 may be used as an alternative to modifier -66.	Variable
-76	*Repeat Procedure by Same Physician:* The physician may need to indicate that a procedure or service was repeated subsequent to the original service. This circumstance may be reported by adding modifier -76 to the repeated service or separate five-digit modifier code 09976 may be used.	Variable
-77	*Repeat Procedure by Another Physician:* The physician may need to indicate that a basic procedure performed by another physician had to be repeated. This situation may be reported by adding modifier -77 to the repeated service, or the separate five-digit modifier code 09977 may be used.	Variable
-78	*Return to the Operating Room for a Related Procedure During the Postoperative Period:* The physician may need to indicate that another procedure was performed during the postoperative period of the initial procedure. When this subsequent procedure is related to the first and requires the use of the operating room, it may be reported by adding the modifier -78 to the related procedure, or by using the separate five-digit modifier 09978. (For repeat procedures on the same day, see -76.)	Variable
-79	*Unrelated Procedure or Service by the Same Physician During the Postoperative Period:* The physician may need to indicate that the performance of a procedure or service during the postoperative period was unrelated to the original procedure. This circumstance may be reported by using the modifier -79 or by using the separate five-digit modifier 09979. (For repeat procedures on the same day, see -76.)	Variable

College Clinic Mock Fee Schedule

Modifier Code No.	Description	Mock Fee ($)
-80	*Assistant Surgeon:* Surgical assistant services may be identified by adding the modifier -80 to the usual procedure number(s) or by using the separate five-digit modifier code 09980.	Variable
-81	*Minimum Assistant Surgeon:* Minimum surgical assistant services are identified by adding the modifier -81 to the usual procedure number or by using the separate five-digit modifier code 09981.	Variable
-82	*Assistant Surgeon* when qualified resident surgeon not available): The unavailability of a qualified resident surgeon is a prerequisite for use of modifier -82 appended to the usual procedure code number(s) or by use of the separate five-digit modifier code 09982.	Variable
-90	*Reference (Outside) Laboratory:* When laboratory procedures are performed by a party other than the treating or reporting physician, the procedure may be identified by adding the modifier -90 to the usual procedure number or by using the separate five-digit modifier code 09990.	Variable
-99	*Multiple Modifiers:* Under certain circumstances two or more modifiers may be necessary to completely delineate a service. In such situations modifier -99 should be added to the basic procedure, and other applicable modifiers may be listed as part of the description of the service. Modifier code 09999 may be used as an alternative to modifier -99.	Variable

Code No. and Description		Mock Fees	Medicare Participating	Medicare Non-participating	Medicare Limiting Charge
EVALUATION AND MANAGEMENT*					
OFFICE	New Patient				
99201	Level I	33.25	30.43	28.91	33.25
99202	Level II	51.91	47.52	45.14	51.91
99203	Level III	70.92	64.92	61.67	70.92
99204	Level IV	106.11	97.13	92.27	106.11
99205	Level V	132.28	121.08	115.03	132.38
Established Patient					
99211	Level I	16.07	14.70	13.97	16.07
99212	Level II	28.55	26.14	24.83	28.55
99213	Level III	40.20	36.80	34.96	40.20
99214	Level IV	61.51	56.31	53.49	61.51
99215	Level V	96.97	88.76	84.32	96.97
HOSPITAL	Observation Services (new or est pt)				
99217	Discharge	66.88	61.22	58.16	66.88
99218	D hx/exam SF/LC DM	74.22	67.94	64.54	74.22
99219	C hx/exam MC DM	117.75	107.78	102.39	117.75
99220	C hx/exam HC DM	147.48	134.99	128.24	147.48
Inpatient Services (new or est pt)					
99221	30 min	73.00	66.82	63.48	73.00
99222	50 min	120.80	110.57	105.04	120.80
99223	70 min	152.98	140.03	133.03	152.98
Subsequent Hospital Care					
99231	15 min	37.74	34.55	32.82	37.74
99232	25 min	55.56	50.85	48.31	55.56
99233	35 min	76.97	70.45	66.93	76.97
99238	Discharge	65.26	59.74	56.75	65.26

Table continued on following page

*See Tables 4–1 and 4–2 in the Handbook for more descriptions on E/M codes 99201 through 99499.

Code No. and Description		Mock Fees	Medicare Participating	Medicare Non-participating	Medicare Limiting Charge
CONSULTATIONS Office (new/est pt)					
99241	Level I	51.93	47.54	45.16	51.93
99242	Level II	80.24	73.44	69.77	80.24
99243	Level III	103.51	94.75	90.01	103.51
99244	Level IV	145.05	132.77	126.13	145.05
99245	Level V	195.48	178.93	169.98	195.48
Inpatient (new/est pt)					
99251	Level I	53.29	48.78	46.34	53.29
99252	Level II	80.56	73.74	70.05	80.56
99253	Level III	106.10	97.12	92.26	106.10
99254	Level IV	145.26	132.96	126.31	145.26
99255	Level V	196.55	179.91	170.91	196.55
Follow-up Inpatient (new/est pt)					
99261	Focused	29.66	27.15	25.79	29.66
99262	Expanded	50.57	46.28	43.97	50.57
99263	Detailed	76.36	69.90	66.40	76.36
Confirmatory 2nd-3rd opinion (new/est pt)					
99271	Focused	45.47	41.62	39.54	45.47
99272	Expanded	67.02	61.35	58.28	67.02
99273	Detailed	95.14	87.08	82.73	95.14
99274	Comprehensive	125.15	114.56	108.83	125.15
99275	Comprehensive	172.73	158.10	150.20	172.73
EMERGENCY DEPARTMENT (new/est pt)					
99281	PF hx/exam SF DM	24.32	22.26	21.15	24.32
99282	EPF hx/exam LC DM	37.02	33.88	32.19	37.02
99283	EPF hx/exam MC DM	66.23	60.62	57.59	66.23
99284	D hx/exam MC DM	100.71	92.18	87.57	100.71
99285	C hx/exam HC DM	158.86	145.41	138.14	158.86
CRITICAL CARE SERVICES					
99291	First hour	208.91	191.22	181.66	208.91
99292	Each addl. 30 min	102.02	92.46	87.84	102.02
NEONATAL INTENSIVE CARE					
99295	Initial	892.74	817.16	776.30	892.74
99296	Subsequent unstable case	418.73	383.27	364.11	418.73
99297	Subsequent stable case	214.68	196.50	186.68	214.68
NURSING FACILITY					
99301	30 min	64.11	58.68	55.75	64.11
99302	40 min	90.55	82.88	78.74	90.55
99303	50 min	136.76	125.18	118.92	136.76
Subsequent (new/est pt)					
99311	15 min	37.95	34.74	33.00	37.95
99312	25 min	55.11	50.44	47.92	55.11
99313	35 min	69.61	63.72	60.53	69.61
DOMICILIARY, REST HOME, CUSTODIAL CARE New patient					
99321	PF hx/exam LC DM	46.10	42.20	40.09	46.10
99322	EPF hx/exam MC DM	65.02	59.52	56.54	65.02
99323	D hx/exam HC DM	86.18	78.88	74.94	86.18
Established patient					
99331	PF hx/exam LC DM	37.31	34.15	32.44	37.31
99332	EPF hx/exam MC DM	49.22	45.05	42.80	49.22
99333	D hx/exam HC DM	60.61	55.47	52.70	60.61
HOME SERVICES New patient					
99341	PF hx/exam LC DM	70.32	64.37	61.15	70.32
99342	EPF hx/exam LC DM	91.85	84.07	79.87	91.85
99343	D hx/exam HC DM	120.24	110.06	104.56	120.24

Table continued on following page

Code No. and Description		Mock Fees	Medicare* Participating	Medicare* Non-participating	Medicare* Limiting Charge
Established patient					
99351	PF hx/exam LC DM	54.83	50.19	47.68	54.83
99352	EPF hx/exam LC DM	70.06	64.13	60.92	70.06
99353	D hx/exam HC DM	88.33	80.85	76.81	88.33
PROLONGED SERVICES WITH CONTACT Outpatient					
99354	First hour	96.97	88.76	84.32	96.97
99355	Each addl. 30 min	96.97	88.76	84.32	96.97
Inpatient					
99356	First hour	96.42	88.25	83.84	96.42
99357	Each addl. 30 min	96.42	88.25	83.84	96.42
PROLONGED SERVICES WITHOUT DIRECT CONTACT					
99358	First hour	90.00			
99359	Each addl. 30 min	90.00			
PHYSICIAN STANDBY SERVICE					
99360	Each 30 min	95.00			
CASE MANAGEMENT SERVICES Team Conferences					
99361	30 min	85.00			
99362	60 min	105.00			
Telephone Calls					
99371	Simple or brief	30.00			
99372	Intermediate	40.00			
99373	Complex	60.00			
CARE PLAN OVERSIGHT SERVICES					
99375	30–60 min	93.40	85.49	81.22	93.40
99376	greater than 60 min	118.00			
PREVENTIVE MEDICINE New patient					
99381	Infant under age 1 year	50.00			
99382	1–4 years	50.00			
99383	5–11 years	45.00			
99384	12–17 years	45.00			
99385	18–39 years	50.00			
99386	40–64	50.00			
99387	65 yrs and over	55.00			
Established patient					
99391	Infant under age 1 year	35.00			
99392	1–4 years	35.00			
99393	5–11 years	30.00			
99394	12–17 years	30.00			
99395	18–39 years	35.00			
99396	40–64 years	35.00			
99397	65 yrs and over	40.00			
COUNSELING (new/est pt)					
Individual					
99401	15 min	35.00			
99402	30 min	50.00			
99403	45 min	65.00			
99404	60 min	80.00			
Group					
99411	30 min	30.00			
99412	60 min	50.00			
Other preventive medicine services					
99420	Health hazard appraisal	50.00			
99429	Unlisted preventive med serv	variable			
NEWBORN CARE					
99431	Birthing room delivery	102.15	93.50	88.83	102.15

Table continued on following page

* Some services and procedures may not be considered a benefit under the Medicare program, and when listed on a claim form, no reimbursement may be received. However, it is important to include these codes when billing because Medicare policies may change without an individual knowing of a new benefit. For this reason, some of the services shown in this mock fee schedule do not have any amounts listed under the three Medicare columns.

Code No. and Description		Mock Fees	Medicare Participating	Medicare Non-participating	Medicare Limiting Charge
99432	Other than birthing room	110.16	100.83	95.79	110.16
99433	Subsequent hospital care	54.02	49.44	46.97	54.02
99440	Newborn resuscitation	255.98	234.30	222.59	255.98
99499	Unlisted E/m service	variable			
ANESTHESIOLOGY					
Anesthesiology fees are presented here for CPT codes. However, each case would require a fee for time, e.g., every 15 minutes would be worth $55. Some anesthetists may list a surgical code on a subsequent line for carriers that do not acknowledge anesthesia codes.					
99100	Anes for pt under 1 yr/over 70	55.00			
99116	Anes complicated use total hypothermia	275.00			
99135	Anes complicated use hypotension	275.00			
99140	Anes complicated emer cond	110.00			
Physician Status Modifier Codes					
P-1	Normal healthy patient	00.00			
P-2	Patient with mild systemic disease	00.00			
P-3	Patient with severe systemic disease	55.00			
P-4	Patient with severe systemic disease (constant threat to life)	110.00			
P-5	Moribund pt not expected to survive for 24 hr with or without operation	165.00			
P-6	Declared brain-dead pt, organs being removed for donor	00.00			
Head					
00160	Anes for proc nose & accessory sinuses: NOS	275.00			
00172	Anes repair cleft palate	165.00			
Thorax					
00400	Anes for proc ant integumentary system of chest, incl SC tissue	165.00			
00402	Anes breast reconstruction	275.00			
00546	Anes pulmonary resection with thoracoplasty	275.00			
00600	Anes cervical spine and cord	550.00			
Lower Abdomen					
00800	Anes for proc lower ant abdominal wall	165.00			
00840	Anes intraperitoneal proc lower abdomen; NOS	330.00			
00842	Amniocentesis	220.00			
00914	Anes TURP	275.00			
00942	Anes colporrhaphy, colpotomy, colpectomy	220.00			
Upper Leg					
01210	Anes open proc hip joint; NOS	330.00			
01214	Total hip replacement	440.00			
Upper Arm and Elbow					
01740	Anes open proc humerus/elbow; NOS	220.00			
01758	Exc cyst/tumor humerus	275.00			
Radiologic Procedures					
01922	Anes CAT scan	385.00			
Miscellaneous Procedure(s)					
01999	Unlisted anes proc	variable			

Table continued on following page

Code No.	Description	Mock Fees	Medicare Participating	Medicare Non-participating	Medicare Limiting Charge	Medicare Follow-Up Days[1]
10060*	I & D furuncle, onychia, paronychia; single	75.92	69.49	66.02	75.92	10
11040*	Debridement; skin, partial thickness	79.32	75.60	68.97	79.32	10
11044	Debridement; skin, subcu. muscle, bone	269.28	246.48	234.16	269.28	
11100	Biopsy of skin, SC tissue &/or mucous membrane; 1 lesion	65.43	59.89	56.90	65.43	10
11200*	Exc, skin tags; up to 15	55.68	50.97	48.42	55.68	10
11401	Exc, benign lesion, 0.6–1.0 cm trunk, arms, legs	95.62	87.53	83.15	96.62	10
11402	1.1–2.0 cm	121.52	111.23	105.67	121.52	10
11403	2.1–3.0 cm	151.82	138.97	132.02	151.82	10
11420	Exc, benign lesion, 0.5 cm or less scalp, neck, hands, feet, genitalia	75.44	69.05	65.60	75.44	10
11422	Exc, benign lesion scalp, neck, hands, feet, or genitalia; 1.1–2.0 cm	131.35	120.23	114.22	131.35	10
11441	Exc, benign lesion face, ears, eyelids, nose, lips, or mucous membrane; 0.6–1.0 cm dia or less	119.08	109.00	103.55	119.08	10
11602	Exc, malignant lesion, trunk, arms, or legs; 1.1–2.0 cm dia	195.06	178.55	169.62	195.06	10
11700*	Debridement of nails, manual	32.58	29.82	28.33	32.58	0
11710*	Debridement of nails, electric	32.58	29.82	28.33	32.58	0
11730*	Avulsion nail plate, partial or complete, simple repair; single	76.91	70.40	66.88	76.91	0
11750	Exc, nail or nail matrix, partial or complete	193.45	177.07	168.22	193.45	10
12001*	Simple repair (scalp, neck, axillae, ext genitalia, trunk, or extremities incl hands & feet); 2.5 cm or less	91.17	83.45	79.28	91.17	10
12011*	Simple repair (face, ears, eyelids, nose, lips, or mucous membranes); 2.5 cm or less	101.44	92.85	88.21	101.44	10

Table continued on following page

[1] Data for the surgical follow-up days from St. Anthony's CPT '96 Companion: a Guide to Medicare Billing

* Codes marked with an asterisk appear in CPT marked as shown. See *Handbook* Chapter 4 for detailed information.

Code No.	Description	Mock Fees	Medicare Participating	Medicare Non-participating	Medicare Limiting Charge	Medicare Follow-Up Days
12013*	2.6–5.0 cm		113.48	107.81	123.98	10
12032*	Repair, scalp, axillae, trunk (intermediate)	169.73	155.36	147.59	169.73	10
12034	Repair, intermediate, layer closure of wounds (scalp, axillae, trunk, or extremities) excl hands or feet; 7.6–12.5 cm	214.20	196.06	186.26	214.20	10
12051*	Repair, intermediate, layer closure of wounds (face, ears, eyelids, nose, lips, or mucous membranes); 2.5 cm	167.60	153.41	145.74	167.60	10
17000*	Cauterization of wart; 2 lesions or less	52.56	48.11	45.70	52.56	10
17001	Caut. second and third lesions, each	19.41	17.77	16.88	19.41	10
17100*	Destruction, any method, skin lesion (benign) any area except face—one	44.86	41.06	39.01	44.86	10
17101	Second lesion	15.21	13.93	13.23	15.21	10
17102	Over two lesions, ea. additional up to fifteen	9.59	8.78	8.34	9.59	10
19020	Mastotomy, drainage/exploration deep abscess	237.36	217.26	206.40	237.36	90
19100*	Biopsy, breast, needle	96.17	88.03	83.63	96.17	0
19101	Biopsy, breast, incisional	281.51	257.67	244.79	281.51	10
20610*	Arthrocentesis, aspiration or injection joint (should, hip, knee) or bursa	52.33	47.89	45.50	52.33	0
21330	Nasal fracture, open treatment complicated	599.46	548.71	521.27	599.46	90
24066	Biopsy, deep, soft tissue, upper arm, elbow	383.34	350.88	333.34	383.34	90
27455	Osteotomy, proximal tibia	1248.03	1142.36	1085.24	1248.03	90
27500	Treatment closed femoral shaft fracture without manipulation	554.90	507.92	482.52	554.90	90
27530	Treatment closed tibial fracture, proximal, without manipulation	344.24	315.09	299.34	344.24	90
27750	Treatment closed tibial shaft fracture without manipulation	400.94	366.99	348.64	400.94	90
27752	With manipulation	531.63	486.62	462.29	531.63	90
29345	Appl long leg cast (thigh to toes)	123.23	112.80	107.16	123.23	0
29355	Walker or ambulatory type	133.75	122.42	116.30	133.75	0
29425	Appl short leg walking cast	102.10	93.45	88.78	102.10	0
30110	Excision, simple nasal polyp	145.21	132.92	126.27	145.21	10
30520	Septoplasty	660.88	604.93	574.68	660.88	90
30903*	Control nasal hemorrhage; unilateral	118.17	108.17	102.76	118.17	0
30905*	Control nasal hemorrhage, posterior with posterior nasal packs; initial	190.57	174.43	165.71	190.57	0

30906*	Subsequent	173.01	158.36	150.44	173.01	
31625	Bronchoscopy with biopsy	312.87	286.38	272.06	312.87	0
32310	Pleurectomy	1234.79	1130.24	1073.73	1234.79	90
32440	Pneumonectomy, total	1972.10	1805.13	1714.87	1972.10	90
33020	Pericardiotomy	1289.25	1180.09	1121.09	1289.25	90
33206	Insertion of pacemaker; atrial	728.42	666.75	633.41	728.42	90
33208	AV sequential	751.57	687.89	653.50	751.57	90
35301	Thromboendarterectomy, with or without patch graft; carotid, vertebral, subclavian, by neck incision	1585.02	1450.82	1378.28	1585.02	90
36005	Intravenous injection for contrast venography	59.18	54.17	51.46	59.18	0
36248	Catheter placement (selective) arterial system, 2nd, 3rd and beyond	68.54	62.74	59.60	68.54	0
36415*	Routine venipuncture for collection of specimen(s)	10.00	—	—	—	XXX
38101	Splenectomy, partial	994.44	910.24	864.73	994.44	90
38510	Biopsy/excision deep cervied node/s	327.42	299.69	284.71	327.42	90
39520	Excision tumor, mediastinal	1436.50	1314.87	1249.13	1436.50	90
42820	T & A under age 12 years	341.63	312.71	297.07	341.63	90
42821	T & A over age 12 years	410.73	375.96	357.16	410.73	90
43234	Upper GI endoscopy, simple primary exam	201.86	184.77	175.53	201.86	0
43235	Upper GI endoscopy incl esophagus, stomach, duodenum, or jejunum; complex	238.92	218.69	207.76	238.92	0
43456	Dilation esophagus	254.52	232.97	221.32	254.52	0
43820	Gastrojejunostomy	971.86	889.58	845.10	971.86	90
44150	Colectomy, total, abdominal	1757.81	1608.98	1528.53	1757.81	90
44320	Colostomy or skin level cecostomy	966.25	884.44	840.22	966.25	90
44950	Appendectomy	568.36	520.24	494.23	568.36	90
45308	Proctosigmoidoscopy for removal of polyp	135.34	123.88	117.69	135.34	0
45315	Multiple polyps	185.12	169.44	160.97	185.12	0
45330	Sigmoidoscopy, diagnostic (for biopsy or collection of specimen by brushing or washing)	95.92	87.80	83.41	95.92	0
45380	Colonoscopy with biopsy	382.35	349.98	332.48	382.35	0
46255	Hemorrhoidectomy int & ext, simple	503.57	460.94	437.89	503.57	90
46258	Hemorrhoidectomy with fistulectomy	636.02	582.17	553.06	636.02	90

Table continued on following page

[1] Data for the surgical follow-up days from St. Anthony's CPT '96 Companion: a Guide to Medicare Billing

* Codes marked with an asterisk appear in CPT marked as shown. See *Handbook* Chapter 4 for detailed information.

Code No.	Description	Mock Fees	Medicare Participating	Medicare Non-participating	Medicare Limiting Charge	Medicare Follow-Up Days[1]
46600	Anoscopy; diagnostic	32.86	30.07	28.57	32.86	0
46614	With coagulation for control of hemorrhage	182.10	166.68	158.35	182.10	0
46700	Anoplastic, for stricture, adult	657.39	601.73	571.64	657.39	90
47600	Cholecystectomy	937.74	858.35	815.43	937.74	90
49505	Inguinal hernia repair, age 5 or over	551.07	504.41	479.19	551.07	90
49520	Repair, inguinal hernia, any age; recurrent	671.89	615.00	584.25	671.89	90
50080	Nephrostolithotomy, percutaneous	1323.93	1211.83	1151.24	1323.93	90
50780	Ureteroneocystostomy	1561.23	1429.84	1357.59	1561.23	90
51900	Closure of vesicovaginal fistula, abdominal approach	1196.82	1095.48	1040.71	1196.82	90
52000	Cystourethroscopy	167.05	152.90	145.26	167.05	0
52601	Transurethral resection of prostate	1193.53	1092.47	1037.85	1193.53	90
53040	Drainage of deep periurethral abscess	520.11	476.07	452.27	520.11	90
53230	Excision, female diverticutum (urethral)	859.69	786.91	747.56	859.69	90
53240	Marsupialization of urethral diverticulum, M or F	520.11	476.07	452.27	520.11	90
53620*	Dilation, urethra, male	100.73	92.20	87.59	100.73	0
53660*	Dilation urethra, female	48.32	44.23	42.02	48.32	0
54150	Circumcision–newborn	111.78	102.32	97.20	111.78	10
54520	Orchiectomy, simple	523.92	479.56	455.58	523.92	90
55700	Biopsy of prostate, needle or punch	156.22	142.99	135.84	156.22	0
55801	Prostatectomy, perineal subtotal	1466.56	1342.39	1275.27	1466.56	90
57265	Colporrhaphy AP with enterocele repair	902.24	825.85	784.56	902.24	90
57452*	Colposcopy	84.18	77.05	73.20	84.18	0
57510	Cauterization of cervix, electro or thermal	115.15	105.40	100.13	115.15	10
57520	Circumferential (cone) of cervix with or without D & C, with or without Sturmdorff-type repair	387.08	354.30	336.59	387.08	90
58100*	Endometrial biopsy	71.88	65.79	62.50	71.88	0
58120	D & C, diagnostic and/or therapeutic (nonOB)	272.83	249.73	237.24	272.83	10
58150	TAH w/without salpingo-oophorectomy	1167.72	1068.85	1015.41	1167.72	90
58200	Total hysterectomy, extended, corpus cancer, including partial vaginectomy	1707.24	1562.69	1484.56	1707.24	90

58210	With bilateral radical pelvic lymphadenectomy	2160.78	1977.83	1878.94	2160.78	90
58300*	Insertion of intrauterine device	100.00	—	—	—	0
58340*	Hysterosalpingography with inj proc	73.06	66.87	63.53	73.06	0
58720	Salpingo-oophorectomy, complete or partial, unilateral or bilateral	732.40	670.39	636.87	732.40	90
	Surgical treatment of ectopic pregnancy					
59120	Salpingectomy and/or oophorectomy	789.26	722.43	686.31	789.26	90
59121	without salpingectomy and/or oophorectomy	638.84	584.75	555.51	638.84	90
59130	abdominal pregnancy	699.12	639.93	607.93	699.12	90
59135	Total hysterectomy, interstitial, uterine pregnancy	1154.16	1056.44	1003.62	1154.16	90
59136	Partial uterine resection, interstitial uterine pregnancy	772.69	707.26	671.90	772.69	90
59140	cervical, with evacuation	489.68	448.22	425.81	489.68	90
59160	D & C postpartum hemorrhage (separate proc)	293.46	268.61	255.18	293.46	10
59400	OB Care–routine, inc. antepartum/ postportum care	1864.30	1706.45	1621.13	1864.30	N/A
59515	C–section, low cervical, incl in-hosp postpartum care (separate proc)	1469.80	1345.36	1278.09	1469.80	N/A
59510	Including antepartum and postpartum care	2102.33	1924.33	1828.11	2102.33	N/A
59812	Treatment of incompl abortion, any trimester; completed surgically	357.39	327.13	310.77	357.39	90
61314	Craniotomy infratentorial	2548.09	2332.35	2215.73	2548.09	90
62270*	Spinal puncture, lumbar; diagnostic	77.52	70.96	67.41	77.52	0
65091	Excision of eye, without implant	708.22	648.25	615.84	708.22	90
65205*	Removal of foreign body, ext eye	56.02	51.27	48.71	56.02	0
65222*	Corneal, with slit lamp	73.81	67.56	64.18	73.81	0
69420*	Myringotomy	97.76	89.48	85.01	97.76	10

Table continued on following page

[1] Data for the surgical follow-up days from St. Anthony's CPT '96 Companion a Guide to Medicare Billing

* Codes marked wiht an asterisk appear in CPT marked as shown. See handbook Chapter 4 for detailed information.

Code No. and Description		Mock Fees	Medicare Participating	Medicare Non-participating	Medicare Limiting Charge
RADIOLOGY, NUCLEAR MEDICINE, AND DIAGNOSTIC ULTRASOUND					
70120	X-ray mastoids, 2 views	38.96	35.66	33.88	38.96
70130	X-ray mastoids, 3 views	56.07	51.33	48.76	56.07
71010	X-ray chest, 1 view	31.95	29.24	27.78	31.95
71020	Chest x-ray, 2 views	40.97	37.50	35.63	40.97
71030	Chest x-ray, compl, 4 views	54.02	49.44	46.97	54.02
71060	Bronchogram, bilateral	143.75	131.58	125.00	143.75
72100	X-ray spine, LS; AP & lat views	43.23	39.57	37.59	43.23
72114	Complete, incl bending views	74.97	68.62	65.19	74.97
73100	X-ray wrist, 2 views	31.61	28.94	27.49	31.61
73500	X-ray hip, 1 view	31.56	28.88	27.44	31.56
73540	X-ray pelvis & hips, infant or child, 2 views	37.94	34.73	32.99	37.94
73590	X-ray tibia & fibula, 2 views	33.35	30.53	29.00	33.35
73620	Radiologic exam, foot; AP & lat views	31.61	28.94	27.49	31.61
73650	X-ray calcaneus, 2 views	30.71	28.11	26.70	30.71
74241	Radiologic exam, upper gastrointestinal tract, with/without delayed films with KUB	108.93	99.71	94.72	108.93
74245	Upper GI tract with small bowel	161.70	148.01	140.61	161.70
74270	Barium enema	118.47	108.44	103.02	118.47
74290	Oral cholecystography	52.59	48.14	45.73	52.59
74400	Urography (pyelography), intravenous, with or without KUB	104.78	95.90	91.11	104.78
74405	Urography (pyelography), intravenous with spec hypertensive contrast concentration	118.36	108.34	102.92	118.36
74410	Urography, infusion	116.76	106.87	101.53	116.76
74420	Urography, retrograde	138.89	127.13	120.77	138.89
75982	Percutaneous placement of drainage catheter	359.08	328.67	312.24	359.08
76090	Mammography, unilateral	62.57	57.27	54.41	62.57
76091	Mammography, bilateral	82.83	75.82	72.03	82.83
76805	Echography, pregnant uterus, B-scan or real time; complete	154.18	141.13	134.07	154.18
76810	Ecography, pregnant uterus, complete: multiple gestation, after first trimester	306.54	280.59	266.56	306.54
76946	Ultrasonic guidance for amniocentesis	91.22	83.49	79.32	91.22
77300	Radiation dosimetry	97.58	89.32	84.85	97.58
77315	Teletherapy, isodose plan, complex	213.59	195.51	185.73	213.59
78104	Bone marrow imaging, whole body	230.56	211.04	200.49	230.56
78215	Liver and spleen imaging	160.44	146.85	139.51	160.44
78800	Tumor localization, limited area	191.53	175.32	166.55	191.53

PATHOLOGY AND LABORATORY[1]

Laboratory tests done as groups or combination "profiles" performed on multichannel equipment should be billed using the appropriate code number (80002 through 80019). Following is a list of the tests. The subsequent listing illustrates how to find the correct code.

Alanine aminotransferase (ALT, SGPT)
Albumin
Aspartate aminotransferase (AST, SGOT)
Bilirubin, direct
Bilirubin, total
Calcium
Carbon dioxide content
Chloride
Cholesterol
Creatinine
Glucose (sugar)
Lactate dehydrogenase (LD)
Phosphatase, alkaline
Phosphorus (inorganic phosphate)
Potassium
Protein, total
Sodium
Urea nitrogen (BUN)
Uric acid

[1] Mock fees for laboratory tests presented in this schedule may not be representative of fees in your region due to the variety of capitation and managed care contracts as well as discount policies made by laboratories. At the time of this edition, Medicare guidelines may or may not pay for automatic multichannel tests where a large number of tests are performed per panel. Some cases require documentation and a related diagnostic code for each test performed. Provider must have the CLIA level of licensure to bill for tests and test results must be documented.

Code No. and Description		Mock Fees	Medicare Participating	Medicare Non-participating	Medicare Limiting Charge
AUTOMATIC MULTICHANNEL TEST					
80002	1 or 2 clinical chemistry tests	10.00	9.80	8.88	12.03
80003	3 clinical chemistry tests	15.00	14.60	13.87	16.64
80004	4 clinical chemistry tests	20.00	19.20	15.99	21.87
80005	5 clinical chemistry tests	20.00	19.20	15.99	21.87
80006	6 clinical chemistry tests	25.00	20.99	19.94	23.93
80007	7 clinical chemistry tests	25.00	20.99	19.94	23.93
80008	8 clinical chemistry tests	27.00	25.00	20.88	24.98
80009	9 clinical chemistry tests	27.00	25.00	20.88	24.98
80010	10 clinical chemistry tests	30.00	28.60	25.97	32.16
80011	11 clinical chemistry tests	30.00	28.60	25.97	32.16
80012	12 clinical chemistry tests	32.00	30.70	27.54	34.15
80016	13–16 clinical chemistry tests	32.00	30.70	27.54	34.15
80018	17–18 clinical chemistry tests	35.00	33.55	31.87	38.24
80019	19 or more clinical chemistry tests	35.00	33.55	31.87	38.24
81000	Urinalysis, non-automated, with microscopy	8.00	7.44	5.98	8.84
81001	Urinalysis, automated, with microscopy	8.00	7.44	5.98	8.84
81002	Urinalysis, non-automated without microscopy	8.00	7.44	5.98	8.84
81015	Urinalysis, microscopy only	8.00	7.44	5.98	8.84
82565	Creatinine; blood	10.00	9.80	8.88	12.03
82951	Glucose tol test, 3 spec	40.00	41.00	36.80	45.16
82952	Each add spec beyond 3	30.00	28.60	25.97	32.16
83020	Hemoglobin, electrophoresis	25.00	20.00	19.94	23.93
83715	Lipoprotein, blood; electrophoretic separation	25.00	20.00	19.94	23.93
84478	Triglycerides, blood	20.00	19.20	15.99	21.87
84479	Triiodothyronine (T–3)	20.00	19.20	15.99	21.87
84520	Urea nitrogen, blood (BUN); quantitative	25.00	20.99	19.94	23.93
84550	Uric acid, blood chemical	20.00	19.20	15.99	21.87
84702	Gonadotropin, chorionic; quantitative	20.00	19.20	15.99	21.87
84703	Qualitative	20.00	19.20	15.99	21.87
85022	Complete blood count, manual, diff with WBC count	20.00	19.20	15.99	21.87
85025	Complete blood count (hemogram), platelet count, automated, differential WBC count	25.00	20.00	19.94	23.93
85031	Complete blood count, manual	25.00	20.00	19.94	23.93
85095	Bone marrow, aspiration only	73.52	67.29	63.93	73.52
85102	Bone marrow aspiration (biopsy)	90.65	82.98	78.83	90.65
85345	Coagulation time; Lee & White	20.00	19.20	15.99	21.87
85590	Platelet count (Rees-Ecker)	20.00	19.20	15.99	21.87
86038	Antinuclear antibodies	25.00	20.00	19.94	23.93
87081	Culture, bacterial, screening for single organisms	25.00	20.00	19.94	23.93
87181	Sensitivity studies, antibiotic; per antibiotic	20.00	19.20	15.99	21.87
87184	Disk method, per plate (12 disks or less)	20.00	19.20	15.99	21.87
87210	Smear, primary source, wet mount with simple stain, for bacteria, fungi, ova, and/or parasites	35.00	48.35	45.93	55.12
88150	Papanicolaou cytopath	35.00	48.35	45.93	55.12
88302	Surgical pathology, gross & micro exam (skin, fingers, nerve, testis)	24.14	22.09	20.99	24.14
88305	Bone marrow, interpret	77.69	71.12	67.56	77.69

Table continued on following page

Code No. and Description		Mock Fees	Medicare* Participating	Medicare* Non-participating	Medicare* Limiting Charge
MEDICINE PROCEDURES					
Immunization Injections					
90701	Diphtheria, tetanus, pertusis	34.00			
90703	Tetanus toxoid	28.00			
90712	Poliovirus vaccine, oral	28.00			
Therapeutic injections					
90782	IM or SC medication	4.77	4.37	4.15	4.77
90784	IV	21.33	19.53	18.55	21.33
90788	IM antibiotic	5.22	4.78	4.54	5.22
Psychiatry					
90825	Psychiatric consult, psychometric tests	175.00			
90843	Psychotherapy 20–30 min	60.25	55.15	52.39	60.25
90844	Psychotherapy 45–50 min	93.71	85.78	81.49	93.71
90853	Group therapy	29.22	26.75	25.41	29.22
Hemodialysis					
90935	Single phys evaluation	117.23	107.31	101.94	117.23
90937	Repeat evaluation	206.24	188.78	179.34	206.24
Gastroenterology					
91000	Esophageal intubation	69.82	63.91	60.71	69.82
91055	Gastric intubation	87.41	80.01	76.01	87.41
Ophthalmologic Services					
92004	Comprehensive eye exam	90.86	83.17	79.01	90.86
92100	Tonometry	47.31	43.31	41.14	47.31
92230	Fluorescein angioscopy	55.49	50.79	48.25	55.49
92275	Electroretinography	81.17	74.29	70.58	81.17
92531	Spontaneous nystagmus	26.00			
Audiologic Function Tests					
92557	Basic comprehensive audiometry	54.33	49.73	47.24	54.33
92596	Ear measurements	26.81	24.54	23.31	26.81
Cardiovascular Therapeutic Services					
93000	Electrocardiogram (ECG)	34.26	31.36	29.79	34.26
93015	Treadmill ECG	140.71	128.80	122.36	140.71
93040	Rhythm ECG, 1–3 leads	18.47	16.90	16.06	18.47
Pulmonary					
94010	Spirometry	38.57	35.31	33.54	38.57
94060	Spirometry before and after bronchodilator	71.67	65.60	62.32	71.67
94150	Vital capacity, total	13.82	12.65	12.02	13.82
Allergy and Clinical Immunology					
95024	Intradermal tests	6.58	6.02	5.72	6.58
95044	Patch tests	8.83	8.08	7.68	8.83
95115	Treatment for allergy, corticosteroids, single inj.	17.20	15.75	14.96	17.20
95117	Treatment for allergy, two or more inj.	22.17	20.29	19.28	22.17
95165	Allergen immunotherapy, single or multiple antigens, multiple-dose vials		6.50	6.18	7.11

* Some services and procedures may not be considered a benefit under the Medicare program, and when listed on a claim form, no reimbursement may be received. However, it is important to include these codes when billing because Medicare policies may change without an individual knowing of a new benefit. For this reason, some of the services shown in this mock fee schedule do not have any amounts listed under the three Medicare columns.

Code No. and Description		Mock Fees	Medicare* Participating	Medicare* Non-participating	Medicare* Limiting Charge
Neurology					
95812	Electroencephalogram, Up to one hr.	129.32	118.37	112.45	129.32
95819	Electroencephalogram—awake and asleep	126.81	116.07	110.27	126.81
95860	Electromyography, 1 extremity	88.83	81.31	77.24	88.83
95864	Electromyography, 4 extremities	239.99	219.67	208.69	239.99
96100	Psychological testing (per hour)	80.95	74.10	70.39	80.95
Physical Medicine					
97024	Diathermy	14.27	13.06	12.41	14.27
97036	Hubbard tank, each 15 min	24.77	22.67	21.54	24.77
97110	Physical therapy, initial 30 min	23.89	21.86	20.77	23.89
97260	Manipulation (cervical, thoracic, lumbosacral, sacroiliac, hand, wrist), one area	16.93	15.49	14.72	16.93
Special Services and Reports					
99000	Handling of specimen (transfer from Dr.'s office to lab)	5.00			
99025	Initial surg eval (new pt) with starred procedure	50.00			
99050	Services requested after office hours in addition to basic service	25.00			
99052	Services between 10 p.m. and 8 a.m. in addition to basic service	35.00			
99054	Services on Sundays and holidays in addition to basic service	35.00			
99056	Services normally provided in office requested by pt in location other than office	20.00			
99058	Office services provided on an emergency basis	65.00			
99070	Supplies and materials (itemize drugs and materials provided)	25.00			
99080	Special reports:				
	Insurance forms	10.00			
	Review of data to clarify pt's status	20.00			
	WC reports	50.00			
	WC extensive review report	250.00			

* Some services and procedures may not be considered a benefit under the Medicare program, and when listed on a claim form, no reimbursement may be received. However, it is important to include these codes when billing because Medicare policies may change without an individual knowing of a new benefit. For this reason, some of the services shown in this mock fee schedule do not have any amounts listed under the three Medicare columns.

INDEX

A

B

C

Chest, x-rays	71000–71270
Cholecystectomy	47600–47620
Cholecystography	74290, 74291
Circumcision	54150–54161
Coagulation time	85345–85348
Colectomy	44140–44160
Colonoscopy, fiberoptic	45355–45385
Colostomy, separate procedure	44320
Colporrhaphy	5757240–57265, 57289
Colposcopy	57452–57460
Complete blood count	85022–85031
Conization cervix	57520–57522
Consultation	
confirmatory	99271–99275
during surgery (pathology)	88329–88332
initial	99251–99255
inpatient follow-up	99261–99263
office	99241–99245
telephone calls	99371–99373
telephone, psychiatric patient	99371–99373
with exam and evaluation	99241–99255
Counseling	
group	99411, 99412
individual	99401–99404
Crainotomy	61314
Creatinine	82540, 82565–82570
Critical care	
initial	99291
follow-up visit	99292
neonatal	99295–99297
Culture, bacterial	87040–87088
Custodial care medical services	
established patient	99331–99333
new patient	99321–99323
Cystourethroscopy	52000–52340

D

Debridement	
nails	11700–11710
skin	11040–11044
Destruction benign lesion, any method	
face	17000–17010
other than face	17100–17105
Dentition, prolonged physician attendance	99354-99360
Dilation	
dilation and curettage	57820, 58120, 59160, 59840, 59851
esophagus	43450–43460
urethra, male	53620–53621
urethra, female	53660–53661
Diathermy	97024
Domiciliary visits	
established patient	99331–99333
new patient	99321–99323
Dosimetry	77300, 77331

E

Ear	
excision, benign lesion, external	11440–11446
layer closure, wounds	12051–12057
repair, simple wounds	12011–12018
Echography, pregnant uterus	76805–76816
Electrocardiogram	93000–93042
Electroencephalogram	95819–95827
Electromyography	95858, 95860–95869
Electroretinography	92275
Emergency department services	99281–99288
Endoscopy, gastrointestinal, upper	43234–43264
Esophageal intubation	91000
Excision: see organ, region, or structure involved	
Eye, excision	65091
Eye, removal foreign body	65205–65222
Eyelid	
excision, benign lesion	11440–11446
layer closure of wounds	12051–12057
repair, simple	12011–12018

F

Face	
excision, benign lesion	11440–11446
layer closure, wounds (intermediate)	12051–12057
simple repair, wounds	12011–12018
Feet: see foot	
Fluorescein angioscopy, ophthalmoscopy	92230
Foot	
excision, benign lesion, skin	11420–11426
radiologic exam	73620–73630
repair, simple wounds	12001–12007
Fracture	
femur shaft	27500–27508
nasal	21300–21339
tibia proximal, plateau	27530–27537
tibia shaft	27750–27758

G

Gastric intubation	91055
Gastrointestinal tract, radiologic exam	74210–74340
Gastrojejunostomy	43632, 43820–43825, 43860–43865
Genitalia	
excision, benign lesion	11420–11426
repair, simple	12001–12007
Glucose tolerance test	82951, 82952
Gonadotropin, chorionic	84702, 84703

H

Handling or specimen	99000
Hands	
excision, benign lesion	11420–11426
simple repair, wounds	12001–12007

Hemodialysis	90935-90937
insertion of cannula	36800–36815
placement, venous catheter	36245–36248
Hemoglobin electrophoresis	83020
Hemorrhage, nasal	30901–30906
Hemorrhoidectomy	46221–46262
Hernia,inguinal	49495–49525
Hip, radiologic exam	73500–73540
Home visits	
established patient	99351–99353
new patient	99341–99343
Hospital visits	
discharge day	99238
first day	99221–99223
newborn, initial care	99431
subsequent day	99433
prolonged service	99356, 99357
subsequent care	99231–99233
Hubbard tank	97036, 97113
Hysterectomy	58150–58285
ectopic pregnancy	59135–59140
supracervical	58180
total	58150–58152, 58200–58240
vaginal	58260–58285
Hysterosalpingography	74740
injection procedure for	58340

I

Imaging	
bone marrow	78102–78104
liver	78201–78220
Immunotherapy	95120–95199
Incision and drainage, furuncle	10060
Incision, breast	19000–19030
Injection	
allergies, steroids	95115–95117
antibiotic	90788
arthrocentesis, small joint or bursa	20600–20610
catheter placement	36245–36248
immunization	90700–90749
intravenous	90784
IV for contrast venography	36005
medication, intravenous	90784
medication, subcutaneous or intramuscular	90782
therapeutic	90782–90784
Intrauterine device (IUD)	
insertion	58300
removal	58301

J

Joint fluid, cell count	89050, 89051

K

KUB	74400–74405, 74420

L

Leg, malignant lesion excision	11600–11606
Lip	
benign lesion excision	11440–11446
layer closure of wound	12051–12057
superficial wound repair	12011–12018
Lipoprotein	83715, 83717

M

Mammography	76090, 76091
Manipulation, spine	22505, 97260
Manipulation (physical therapy)	97260, 97261
Marsupialization, urethral diverticulum	53240
Mastoids, radiologic exam	70120, 70130
Mucous membrane, cutaneous	
excision, benign lesion	11440–11446
layer closure, wounds	12051–12057
simple repair, wounds	12011–12018
Myringotomy	69420

N

Nail, excision	11750
Nasal polyp, excision	30110
Neck	
excision, benign lesion	11420–11426
wounds, simple repair	12001–12007
Neonatal critical care	99295–99297
Nephrostolithotomy	50080
Newborn care	99431–99440
Nose	
excision, benign lesion	11440–11446
layer closure	12051–12057
simple repair	12011–12018
Nursing facility care	
assessment	99301–99303
subsequent care	99311–99313
Nystagmus	
optokinetic	92534
opotokinetic test	92544
positional	92532
spontaneous	92531
spontaneous test	92541

O

Obstetric care	59400–59410
Office medical service	
after hours	99050–99054
emergency care	99058
Office visit	
established patient	99211–99215
new patient	99201–99205
service at another location	99056
with surgical procedure	99025

Ophthalmologic examination	92002–92019
Orchiectomy	54520–54535
Osteotomy, tibia	27455, 27457, 27705, 27709
Outpatient visit	
established patient	99211–99215
new patient	99201–99205

P

Pacemaker, insertion	33200–33217, 71090
Papanicolaou cytopathology	88150–88155
Patch skin test	95044–95052
Pathology, surgical gross and microscopic	88302–88309
Pericardiotomy	33020
Physical medicine services	97010–97150
Platelet count	85590
Pleurectomy	32310
Pneumonectomy	32440–32450
Preventive medicine	
established patient	99391–99397
health hazard appraisal	99420
new patient	99381–99387
unlisted	99429
Proctosigmoidoscopy	45300–45321
Prolonged services	
hospital inpatient	99356–99359
office/outpatient	99354, 99355, 99358, 99359
Prostatectomy, perineal, subtotal	55801
Psychiatric evalution of records, reports, and/or tests	90825
Psychological testing	96100
Psychotherapy	
pharmocologic management	90862
family (conjoint)	90847
group medical	90853
individual	90841–90844
multiple-family	90849
Puncture	
lumbar spine	62270, 62272

Q

Quadriceps, plasty	27430

R

Radiology	
dosimetry	77300, 77331
teletherapy	77305–77315, 77321
therapeutic	77261–77799
treatment delivery	77401–77417
Repair: see procedure, organ, structure, or region involved	
Reports, special	99080
Resection, prostate, transurethral	52601–54640

S

Salpingo-oophorectomy	58720
Salpingectomy and/or oophorectomy	59120–59140
excision, benign lesion	11420–11422
layer closure, wounds	12031–12037
simple repair, wounds	12001–12007
Sensitivity studies, antibiotic	87181–87192
Septum, nasal septoplasty	30520
Skin excision, skin tags	11200, 11201
Splenectomy	38100–38115
Smear, primary source	87205–87211
Spine, radiologic exam	72010–72120
Spirometry	94010–94070
Standby services	99360
Supplies and materials	99070, 99071

T

Teletherapy	77305–77321
Thromboendarterectomy	35301–35381
Tibia, radiologic exam	73590
Tonometry	92100
Tonsillectomy	42820–42826
TURP	52601–52648
Treadmill exercise	93015–93018
Triglycerides	84478
Triiodothyronine	84479–84482
Trunk	
excision, malignant lesion	11600–11606
layer closure - intermediate	12031–12037
simple repair	12001–12007
Tumor localization	78800–78803

U

Ureteroneocystostomy	50780–50800
Urethral diverticulum, excision	53230–53235
Uric acid	84550–84560
Urinalysis	81000–81099
Urography	74400–74425

V

Venipuncture	36400–36425
Vescovaginal fistula, closure	51900, 57320, 57330
Vital capacity	94010, 94150, 94160

W

Wrist, radiologic examination	73100, 73110

XYZ

Xenograft	15400
Y-plasty, bladder	51800
Z-plasty	14000, 26121, 41520

APPENDIX B

Medicare Level II HCPCS Codes

The following pages provide a partial alpha/numeric list of the Health Care Financing Administration's Common Procedure Coding System, referred to as HCPCS (pronounced "hick-picks"). These Level 2 codes and modifiers were adopted by the Medicare program in 1984; additional codes and modifiers are added and deleted every year. This system was developed to code procedures not listed in the American Medical Association's *Current Procedural Terminology* (CPT) *Code Book*. This second level is a national standard used by all regional Medicare carriers.

For fees, refer to a comparable procedure in Appendix A. *Example:* J2510, penicillin procaine injection, would be comparable to 90788, IM injection, so the fee is $15.00.

PARTIAL LIST OF THE MEDICARE HEALTH CARE FINANCING ADMINISTRATION'S COMMON PROCEDURE CODING SYSTEM (HCPCS)

In certain circumstances, a code may need a modifier to show that the procedure has been changed by a specific situation. Remember that CPT and national modifiers apply to both CPT and HCPCS code systems. When applicable, indicate the appropriate modifier on the insurance claim form. Sometimes a special report may be needed to clarify the use of the modifier to the insurance company.

Medicare HCPCS Modifiers

Modifier	Description
These one-letter modifiers may be used most often with A codes, transportation services, including ambulance, chiropractic services, medical and surgical supplies, and miscellaneous.	
-D	Diagnostic or therapeutic site other than "H" or "P" when these are used as origin codes
-E	Residential, domiciliary, custodial facility (other than an 1819 facility)
-H	Hospital
-N	Skilled nursing facility (NF) (1819 facility)
-P	Physician's office
-R	Residence
-S	Scene of accident or acute event
-X	(destination code only) Intermediate stop at physician's office on the way to the hospital

Table continued on following page

Medicare HCPCS Modifiers *Continued*

Modifier	Description
A list of two-letter modifiers follows.	
-AA	Anesthesia service personally furnished by anesthesiologist. This modifier affects the fee schedule payment amount received.
-AB	Medical direction of own employee(s) by anesthesiologist (not more than four employees).
-AC	Medical direction of other than own employees by anesthesiologist (not more than four individuals).
-AD	Medical supervision by a physician; more than four concurrent anesthesia procedures. This modifier affects the fee schedule payment amount received.
-AE	Direction of residents in furnishing not more than two concurrent anesthesia services—attending physician relationship met.
-AF	Anesthesia complicated by total body hypothermia. For therapeutic hypothermia, see CPT code numbers 99185 and 99186.
-AG	Anesthesia for emergency surgery on a patient who is moribund or who has an incapacitating system i.e. disease that is a constant threat to life (may warrant additional fee).
-AH	Clinical psychologist.
-AJ	Clinical social worker.
-AK	Nurse practitioner, rural, team member
-AL	Nurse practitioner, non-rural, team member
-AM	Physician, team member service.
-AN	PA services for other than assistant-at-surgery, nonteam member.
-AP	Determination of refractive state not performed in the course of diagnostic ophthalmologic examination.
-AR	Return ambulance trip (when filing for a return trip, the appropriate procedure code should be followed by -AR)
-AS	PA services for assistant-at-surgery (nonteam member).
-AT	Acute treatment (this modifier should be used when reporting service A2000 for acute treatment).
-AU	PA for other than assistant-at-surgery team member.
-AV	Nurse practitioner, rural, nonteam member.
-AW	Clinical nurse specialist, nonteam member.
-AY	Clinical nurse specialist, team member.
-BP	The beneficiary has been informed of the purchase and rental options and has elected to purchase the item.
-BR	The beneficiary has been informed of the purchase and rental options and has elected to rent the item.
-BU	The beneficiary has been informed of the purchase and rental options and after 30 days has not informed the supplier of his/her decision.
-CC	Procedure code change. Use modifier when the procedure code submitted was changed either for administrative reasons or when an incorrect code was filed.
-DD	Powdered enteral formulae. Use modifier when enteral powdered products are supplied.
-EJ	Subsequent claim (for epoetin alfa-epo-infection claim only).
-EM	Emergency reserve supply (for end-stage renal disease [ESRD] benefit only).

Medicare HCPCS Modifiers *Continued*

Modifier	Description
-EP	Service provided as part of Medicaid Early Periodic Screening Diagnosis and Treatment (EPSDT) program.
-ET	Emergency treatment (dental procedures performed in emergency situation should show the modifier -ET). This modifier has no direct effect on reimbursement.
-E1	Upper left, eyelid
-E2	Lower left, eyelid
-E3	Upper right, eyelid
-E4	Lower right, eyelid
-FA	Left hand, thumb
-FP	Service provided as part of Medicaid family planning program.
-F1	Left hand, second digit
-F2	Left hand, third digit
-F3	Left hand, fourth digit
-F4	Left hand, fifth digit
-F5	Right hand, thumb
-F6	Right hand, second digit
-F7	Right hand, third digit
-F8	Right hand, fourth digit
-F9	Right hand, fifth digit
-GA	Waiver of liability statement on file.
-GB	Distinct procedural service: The physician may need to indicate that a procedure or service was distinct or separate from other services performed on the same day. This may represent a different session or patient encounter, different procedure or surgery, different site, separate lesion, or separate injury (or area of injury in extensive injuries). Note: This modifier was used only during 1996. As of January 1997, it has been replaced with modifier -59
-KA	Add-on option/accessory for wheelchair.
-KH	DMEPOS item, initial claim, purchase of first-month rental.
-KI	DMEPOS item, second or third rental.
-KJ	DMEPOS item, parenteral enteral nutrition (PEN) pump or capped rental, months 4 to 15.
-KK	Inhalation solution compounded from an FDA-approved formulation.
-KL	Product characteristics defined in medical policy are met.
-KO	Lower-extremity prosthesis functional level 0—does not have the ability or potential to ambulate or transfer safely with or without assistance and a prosthesis does not enhance their quality of life or mobility.
-K1	Lower-extremity prosthesis functional level 1—has the ability or potential to use a prosthesis for transfers or ambulation on level surfaces at fixed cadence; typical of the limited and unlimited household ambulator.
-K2	Lower-extremity prosthesis functional level 2—has the ability or potential for ambulation with the ability to traverse low-level environmental barriers such as curbs, stairs or uneven surfaces; typical of the limited community ambulator.
-K3	Lower-extremity prosthesis functional level 3—has the ability or potential for ambulation with variable cadence; typical of the community ambulator who has the ability to traverse most environmental barriers and may have vocational, therapeutic or exercise activity that demands prosthetic utilization beyond simple locomotion.

Table continued on following page

Medicare HCPCS Modifiers *Continued*	
Modifier	**Description**
-K4	Lower-extremity prosthesis functional level 4—has the ability or potential for prosthetic ambulation that exceeds the basic ambulation skills, exhibiting high impact, stress or energy levels; typical of the prosthetic demands of the child, active adult or athlete.
-LL	Lease/rental. Use the -LL modifier when durable medical equipment (DME) rental is to be applied against the purchase price.
-LR	Laboratory round trip.
-LS	FDA-monitored intraocular lens implant.
-LT	Left side. Used to identify procedures performed on the left side of the body. This modifier has no direct effect on payment.
-MS	Six-month maintenance and servicing fee for reasonable and necessary parts and labor which are not covered under any manufacturer or supplier warranty.
-NR	New when rented. Use the -NR modifier when DME that was new at the time or rental is subsequently purchased.
-NU	New equipment.
-PL	Progressive addition lenses.
-QB	Physician providing service in a rural HPSA. The -QB and -QU modifiers describe covered Medicare services performed by a physician within the geographic boundaries of a rural or urban hcalth professional shortage area (HPSA).
-QC	Single channel monitoring.
-QD	Recording and storage in soled state memory by a digital recorder.
-QE	Prescribed amount of oxygen less than 1 liter per minute (LPM).
-QF	Prescribed amount of oxygen exceeds 4 liters per minute (LPM), and portable oxygen is prescribed.
-QG	Prescribed amount of oxygen greater than 4 liters per minute (LPM).
-QH	Oxygen-conserving device is being used with an oxygen delivery system.
-QK	Medical direction of two, three or four concurrent anesthesia procedures involving qualified individuals.
-QM	Ambulance service provided under arrangement by hospital.
-QN	Ambulance service furnished directly by hospital.
-QS	Monitored anesthesia care service.
-QT	Recording and storage on tape by an analog tape recorder.
-QU	Physician providing service in urban HPSA. The -QB and -QU modifiers describe covered Medicare services performed by a physician within the geographic boundaries of a rural or urban health professional shortage area (HPSA).
-QX	CRNA service: With medical direction by a physician.
-QZ	CRNA service: Without medical direction by a physician.
-Q1	Certifies evidence of mycosis of the toenail which causes marked limitation of ambulation
-Q2	HCFA/ORD demonstration project procedure service.
-Q3	Live kidney donor: services associated with postoperative medical complications directly related to the donation.
-Q4	Service for ordering/referring physician qualifies as a service exemption.
-Q5	Service furnished by a substitute physician under a reciprocal billing arrangement.
-Q6	Service furnished by a locum tenens physician.

Medicare HCPCS Modifiers *Continued*

Modifier	Description
-Q7	One Class A finding
-Q8	Two Class B findings
-Q9	One Class B and two Class C findings
-RP	Replacement and repair, -RP, may be used to indicate replacement of durable medical equipment, orthotic and prosthetic devices that have been in use for some time. On the claim, show the code for the part, followed by the -RP modifier and the fee for the part.
-RR	Rental. Use this modifier when durable medical equipment is to be rented.
-RT	Right side. Used to identify procedures performed on the right side of the body. This modifier has no direct effect on payment.
-SF	Second opinion ordered by a professional review organization (PRO). 100% reimbursement; no Medicare deductible or coinsurance.
-SG	Ambulatory surgical center facility service.
-TA	Left foot, great toe
-TC	Technical component: Under certain circumstances a charge may be made for the technical component alone. Under those circumstances the technical component charge is identified by adding modifier -TC to the usual procedure number. Technical component charges are institutional charges and not billed separately by physicians. However, portable x-ray suppliers only bill for the technical component and should use modifier -TC. The charge data from portable x-ray suppliers will then be used to build customary and prevailing profiles.
-T1	Left foot, second digit
-T2	Left foot, third digit
-T3	Left foot, fourth digit
-T4	Left foot, fifth digit
-T5	Right foot, great toe
-T6	Right foot, second digit
-T7	Right foot, third digit
-T8	Right foot, fourth digit
-T9	Right foot, fifth digit
-UE	Used durable medical equipment.
-VP	Aphakic patient.

HCPCS Alpha/Numeric Index

Description	Code
A	
above elbow endoskeletal prostheses	L6500
above elbow prostheses	L6250
above knee endoskeletal prostheses	L5320
acetazolamide sodium (Diamox sodium), injection	J1120
Achromycin, injection	J0120
Actinomycin D, injection	J9120
adjustable arms, wheelchair	E0973
adjustable chair, dialysis	E1570

Table continued on following page

HCPCS Alpha/Numeric Index *Continued*

Description	Code
adrenalin, injection	J0170
Adriamycin, injection	J9000
air ambulance	A0030
air bubble detector, dialysis	E1530
air travel and nonemergency transport	A0140
alarm, pressure dialysis	E1540
alcohol	A4244
alcohol wipes	A4245
alternating pressure pad	E0180
aminophylline injection	J0280
amitriptyline (Elavil), injection	J1320
ammonia test papcr	A4774
amobarbital (Amytal sodium), injection	J0300
ampicillin, injection	J0290
amputee adapter, wheelchair	E0959
amputee cheelchair, detachable elevating leg rests	E1170
amputee wheelchair, detachable foot rests	E1200
amygdalin, injection	J3570
anesthetics for dialysis	A4735
ankle prostheses, Symes, metal frame	L5060
ankle prostheses, Symes, molded socket	L5050
antineoplastic drugs, NOC	J9999
antitipping device, wheelchair	E0971
apnea monitor	E0608
appliance, pneumatic	E0655
Aralene HCI, injection	J0390
arm rest, wheelchair	E0994
arms, adjustable, wheelchair	E0973
asparaginase (Elspar), injection	J9020
atropine sulfate, injection	J0460
aurothioglucose (Solganal), injection	J2910
axillary crutch extension	L0978
B	
back, upholstery, wheelchair	E0993
bacterial sensitivity study	P7001
bandage, elastic	A4460
bandages, gauze	A4202
bath conductivity meter, dialysis	E1550
bathroom equipment, miscellaneous	E0179
batteries, wheelchair, deep cycle	E1069
battery charger, wheelchair	E1066
BCNU (carmustine, bischlorethyl nitrosourea), injection	J9050
bed accessories: boards, tables	E0315
bed pan	E0276
below elbow endoskeletal prostheses	L6400
below knee endoskeletal prostheses	L5300
belt, extremity	E0945
belt, ostomy	A4367
belt, pelvic	E0944
bench, bathtub	E0245
benzquinamide HC1 (Emete-Con), injection	J0510
benztropine, injection	J0515
bethanechol chloride, injection	J0520
bicarbonate dialysate	A4705
bilirubin (phototherapy) light	E0202
biperiden (Akineton), injection	J0190
bischlorethyl nitrosourea, injection	J9050
bleomycin sulfate, injection	J9040

HCPCS Alpha/Numeric Index *Continued*

Description	Code
blood, mucoprotein	P2038
blood (split unit), specify amount	P9011
blood (whole), for transfusion, per unit	P9010
blood leak detector, dialysis	E1560
blood pressure monitor	A4670
blood pump, dialysis	E1620
blood strips	A4253
blood testing supplies	A4770
bond or cement, ostomy skin	A4364
brompheniramine maleate (Dehist)	J0945
C	
calcimar, calcitoninsalmon, injection	J0630
calcium disodium edetate (Versenate), injection	J0600
calcium gluconate, injection	J0610
calcium glycerophosphate and calcium lactate (Calphosan), injection	J0620
calcium leucovorin, injection	J0640
calf rest, wheelchair	E0995
calibrator solution	A4256
canes	E0100
carbon filters	A4680
carmustine, injection	J9050
catheter caps, disposable (dialysis)	A4860
catheter insertion tray	A4354
catheter irrigation set	A4355
CCPD supply kit	A4901
cefazolin sodium, injection	J0690
cefonicid sodium, 1 gm, injection	J0695
cellular therapy	M0075
cement, ostomy	A4364
centrifuge	A4650
cephalin flocculation, blood	P2028
cephalothin sodium (Keflin), injection	J1890
cephapirin sodium, injection	J0710
cervical head harness/halter	E0942
cervical pillow	E0943
chair, adjustable, dialysis	E1570
chelation therapy, IV, (chemical endarterectomy)	M0300
chin cup, cervical	L0150
chiropractor, manipulation of spine	A2000
chloramphenicol (chloromycetin sodium succinate), injection	J0720
chlordiazepoxide HC1 (Librium), injection	J1990
chloroprocaine HC1 (Nesacaine), injection	J2400
chlorothiazide sodium (Diuril), injection	J1205
chlorpheniramine maleate (Chlor-Trimeton), injection	J0730
chlorpromazine (Thorazine), injection	J3230
chlorprothixene (Taractan), injection	J3080
chorionic gonadotropin, injection	J0725
clamps, dialysis, venous pressure	A4918
clamps, Harvard pressure	A4920
cleansing agent, dialysis equipment	A4790
clotting time tube	A4771
codeine phosphate, injection	J0745
colchicine, injection	J0760
colistimethate sodium (Coly-Mycin M), injection	J0770
commode seat, wheelchair	E0968
compressor	E0565
compressor, pneumatic	E0650

Table continued on following page

HCPCS Alpha/Numeric Index *Continued*

HCPCS Alpha/Numeric Index *Continued*

Description	Code
estradiol valerate, up to 20 mg (Estraval-2X), injection	J1390
estradiol valerate, up to 10 mg (Estraval P.A.), injection	J1380
estrone, injection	J1435
ethylnorepinephrine HC1 (Bronkephrine HC1), injection	J0590
etoposide, 50 mg, injection	J9181
external ambulatory infusion pump with adm equip	E0781
extremity belt-harness	E0945
F	
faceplate, ostomy	A4361
fentanyl citrate (Sublimaze), injection	J3010
fibrinogen unit	P9013
fistula cannulation set	A4730
flotation mattress	E0184
flotation pad gel pressure	E0185
floxuridine, 500 mg, injection	J9200
fluid barriers, dialysis	E1575
fluorouracil, injection	J9190
fluphenazine decanoate (Prolixin Decanoate), injection	J2680
footplates, wheelchair	E0970
foot rest, for use with commode chair	E0175
forearm crutches	E0110
furosemide (Lasix), injection	J1940
G	
gamma globulin, 1 ml, injection	P9014
Garamycin, injection	J1580
gauze bandages (gauze elastic)	A4202
gauze pads	A4200
gel, conductive	A4558
gel flotation pad	E0185
gentamicin, injection	J1580
globulin, gamma, 1 ml, injection	P9014
globulin, Rh immune, 1 ml, injection	P9015
gloves, dialysis	A4927
glucose test strips	A4772
gold sodium thiosulfate, injection	J1600
Gomco drain bottle	A4912
Grade-Aid, wheelchair	E0974
gravity traction device	E0941
Gravlee jet washer	A4470
H	
hair analysis	P2031
hallux-valgus dynamic splint	L3100
haloperidol (Haldol), injection	J1630
halter, cervical head	E0942
hand rims, wheelchair	E0967
harness, extremity	E0945
harness, pelvic	E0944
harness/halter, cervical head	E0942
Harvard pressure clamp, dialysis	A4920
head rest extension, wheelchair	E0966
heater for nebulizer	E1372
heel or elbow protector	E0191
heel stabilizer	L3170
helicopter ambulance	A0040
hemipelvectomy, endoskeletal prostheses	L5340
hemipelvectomy prostheses	L5280

Table continued on following page

HCPCS Alpha/Numeric Index *Continued*

Description	Code
hemodialysis, monthly capitation	E0945
hemodialysis kit	A4820
hemodialysis unit	E1590
hemostats	A4850
Hemostix	A4773
heparin	A4800
heparin infusion pump, dialysis	E1520
Hexcelite, cast material	A4590
HN_2 (nitrogen mustard)	J9230
hot water bottle	E0220
hyaluronidase (WyDase), injection	J3470
hydralazine (Apresoline HC1), injection	J0360
hydrochlorides of opium alkaloids (Pantopon), injection	J2480
hydrocortisone, injection	J1720
hydrocortisone acetate, up to 25 mg, injection	J1700
hydrocortisone phosphate, injection	J1710
hydrocortisone sodium succinate (Solu-Cortef), injection	J1720
hydromorphone (Dilaudid), injection	J1170
hydroxyzine HC1 (Vistaril), injection	J3410
hyoscyamine sulfate (Levsin), injection	J1980
hypertonic saline solution	J7130
I	
ice cap or collar	E0230
imipramine HC1 (Tofranil), injection	J3270
incontinence clamp	A4356
infusion pump, external ambulatory with adm equip	E0781
infusion pump, heparin, dialysis	E1520
infusion pump, implantable	E0782
installation and/or delivery charges for ESRD equip	E1600
insulin, injection	J1820
intercapsular thoracic endoskeletal prostheses	L6570
interferon, injection	J9213
intermittent peritoneal dialysis (IPD) supply kit	A4905
intermittent peritoneal dialysis (IPD) system, automatic	E1592
intraocular lenses, anterior chamber	V2630
intraocular lenses, iris supported	V2631
intraocular lenses, posterior chamber	V2632
iodine swabs/wipes	A4247
IPPB machine	E0500
iron dextran (Imferon), injection	J1760
irrigation kits, ostomy	A4400
irrigation set, catheter	A4355
IV pole	E0776
J	
jacket, Risser	A4581
K	
kanamycin sulfate, injection	J1840
kanamycin sulfate, up to 75 mg (Kantrex) pediatric, injection	J1850
Kartop patient list, toilet or bathroom	E0625
kit, CAPD supply	A4900
kit, CCPD supply	A4901
kit, hemodialysis	A4820
Kutapressin, injection	J1910
L	
Laetrile, amygdalin (vitamin B_{17}), injection	J3570

HCPCS Alpha/Numeric Index *Continued*

Description	Code
lancets	A4259
lead wires	A4557
leg extension, walker	E1058
leg rest, wheelchair, elevating	E0990
leukocyte-poor blood, each unit	P9016
levorphanol tartrate (Levo-Dromoran), injection	J1960
lidocaine (Xylocaine), injection	J2000
lightweight wheelchair	E1087
lincomycin, injection	J2010
liquid barrier, ostomy	A4363
liver injection	J2050
lubricant, ostomy	A4402
M	
manipulation, of spine, by chiropractor	A2000
mannitol, injection	J2150
measuring cylinder, dialysis	A4921
mechlorethamine, injection	J9230
medical supplies used in DME	A4610
medroxyprogesterone acetate (Depo-Provera), injection	J1050
meperidine, injection	J2175
meperidine and promethazine HC1 (Mepergan), injection	J2180
mephentermine sulfate (Wyamine), injection	J3450
mepivacaine (Carbocaine), injection	J0670
metaraminol (Aramine), injection	J0380
meter, bath conductivity, dialysis	E1550
methadone HC1, injection	J1230
methicillin sodium (Staphicillin), injection	J2970
methocarbamol (Robaxin), injection	J2800
methotrimeprazine (Levoprom), injection	J1970
methoxamine (Vasoxyl), injection	J3390
methyldopate (Adlomet ester HC1)	J0210
methylergonovine maleate (Methergine), injection	J2210
methylprednisolone acetate (Depo-Medrol), injection	J1020
methylprednisolone sodium succinate (Solu-Medrol), injection	
up to 40 mg	J2920
up to 125 mg	J2930
metoclopramide HC1 (Reglan)	J2765
metocurine iodide (Metubine), injection	J2240
microbiology tests	P7001
mini-bus, nonemergency transportation	A0120
miscellaneous dialysis supplies	A4913
mithramycin, injection	J9270
mitomycin (Mutamycin), injection	J9280
monitor, apnea	E0608
monitor, blood pressure	A4670
morphine, injection	J2270
mucoprotein, blood	P2038
Mustargen, injection	J9230
Myotonachol, injection	J0520
N	
nandrolone decanoate, injection, up to 50 mg	J2320
nandrolone decanoate, injection, up to 200 mg	J2322
nandrolone phenporpionate (Anabolin), injection	J0340
narrowing device, wheelchair	E0969
nasal vaccine inhalation	J3530
nebulizer, portable	E1375

Table continued on following page

HCPCS Alpha/Numeric Index *Continued*

Description	Code
nebulizer, with compressor	E0570
nebulizer heater	E1372
needle with syringe	A4206
necdlcs	A4215
needles, dialysis	A4655
neonatal transport, ambulance, base rate	A0225
neostigmine methylsulfate (Prostigmin), injection	J2710
neuromuscular stimulator	E0745
niacin, injection	J2350
nikethamide (Coramine), injection	J3490
nitrogen mustard, injection	J9230
noncovered procedure	A9270
nonmedical supplies for dialysis, (i.e., scale, scissors, stopwatch, etc.)	A4910
nonprescription drugs	A9150
nonprofit transport, nonemergency	A0120
O	
occipital/mandibular support, cervical	L0160
occupational therapy	H5300
Omnipen-N, injection	J2430
opium, injection	J2480
orphenadrine (Norflex), injection	L2360
orthoses, thoracic-lumbar-sacral (scoliosis)	L1200
ostomy supplies	A4421
otymorphone HC1 (Numorphan), injection	J2410
oxacillin sodium (Prostaphlin), injection	J2700
oxytetracycline, injection	J2460
oxytocin (Pitocin), injection	J2590
P	
pacemaker monitor, includes audible and visible check systems	E0610
pacemaker monitor, includes digital/visible check systems	E0615
pad for water circulating heat unit	E0249
pads, flotation, electric, standard	E0192
pail or pan for use with commode chair	E0167
papaverine HC1, injection	J2440
paraffin	A4265
paraffin bath unit	E0235
paste, conductive	A4558
pelvic belt/harness/boot	E0944
penicillin G banzathine (Bicillin), injection	J0540
penicillin G potassium (Pfizerpen), injection	J2540
penicillin procaine, aqueous, injection	J2510
pentazocine HC1 (Talwin), injection	J3070
Percussor	E0480
peritoneal straps	L0980
peroxide	A4244
perphenazine (Trilafon), injection	J3310
personal items	A9190
pessary	A4560
phenobarbital, injection	J2560
phenobarbital sodium, injection	J2515
phentolamine mesylate (Regitine), injection	J2760
phenylephrine HC1 (Neo-Synephrine), injection	J2370
phenytoin sodium (Dilantin), injection	J1165
pHisoHex solution	A4246
phototherapy, light	E0202
phytonadione (AquaMEPHYTON), injection, vitamin K	J3430
pillow, cervical	E0943

HCPCS Alpha/Numeric Index *Continued*

Description	Code
plasma, protein fraction, each unit	P9018
plasma, single donor, fresh frozen, each unit	P9017
platelet concentrate, each unit	P9019
platelet-rich plasma, each unit	P9020
podiatric services, noncovered	A9160
portable hemodialyzer system	E1635
portable nebulizer	E1375
postural drainage board	E0606
pralidoxine chloride (Protopam), injection	J2730
prednisolone acetate, injection	J2650
preparation kits, dialysis	A4914
prescription drug, oral	J7140
prescription drug, oral chemotherapy	J7150
pressure alarm, dialysis	E1540
procainamide HC1 (Pronestyl), injection	J2690
prochlorperazine (Compazine), injection	J0780
progesterone, injection	J2675
prolotherapy	M0076
promazine HC1 (Sparine), injection	J2950
promethazine HC1 (Phenergan), injection	J2550
propiomazine (Largon), injection	J1930
propranolol HC1 (Inderal),injection	J1800
prostheses, above albow, endoskeletal	L6500
prostheses, below elbow, endoskeletal	L6400
prostheses, hemipelvectomy	L5280
prostheses, intercapsular thoracic, endoskeletal	L6570
prostheses, knee, endoskeletal	L5300
prostheses, lower extremity, NOC	L5999
prosthetic services, NOC	L8499
protamine sulfate, injection	J2720
protector, heel or elbow	E0191
Q	
Quad cane	E0105
R	
rack/stand, oxygen	E1355
reciprocating peritoneal dialysis system	E1630
red blood cells, each unit	P9021
regulator, oxygen	E1353
replacement components, ESRD machines	E1640
replacement tanks, dialysis	A4880
restraints, any type	E0710
reverse osmosis water purification, ESRD	E1610
Rh_0 (D) immune globulin, injection	J2790
rib belt	A4572
rims, hand (wheelchair)	E0967
Ringer's, injection	J7120
rings, ostomy	A4404
Risser jacket	A4581
S	
safety equipment	E0700
safety vist, wheelchair	E0980
sales tax, orthotic/proshetic/other	L9999
Sandril, injection	J2820
scale or scissors, dialysis	A4910
seat attachment, walker	E0156
seat insert, wheelchair	E0992

Table continued on following page

HCPCS Alpha/Numeric Index *Continued*

Description	Code
Seconal sodium, injection	J2860
sensitivity study	P7001
serum clotting time tube	A4771
shunt accessories, for dialysis	A4740
sitz bath, portable	E0160
skin barrier, ostomy	A4362
skin bond or cement, ostomy	A4364
sling, patient lift	E0621
slings	A4565
social worker, nonemergency transport	A0160
sodium chloride, injection	J2912
sodium succinate, injection	J1720
sorbent cartridges, ESRD	E1636
spectinomycin dihydrochloride (Trobicin), injection	J3320
sphygmomanometer with cuff and stethoscope	A4660
spinal orthosis, NOC	L1499
splint	A4570
splint, hallux-valgus, night, dynamic	L3100
stand/rack, oxygen	E1355
sterilizing agent, dialysis	A4780
streptokinase-streptodornase, injection	J2995
streptomycin, injection	J3000
streptozotocin, injection	J9320
succinylcholine chloride (Anectine), injection	J0330
suction pump, portable	E0600
surgical brush, dialysis	A4910
surgical stockings, above-knee length	A4490
surgical supplies, miscellaneous	A4649
surgical trays	A4550
swabs, Betadine or iodine	A4247
syringe	A4213
syringes, dialysis	A4655
T	
tape, all types, all sizes	A4454
taxes, orthotic/prosthetic/other	L9999
taxi, nonemergency transportation	A0100
tent, oxygen	E0455
terbutaline sulfate, 0.5 mg, injection	J3105
terminal devices	L6700
testosterone cypionate (Depo-Testadiol), injection	J1060
testosterone enanthate (Deladumone), injection	J0900
testosterone propionate, injection	J3150
testosterone suspension, injection	J3140
tetanus immune globulin (Homo-Tet), injection	J1670
tetracycline, injection	J0120
theophylline (Salyrgan-theophylline), injection	J2810
thermometer, dialysis	A4910
thiethylperazine maleate (Torecan), injection	J3280
thiotepa (triethylenethiophosphoramide), injection	J9340
thiothixene (Navane IM), injection	J2330
thymol turbidity, blood	P2033
thyrotropin (TSH), exogenous, up to 10 IU, injection	J3240
tobramycin sulfate (Nebcin), injection	J3260
toilet rail	E0243
toilet seat, raised	E0244
tolazoline HC1 (Priscoline), injection	J2670
tolls, nonemergency transport	A0170
tool kit, dialysis	A4910

HCPCS Alpha/Numeric Index *Continued*

Description	Code
tourniquet, dialysis	A4910
tracheotomy collar or mask	A4621
traction device, gravity-assisted	E0941
traction equipment, overdoor	E0860
travel hemodialyzer system	E1635
trays, surgical	A4550
triflupromazine HC1 (Vespirin), injection	J3400
trimethaphan camsylate (Arfonad)	J0400
trimethobenzamide HC1 (Tigan), injection	J3250
tube-occluding forceps/clamps, dialysis	A4910
U	
ultraviolet cabinet	E0690
unclassified drugs (contraceptives)	J3490
underarm crutches, wood	E0112
unipuncture control system, dialysis	E1580
upholstery, reinforced seat, wheelchair	E0975
upholstery seat, wheelchair	E0991
Ureaphil, injection	J3350
Urecholine, injection	J0520
urinary drainage bag	A4357
urinary leg bag	A4358
urinary suspensory	A4359
urine control strips or tablets	A4253
urine sensitivity study	P7001
V	
vancomycin (Vancocin), injection	J3370
vaporizer	E0605
vascular catheters	A4300
vinblastine sulfate, injection	J9360
venous pressure clamps, dialysis	A4918
ventilator, volume	E0450
vest, safety, wheelchair	E0980
vinblastine sulfate (Velban), injection	J9360
vitamin B_{12}, injection	J3420
vitamin K, injection	J3430
volume ventilator, stationary or portable	E0450
W	
WAK (wearable artifical kidney)	E1632
walker, wheeled, without seat	E0141
walker attachments, platform	E0154
warfarin sodium (Coumadin), injection	J3490
washed red blood cells, each unit	P9022
water, ambulance	A0050
water softening system, ESRD	E1625
water tanks, dialysis	A4880
wearable artificial kidney	E1632
wheel attachment, walker	E0977
wrist disarticulation prostheses	L6060
Y	
youth wheelchair	E1091

APPENDIX C

Medi-Cal

Key Abbreviations

Your instructor may wish to select some specific abbreviations pertinent to this chapter for a test. Key terms for this chapter may be found in the Handbook Chapter 11.

Abbreviation	Interpretation
AB	Aid to the Blind
A/R	accounts receivable
AEVS	automated eligibility verification system
AFDC	Aid to Families with Dependent Children
ATD	Aid to the (permanently) Disabled
BIC	Benefits Identification Card
Cal-MAP	California Medical Assistance Program
CCN	claim control number
CCS	California Children's Services
CERTS	claims and eligibility real-time system
CHDP	Child Health and Disability Prevention Program
CIF	Claims Inquiry Form
CMC	computer media claims
CMSP	County Medical Services Program
CNN	claim control number
CPSP	Comprehensive Perinatal Services Program
DME	durable medical equipment
EDS	Electronic Data Systems Corporation
EFT	electronic funds transfer
EVC	eligibility verification confirmation
GHPP	Genetically Handicapped Persons Program
ICF	intermediate care facility
MI	medically indigent
MN	medically needy
OASHDI	Old-Age, Survivors, Health and Disability Insurance Program
PE	presumptive eligibility
PHP	prepaid health plan
POS	point of service device
PTN	Provider Telecommunications Network
RAD	Remittance Advice Details (formerly EOB/RA)
RTD	Resubmission Turnaround Document
SNF	skilled nursing facility
SOC	share of cost
SSN	Social Security number
TAR	Treatment Authorization Request Form
VDTS	Voice Drug TAR System

Performance Objectives

The student will be able to

- Define and spell the key terms for this chapter, given the information from the textbook Glossary, within a reasonable period of time and with enough accuracy to obtain a satisfactory evaluation.
- Answer the review questions after reading the chapter, with enough accuracy to obtain a satisfactory evaluation.

See Chapter 11, Medicaid and Other State Programs for assignments in completing the HCFA–1500 insurance claim form for billing, for posting to ledger cards, and for additional assignments on key terms and abbreviations.

Study Outline

Introduction
Medi-Cal Reform
Eligibility
Benefits
Fiscal Intermediaries
Identification Card
Share of Cost
Eligibility Verification
Co-Payment
Prior Approval
  Treatment Authorization Request (TAR)
  Instructions for Completing the Treatment Authorization Request Form 50–1
Telecommunications Networks
Time Limit
Claim Procedure
  Health Insurance Claim Form HCFA–1500
  UB–92 Claim Form
  Instructions for Completing the UB–92 Claim Form
Computer Media Claims
Remittance Advice Details
Adjustments
Approvals
Denials
Suspends
A/R Transactions
Electronic Fund Transfer
Resubmission Turnaround Document (RTD)
  Instructions for Completing the Resubmission Turnaround Document
Claims Inquiry Form (CIF)
  Instructions for Completing the Claims Inquiry Form
Medi-Cal and Other Coverage
Medi-Cal and CHAMPUS
Medi-Cal and Medicare

Review Questions

Review the objectives, key abbreviations, chapter information, and figures in Appendix C before completing the following review questions.

1. It is July 14 and a Medi-Cal established patient comes in the office for a Level 3 office visit. What is the first step to perform? ______________________

   ____

2. A Medi-Cal patient was seen in the office late on May 1 and was scheduled for an emergency appendectomy in the wee hours of May 2. You verified Medi-Cal eligibility when the patient was in for the office visit. What additional task must be performed to complete the billing to Medi-Cal?

   ____

3. A Medi-Cal new patient arrives for an appointment and also has health insurance from Pacific Mutual. You verify eligibility. What else do you need from the patient?

   ____

4. A Medi-Cal patient came in for an office visit and the physician said the patient needed to have a cholecystectomy within the next 6 weeks to 2 months and that it needed to be scheduled when convenient (aka elective surgery). Before scheduling surgery, what do you do? ______________________
After you have completed this procedure, the patient is scheduled for the cholecystectomy. After surgery you bill Medi-Cal noting ______________________ and ______________________ on the claim form. Do you need to send any information to the hospital? ______________________
5. A Medi-Cal patient also has CHAMPUS. What billing procedure do you follow? Be exact in your steps for a dependent of an active military man.
   a. ______________________
   b. ______________________
6. What is the time limit for submitting a Medi-Cal claim? ______________________
7. What do these abbreviations mean?

PE	______________	TAR	______________
RA	______________	MN	______________
BIC	______________	POS	______________

8. A Medi-Cal patient seen today needs chronic hemodialysis services. You telephone for a TAR to get verbal approval. What four important items must you have to complete the written TAR?

a.	______________	c.	______________
b.	______________	d.	______________

If the patient is having dialysis as an outpatient at the hospital, what form is used by the hospital to submit the claim to Medi-Cal? ______________________
9. A program offering a large number of services to pregnant Medi-Cal recipients is called ______________, and the program designed for easy access to prenatal care for low-income women pending Medi-Cal acceptance is known as ______________________
10. State four ways to verify Medi-Cal eligibility.
    a. ______________________
    b. ______________________
    c. ______________________
    d. ______________________
11. Name two Medi-Cal telecommunication voice-response networks for obtaining information.
    a. ______________________
    b. ______________________